The King's Other Body

The King's Other Body
María of Castile and
the Crown of Aragon

Theresa Earenfight

PENN
University of Pennsylvania Press
Philadelphia

THE MIDDLE AGES SERIES

Ruth Mazo Karras, Series Editor

Edward Peters, Founding Editor

A complete list of books in the series is available from the publisher.

Copyright © 2010 University of Pennsylvania Press

All rights reserved. Except for brief quotations used for purposes of review or scholarly citation, none of this book may be reproduced in any form by any means without written permission from the publisher.

Published by
University of Pennsylvania Press
Philadelphia, Pennsylvania 19104-4112

Printed in the United States of America on acid-free paper

10 9 8 7 6 5 4 3 2 1

Library of Congress Cataloging-in-Publication Data

Earenfight, Theresa, 1954–
The king's other body : Maria of Castile and the crown of Aragon / Theresa Earenfight.
  p. cm.—(The Middle Ages series)
Includes bibliographical references and index.
ISBN 978-0-8122-4185-3 (alk. paper)
  1. Maria, of Castile, Queen, consort of Alfonso V, King of Aragon, 1401–1458.
2. Aragon (Spain)—History—Alfonso V, 1416–1458. 3. Aragon (Spain)—Kings and rulers—Biography. 4. Monarchy—Spain—Aragon—History—To 1500.
5. Political culture—Spain—Aragon—History—To 1500. 6. Alfonso V, King of Aragon, 1396–1458. I. Title.
DP133.1.E23 2009
946'.02092—dc22   2009004269

Frontispiece: Bernat Martorell, untitled illuminated miniature, 1448, in "Comentaria super Usaticis Barchinonae" (frontispiece), Arxiu Històric de la Ciutat de Barcelona.

This book is dedicated to the memory of my parents,
John and Norma Earenfight

Contents

A Note on Proper Names   ix

Maps   xi

1. *Alter Nos*: The Lieutenancy of María of Castile   1
2. From Castilian Princess to Aragonese Queen   19
3. From Queen to Queen-Lieutenant, 1420–35   41
4. A Permanent Lieutenancy, 1436–48   71
5. The Struggle to Liberate the *Remença* Peasants, 1448–53   102
6. Queenship, Kingship, and the Dynamics of Monarchy   131

Genealogy: The Trastámara Family in the Crown of Aragon   145

Abbreviations   149

Notes   151

Bibliography   215

Index   237

Acknowledgments   241

A Note on Proper Names

Medieval Spain encompassed several realms that spoke distinct languages, a fact that poses difficulties for English-speakers. These problems are minimized in the early modern period, after the marriage of Isabel of Castile and Fernando of Aragon when the realms—the Crown of Aragon, Castile, León, and Navarre—were united under a single Castilian dynasty that tried, more or less successfully, to impose linguistic unity over their various subjects. This is particularly problematic for the realms of the Crown of Aragon that constituted a federative empire spanning the western Mediterranean, each entity with its language. Some rulers were Catalan by birth, others Aragonese; Alfonso V, María, and Juan of Navarre were part of the Castilian Trastámara family. Moreover, regnal numbers can be confusing because since 1162, the kings bore the regnal numbers of an Aragonese dynasty. Catalan historians, however, consider the House of Barcelona to have originated earlier, so that a Catalan scholar will refer to the king who ruled from 1416 to 1458 not as Alfonso V, but Alfons IV.

Respecting the languages spoken by the queens and kings of Castile and the Crown of Aragon, I have chosen to use the language and regnal numbers that best convey the speech of the actors. Therefore, Castilian forms are used for all the Trastámara kings and princes who ruled the Crown of Aragon after 1412: Fernando I "de Antequera," Alfonso V "the Magnanimous," and Juan II (Juan of Navarre before 1458), because they were from a Castilian dynasty and most writers refer to them as they would have called themselves.

The most potentially confusing common names are the following, rendered first in Catalan, then the Castilian form, and finally in English.

Alfons, Alfonso, Alphonse
Elionor, Leonor, Eleanor
Enriq, Enrique, Henry
Joan, Juan, John
Maria, María, Maria
Martí, Martín, Martin

Pere, Pedro, Peter
Violant, Yolande, Yolanda

I have translated Latin, Spanish, and Catalan texts into modern standard English. Toponyms are given in the modern forms. This may cause some confusion among readers more familiar with the French Rousillon rather than the Catalan Rosselló, but this system has the advantage of underscoring the coherence of the realms of the Crown of Aragon. Throughout this study, I use the Catalan spelling of *remença* (plural, *remences*); *remensa* (*-as*) is the Castilian spelling.

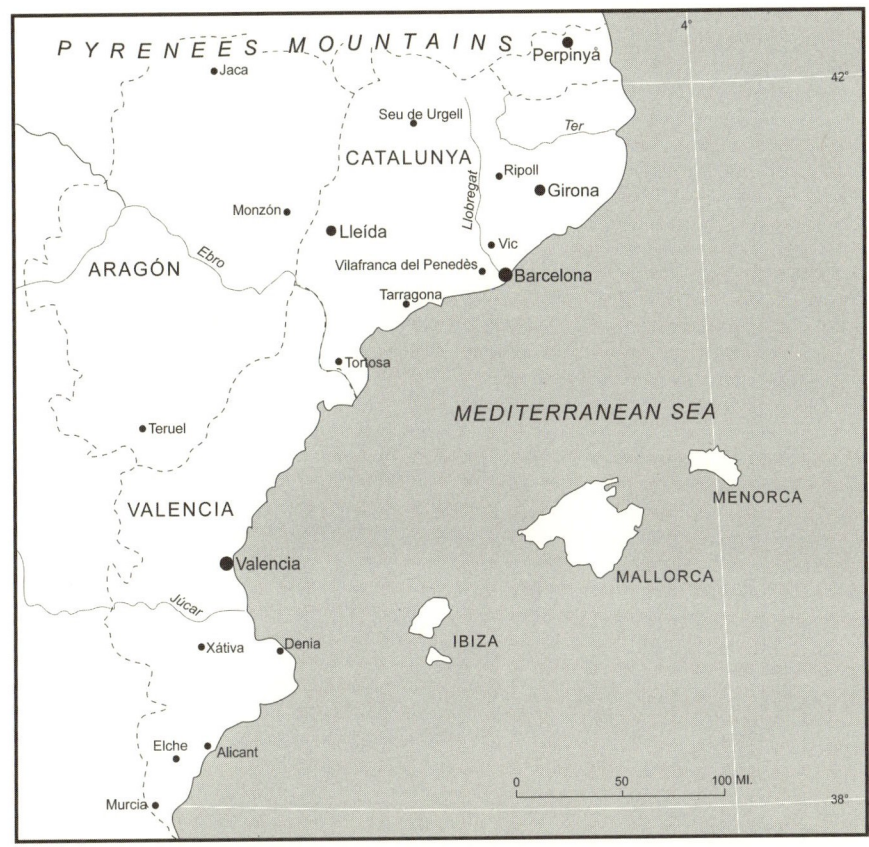

Map 1. The Mediterranean realms of the Crown of Aragon in the fifteenth century. Drawn by Tiffany Ta.

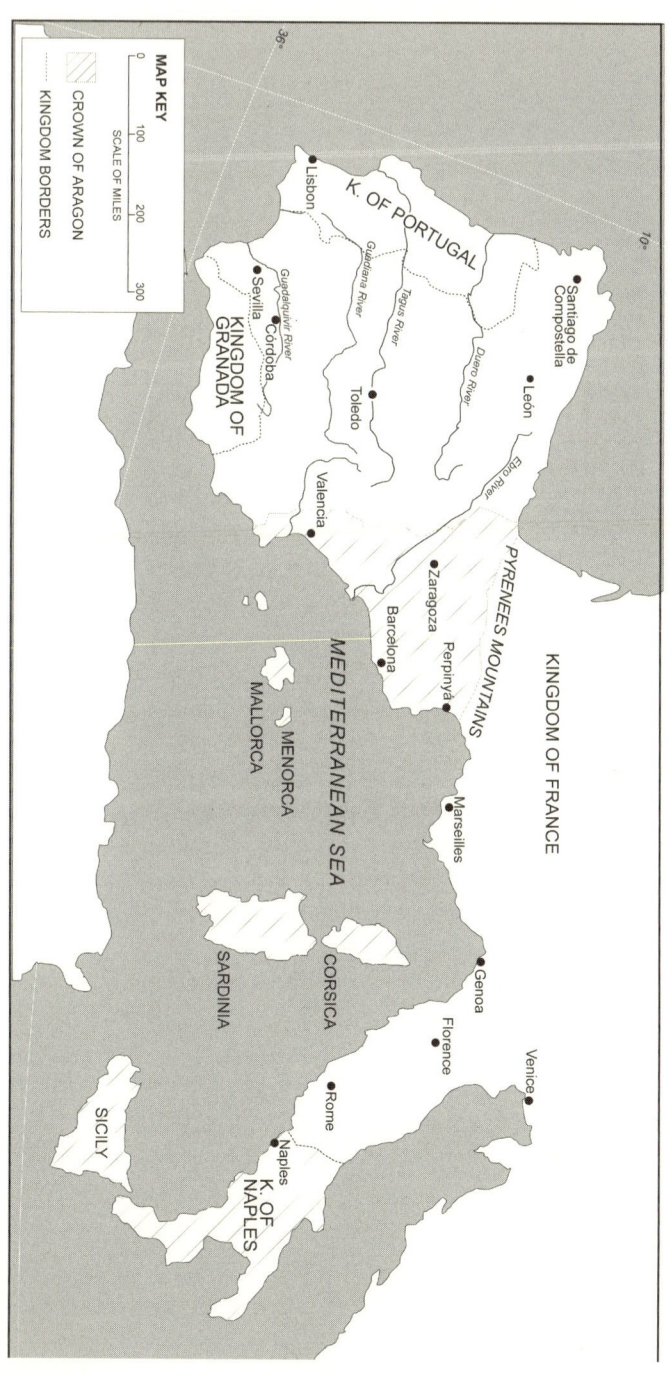

Map 2. The Iberian realms of the Crown of Aragon. Drawn by Tiffany Ta.

Chapter 1

Alter Nos: The Lieutenancy of María of Castile

QUEEN MARÍA OF CASTILE,[1] wife of Alfonso V "the Magnanimous," king of the Crown of Aragon (1416–58),[2] governed Catalunya from 1420 to 1423 and again from 1432 to 1453 while her husband was occupied with the conquest and governance of the kingdom of Naples.[3] For twenty-six years she had control over the provincial governors, prelates and religious orders, the nobility, the army, the municipal government, and all other subjects regardless of legal status. She could grant constitutions and make laws in accordance with royal authority and could sign letters in her own hand according to her own conscience. She was empowered to carry out justice, both civil and criminal, and to name judges and delegates. Assisted by a royal council separate from the king's, she had full royal authority in Catalunya.[4]

Such legitimately sanctioned political authority in the hands of a queen is remarkable because María governed Catalunya not as queen in her own right, or even as queen-regent, but rather as lieutenant general (*lloctinent general*).[5] In the *privilegios* that named María lieutenant, Alfonso clearly stated that her powers as lieutenant should be equivalent to his own as king, referring to her as his *alter nos*. María was clearly more than just a wife offering advice: She held the highest political office in the most important of Alfonso's Iberian realms and, in political terms, was second only to the king himself. For a medieval queen, this combination of exalted royal status plus official political appointment was not common and may not have existed outside the realms of the Crown of Aragon. But in the Crown a unique contractual form of kingship and government had developed that relied heavily on delegated authority to rule the far-flung constituent territories in the Mediterranean. Established in the thirteenth century, the lieutenancy was both an ad hoc adjunct to the king and a training ground for princes to rule one or more of the constituent realms of the Aragonese crown. The institution was the by-product of innovation brought on by rapid territorial acquisition during the thirteenth and fourteenth centuries—encompassing the kingdom of Aragón, the county of Catalunya, the Balearic Islands (Mallorca, Menorca, and Ibiza), Valencia, Sardinia, and Corsica—that stretched across the western Mediterranean.[6] This widely dispersed geography forced the kings to travel frequently and delegate authority normally reserved to the king to their wives, sons, and brothers. As an official form of co-rulership it is, to my knowledge, unique.[7]

The embodiment of the king's personal authority and a custodian of the realm, a royal lieutenant governed both in place of and with an adult king who was fully capable of ruling but, for any number of reasons, was unable to govern a particular territory or territories. Lieutenants governed for continuous periods of time and were actively involved in all aspects of government, including convocation of parliamentary assemblies (known in Catalan as *Corts*) and direction of military matters. The office was flexible enough so that each king could customize it to allow an individual lieutenant some leeway while remaining under the king's supervision. The mainstay of the Aragonese monarchy, the lieutenancy allowed kings to expand their territorial horizons without losing effective political control.

Elsewhere in Europe this office was staffed regularly by men, but in the realms of the Crown of Aragon the lieutenancy developed into a permanent institution that explicitly and officially delineated a queen's official capacity to govern.[8] Until recently, little was known about the careers of most of these queens, many of whom held the office intermittently, usually during an emergency or until their eldest son reached his majority. Complicating matters further, the office of the Aragonese queen-lieutenant, considered incidental to monarchy, has received little scholarly treatment. But it was hardly unimportant to the Crown: over the course of two centuries, seven queens served as lieutenants. The scope of María's authority and the duration of her tenure were unprecedented. In addition to her ordinary powers, María had something her predecessors did not: She maintained a royal court and council separate from and roughly equivalent to Alfonso's court in Naples. Her discretionary power to choose her staff and their compensation was key to the operations of patronage in the public political sphere.[9] María took council from her own council of close advisors (*sacrum consilium*), which paralleled the structure of Alfonso's in Naples—minus the military—complete with chancery, secretaries, and a full complement of official seals; household officials; a judicial tribunal; and high-ranking financial officers. This council reinforced her status and political authority and facilitated her dealings with the royal, regional, comital, episcopal, and municipal officials of Catalunya. She routinely convoked and presided over parliamentary assemblies—eight in Catalunya,[10] two in Aragón,[11] and two in Valencia.[12] The most important issues of the day were played out in the Corts—the election of a king in 1412, the cost of warfare in Italy, the debate over manumission of the semiservile *remença* peasants in the late 1440s, and the reform of urban government in Barcelona in 1454.[13]

This bare outline of her reign tells us much about rulership in the Crown of Aragon in the later Middle Ages. But more broadly it makes a compelling argument for a reformulation of our understanding of the place of queenship in the institution of monarchy. María of Castile, and an Aragonese queen-lieutenant in general, may be unfamiliar to most scholars of the Middle Ages, and she may seem anomalous and her experience ungeneralizable to the rest of Europe, but her case exposes the limitations of current explanatory models of queenship. She did not rule in her own right, so comparisons with female rulers like Urraca of Leon-Castile, Isabel of Castile, and Juana of Castile are misleading.[14] Even though she married an Aragonese prince and derived her office as queen-lieutenant from her marriage, she does not fit the typologies that analyze queenly power in the context of marriage and motherhood—queen-consort, queen-mother, queen-regent, and queen-dowager.[15] She had no children and thus could not be queen-regent for them in their minorities and could not exercise a queen-mother's privilege to act as diplomat when arranging the marriages of her children and grandchildren.[16] She could she serve as queen-dowager because she died a few months after Alfonso and his brother succeeded him immediately. María's reign typifies the idiosyncratic character of the office of queenship, poised ambiguously between family and bureaucracy.[17]

But María's reign offers more than just the possibility of a reconsideration of queenship. Her exercise of public authority and political power cannot be dismissed as simply the context for her husband's reign, or an exception to the rule, or a separate issue altogether, peripheral to the study of monarchy as a whole. Her reign exposes the weakness of our current understanding of the dynamic operations of queenship and kingship. It prompts a reconsideration of the institution of monarchy itself by compelling us to make sense of public political authority exercised by a queen-consort who governed alongside a fully capable, completely healthy, competent male king. It necessitates a careful examination of the practical limits of the theoretical boundaries of kingly power and the rightful place of a female ruler in society within the institutional context of monarchy. It provides an opportunity to consider monarchy as the domain not just of a masculine prince, but many princes, who could just as easily be a queen as a king. Because María's lieutenancy can only be understood when analyzed from within the institution of monarchy rather than from the margins, it prompts a reconsideration of long-held notions of power, statecraft, personalities, and institutions.

Seen from this perspective, monarchy no longer appears as sole rule by a man but as a partnership between king and queen. The densely interconnected personal, cultural, social, economic, and political milieu of queenship is part of a gender system of political action that is not culturally static, but rather has a political dimension that varied geographically and temporally. These variations made the practice of queenship appear more ad hoc than kingship, and they have confounded scholars who seek a uniform definition of an institution. But María's lieutenancy makes it clear that monarchy is best understood as a repertoire of collective norms, institutional structures, and strategies for women's participation in the public political sphere of monarchy that included, but was not limited to, governance. In the Crown of Aragon, the configuration of queenship as part of the lieutenancy resulted in an office with considerable political authority and power.

This book, therefore, is a study of the institution of monarchy as much as it is a theoretical reconsideration of modern understanding of the operations of gender in monarchy. It is a biography of María and an analysis of her political partnership with Alfonso. It is attentive to the dynamic relationship of queenship and kingship and the circumstances and theories that shaped the institution that she inhabited. It takes into account three political cultures and traditions that informed María's practice—the broad context of late medieval Western European monarchy and queenship, the narrower Anglo-Castilian political context that shaped María's instruction in queenship, and the specifically Aragonese context of the queen-lieutenant.

Biography and Historiography

Everything in María of Castile's early life—her family, education, and marriage—prepared her for a politically and publicly active reign as queen,

She was born in Segovia in 1401, the eldest daughter of Enrique III of Castile (1379–1406), and Catalina of Lancaster (1372–1418), two families legendary in their audacious pursuit of outsize ambitions.[18] Enrique was the third king of Castile from the Trastámara dynasty; his grandfather, Enrique, murdered his half-brother King Pedro I "the Cruel," reputedly by stabbing him in the eye after the battle of Montiel in 1469. Catalina was the daughter of Constanza (and the grand-daughter of Pedro "the Cruel") and John of Gaunt, duke of Lancaster and self-styled king of Castile, whose marriage was the result of English intervention in civil wars in Castile and the fortunes of the Hundred Years' War.[19] To cement their power throughout Spain, the Trastámara family used a network of complicated and often consanguineous marital alliances that necessitated many papal dispensations. So, to no one's surprise, María was married at age fourteen to her first cousin, Alfonso of Aragón. A year later, he succeeded his father, Fernando of Antequera (Enrique III's brother), as king. Four years later, María began her first tenure as lieutenant general of Catalunya; this was followed by another tenure, from 1432 until 1453. Within a decade into her long career as queen-lieutenant, María, a Castilian princess with an English heritage whose brother, Juan, was king of Castile (1406–54), did indeed become an Aragonese queen. She spoke Catalan fluently enough to please her Catalan subjects and skillfully practiced a form of queenship that was more Aragonese than the kingship of her husband, who left his peninsular realms for Naples and governed in an authoritarian manner more closely akin to his counterparts in Renaissance Italy.

María was married to Alfonso for thirty-two years, and as successful as their marriage was in terms of governance, it was a dynastic failure. She had no children and may never have been pregnant, although Alfonso had three illegitimate children.[20] While separated from her husband for decades—in total, they lived together for just over fourteen years—she was circumspect in her private life and, as far as I have been able to discern, had no extramarital sexual relations. She was never implicated in a scandal. Her power has not been attributed to great beauty or sexual charisma. She was dutiful, hard working, pious, and attentive to the needs of her subjects. In her demeanor and comportment, she conformed to the prevalent expectations for an elite woman in late medieval Catalunya. She governed like a king and lived like a saint.[21] Her place in the public political sphere was determined not by her own right to rule, but as a member of the royal family, as the wife of the king. For María, queenship was defined by governance.

María governed forcefully during a difficult period in Catalan his-

6   Chapter 1

tory, filled with warfare and peasant unrest, but despite this considerable power and authority, she is an unfamiliar figure, even to scholars of medieval Spain.[22] Historians' neglect of María started early, when contemporary chroniclers neglected to include her in their accounts. In 1438 Pere Tomich finished his rather brief narrative history of the Aragonese kings, *Histories e conquestes dels reys d'Aragó e comtes de Catalunya*; in it he mentioned María only in passing reference as Alfonso's queen.[23] Gabriel Turell's *Recort*, published in 1476, glossed over Alfonso's reign and María's role in it.[24] Geronimo Zurita, writing the *Anales de la Corona de Aragón* in the mid-sixteenth century, mentions María in passing often, but focuses on her in detail when she was married in 1415, when she convoked parliaments in 1435 and 1441, left for Castile and then Valencia in 1453, and when she died in 1458.[25] Women in general are given little attention in Zurita's chronicle, but it is significant that he neglects a queen so involved in governance. He followed the actions of the king, and when Alfonso went to Italy, so did the narrative. He was interested in Alfonso's Italian government and discussed affairs in Aragón, Catalunya, Mallorca, and Valencia only when they touched on Italian politics or, as in the case of war with Castile, were too important to pass over. He spends considerable attention on the Council of Constance and Crown embassies to other monarchies, but the political actions of a queen are treated superficially. The best chronicles of Alfonso's reign were written by the Italian Renaissance humanists Antonio Beccadelli and Lorenzo Valla who naturally focused on the king's exploits in Italy. María and government in the Iberian realms are seen only from afar.[26]

The neglect of a busy queen cannot be attributed to lack of archival material, which exceeds 10,000 documents contained in the royal archives in Barcelona and Valencia for the period. Despite this mountain of material, there is a distinct void in the historiography for the Crown of Aragon from roughly 1430 until 1458 and, until recently, both king and queen were poorly served by historians. This is due in part to national sympathies. Catalan historians have long considered Alfonso an "Italian" king with a Renaissance sensibility and have played down his role in Iberian politics while Italian historians rarely concern themselves with his non-Italian activities.[27] In his biography of Alfonso, Alan Ryder intersperses the governance of Aragón, Catalunya, Valencia, and the Balearics throughout the text, but devotes only a single chapter entitled "Some Questions of Kingship" to the lieutenancy that made possible his governance of Naples.[28] The problem shared by medieval chroniclers and modern political biographers is their narrow definition of monarchy. They assume that María governed more in name than in fact and did little more than carry out Alfonso's direct orders.

This is a historically reckless assumption. Ignorance of María's role in governance has left, at best, serious gaps in the historiography of fifteenth-century Spanish history and at worst, has led to grave misunderstandings of the catastrophic civil war that broke out in Catalunya four years after the deaths of both Alfonso and María in 1458.[29] Ten years of violent strife tore apart the political, social, and economic fabric, leaving the once-powerful Mediterranean commercial and political power in a depressed state from which it would not recover until well into the modern era. Economic and political historians differ in their interpretations of the causes and impact of the war and the subsequent "decline of Spain." In an influential economic analysis, Pierre Vilar investigated the structural shifts that mark this decline. He attributed its causes to the failure of key economic structures for maintaining Catalunya's dominance in the Mediterranean.[30] Vilar's thesis was affirmed by the extensive research into the economies of Christian Spain as a whole by Jaime Vicens Vives,[31] and substantially reinforced and refined by the regional studies of Claude Carrère[32] and Carme Batlle i Gallart.[33] These interpretations were challenged by Mario del Treppo, who has observed a closer connection between political events and economic trends, especially during Alfonso's reign.[34]

Political historians picked up where del Treppo left off, and have focused their attention on what they perceive as the problem of royal absenteeism, the fact that Alfonso spent more than half his reign in Italy. Luis Suárez Fernández felt that Alfonso's lengthy personal absence from his Iberian realms was "truly fatal."[35] To Thomas Bisson it was "disastrous."[36] They contend that the king's absence, coupled with his general neglect of peninsular affairs, led the independent-minded Catalans to take advantage of the situation by strengthening their own political power at the expense of the monarchy, which in turn led to the devastations of the civil war. These same scholars admit, however, that somehow Alfonso managed to keep a firm grip on Catalan government and that peace prevailed throughout his reign. Ryder disagrees with both of them, noting that sufficient "administrative procedures were devised to cope with the problems . . . Spaniards demanded his presence from a sense of injured national pride and with an oligarchic hope of forcing concessions from him, not because all progress had ground to a halt in his absence."[37] These contradictory opinions prompted my initial research questions: Which was

8   Chapter 1

it? Anarchy or autocracy? Incipient civil war or orderly government? Who
is right?

When I first began to study these questions, María did not immediately spring to my mind. Trained as a political and institutional historian, steeped in kingship ideology, at first I, too, took it for granted that
Alfonso, his brother Juan, and his advisors continued to rule Catalunya
from Naples.[38] Ryder argued that Alfonso "closely supervised" María and
wanted to approve the substance of her actions, which he felt were limited to approvals of his appointments and minor details.[39] Bisson credited
María for her "political sagacity . . . patience and fidelity," but nonetheless
he implies that Alfonso remained directly in charge of government.[40] I was
troubled by these conclusions because there was no detailed study of the
political events or issues in Catalunya during María's lieutenancy.[41] Bisson,
Ryder, and Vicens Vives relied principally on archival material specific to
Alfonso and three studies for their assertions about María's role in governance. Andrés Giménez-Soler's 1901 study was brief, almost hagiographi-
cal, and typical of late nineteenth-century romantic Spanish impulse to
find examples of "valores madres," or valiant women ancestors. Its greatest value is the use of unpublished material contained in the Aragonese
royal archives (Arxiu de la Corona d'Aragó).[42] Ferran Soldevila, writing
two decades later, relied on chronicles and Giménez-Soler's research, and
looked in greater detail at María's role in contemporary politics. But he
was primarily interested in her intellectual contributions to medieval Catalan culture.[43] In her 1959 dissertation, Francisca Hernández-León de
Sánchez examined previously untapped resources of the royal Valencian
archives but, regrettably, failed to include transcriptions or translations of
documents. She admitted that she was more interested in María's character than in her role in government and was true to her word. Hernández-
León de Sánchez spent less than one-fifth of her monograph discussing
María's twenty-six years as lieutenant, while devoting the remainder to
María's physical appearance, her personal possessions, and her literary,
cultural, and religious patronage. The works of Soldevila and Hernández-
León de Sánchez are important because the exercise of patronage was a
key component of medieval queenship. Like most queens, María was a
significant patron of religious foundations. With Alfonso, she supported
the construction of a hospital and chapel of Sant Antoni in Barcelona in
1430. She took a special personal interest in the Trinitarian and Jeronimite
orders. One of her confessors late in her reign was the prior of the monastery of Sant Jeroni de la Vall d'Hebron; she sponsored the construction

of that monastery's cloister and was a frequent guest there during the heat of summer.[44] She was especially devoted to the Franciscans. She supported the Clarissan convents of Sant Trinitat in Valencia and Santa Clara in Gandía; she encouraged her niece, Isabel de Villena, the illegitimate daughter of the Castilian noble writer Enrique de Villena, to enter Sant Trinitat and paid her entrance fee; and she was influential in obtaining Alfonso's support for the movement for stricter observance of the Franciscan rule.[45] She was an important patron of Valencian writers and the center of a literary circle that included Joanot Martorell, author of the chivalric novel, *Tirant lo Blanc*; Jaume Roig, María's personal physician at Sant Trinitat and author of *L'Espill*, a misogynist treatise; and Isabel de Villena, who wrote a *Vita Christi* dedicated to Queen Isabel of Castile that included a defense of women in response to Roig.[46] This is a vibrant cultural milieu, and María's role in it needs further study, but her reign was much more important than her confessors, what books she owned, what authors she supported, what she wore, and to whom she made pious donations.

Sources and Methods

Hernández-León de Sánchez's work is long on details of María's court and piety but short on a discussion of her official role in governance. This study is the opposite: It is long on governance and short on culture and ceremony. It is both empirical and theoretical, a political biography and an institutional history. It adheres closely to the archival material pertinent to María's lieutenancy in order to fill in the blank spots in Alfonso's reign in Spain while reevaluating the conclusions of Ryder, Bisson, and Vicens Vives in light of postmodern theories on gender and power. It is the first study of the period that looks at events from María's perspective while tracing the development of the working relationship between María and Alfonso. Although I look at her entire reign, I will concentrate primarily on her two separate tenures as lieutenant general of Catalunya. The first, from 1420 to 1423, was brief and she was more supervised than governing; the bulk of this book focuses on the second, longer and more influential lieutenancy, from 1432 to 1453.

Abundant extant archival materials in three archives, hundreds of registers containing thousands of documents issued during María's lieutenancy, provide insight into the administrative mechanics of the queen-lieutenancy and how it fit into existing Catalan government. The Arxiu de la Corona d'Aragó (ACA) in Barcelona is the principal repository of the documentary collection for the Crown of Aragon, while the Arxiu Reial de Valencia (ARV) contains the records of royal government that pertain specifically to the kingdom of Valencia.[47] The Arxiu Històric de la Ciutat de Barcelona (AHCB) houses the official records of municipal government in Barcelona. The bulk of the documentation used in this study consists of letters between María and Alfonso and their royal officials, legal briefs, petitions, judicial sentences, grants, and instructions to advisors, from which can be constructed an almost complete circle of correspondence. Almost none of this material, which provides a nearly day-to-day chronicle of the events, has been published.

The Arxiu de la Corona d'Aragó and the Arxiu Reial de Valencia provide the royal perspective on events, with the most important documents in the Chancery (*Cancillería*) section.[48] Six *Secretorum* registers, each concerned with a specific topic (for instance, warfare, peasant unrest, Muslims) contain letters close issued under María's secret seal, sent to Alfonso the magnates, high-ranking prelates, leading townspeople, and other members of royal families. Numerous *instruccios* or memorials, itemized lists of instructions to royal officials in Catalunya or to the queen's messengers to present personally to Alfonso in Naples permit a close look at how decisions were made and who made them. Most of the letters sent by María to Alfonso, her royal advisers and officials, members of town councils, and prelates appear in fifty-five *Curiae* registers. *Comune* registers, the largest (165 registers) and most complete chronological series in the ACA, contain the judicial records issued by the queen as queen and as queen-lieutenant in her royal *Audiència*, or court of justice. Three registers, *domine Regine*, contain records of her work from 1416 until 1419, before she was lieutenant. An official listing of appointments, grants, sentences, safe-conduct letters, and other routine official business can be found in forty-seven *Diversorum* registers. Alfonso's side of the correspondence is located in the ACA *Cancilleria* registers that include material from his chancery in Naples that contained his official correspondence sent to María, their royal officials, nobles and prelates in Catalunya.[49] The smaller collection in the ARV houses records from María's lieutenancy in Valencia and the original royal grants that specified María's powers as lieutenant general in the *Mestre Racional* (financial office) section.[50] The last set of royal sources I consulted are the *Lletres Reials Originals* in the Arxiu Històric de la Ciutat de Barcelona, 407 original, mostly unpublished and unedited autograph letters sent from

Alfonso and María to the executive committee of the town council (Consell de Cent) of Barcelona.

The attitudes and intentions of the prominent nobles, prelates, and the urban elites in Barcelona who worked with, and frequently against, María in governing Catalunya are revealed in documents in the *Generalitat* registers of the ACA, particularly the letters sent by the Diputació del General. This powerful watchdog committee of the Corts, the Catalan parliamentary assembly, was charged with guarding traditional privileges against royal actions that threatened their interests.[51] In the Arxiu Històric de la Ciutat de Barcelona, the *Lletres Closes*, are registers of letters sent from the town council to various individuals—Alfonso, María, nobles, burgesses, crown officials, municipal and provincial administrative officials, prelates and members of religious orders—as well as to other town councils or representative bodies such as the Corts or the Diputació. Last, the *Lletres Comunes Originales* are original autograph letters sent from various persons and governmental bodies to the town council of Barcelona.[52]

Two editions of printed primary sources proved indispensable. The proceedings of the Corts of Catalunya includes not only the petitions, proceedings, and official acts of the Corts but also letters from Alfonso, María, and other participants, informs the discussion of María's dealings with the Corts.[53] José María Madurell Marimón's edition of 544 letters documents relations between the Consell de Cent of Barcelona and Alfonso between 1435 and 1458.[54] The collection is a mixed bag, with letters of credential, notices of official appointment of several notaries in Barcelona, news of battles in Italy, reports of diplomatic missions interspersed with petitions to Alfonso, reports of meetings with the king, descriptions of court festivities, and highly personal opinions of current events.

This material enabled me to look carefully at the debates and discussions among the king, the queen and the high-ranking nobles, clerics, and urban elites who had political authority in Catalunya and construct a narrative outline for María's lieutenancy. The drawback to relying on administrative sources is that the letters, written in official rhetoric, are dry and dense. A cursory glance might lead one to conclude that the king and queen were bureaucratic paper-pushers tethered to their secretaries. A shrewd and savvy king or queen reveals more to a courier's ear than to a secretary's pen. But a careful reading of the full series of documents in chronological order reveals subtle hints about their personalities and temperaments. For instance, early in her reign, María refers to herself as *primogénita de Castilla* and both Alfonso and María are noted as the

12   Chapter 1

originators of the letters: "Nos Alfonso e nos dona e nos la dita reyna
Maria primogenita de Castella con licencia e auctoritat e expresso con-
sentimiento."[55] But after 1420, she drops this and uses *lloctinent general,*
indicating her confidence and that she has a secure place in the governance
of the Crown of Aragon.[56] It was, paradoxically, easy to cut through the
formal prose and detect subtle shifts in tone in a letter or memorandum
dutifully written by a secretary, especially with an issue as sensitive as the
manumission of the *remença* peasants. The occasionally vivid and sometimes personal statements convey far more than just the bare facts—they
are witnesses to the seriousness of the growing crisis in the towns and the
countryside. The letters between Alfonso and María are especially important because they expose their will and temperament in ways rarely seen
in official correspondence and permit a careful analysis of their working
relationship. Anyone expecting either eloquent prose or sentiment would
be advised to look elsewhere, but it is a rich archive for anyone interested
in the operations of monarchy.

Reformulating the Theory and Practice
of Queenship in Monarchy

While there are many theoretical considerations of the mechanisms of gender in the practice of queenship, similar analyses of gender in medieval and
modern theories on monarchy have not been regarded as an important dimension of medieval intellectual and political history.[57] No matter what the
approach—comparative studies of medieval institutions, legal and political
studies, or anthropology—queens are rarely part of the discussion.[58] Narrow and partial ideas on monarchy are derived from early modern theories
on divine right of kings and post-Enlightenment attitudes about women
and power that obscure the theory and practice of medieval queenship.
Ernst Kantorowicz is a key case in point.[59] His influential study of medieval political theology is still essential reading for all scholars of monarchy,
but his linkage of the king's body and the royal office, and of the secular
and priestly functions of rulership, focused on kings and illuminates bril-
liantly the origins of the persistent exclusion of women from high office.
To Kantorowicz and his contemporaries, queenship, when they discussed
it, was entirely separate from kingship, merely a corollary. But they mistak-
enly equated rulership with kingship. They framed narratives of monarchy
around a gendered division of the labor of governance that was not neces-

sarily or universally operative.[60] Politics is not gender-blind, as Kantorowicz was when he argued that "in the body politic there is no sex," but failure to consider queens as integral to the mechanisms of monarchy is to be blind to the real gendered forces that shape political culture.[61]

These forces were very real and very powerful.[62] Patristic and medieval philosophers and theologians, principally Augustine and Aquinas, regarded women as physically and intellectually unfit for priestly, and therefore secular, office.[63] Like most medieval theorists and many of their modern counterparts, they regarded women and rulership as incompatible. This view resulted in a bifurcation of royal work—kings philosophize, govern, and make war while queens manage the household, provide sex and children, and plead for peace. Marriage, sexuality, and motherhood,[64] Marian piety,[65] intercession and peacemaking were a queen's work, but most queens did all that and more.[66] Anglo-Saxon and early Anglo-Norman queens,[67] Adela of Blois,[68] the Empress Matilda,[69] Matilda of Flanders,[70] Eleanor of Aquitaine,[71] Blanche of Castile,[72] Catalina of Lancaster,[73] Margaret of Anjou,[74] and María of Castile either ignored altogether whatever gendered division of labor that might have been operative, or ignored it selectively, when it suited their purposes. Although there are significant temporal and geographic differences among these queens that make sweeping generalizations dangerous, it is safe to say that models of monarchy predicated on a division of labor that separate kingship and queenship simply do not explain the many queens whose work encompassed both masculine and feminine aspects.

In order to understand María's legitimate exercise of political authority, the office of the queen-lieutenant must be analyzed from within the institution of monarchy. Doing this reveals the relational and dialectical character of kingship and queenship. It critiques the traditional ascending and descending theories of power as unrepresentative of the actual mechanisms of politics and shows instead that monarchical power was a dynamic and shifting set of force relations that circulated and passed back and forth among the political actors.[75] The partnership of María of Castile and Alfonso V challenges conventional ideas of monarchy as sole rulership by a king and reveals the corporate character of monarchy. It illuminates the collaborative character of monarchical rule by emphasizing how medieval monarchy admitted a plurality of power arrangements that permitted a range of power-sharing options situated in dispersed and localized sites clustered around the king.

Chapter 2, the most biographical section of the book, takes up the question of how a Castilian princess with a famous English grandfather became an Aragonese queen. She came to the Crown of Aragon not as a very young child but at the age of fourteen. She learned queenship primarily from her mother, Catalina of Lancaster, and to a lesser extent from her mother-in-law, Leonor of Albuquerque, but both Catalina and Leonor were Castilian. María gained knowledge of Aragonese customs and practices through on-the-job training, with carefully selected advisors and sophisticated bureaucratic officers who smoothed the transition by providing institutional continuity. María's contemporaries regarded her as a capable, just, and fair queen, and preferred her to her husband, whom the Catalans resented for his abandonment of them and his neglect of their concerns.[76] Although she bore no children, this was considered not as a strike against her, but against Alfonso, whom the Catalans often criticized for failing in his marital duties. The Catalans may have thought that she would have been weaker and easier to manipulate than Alfonso would have been (or was), but she proved her toughness and resilience through her handling of two thorny issues—her right to convoke and preside over the parliamentary assemblies and her attempts to grant manumission to the *remença* peasants. She possessed, in the words of one of her contemporaries, "good sense and virtue, was very honest throughout her life, fearing God and loving justice and administering it."[77] No matter how formulaic such official comments may sound to modern ears, the fact remains that few medieval queens were noted for their administration of justice or governmental skills. Her actions as queen-lieutenant general reflect this combination of natal, marital, and bureaucratic influences, and contributed greatly to her longevity and success.

Subsequent chapters link political theory with practice. Chapter 3 examines the institution of the lieutenancy from its mid-thirteenth-century origins and its development from an ad hoc office to a permanent part of Aragonese monarchy and queenship. María was the sixth of seven queens-consort who ruled the Crown as a governmental lieutenant (distinct from the more familiar military form). Often foreign-born, with some limited fluency in Catalan, these queens were far from silent, hardly powerless, and certainly not absent from the political sphere. On the contrary, it was the kings who were absent. By the fourteenth century, conquest and adroit marriage alliances brought the Crown a variety of possessions that stretched across the western Mediterranean, forcing the kings to travel almost continuously and delegate key aspects of royal authority to trusted officials. During their frequent and often lengthy absences from the principal royal court in Barcelona, the kings of this federative realm relied increasingly on governmental lieutenants to govern in their place. With the office came the instruments of government—royal council, the chancery, fiscal, and parliamentary institutions. As the office of the queen-lieutenancy developed, the contractual character of Aragonese kingship adjusted, which resulted in a transformation of the political culture in of the Crown of Aragon.

Her first tenure as lieutenant, from 1420 to 1423, set the tone for what was to be the defining feature of her lieutenancy, her convocation of the Corts of Catalunya. In all, María presided over eight separate sessions of the Corts of Catalunya between 1435 and 1458, most of which were highly charged events. Two separate issues were central to the dispute over a queen-lieutenant routinely presiding over the Corts: first, the legality in general of such a delegation of authority to a lieutenant, and second, the question of what it meant to the Catalans to have a woman stand in for the king in such a weighty matter. The authority to convoke the Corts by the king, in person, was central to Aragonese kingship, and the pertinent question was juridical, whether that right was transferable to his lieutenants. Alfonso's *privilegios* are unambiguous, but the convocation of Corts by a lieutenant who was also a queen inverted the political order by substituting a female royal body for a male one and generated an important body of Catalan legal theory.[78]

The key point of change was 1435 when her husband and his brothers were captured at the battle of Ponza. It was then that María's training as lieutenant was put to the test, and when, as I discuss in Chapter 4, she demonstrated that she clearly had mastered the art of Aragonese governance.[79] After his release by the Genoese, Alfonso remained permanently absent from his peninsular realms, never to return. From 1436 until 1448, María assumed a much greater role in government than during her first tenure as lieutenant, when she relied on high-ranking nobles, clerics, townsmen, and court bureaucrats to assist her. She began to assert herself and govern more and more without Alfonso's direct involvement in the day-to-day governing of Catalunya, while he was preoccupied with military campaigns both in Spain and in Italy and in trying to raise money to pay for them. By the mid 1440s he had established a royal court in Naples and it was soon apparent to him that he needed to systematize his long-distance government.[80] In the day-to-day rhythms and patterns of government we get a sense of their working relationship when it had reached its institutional maturity. María's convocations of the Corts became increasingly controversial because they were regular and frequent, the issues were contentious, and because Alfonso made no serious attempt to come personally to Catalunya. Her actions were opposed by the Diputació del General.[81] Alfonso's lengthy delegation to his wife of this authority over the Corts had important ramifications and affected María's ability to carry out her other duties as lieutenant under even the most difficult circumstances. Beyond her key role in the events of the period, the circular correspondence—among the king, queen, prelates, nobles, townspeople, and peasants—reveals the discursive nature of queenship, kingship, and monarchy and the presence of a dynamic, vibrant public sphere.

Chapter 5 discusses the last years of their partnership in Catalunya, 1448–53, when it was at its most stressful and difficult. The final sessions of Corts over which María presided dealt with the manumission of the *remences*, peasants tied to the land in an archaic quasifeudal agrarian system. The issue had been brewing for decades, came to the fore in 1447, occupied everyone concerned for the next six years, and was the motive force behind the civil war of 1462–72. Ultimately, the issue became not simply peasant manumission, but who was to decide the issue itself? The king? The lieutenant general? The Corts? The *remença* dispute is emblematic of the wider theoretical issues of Aragonese kingship, the scope of the office of the lieutenant general, and ultimately, of co-rulership. The struggle for the manumission of the *remença* peasants demonstrates María's clear and forceful authority as queen-lieutenant. Her handling of this contentious and difficult crisis that was one of the root causes of the civil war and Alfonso's efforts to resolve the situation were opposed by influential nobles and wealthy urban landlords who controlled the town council of Barcelona.[82] The manumission of the *remences* was not an issue the queen took lightly. She strongly supported the efforts of the *remences* and did not hesitate to say so. She met personally with the delegated representatives (*sindichs*) of the *remences*, forcefully implemented the royal decrees in favor of *remença* manumission, and punished any lord—secular or ecclesiastical—who impeded her work. Nobles and landlords strenuously resisted royal authority and were especially hostile to María's attempts to resolve the matter. The crisis polarized Catalan society, dominated political discourse, and nearly halted government at times as it dragged on from 1447 to 1453. Through it all, María recognized Alfonso's authority as superior to hers and carried out his orders until the summer of 1453 when, frustrated by his decision to revoke the *remença* decrees, she resigned her post and went to Castile to negotiate a peace treaty between her brother, Juan II of Castile, and her husband. Her resignation was extraordinary, without precedent in the history of the office. Her handling of this controversial question—indeed, the fact that she handled it at all—testifies to the existence of a strong governing partnership between Alfonso and María. Moreover, it reveals a great deal about women and the exercise of political power in the later Middle Ages. It is her greatest legacy and was more than just one of the inflammatory issues of the day. It persisted well into the sixteenth and seventeenth centuries as Isabel and Fernando struggled with the problems of servitude and slavery, when critics like Bartolomé de las Cases spoke out against the mistreatment of the indigenous peoples of the Americas and Asia.

María was more than just sage, patient, and faithful, she was indispensable to the effective monarchical rulership of Catalunya. She possessed genuine talents for rulership—she was intelligent and well educated, tough-minded and shrewd, with sound political instincts and a generous measure of diplomacy. She was expert at developing and maintaining personal circles of associates both companionate and political who formed the core of her court. Although the long distance between Barcelona and Naples slowed things down and impeded quick decision-making, it also cooled tempers and provided much-needed time to think clearly and proceed carefully. She adeptly used time and distance to her advantage and proved to be a skillful staller who used the delays in mail delivery to buy time. It became clear to me, as I read the archival documents, that Alfonso's absenteeism was not the fatal blow in Spanish medieval economic and political power. The government of Alfonso and María ran smoothly and effectively until the 1440s and faltered only under the tremendous pressure of an impending peasant rebellion. Alfonso ultimately refused, against María's advice, to grant manumission to semiservile peasants in Catalunya. His policies, and not his absenteeism, created an untenable situation that worsened under his successor, his brother Juan II (1458–79), whose style of authoritarian rulership clashed violently with local customs. The civil war of 1462–72 was about many things—structural changes in the European economy, a violent peasant uprising, Juan's stubbornly bellicose actions—but it was not simply about an absent king. I do not presume to have all the answers to questions about the causes of the sixteenth-century economic and political decline of Catalunya. For that, we need much more research into the reign of Juan II and Juana Enríquez, his queen-lieutenant.

But this much is clear: María governed at this pivotal moment in the political and institutional transition from the medieval kingdom to the early modern state. Her nephew and niece, Fernando and Isabel, married in 1469 and united Castile and the Crown of Aragon. Their reign ushered in the fundamental political and economic transformations of the later Middle Ages and early Renaissance. The government they crafted was based on institutional models of delegated authority and contractual rulership devised by medieval Aragonese kings and carried out by Aragonese queens-lieutenant. Their early modern heirs governed a complex state consisting of Spain, Naples, the Austro-Burgundian realms, the Americas, and they faced a problem that was common in the medieval Crown of Aragon—how to reconcile local particularism with expansionist tendencies. The study of Aragonese queen-lieutenant has much to tell us about delegated authority, royal absenteeism (what José Nieto Soria terms the "hidden" king), and what John Huxtable Elliott calls the "composite monarchy."[83] These are vitally important issues in any study of the Spanish Habsburgs. The administrative instruments of delegated authority, the *consejo* system and the viceroyalty, employed by the Habsburgs to rule the Americas are the direct descendants of the office of the lieutenant that Aragonese queens occupied for over two centuries. Thus, the more we know about queens, queenship, and the attendant shifts in attitudes toward women and political power in general and how this affected men's exercise of political authority, the more we will be able to make sense of medieval Europe and its impact on the wider world after 1500.

Chapter 2
From Castilian Princess to Aragonese Queen

How did the Castilian *infanta* María of Castile learn to be an Aragonese queen? How did she learn the conventions and standards of monarchy in her husband's realms? More fundamentally, how does any princess or countess or duchess learn to be a queen? In addition to the general European context of queenship and monarchy outlined in Chapter 1, María's understanding of the practice of queenship stemmed from two similar, yet rather different forms of political culture of Castile and the Crown of Aragon. Norms and practices of queenship were conveyed to her by the training and example of her mother and her mother-in-law, who were duty bound to instruct the young bride in queenship particular to each realm, and by her advisors at court who taught her how to be a queen in the Crown of Aragon. Her Anglo-Castilian heritage shaped her early life in Castile, and this informed her education in Aragonese queenship and rulership from the first years of her marriage until her first tenure as lieutenant of Catalunya in 1420. Castile and the Crown of Aragon may have had distinct political cultures, but María's complex family history resulted in a genealogy with horizontal and vertical lines of affiliation and intermarriage so densely interwoven that it resembles a spider web. The marriage of the English Lancastrian duke John of Gaunt (1340–99) and the Trastámara princess Constanza of Castile (1354–94) linked two wildly ambitious families and changed the political dynamics of the entire Iberian peninsula.[1] John of Gaunt, with his brother Edward, Prince of Wales, allied with the Castilians during the Hundred Years' War. Gaunt staked a claim to the Castilian crown by marrying Constanza, whose father, King Pedro was murdered by his half-brother Enrique of Trastámara in 1369; in 1388, he secured the marriage of his daughter Catalina (1372–1418) to Enrique's grandson, Enrique (1379–1406). This union mended the damage done by Pedro's death and assured Trastámaran dominance in Castile for the next century, and their power was augmented by the accession of Enrique's younger brother, Fernando of Antequera (1379–1416), to the Crown of Aragon. Fernando then arranged the marriage of his son, Alfonso V, "the Magnanimous," to Catalina's and Enrique's daughter, María of Castile, which extended this incestuous hegemony to the Crown of Aragon.

This story has all the elements of popular fiction, but what interests me is what María would have learned about Castilian queenship theory, inheritance law, rulership, and queenship first from her mother, Catalina of Lancaster, and later, after she married Alfonso, then heir to the Crown of Aragon, from her mother-in-law (and aunt), Leonor of Albuquerque (1374–1435). Catalina's education in English and Castilian ideas on rulership prepared her well for her two tenures as regent, once for her young husband, Enrique, and then again as co-regent with her brother-in-law for her minor son, Juan. These experiences shaped María's understanding of a queen's rightful place in monarchy and the dynamics of shared rule. Leonor, on the other hand, ruled vigorously and openly alongside her husband, Fernando, and she provided María with an introduction to Aragonese political culture. Both Catalina and Leonor shared a complicated political history that was deeply rooted in the Castilian experience of reconquest and war. Women, deemed unsuited to military pursuits, were excluded from knighthood and rarely mustered or led an army.[2] Even into the later Middle Ages a Spanish king's right to rule stemmed in large part from his military success in the reconquest, but women were not excluded from the inner circle of power.[3] These pragmatic kings governed alongside with queens who exercised authority in official and unofficial roles.[4] Castilian monarchy was mildly theocratic but had well developed constitutional institutions.[5] As sisters-in-law, Catalina and Leonor also shared a family history that culminated later with the marriage of Fernando of Aragon and Isabel of Castile. Both women were regarded as foreigners by the subjects they ruled, both were closely associated in rulership with their husbands, and both bequeathed to María decidedly Castilian ideas, both theoretical and practical, on the queen's role in politics.

María of Castile's Anglo-Castilian Heritage

Born and raised in England, Catalina of Lancaster was educated by her relative, Joan Lady Wake, and lived for a time in her household of Lady Mohun, an influential member of the king's court. Joan Burghersh was a companion whose family was close to that of Edward, the Black Prince, and his uncle, John of Gaunt. She was a cultural amalgam. To the English she was "Katerine d'Espaigne" but she spoke English well (John of Gaunt was a patron of Chaucer), and learned French and Latin. She absorbed English ideas on a woman's role in politics derived from legal traditions that granted women considerable latitude in terms of possession of titles and rights to exercise lordship. Catalina would surely have been aware of earlier English queens who exercised considerable power as queen in various capacities—Eleanor of Aquitaine, Eleanor of Provence, and Eleanor of Castile.[6] These queens had ample space to maneuver when the king was alive and physically and mentally healthy, but fear of powerful regents prompted Parliament in the mid-fourteenth century to limit the power of queens-regent Margaret of Anjou, Elizabeth Woodville, and Elizabeth of York.[7]

Catalina witnessed, or at the very least knew of, the tumultuous rule of Richard II, her own father's machinations in Richard's deposition and death, and the formidable power of English nobles. From this, she learned that even the most authoritarian kings never ruled alone, that they typically took counsel from secular and ecclesiastical lords, and that they relied on an inner circle composed of a few trusted intimates who often were family members.[8] Thomas Aquinas recognized this when he noted that the title of king is autonomastic, by which he meant that it is a noun properly belonging to a whole species of things that becomes applied to a single individual.[9] Aquinas would not have considered Catalina (or any other queen) to be part of the "species of things" that constitutes monarchy; far from it. But recognizing the collective character of monarchy admits queenship within range of power-sharing options that fall under the general rubric of monarchy and provides a fuller definition of the term.

Catalina's mother made certain that her Englishness was offset and complemented by a strong presence of Castilians in her household because Catalina was an *infanta*, with a legitimate claim to the crown of Castile.[10] Yet she held on to her connections with England throughout her life in Castile through regular correspondence with her English relatives and she advanced a pro-Lancastrian and pro-English agenda, especially concerning the papal schism. With her sister Philippa, queen of Portugal, she supported Portuguese alliances with England and Castile.[11]

Catalina moved to Castile in 1386 at the age of fourteen to marry her cousin Enrique, then seven years old. With her marriage in 1388 she received the title *princesa de Asturias*, an innovation in Castilian royal nomenclature that closely parallels English practice since the naming of Edward, the Black Prince, as the Prince of Wales.[12] It is noteworthy that Catalina formally gave her consent to the marriage and renounced her inheritance rights and all claims to rule Castile in her own right.[13] Her claim was weak, based on her father's pretensions to the crown through his marriage to Constanza, and the strength of her mother's Trastámara relatives prevented John of Gaunt from seizing power. Nevertheless, Catalina's right to rule had a sound legal basis. In both Castile and the Crown of Aragon, testamentary succession was common and customary law left property decisions to the option of the head of the family.[14] In Castile, the royal couple were considered one by law and princesses could be designated their fathers' legitimate successors.[15] Because a woman could legitimately inherit in the absence of a legitimate male heir, two princesses did succeed and ruled in their own right.[16] Alfonso VI of León (r. 1065–1109) designated his daughter Urraca as his successor and she ruled from 1109 until 1126. Married twice to powerful men, including Alfons I of Aragón (r. 1104–34), Urraca defied the expectation that a man who married a ruling queen should automatically share in the governance of his wife's realms.[17] And Isabel "la Católica" (r. 1474–1504) held her realms separate from those of her husband, Fernando II of Aragon (r. 1479–1516), who ruled the Crown of Aragon in his own right but did not have sovereign power over Isabel; not even after her death could he rule as king of Castile.[18] Urraca and Isabel owed their crowns to those same twists of fate that made kingship ad hoc—the untimely deaths, the succession crises, and the mental and physical debilities that smoothed the pathway to the throne. They could rule, or transmit a right to rule, because they were only means of continuing a lineage. During the three centuries that separate them, generations of healthy male babies were born in both Castile and Aragon, combined with brute force and adroit political manipulation, rendered rulership by right moot for princesses.

Still, Catalina expected to be an active partner in governance, in both official and unofficial capacities, with Enrique. A crowned queen-consort's intimate association with the powerful mythical quality of royalty transmitted enormous power.[19] The idea of the "harmonious" union of a king and queen was stated explicitly in the *Siete Partidas*, the fundamental thirteenth-century law code created during the reign of Alfonso X of Castile (r. 1252–84). By this Alfonso meant more than just the reciprocity of the marriage relationship, he meant also that both king and queen should share their responsibilities in both the public and private realms.[20] His wife Violante acted like a lieutenant for her husband when he was ill but had no special title. She certainly was busy. She frequently advised her husband on political matters such as taxation; she interceded between her father, Jaume I of the Crown of Aragon (r. 1213–76), and her husband over the revolt of the Mudéjars in 1264; she participated in sessions of the Cortes and was appointed by her husband to a commission to the Cortes of Burgos in 1272 to negotiate with rebellious nobles.[21]

Castilian theories and precedents for rulership were made real for Catalina in 1390 when Juan I of Castile died, and at age eighteen she became regent for her eleven-year-old husband. Like all queens, she would have been familiar with the regency, the most common means by which a queen could participate in government. Throughout Europe, the queen-regent's political authority was accepted, at least in theory, as an extension of her maternal rights as the guardian of her children.[22] And, Catalina had many Castilian predecessors. María de Molina, widow of Sancho IV was regent for both her son, Fernando IV (r. 1295–1312), and grandson, Alfonso XI (r. 1312–50).[23] Berenguela, daughter of Alfonso VIII of Castile (r. 1158–1214), regent for her son Fernando III (r. 1217–52), maintained order in Castile in the face of threat of invasion by her ex-husband (Alfonso IX of León, r. 1188–1230) and civil war.[24] In Navarre, Toda Asnúrez, was regent for her son García I Sánchez (r. 926–70); Urraca Fernández and Jimena González, grandmother and mother respectively, were regents for Sancho III Garcés, el Mayor (r. 1000–1035).[25]

It was rare, however, for a queen to be regent for her young husband. Despite her youth, she had already spent two years, and would spend two more years of her three-year regency, with her mother-in-law, Beatriz of Portugal learning the fundamentals of Castilian queenship. But it proved to be a difficult minority and eventful regency, punctuated by struggles within the regency council itself and opposition from the powerful Castilian nobility and clergy. Catalina mostly stayed in "tactful retreat," and between 1401 and 1406 she bore Enrique three children: María (1401), Catalina (1403), and Juan (1405). She intervened in political matters only once, when she tried unsuccessfully to appoint officers for *infante* Juan's chamber.[26] Enrique's personal reign was short, but he proved himself an effective ruler who found war distasteful and limited his military involvements as much as possible in an age of nearly continuous warfare. His peaceful goals were compromised, however, by the violent pogroms against the Jews in 1391. He dismantled the power of the high-ranking nobles who threatened Trastámara dominance but could not stop the rise of the lesser nobles who scrambled to take their place. His efforts to resolve papal schism and curb Ottoman Turkish threats in eastern Mediterranean were cut short by his death in 1406, at age twenty-seven.[27] Catalina became regent again, this time for her infant son, Juan (r. 1406–54). She moved out of the shadows and into the contentious and controversial public arena of Trastámara politics.

This second regency was especially difficult because she shared rulership with her brother-in-law, Fernando de Antequera, who became king of the Crown of Aragon in 1412 after a two-year interregnum and a disputed succession that Catalina mediated. In addition to Fernando de Antequera, who claimed throne rights as grandson of Pere IV (r. 1336–87), the contestants were Fadrique de Aragón, the count of Luna and Martí's illegitmate grandson; Jaume, count of Urgell, great-grandson of Alfonso IV, and married to a daughter of Pere IV; Louis of Anjou, duke of Calabria and grandson of Joan I; and her son, Juan, who by then had succeeded his father as king of Castile. Fernando was determined to claim his rights, but he needed legal and economic support from Castile. Catalina called a commission of experts to determine the most qualified claimant, but Fernando skillfully manipulated the proceedings, and in an act known as the Compromise of Caspe he became the first Trastámara king of the Crown of Aragon (r. 1412–16).[28] Although he had difficulties ruling the Crown, Fernando assumed almost undisputed authority in Castile over every matter dealing with war and the monastic military orders until his death in 1416. For the next two years, Catalina was sole regent of Castile, and she worked to depose Benedict XIII at the Council of Constance (1416), concluded a series of truces between England and Castile (1416), made peace with Granada (1417), and smoothed relations with Castilian Jews that had been tense since the pogroms of 1391. She finally turned power over to Juan when he reached his majority, just a few months before her own death in 1418.[29] Catalina could step into these institutional gaps and govern because monarchical power in premodern Europe was never isolated in one person. It was not "the rule, whole or partial, of one person over a political unit."[30] Monarchy had a "corporational character—with the king as guardian, though again not with the king alone, but with the composite body of king and magnates who together were said to represent the Crown."[31] Because monarchy was a family affair, the queen was a vital component of the royal institutional composite, although her ability to exercise any power depended on personality and circumstance.

As the eldest child in the royal family, María was designated *princesa de Asturias*, just as her mother was, but she possessed a title her mother did not. At the Cortes of Toledo on 6 January 1402, Enrique designated María the *primogénita al trono*, his legitimate heir to the kingdom of Castile.[32] María soon found out that it is one thing to inherit, but another to rule.[33] The birth of her brother, Juan, in 1405 and his designation as the *primogénito* in 1406 left María an *infanta* without an expectation of ruling in her own right. She certainly was not the first Castilian princess-heiress who lost her claim to the crown. Berenguela of León (1180–1246) was named *primogénita* and legal heir after the death of her father, Alfonso VIII of Castile, but renounced her rights in favor of her son Fernando III (r. 1217–52).[34] Alfonso IX may have named his daughters Sancha and Dulce as his successors, but they renounced their claims in favor of their half-brother Fernando, resulting in the union of the Leonese and Castilian realms.[35] But María did expect to marry a king and share in the responsibilities of governance.

María's designation as *princesa de Asturias* sharply distinguishes Castilian practice from that of the Crown of Aragon, where women were excluded from the succession by their fathers' wills and only one queen, Petronila (1137–62), daughter of King Ramiro II (r. 1134–7), inherited and ruled in her own right.[36] Petronila was only one year of age when she inherited the kingdom in 1137 on the occasion of her betrothal to the older (by perhaps twenty-five years) and more politically experienced Ramon Berenguer IV, count of Barcelona. Their marriage was both a marital and a political union. Shortly after the marriage, Ramiro retired to a monastery and Ramon Berenguer acknowledged his status in Aragón not as king but as prince-consort. Due to her youth, however, Petronila ruled more in name than in fact (she and Ramon were not formally married until 1150). When Ramon Berenguer died in 1162, she ceded her throne-rights to the united realms of Aragón and Catalunya to their son, Ramón with the provision that if he died without a male heir, his younger brother would succeed. Petronila remained regent for her son, renamed Alfons II (r. 1162–96), until 1164. Testamentary exclusion of women from the Aragonese succession was reinforced by the will of Jaume I in 1272, but the right of women to transmit throne rights was upheld.[37] This loophole in Aragonese law was tested in 1347 when Pere IV, whose first wife, María of Navarre, had borne only daughters, encouraging his brother Jaume to hope that he might inherit the Crown. Pere named his daughter, Constança, his heir, arguing that the idea came to Us to see if We could legally establish that Our daughter, Constança, Our first born, in case We died without male children, should succeed Us in Our kingdom and our lands. And We discovered, through the sayings of masters of theology, doctors, learned men and great clerics, experts in canon law as well as civil, that, according to divine and human law, Our daughter could become Our universal heiress, should We die without male children. On this question, many and divers arguments were made on the side of Our daughter, although some learned men held the contrary view.[38]

Pere's "learned men" were correct: There was no explicit statement in Catalo-Aragonese law that prohibited women from inheriting and ruling. But he was overruled by other of his own jurists, influenced by French application of the Salic Law, who determined in 1347 that Pere could not name his daughter, Constança, his heir.[39] The birth of a son to Pere's third wife rendered Constança's claims moot, and no subsequent Aragonese princess would claim to inherit or rule the Crown of Aragon.

Unpredictable messiness was not a problem just for the Aragonese. Medieval monarchy was hardly the rational ordering of the divinely ordained principles of dynastic succession. The study of dynastic monarchy is the story the pragmatic resolution of one messy and contested succession crisis after another.[40] Primogeniture, which was not a fully formed juridical theory until the twelfth or thirteenth century, worked only when nature cooperated with an ample provision of healthy sons who survived to adulthood. The "ordinary" pattern of inheritance—firstborn sons succeeding fathers, generation after generation, in an orderly manner—was, in fact, "extraordinary" in most Christian kingdoms, and these extraordinary conditions were the norm.[41]

What makes the Aragonese situation distinctive is the fact that queens were expected to be partners with their husbands in domestic and local politics and governance of the realm.[42] The precedent for partnership was established at least as early as the reign of Jaume I. In his autobiographic work, the *Llibre dels Feyts*, Jaume distinguishes himself from his son-in-law Alfonso X of Castile, when he describes his second wife, Violant of Hungary, as embodying the ideal qualities in a queen a king should seek. Jaume portrays the queen as a strong, tough, loving partner, yet makes it clear that he is dominant and the queen is his subordinate. He says that he never made an important decision without first consulting Violant, but then he goes on to say that she was quite different from his first wife, Leonor of Castile, whom he divorced because she did not support him properly. Ultimately, the *Llibre dels Feyts* is, in Marta VanLandingham's apt phrase, a "portrait as a construct," as much political theory as kingship ideology, a blend of fact and fiction.[43] When Alfonso and Jaume speak officially of their wives, it is a flattering portrait not only of the queen, but also of the king, and it is far more favorable than what their partisans or enemies write of the queens.[44] Like the *Siete Partidas*, the *Llibre dels Feyts* reflects a truth of queenship and monarchy, but like all mirrors such reflections are only fragments of the panorama as a whole.

The Education of a Castilian *Infanta*

María grew up in an entirely Castilian household and, unlike many princesses destined to marry a foreign prince, lived there until her marriage. Her godmother was María de Ayala, a nun and daughter of Pedro I of Castile and his mistress, Teresa de Ayala; her wet nurse was Juana de Zúñiga, wife of Fernando López de Estúñiga, *alcaide* (mayor) of Burgos, and later their daughter Mencía. Her education was supervised by the Great Steward Pedro González de Mendoza, and her governess was Inés de Ayala, a member of the chancellor's family.[45] By all accounts, her childhood was tranquil. Her father's death when she was barely four did not appear to leave any lasting scars. The illnesses that would trouble her in adulthood were nowhere evident until she was in her teens and married.[46] During Catalina's second regency María was able to observe firsthand a queen regent whose actions in the political realm influenced the young princess's own notions of the duties, responsibilities, rights, and prerogatives of a queen. She was close to her mother until her own marriage in 1415 and remained in frequent correspondence with her during the first few years of marriage until Catalina's death in June 1418.[47] María was in Aragón when she received news that her mother had died, but because she was seriously ill, she did not attend her funeral.[48]

On 12 June 1415, in Valencia, in a ceremony presided over by Pope Benedict XIII who also provided the necessary dispensation for the couple to wed, María married her first cousin, Alfonso. It was a sumptuous two-day celebration that included bonfires, fireworks, jousting, and public dancing in which the couple participated.[49] The marriage had been arranged at the time of her designation as *princesa de Asturias* as a way to stabilize her succession to the Castilian crown. It was reiterated in Enrique's will, but the betrothal was not formalized until she was seven, at which point her succession was moot because her brother Juan had been designated the heir.[50] The marriage was part of a triple alliance that rendered everyone but the Portuguese and Navarrese subjects of Trastámara rule.[51] Alfonso's sister, María of Aragón, married María's brother, Juan II of Castile, in 1418, and María's sister, Catalina, married Alfonso's brother, Enrique in 1420.[52] Family squabbles, and there were many, became international incidents as a result of the monarchical politics of Fernando of Antequera and Leonor of Albuquerque, five years older than her husband and his aunt, as well. Especially problematic for the Aragonese crown, and most pertinent to María's lieutenancy, were their meddlesome younger sons Juan (king of Navarre, 1425–79 and king of the Crown of Aragon, 1458–79), Enrique (Catalina's husband, master of Santiago; died 1445), and Pedro (died 1439), known collectively as the *infantes de Aragón*.[53] María's dower from Alfonso was 30,000 *doblas*; her dowry from her family was the marquisate of Villena, the revenues of Andújar and Medellín, and the lordship and revenues of the towns of Aranda and Portillo. She was also to receive 560,000 *maravedís* per year in rents from Seville, plus smaller, token sums from various Castilian towns.[54] Alfonso was elevated in rank to *infante* of Castile and was granted the title of duke (restricted to members of the royal family), was given a household to match his new status, including the bishop of León as his chancellor.[55]

According to the terms of the betrothal documents drawn up shortly after María was designated *princesa de Asturias*, by Enrique III and Fernando of Antequera, the lordship of Villena could not be alienated from the Castilian patrimony, and so the land was converted to a cash payment of 200,000 *doblas*. Dowries were key components of the fisc, but in the later Middle Ages kings like Enrique III often chose to pay the dowry in cash rather than landed estates.[56] There are several reasons for this strategic shift from earlier practices. First, whereas revenue from estates trickled in, cash from a dowry was preferred as a way to quickly infuse a treasury as sorry as that of the Crown of Aragon. Second, since the thirteenth century, preservation of royal patrimony was an important consideration, especially in light of laws strictly regulating nonpartible inheritance, primogeniture, and the creation of royal apanages.[57] Third, kings learned to think twice before they gave a gift of land to a loved one, as Alfons IV of Aragon did in 1338 when an enraged outcry ensued because he granted lands in Tortosa and Valencia to his second wife, Leonor of Castile and their sons Fernando and Juan.[58] Converting landed endowments into a cash payment, which is legally a temporal, not a perpetual grant, left the Crown patrimony intact. María's substantial dowry was to be paid within two years but the final payment was not received until after 1420, and only then after considerable foot-dragging by her brother Juan, who complained that it was the largest dowry ever given a Castilian princess.[59]

On 1 April 1416, less than one year after the marriage, King Fernando I died and the Crown of Aragon passed to Alfonso. Unlike his father and most Aragonese kings before him, he did not have a formal coronation.[60] The absence of a coronation could not have gone unnoticed by his subjects when his father's coronation combined political propaganda and legal legitimation in a grand spectacle that faithfully preserved Catalan and Aragonese rituals and traditions.[61] The terms of the Compromise of Caspe that brought his father to power legally validated the Trastámara dynasty as the legitimate rulers of the Crown and although there was no apparent opposition to Alfonso's succession, there were still some partisans of the Luna and Urgell families who posed a threat. Alfonso took care to be formally proclaimed heir by the regional assemblies just before his father's death, and he was happy to use the promise of a coronation as leverage when necessary and happily collected several coronation taxes, but he was never crowned king.[62]

Alfonso's deliberate omission of the rites of coronation is a vexing problem, not only for his subjects who made their sentiments clear time and again when, but also over the course of his reign and María's lieutenancy, they demanded that he return to Catalunya and Aragón to reiterate his promises to uphold their privileges as part of a formal coronation. Scholars struggle with what Teofilo Ruiz has argued is an "unsacred monarchy" that Spanish kings forged through the reconquest. Coronations in all the Christian monarchies in Spain were erratic at best. Most Spanish kings—Castilian or Aragonese—used the coronation only when their own legitimacy, or the queen's, was called into question.[63] It is possible that by choosing not to be crowned, Alfonso was behaving like a Castilian king who believed that a coronation was not an absolute necessity, that he was simply reluctant to have a coronation because they feared appearing to owe their kingship to anyone—bishop or noble.[64] As king of the Crown of Aragon, his lack of coronation signals a belief that his right to rule came from his father, whose rights of inheritance were confirmed by the Compromise of Caspe. He met with the Catalan Corts in September 1416 and took oaths to observe the laws of the principality, and he would repeat this at various times, but he would go no further. Alfonso very clearly signaled to his subjects that he regarded the Crown as his patrimony and that his subjects had no legal standing to determine the legitimacy of his claim.[65]

Alfonso's later actions, and most clearly his strong distaste for the Crown's contractual monarchy that put clear limits on him, were just the first salvos in a long fight for control. By going against tradition, even one as weak as coronation, Alfonso risked the wrath of his subjects who were famously independent and suspicious of strong kings. In each constituent realm of the Crown of Aragon, royal authority was counterbalanced by the equal strength of the Corts, composed of nobles, clerics, and, since the fourteenth century, the townspeople. The wealth and vigor of this group, particularly the nobles and the urban patriciate (known collectively as the *ciutadans honrats*) who dominated regional government in Barcelona, enabled them to resist any royal actions that they interpreted as an attempt to limit their political privileges and economic freedom.[66] The relationship between the king and the governed, known as *pactism*, was a form of contractual government that specifically called for a monarchy limited by law and powerful only when united in purpose with the people.[67] In theory, it was a working version of "primus inter pares" in which the status of the king was of a superior and directing, but by no means absolute, authority. In practice, however, the king's authority superseded all others, and this carefully balanced political equilibrium was based more on mutual wariness than on trust.

It is not surprising, then, that María did not have a formal coronation, either. But, unlike Alfonso's overtly political snub, this was not unusual for Aragonese queens. Unlike their counterparts elsewhere in Europe, it was marriage, not coronation, and especially after 1300, the office of the lieutenancy that legitimized the Aragonese queen.[68] Prominent uncrowned queens of the Crown of Aragon wielded significant political power—Elionor of Sicily, Violant of Bar, Juana Enríquez—and like María of Castile they were uncrowned queens with considerable political authority.[69] Of twenty-six queens of the Crown of Aragon, only five were formally crowned and all had particular reasons for doing so. The coronation of Constança of Sicily, wife of Pere III (r. 1276–85), legitimized the acquisition of Sicily.[70] The marriage of Blanca of Naples in 1295 to Jaume II (r. 1291–1327) further cemented Aragonese power in the Mediterranean and her coronation legitimized the custom of primogeniture.[71] Sibila de Fortià, a widow, became the fourth wife of Pere IV (1336–87) in 1377 after first being his mistress and bearing him a daughter. Her extravagant coronation was a bold assertion of her status that signaled her dislike of her stepchildren, and was clearly an attempt to shield her from enemies who considered her a dangerous upstart whose crown was strictly for show.⁷² Martí (r. 1396–1410), king of Sicily who succeeded to the Crown of Aragon after the death of his brother, Joan I (r. 1387–96), personally crowned his wife, Maria de Luna, in an ornate and well-publicized ceremony in 1399. By then, she had secured the Crown for him while he settled his affairs in Sicily, summoned the Corts, pacified the kingdom, and governed as his lieutenant for a year. Her coronation legitimated all her actions before Martí's return, but more than that, it was a formal "thank you" from the king and a clear assertion of his presence in the kingdom and his role in the ruling partnership.⁷³ The last Aragonese queen to be crowned was Leonor of Albuquerque in 1414, one month after Fernando and fully two years after the Compromise of Caspe legally secured his rights to the Crown. Their coronations symbolized and legitimated the arrival of a new dynasty to the Crown Aragon, and Alfonso's snubbing of the coronation rite just a few years later reveals a style of rule that would gradually become more authoritarian over time.

Alfonso, from the day he was born and throughout his education as a prince, was expected to rule. He was regarded as the defender of the realm, a lord in God's image, and the natural successor to his father. His entire education, from his infancy when he was guided by his mother to his youth when he was formally educated and often supervised directly by the king, was directed toward the day he would succeed his father. María should have received training in the duties, responsibilities, rights, and prerogatives of an Aragonese queen at court and by observing how her mother-in-law operated in the political realm. But there is little evidence that she received guidance from Leonor of Albuquerque, who owed her political power to her prodigious family connections, her vast estates in southern Castile, and a happy marriage to her husband, who was both five years younger and her nephew. Moreover, she had little time to devote to training her young daughter-in-law how to be an Aragonese queen, occupied as she was with supervising her seven children and managing her estates.⁷⁴ Leonor, a charismatic and prodigiously talented woman, could have given much advice on queenship, but very little would have been particular to the Crown of Aragon because she was far more familiar with Castilian institutions and procedures. Leonor was active in all areas of governance during her brief four years as queen as her husband's right hand and was a careful tutor to her son, but she was hardly a typical Aragonese queen. She and Fernando were rarely apart while he was king of the Crown of Aragon, and Alfonso, not his mother, served as the royal lieutenant. During Fernando's final illness and the first years of Alfonso's reign, Leonor was ever-present in Aragonese government.[75] Leonor was kept busy by her sons, the *infantes of Aragón*, and their intrigues in Castile, and devoted herself to advising Alfonso on matters of state. All of this left little room for her daughter-in-law and even less time to train her.[76] Illness compounded matters, as María and many others in the royal court suffered from various maladies during most 1416. Fearful of contagions, Alfonso ordered her to stay away from her father-in-law's deathbed and she was unable to attend his funeral at Poblet.

The Queen's Court and Household

María's education in Aragonese queenship took place in earnest in the Aragonese court and household itself. Unlike many royal brides who lived in their prospective husband's household for education and acculturation, she lived in the Castilian court until her marriage. A young newcomer to the Aragonese court, overshadowed by her formidable mother-in-law, María was absent from government, appearing publicly only when bidden and deferring to her mother-in-law, who continued to govern alongside Alfonso.[77] She appeared in 1417 with Alfonso and Leonor at a tourney in Valencia, and later with her husband in Teruel. Around 1418, when Leonor's poor health limited her public role, María moved into the public eye. She did so, as all queens did, in the curious and contradictory, public and private, space of the royal court. As Rita Costa Gomes observes, the medieval court was a mixture of *domus* and *res publica*, a physical, social, and temporal space. It is a "human configuration that is the central site of a larger structure, connecting the monarch to the kingdom through a group of complex relations, and by this implying a system of institutions" that mediate the king's and queen's power.[78] The late medieval court consisted of complex bureaucratic offices governing justice and administration, fisc and patrimony, and the chancery, which in most kingdoms pertained to the king alone.

In the late medieval Crown of Aragon, this tidy structure was augmented and complicated by a parallel structure for the queen-lieutenant. Like all queens, she had the usual complement of personal attendants as well as tailors, jewelers, cooks, and host of servants to tend to her personal needs. She also had governmental officials who served her as the queen-lieutenant. There could be considerable overlap of offices, which may appear confusing to us, but was quite normal for an Aragonese queen. After

1420, when she was first named lieutenant, she was the chief official of a complex federative Crown, and moved her court and household at least every four months and more, depending on circumstances. Like all medieval queens, she took her personal household attendants with her wherever she went, but many members of the administrative staff remained in regional capitals, while her chief advisers accompanied her. Barcelona, the historic site of Aragonese royal government, was the primary royal residence for most of María's tenure as lieutenant, second only to Valencia, the site of the royal winter palace. She also maintained a summer palace at Perpinyà, but it was never used as a permanent residence.[79]

María's royal court and household in Catalunya were managed much as they had been since the reforms of Pere IV in 1344.[80] Pere's reforms regulated and stabilized all aspects of the royal household and the offices of judicial and financial administration. His first goal was to reduce the number and influence of nobles in government. Catalan nobles were contentious, prone to bitter political-familial factions, and not always diligent servants of the Crown. Pere turned to a cadre of professionally trained lawyers and *familiares*—clerics, some lay officials, and non-nobles who were loyal only to him. His second goal was to strengthen central administration as a means of holding together his disparate realms, which, with their distinct languages, local institutions, and cultures, tended toward fragmentation. Until then, the main constituent states of the Crown of Aragon—Aragón, Catalunya, Mallorca, Valencia—were united principally in the person of the king himself, and Pere's reforms created an institutional umbrella that covered all the realms.[81] To these ends, Pere organized royal government into four main departments under a single office. Two were household officials, the majordomo (*mayordomen*), responsible for provisioning and staffing the royal household, and the chamberlain (*camarlench*), responsible for the royal personage, including jewels, clothing, and other personal valuable items.[82] Two were governmental offices, the chancellor, the head of the chancery and royal council, and the mestre racional, chief fiscal officer. The royal chapel fell under the purview of the chancellor, who by the later Middle Ages often was a high-ranking cleric.[83] In each realm, a local branch of each department was established and then supervised by an official with delegated authority. The court and household thus formed the principal administrative bond among the constituent states, and officials who traveled with the king and the queen-lieutenant on their tours of the realm kept a close eye on the local offices. For the officials themselves, physical proximity likewise meant access to the king and queen through their ex officio membership in the royal council and, often, a personal friendship.

As the main household official, each majordomo was responsible for feeding and provisioning the household, maintaining the royal stables and the hunting dogs and birds. Majordomos had to be noble knights (*nobles cavallers*), and because they were responsible for both the body and the residence of the royal family, they were among the king's and queen's closest advisers. The precedence among them was determined by the realm in which the king was residing, which meant that for most of Alfonso's reign the majordomos who followed him to Naples were officially higher in status than María's in Barcelona.[84] The two chamberlains, also knights, were in charge of the care of the royal chamber, its contents, and the physical well-being of the king and the royal family. The chamberlain later was granted a limited jurisdiction over the administration of Crown revenues such as those derived from the king's lordship in the royal demesne, from those lands he held as tenant-in-chief, and from his sovereign rights, including mints (which had their own courts), saltworks, monopolies, shipwrecks, and customs dues.[85] Authority in the royal household naturally implied jurisdiction over the courtiers and their staff. So, for instance, the chamberlain supervised the royal secretaries and the *algutzirs* (constables), royal appointees who were also knights and whose criminal and civil jurisdiction extended to include the royal household.[86]

The extent of a queen's ability to exercise her prerogative to appoint her own staff of officials and advisers is a critical measure of a queen's power, relative to that of her husband.[87] In the case of María and Alfonso, this is the barometer that records the shifting dynamics of their political and marital partnership, especially later in the reign, when she was more assertive and less willing to bend to his will. Like her mother and mother-in-law, María developed and maintained personal circles of associates both companionate and political. They formed the core of her household, her court, and the administrative staff of her lieutenancy. María worked almost exclusively with Catalans or Valencians, a practice that differed from that of her husband, who preferred a Castilian household retinue and liked to appoint Catalans to Aragonese offices, and vice versa.[88] This practice may have been purely practical, because the men she worked with were seasoned professionals with extensive experience with Catalan law and customs. It may also have been a political tactic, a sign of recognition that she was building alliances by working with locals. Her personal retinue and friends included many Castilians, but in matters of government she took care to work with Catalans, and this no doubt contributed to the smooth functioning of her court. She tended to rely on a small group of household officers who moved from job to job in her court, and worked very closely with two, Berenguer de Montpalau (who served until 1452) and her own appointee, Hug de Puigpardines (1450–53).[89] Among her majordomos were Berenguer de Hostalrich, Joan de Próxida, and Guillem de Vic, who also served at other times as chamberlains. Because they served at her pleasure and they literally shared the same roof, bonds of loyalty and perhaps even friendship formed.

María had an additional household official, the *governador de la Cambra de la Reyna*, a sort of cabinet member without a portfolio, theoretically in charge of her personal court, especially her finances, but distinct from her chamberlain. Berenguer de Montpalau held this office most often, especially during the late 1440s and early 1450s. Montpalau's job was complicated because as queen-lieutenant María's personal finances as queen were distinct from those she administered as lieutenant of Catalunya, and each were managed separately. The maestre racional handled the treasury and accounting for the office of the lieutenant, while income specifically earmarked to support the queen's household income as queen, derived from personal wealth and her dowry, was handled by the financial office known as the *Cambra de la Reyna*.[90] The queen's lands during the fifteenth century included reveneues from the Jewish and Muslim communities of Montblanc, Tarrega, and Tortosa in Catalunya; Huesca, Calatayud, Borja, Magallón, and Tarazona in Aragón; Játiva, Alcira, Burriana, Crevillente, Elche, Eslida, Morella, and Murviedro in Valencia; the Jewish *aljamas* of Barcelona and Valencia; and estates in Sicily.[91] The lands in the Cambra de la Reyna were governed as direct lordship, comparable to similar arrangements in England and France.[92] The lands themselves and the revenues were not held by a single person but rather the queen qua queen and thus were not permitted to be included in any bequests or endowments.[93]

Berenguer de Montpalau's title alone does not tell the whole story of his importance to her, however. He went where she could not go and did what she could not do, either because she was a woman or because of illness. She placed him in charge of collecting an unpopular 1449 subsidy that Alfonso levied to celebrate the marriages of his illegitimate children (the *maridatge*);[94] and he handled her personal finances, often traveling to Naples to justify certain expenses or requests for additional funds for the queen's court.[95] He functioned as her eyes and ears in the court, the

Corts,[96] and in her dealings with local officials, and was invaluable to her later, especially during the *remença* dispute.[97]

A Political Marriage

María and Alfonso's marriage created a political partnership but little else. What moments of personal happiness they may have had together occurred early in the marriage. Catalina fretted over the time the couple spent apart, but María assured her mother that all was well.[98] As it turns out, her mother's concerns were not groundless. María's health was fragile, perhaps due to epilepsy, and a bout of smallpox in 1423 left her permanently scarred. Most important, she bore Alfonso no children. María did not have her first menstrual period until she was sixteen, two years after their marriage, which forced the couple to delay consummating their marriage.[99] This could not have been easy for either of them. but especially for Alfonso, an active, athletic man who loved hunting and physical activities, and made no attempt to conceal his sexual adventures.[100] Whatever the cause of their childlessness—María's ill health or Alfonso's lengthy absences—the fact that there was neither son nor daughter to inherit the Crown profoundly affected the course of their marriage and, above all, the reign.

The cracks in their personal relationship began to surface as early as 1423, when Alfonso returned from Italy. Their difficulties had both public and personal dimensions. The meddling of the *infantes* Juan, Enrique, and Pedro in Castile nearly resulted in war in 1424 and distressed María greatly.[101] As important as war was, the lack of a legitimate heir, male or female, was even more troubling. After nearly ten years of marriage, with two spent waiting for María to mature sexually and over three years apart, María and Alfonso had no children together.[102] The problem was clearly not Alfonso's, for in June 1425, Gueraldona Carlina Reverdit, one of his mistresses and the wife of a high-ranking Barcelona citizen, bore the king his only son, Ferran.[103] The strains on their marriage became publicly evident in October 1424, when María summoned the city councilors of Barcelona to tell them that she had news that Alfonso's mother, Leonor, had died, and instructed them to convey this information to Alfonso.[104] The king, who was extremely close to his mother, ordered his household into mourning and began funeral preparations, only to learn that the information was false. It is unclear whether María made up the story or spread a false rumor, either willingly or unwillingly, but it was a stunning move. Ryder attributes María's actions to "exasperation, perhaps malice," and notes that the revelation that Alfonso had a new mistress may have prompted the queen to inflict pain on her husband. If nothing else, it is an indication of how cool relations were between María and Leonor, whose own brood must have been a rebuke to María's inability to conceive. Whatever struggles there were between the two women, it is not evident in the documents. This one moment is the only public indication of stress between the two women. It is also significant that María spread the false story of her mother-in-law's death at around the same time that Alfonso's illegitimate son was conceived.[105] Other rumors surrounded their marriage, all concerning Alfonso's extramarital sexual behavior and all underscoring María's failure to produce an heir. One particularly vivid story, often repeated but never substantiated, has María personally strangling one pregnant mistress, Margarita de Hijar, in her bed with her own embroidered belt. Some accounts say she was smothered, not strangled; some say Hijar was a high-ranking lady-in-waiting at María's court, others say she was a prostitute.[106] I have found no evidence to prove the story's veracity, and on the basis of María's careful, prudent, and circumspect life in later decades, I am inclined to agree with both Soldevila, who does not believe that Alfonso ever had an affair with Hijar, and Ryder, who says that "of neither Alfonso nor María does this tale ring true."[107] But the existence of such rumors reflected both the sad state of their affections and the general opinion of the court and household that the royal marriage was not a happy one. This is borne out by the births, around 1430, of two more illegitimate children, his daughters María and Leonor on whom Alfonso lavished money, affection, and attention. All three children eventually lived with him in Italy. Ferran was later granted the duchy of Calabria and both daughters married influential Italian princes.[108] Divorce was not an issue, with their marriage a key piece of Trastámara strategy in Spain, and so they stayed together but kept their distance. Alfonso left Spain shortly after Hijar's death in 1430 and never returned. For the next twenty-eight years their marriage was consumed with governance not sentiment.

But political, not personal, tensions were foremost in May 1420. From the outset of his reign, Alfonso's dealings with the Catalans were stormy, especially with the Catalan nobles who played a key role in the Compromise of Caspe that made Fernando of Antequera king of the Crown of Aragon.[109] Fernando owed his crown to his nobles in the Corts who agreed to the Compromise and they never let him, or his son, forget it. Even though Alfonso had been his father's lieutenant in various Aragonese realms before becoming king in 1416, he was considered by many Catalans to be a foreign prince. He remained close to his Castilian heritage and language, often preferring Castilians as his closest advisors. His choice of a Castilian bride, even one who quickly became fluent in Catalan, reinforced this sentiment. He tried to mute the influence of the Catalans in royal administration by appointing Aragonese officials to Catalan posts and vice versa. He played urban mercantile interests against powerful Catalan noble families who had long formed the inner circle of the king's court and soon found themselves outside the center of power.[110] He created new noble families and brought others from Aragón and Valencia into his council.[111] But the Catalans' ingrained wariness of royal power had hardened into belligerence, and was matched in turn by Alfonso's increasing tendency toward absolutism.[112]

And so, when Alfonso boarded the royal galley docked at Alfachs in the bay at the mouth of the Ebro River near Tortosa and set sail for Sardinia, Italy was not his only destination, nor was the need to subdue incipient civil war his only goal. The lure of Italy was a respite from seemingly endless confrontations with the Catalans, an opportunity for military action instead of debate and legislation cloaked in dynastic ambition. This was not an impulsive gesture. He had made plans to build a royal navy in 1417, and construction of the fleet began in February 1419.[113] In spite of his stated goal to save Sardinia from the "perfidious Sards," he was drawn to Italy by the allure of a dynastic vacancy in the kingdom of Naples that tempted him with the prospect of adding another Mediterranean realm to the Crown of Aragon.[114] Queen Giovanna II (r. 1414–35), elderly and childless and a puppet of the Neapolitan barons, was willing to name Alfonso as her heir in return for Aragonese military support. His claim was contested by Louis III of Anjou and his Sforza family allies; as a result, Alfonso's initial attempt to gain Naples was unsuccessful and he became engaged in sporadic warfare until 1423.[115] He persuaded the Catalan merchants and bankers that Naples would be a lucrative mercantile entrepôt in Italy that would give them an edge in the long-standing commercial rivalry between Barcelona and Genoa, Pisa, and Florence.[116] Convinced, the Corts granted him a generous subsidy to pay for the military campaigns, leaving Alfonso with only the problem of the governance of Catalunya to resolve.[117]

To govern his peninsular realms, Alfonso turned naturally to the lieutenancy, but he faced a problem that his predecessors did not have. He had a wife but no legitimate sons to enlist as lieutenant. His three brothers, the *infantes de Aragón*—Enrique, Pedro, and Juan, king of Navarre— were ambitious and not completely trustworthy siblings. Pedro would later prove to be one of Alfonso's most trusted military advisors, but he was only eleven years old in 1420. Juan and Enrique, in particular, were frequent co-conspirators who interfered in Castilian politics, especially against the powerful Alvaro de Luna. On more than one occasion they brought Castile and the Crown of Aragon to the brink of open warfare.[118] Alfonso was reluctant to give the job to any of his brothers, even though Juan of Navarre was Alfonso's designated heir.[119] But in 1420 Juan was in Castile and Alfonso was unwilling to leave his peninsular realms in the hands of Pedro or Enrique, so he followed the precedent of four of his predecessors and left María, then nineteen years old, in charge.[120]

Given the tension between the king and the Catalan ruling elites, it is remarkable that he left the kingdom at all, much less leave its governance in the hands of someone so young and inexperienced in government. Ryder believes that Alfonso's impatience with the pace of politics in Catalunya made him long for military action and led him to take risks that other kings might have considered imprudent.[121] It was, however, a period of relative calm, and hindsight proves that he read the situation correctly. He made certain that the people most likely to take advantage of his absence accompanied him to Italy by promising them a piece of the mercantile riches there. He trusted that those subjects who remained would not seize power in his absence and, after five years of marriage, he had tremendous confidence in María. Their marriage was still steady; their problems still distant. And, he no doubt took comfort in knowing that his mother, Leonor, whom he trusted completely, could be called on to assist if the need arose.

Prior to his departure, on 2 May 1420 at Castellón de la Plana (Valencia), Alfonso issued a *privilegio* that named María as lieutenant general and delegated to her full governmental powers over the kingdoms of Aragón and Valencia, the principality of Catalunya, and the island of Mallorca.[122]

Dirigere Nos opportet et a regnis nostris Aragonum, Valencie et Maioricarum ac Principatu Cathalonie per consequens absentare, dignumque esse personam talem dimittere in eisdem que maiestatem Nostram in omnibus representet: Tenore presentis, de certa sciencia et consulte Vos, illustrem Reginam Mariam consortem nostram carissimam, regimini dictorum regnorum Principatus ac insularum adjacencium regno Maioricarum predicto et omnium subditorum nostrorum in eis presencium preficimus et in eisdem nostram generalem locumtenentem creamus,

Chapter 2

constituimus et eciam ordinamus, concedentes Vobis expresse et potestatem plenariam tribuentes quod regatis et gubernetis ac regere et gubernare possitis dicta regna, Principatum et insulas, quamdiu Nos abesse contigerit ab eisdem; et utamini et possitis uti mero et mixto imperio cum plenissima gladii potestate, omnique jurisdiccione civili et criminali eaque exercere libere valeatis et facere exerceri tam in terra quam in mari quam eciam aqua dulci.[123]

This *privilegio* stipulated that her powers as lieutenant general should be equivalent to his own as king, and that she had the authority to rule independently. As the highest judicial authority in Catalunya, María had full sovereign power over all civil and criminal jurisdictions in all four realms, including the army and the military orders. Her authority superseded all the royal, seigneurial, regional, and local officials; provincial governors; prelates and religious orders; the nobility, townspeople, peasants, and all other subjects regardless of status. She had the authority to summon, convoke, and preside over the Corts, the regional parliamentary assemblies.[124] The formulaic chancery language of the *privilegio* is consistent with Aragonese chancery practice and resembles other grants of lieutenancy in content and organization. It may have been written in a rush; for instance, Alfonso granted María military authority (*gladii potestate*) but it is unlikely that he seriously intended that she would take charge of an army.[125] The explicit statement of the scope and duration of the governmental authority makes it clear that her authority was held at the king's discretion. Just as the king could give her political power, so too could he take it away. Her authority was equivalent to the king's in the realms stipulated by the *privilegio*, but he nevertheless retained the ultimate authority. She governed, but he held dominion.[126]

From his mother's example and his own experience as his father's lieutenant, Alfonso assumed that he and María would govern as partners, so when he left for Naples in 1420 he was comfortable leaving his young wife as lieutenant. Moreover, his goals in 1420 were strictly military, and he was confident that his Italian campaigns would be brief and he planned to return shortly.[127] Whatever his personal feelings toward her may have been, he trusted María to take his place at the head of the government of the principality of Catalunya, the kingdom of Mallorca and at various times, the kingdoms of Aragón and Valencia.

Chapter 3
From Queen to Queen-Lieutenant, 1420–35

THE FACT THAT ALFONSO'S BROTHERS, the *infants de Aragón*, did not protest María's appointment as lieutenant may seem surprising. They were ambitious young men, but they were receptive to rule by a woman because by 1420 a queen-lieutenant was a fairly common occurrence.[1] Five queen-consorts ruled as lieutenants in the Crown of Aragon before María did: Blanca of Naples, wife of Jaume II, in 1310[2]; Teresa d'Entença, wife of Alfons III, lieutenant from 1324 to 1327[3]; Violant of Bar, third wife of Joan I, 1388–95[4]; Maria de Luna, first wife of Martí, 1396–1401[5]; and Margarida of Prades, second wife of Martí, 1412–21.[6] María of Castile would be the sixth, followed by Juana Enríquez, second wife of Juan II, 1461–77 and the last queen-lieutenant.[7] The *infantes* recognized the strength of precedent, the competency of earlier queens-lieutenant, and could take for granted María's legitimacy. This also explains the matter-of-fact acceptance of her lieutenancy by the nobles, clerics, and townspeople of Catalunya, who seemed unbothered, or at least acquiescent.[8] The absence of protests concerning her appointment does not mean that María did not face serious challenges to her authority, because she did. But these protests came later in her lieutenancy and were confined to one very specific action—the convocation of the Corts—and not to the many other duties and functions of governance that she performed, such as judicial and financial administration. This issue—whether a queen, or anyone, could take the king's place in the Corts and whether the king had, in fact, the right to delegate that authority—touched the heart of Aragonese kingship and dominated her tenure as lieutenant. The protests were rooted in long-held notions of kingship and law. Although they were not an attack on her abilities and they did not question the overall legitimacy of her lieutenancy, they reflect very clearly the limits of a queen-lieutenant's power, regardless of the official extent of her authority and the force of her personality.

Political institutions such as the lieutenancy rarely are subjected to gendered analysis, perhaps because they were so often staffed by men that we presume women were officially excluded, and that the exercise is futile. Yet institutions are empty shells that a society fills with cultural presumptions and that shift shape to accommodate changing needs. The particular gender norms in the late medieval Crown of Aragon play a key role in understanding the lieutenancy of María of Castile and, more broadly, the Aragonese monarchy. To study the gender of an institution means to ask questions such as, what does it mean when a woman occupies the office and exercises the authority? In the case of the lieutenant, what does it mean to delegate official authority to a woman? How does this affect governance and political theory? How does this affect the operations of kingship and queenship? How do other people react? What does it mean to have a queen at the head of a complex set of political institutions—royal, regional, and municipal—that were highly developed with a precision unmatched anywhere else in Europe at the time.[9] How does this affect the operations of gender in other spheres, such as economics, law, social relations, and religion?

Answers to some of these questions can be found in the institution itself, its development, and its adaptation over time from a training ground for princes to a key component in queenship. But real insight is found best in how the theory and precedent and institutional bureaucracy actually operated during her long tenure. Her first, short stint as lieutenant from 1420 to 1423 serves as a springboard for a discussion of the tools of office—council, chancery, justice, and financial administration—and an examination of how the office worked with regional and municipal institutions—Corts, Diputació del General, and Consell de Cent of Barcelona. In the chapters that follow I explore these issues by continuing to follow the trajectory of her long tenure as lieutenant from 1432 to 1453.

Representation and Delegation of the King's Authority

The office of the governmental lieutenant was not an innovation, nor was it unique to the Crown of Aragon. Similar institutions appeared at roughly the same time in England and France under a variety of Latin names—*gerenti vices, custos, procurator, locumtenens*—each slightly different but all of them fall under the same rubric. Vernacular nomenclature is confusing—titles changed over time in the Crown of Aragon, from *procurador* to *gobernador* to *lloctinent*—and the only way to clearly distinguish one from the other is to focus on actual jurisdiction. Sometimes a male lieutenant was head of both the government and the army, but a governmental lieutenant must not be confused with a military rank. In the Crown of Aragon the lieutenancy was never solely military in character although the direction of military affairs often fell under the jurisdiction of the lieutenant. But a lieutenant was, in the literal definition of the Latin phrase *locum tenens*, someone who occupied the place of another person, in this case, the king. This meaning is clearly retained in all its Romance cognates: the French *lieutenant*, the Castilian *lugarteniente*, the Italian *tenente*, and the Catalan *lloctinent*.[10] Lieutenancies developed as a consequence of theories of representation that stemmed from late twelfth- and early thirteenth-century legal decisions prompted by the rapid growth of both papal and secular government. Rules 68 and 72 of the "Liber Sextus" and Pope John XXII's decretal, "Super gentes," determined that the pope could delegate his authority.[11] Secular rulers, whose realms expanded due to conquest, annexation, inheritance, or dowry recognized that they could empower an official to govern those places where they could not be physically present, without losing legal regal status. The growth of the lieutenancy as an institution coincided with, and contributed to, the development of political theories that drew a distinction between the person of the king from the office of the king.[12] Popular resistance to rule by a lieutenant was minimal because the office was not an innovation but simply an extension of the powers of an existing office. Delegated authorities such as regents, protectors, justiciars, or seneschals were especially important for those kings who governed territories abroad, notably the English and the Aragonese.

A brief comparison of the governance of the Crown of Aragon's Mediterranean realms with the more familiar case of the Plantagenet family during and after the reign of Henry II (1152–89) highlights the distinctiveness of the Aragonese realms and the office of the queen-lieutenant.[13] In both cases, royal realms encompassed a wide geographic sweep of territories acquired via marriage and conquest. For Henry II and his sons, this included England and most of western France (which at varying points in time included the duchies of Anjou, Aquitaine, Brittany, Gascony, Maine, and Normandy, and the counties of Poitou and Touraine).[14] The lands of the Crown of Aragon at its greatest extent in the mid-fifteenth century consisted of the kingdoms of Aragón, Naples, and Valencia, the principality of Catalunya, the Balearic Islands, Sicily, Sardinia, and Corsica.[15] The Plantagenet monarchs were wealthier, but the rulers of the Crown of Aragon exerted hegemony over their domains far longer than their Anglo-Norman peers, who acquired their lands quickly and lost them in short order. By the end of the reign of King John in 1216, much of his inheritance from Henry II had been lost to Philip Augustus.[16] The medieval Crown of Aragon, on the other hand, took shape between 1137 and 1436, and remained a coherent distinct political entity until 1479 when the succession of Isabel and Fernando joined the Crown with Castile.[17] Finally, both the English and the Aragonese monarchs shared an extensive reliance on governmental lieutenants and viceroys to rule these dispersed realms, but the differences here are as notable as the similarities.

Even before the office of the Aragonese queen-lieutenant was created in the early fourteenth-century, the lieutenant general in the Crown of Aragon was unlike any other royal office. A lieutenant was the embodiment of the king's personal authority and custodian of the realm, a co-ruler with an adult king, fully capable of ruling, who, for any number of reasons, could not govern a particular territory or territories. Although chancellors and governors performed very specific tasks, often for a specific length of time, at the king's command, they were still subject to his will: They worked for the king. A lieutenant, on the other hand, worked in place of the king. Because of the lieutenant's intimate association with the king's body, he or she could take the place of that body only and no other. The lieutenant's term expired when the king did, but the lieutenancy could continue at the new king's discretion, like a chancellor who could remain in office during the interregnum or from king to king. It is the nature and scope of the official jurisdiction that distinguishes the two offices. The chancellor could advise the king and he could prepare a writ on the king's order for the king's signature, but that was the extent of his authority. A lieutenant acted in concert with the king as well as in place of the king and thus could order the writ and sign it. In theory, lieutenants were empowered to act freely in all circumstances, but in practice all kings retained the power to withhold assent or revoke the title.[18] Substitution of a lieutenant for a king was acceptable to their subjects because although the king was free to name anyone he wanted, he most often chose his eldest son or, in the case of the Crown of Aragon, the queen. It was not an equal substitution, of course, but one royal body did replace another regardless of gender. Because of this association with the royal family, the lieutenant personified royal power more perfectly than any other office and thus had a higher dignity than all others. The increased acceptance of primogeniture as a means of determining the succession,[19] anticipatory association of the heir,[20] and coronation ceremonies for queens all combined to make the substitution more palatable to the local population subject to the lieutenant's immediate jurisdiction.[21]

A member of the royal family with broad jurisdiction resembles a regent or an apanaged (cadet) prince, but these are distinct entities. A lieutenant was appointed to a permanent office by a very much alive and well king who ruled with him, in his place, in far-flung territories or newly conquered realms, and held the office at the king's discretion, sometimes for life.[22] A regent (or regency council) or protector governed because youth or illness or captivity impaired a king's ability to rule. Like lieutenants, regents and protectors held nonheritable custodial offices with an official scope but they served only until the king reached his majority or was otherwise capable of returning to work full time.[23] For example, Richard, duke of York, was named "protector and defender of the realm" due to Henry VI's (1422–61) insanity and his son's minority. His title implied a personal duty for the defense of the land and the appointment continued only until the prince came of age.[24] In France, the regency functioned like the lieutenancy, as when a very healthy and sane Philip Augustus (1180–1223) went on Crusade in 1190 and left France in the hands not of a lieutenant but of a regency council led by his mother, Adéle of Champagne.[25]

On the other hand, an apanaged prince, like a lieutenant, protector, or regent, was a member of the royal family with a broad jurisdiction superseded only by the king himself, but with one important difference. But the apanage was not just an office, it was an inheritance, and the pressures of the blood tie made an apanage a new kind of fief. It was not just a way to govern newly acquired lands, it was a grant of land. It was not custodial, it was seigneurial. The king rarely exercised direct control or administration over apanage lands and they were not necessarily represented at royal assemblies. An apanage brought with it a title, such as duke or earl, whereas a lieutenant, already a duke, earl, or queen, had one.[26] The holder of an apanage could collect the revenues as his own and thus maintained a semi-autonomous financial position. Conversely, the lieutenant collected revenues from the king's lands in the name of the king and had limited control over treasury disbursements. The lands, titles, incomes, and jurisdiction of an apanage reverted to the crown if there were no male heirs to succeed, but lands governed by a lieutenant were never alienated from Crown patrimony.[27]

Like the lieutenant, the justiciar, created by King Henry I (1100–35) of England, occupied a permanent office and had the power to issue writs and to preside over a central court of Exchequer. Henry II (1154–89) whose realms comprised five separate administrations, left the justiciar in charge of England and his seneschals (the Norman equivalent of a justiciar) in charge of his French territories.[28] He sent his son John as quasi-viceroy to govern Ireland in 1185 (although Henry retained a firm grip on policy) and set a precedent for associating the office with a member of the royal family.[29] In France, Philip Augustus delegated authority to bailiffs and seneschals who, like the English justiciar, were not members of the royal family, but whose jurisdiction was limited.[30] In France, as in the Crown of Aragon, the king brought a province (Languedoc or Normandy, for instance) under his direct control, he preserved intact its customs and institutions but staffed all the higher offices with his own men from Paris. By the late fourteenth century, the lieutenancy, or some variant of it, became integral to a prince's education.[31] The Valois kings used the office of the lieutenant as a training ground for the dauphin.[32] Charles V of France (1364–80) served as *lieutenant du roi* after the capture of his father, Jean (1350–64), at the battle of Poitiers in 1356. Because his father was unable to rule, this seems more like a regency than a lieutenancy, but after Jean's release in 1360, Charles remained active in government until his father's death.[33] The lieutenancy was especially important to the English because of their extensive continental territories. During the Hundred Years' War there were several English lieutenants—John Beaufort, duke of Somerset (1372–1410), John of Lancaster, duke of Bedford (1389–1435), and María's own grandfather, John of Gaunt—but none more famous than Edward, Prince of Wales, the "Black Prince." As lieutenant in Gascony (1355–63) he had complete administrative control; as lord of Aquitaine (1363–70), he had similar powers, except that he was to be lord for life.[34]

Aragonese Lieutenants in the Thirteenth and Fourteenth Centuries

Unlike their English and French contemporaries, the Aragonese kings faced a vexing long-term challenge. With far-flung territories stretching across the western Mediterranean, they needed an institution with the stature and clout of the regency but one with sufficient flexibility to enable the king to respond quickly to changing circumstances, and the governmental lieutenancy suited their needs.[35] Originally established in the thirteenth century as both an ad hoc adjunct to the king and a training ground for princes, it was a well-established institution by the fifteenth century. A governmental lieutenant in the Crown of Aragon was, in the terminology of the documents, the king's alter ego (in Catalan, *alter nos*), occupying the king's place when he was absent and relinquishing the office when he died. At that point, the eldest son would succeed his father as king and any other siblings remained lieutenants at the discretion of the new king. During the fourteenth century, when all of a king's sons were lieutenants in various realms, the lieutenancy became firmly established as part of the institutional structure of the Crown of Aragon.[36]

Once the Aragonese kings acquired dominions in the Mediterranean that were not contiguous, they were compelled to take the lieutenancy a step further than anyone else. Whereas Edward, the "Black Prince," could govern personally much of southern France, it was almost impossible for one person to rule the sprawling Crown that consisted of Aragón, Catalunya, Valencia, Majorca, Sicily, Corsica, and Sardinia.[37] Because the office could be easily modified it to suit changing needs, the Aragonese rulers used the lieutenancy continuously. They blended innovation with local practice when they equipped each new territorial addition with institutions modeled on, but not quite identical to, those of Aragón and Catalunya, the core of the Crown. The lieutenant provided institutional consistency, an administrative bond, and a close tie with the charisma of the royal family that linked the diverse and distant realms that made it possible for the royal household to easily pack up and move whenever necessary in order to convoke a regional assembly, to settle a dispute, or simply to make the royal presence felt.[38] The resultant office thus resembles its English and French counterparts, but it differs from them in the continuous and often lengthy tenure and its close association with Aragonese queenship. At no other time in the Middle Ages and in no other kingdom did this form of co-rulership acquire the institutional importance of the lieutenant general of the Crown of Aragon.

The office of the lieutenant, originally called the *procurador general*, first appeared in the Crown of Aragon during the reign of Jaume I (1213–76), who intended it as an adjunct to royal rule.[39] Jaume appointed his sons to rule the home territories of Aragón and Catalunya while he conquered, pacified, and then established a government in the realms of Valencia and Majorca. His son Pere (later Pere III, 1276–85) was *procurador general* in the principality of Catalunya in 1257 and later the kingdom of Aragón until his accession in 1276.[40] The first procuradors handled routine matters of government in nearby realms while the king moved from one kingdom to another according to the demands of government, especially for the convocation of regional *Corts* (*Cortes* in Aragón) which by law demanded the king's physical presence. In 1302, the procurador's duties were more clearly defined and charged with a wider territorial jurisdiction. At this early stage, none of these officials acted as true proxies for the king, and even the procurador general continued to carry out his functions in the presence of the king. The term lieutenant first designated anyone who was appointed to rule more distant realms such as Mallorca and Valencia but the jurisdiction was local and the term of office was limited.[41] Changes in nomenclature signal the development of the office from an ad hoc post to a permanent fixture of government. When Sicily was annexed in 1282 and government became a truly long-distance affair, Pere III expanded the older lieutenancy and renamed the office lieutenant general of Sicily.[42] The designation "general" distinguished it from earlier lieutenants and indicates that the office had an even wider jurisdiction within a single territory, and may have had an increased military role. He gave the job to his eldest surviving son Jaume (later Jaume II, 1291–1327), who governed Sicily for eight years until his accession to the Aragonese throne.[43]

At this point, distance, coupled with extended periods of time, resulted in an institutional innovation that is distinctive in western Europe in the Middle Ages—the queen-lieutenant. The queen first became associated with the lieutenancy in April 1310 when Jaume II appointed his wife, Blanca of Naples, to serve as his lieutenant while he was on crusade in Almería.[44] Her tenure was brief, no more than two months, and little is known of her actions, but her exercise of legitimate political authority set the precedent for six subsequent Aragonese queens-lieutenant. A generation later, Teresa d'Entença governed for her husband, Alfons IV, in 1327 certainly, and perhaps earlier, but the documentation for her reign is unclear. There is no official *privilegio* or other document naming her lieutenant, and she may have been more a regent than a lieutenant.[45] The old office of the procurador general, which had a limited territorial jurisdiction and thus was ill-suited to the needs of such a dispersed kingdom, had disappeared altogether and its duties were assumed by lieutenants.[46]

During subsequent decades, territorial expansion continued and each realm—Catalunya, Aragón, and Valencia—developed separate parliamentary assemblies that could meet together as a Cort General or separately.[47] The king traveled from place to place, opened a session in one realm,

From Queen to Queen-Lieutenant, 1420–35

turned it over to a lieutenant (or vice chancellor) in that realm, moved on to the next stop, and repeated the process. This peripatetic governance kept the rulers in touch with their subjects, but personally convoking an assembly was expensive, cumbersome, and exhausting.[48] By the fourteenth century the kings began to reside more continuously in Barcelona. Because of this, the kings needed a lieutenant general less often in Catalunya, which in turn made the Catalans unaccustomed to rule by lieutenants and fostered among them a sense that they were the favored partners of the kings. Furthermore, roughly half the taxable wealth of the kingdom derived from Catalunya, and royal policy in the Mediterranean could easily be seen as an extension of Catalan interests. The Catalans, more than any other royal subjects, resented the king's absences and made governance difficult for any lieutenant in Catalunya, male or female.

In 1358 Joan (later Joan I, 1387–96) became the first lieutenant fully empowered to rule in the king's place when his father, Pere IV (1336–87), named him lieutenant general.[49] For the first time, the designation "general" truly signified both wide governmental powers and wide territorial jurisdiction. The first lieutenant to preside over the Cortes in Aragón, he took over because, after a series of lengthy delays, Pere was unavailable by the time the Cortes actually met.[50] Joan was instructed by Pere to "prorrogar, continuar, e encara celebrar la dita Cort."[51] Joan's actions did not raise any eyebrows, probably because the law specified that he could do so with the formal consent of the king and the three estates in the Corts, and because it was customary for the heir to do so in the absence of the king.[52] What was customary for a prince could be controversial for a queen. Pere IV's third wife, Elionor of Sicily, took over for him, in his name and at his expressed request, at the Corts of Catalunya on 22 January 1364 because he was on the battlefield in Castile. She did so without official capacity—she never held the office of lieutenant—and simply stepped in when needed and stepped aside when he returned to preside personally.[53] Joan took over briefly for his mother when she joined Pere to celebrate Christmas in 1364.[54] The state of emergency, the brevity of her convocation, and the proximity of the king no doubt smoothed over any opposition to her actions and calmed any suspicion of institutional innovation. In another significant development, the lieutenancy became firmly associated with immediate members of the royal family. The Corts of Aragón at Tamarit in 1367 legally formalized the customary linkage of the office with the first-born son and heir (*primogénito*) by decreeing that he could automatically serve as lieutenant once he reached the age of fourteen.[55]

But precedent and the force of the king's will to work in partnership with his wife strengthened the office of the queen-lieutenant. Violant of Bar, the politically astute third wife of Joan I, was his lieutenant from 1388 to 1395. She governed ably for and with her husband during his frequent illnesses, stood in for him at the Cortes of Zaragoza in 1388, and calmed the unrest in the Crown of Aragon during the anti-Jewish riots in 1391.[56]

Violant's tenure as lieutenant is intertwined with that of Maria de Luna, queen-lieutenant for her husband Martí (r. 1395–1410) from 1396 to 1397 and again in 1401.[57] Maria was a forceful queen who served first as her husband's regent and later as his lieutenant general. Martí was king of Sicily when Joan I, his brother, died in May 1395 without leaving adult sons to succeed him. His widow Violant falsely claimed to be pregnant and as regent, Maria had to secure official recognition for Martí.[58] She summoned and convoked two sessions of the Parlament of Barcelona, a local parliamentary assembly, to legitimize Martí's right to succeed, determine whether Violant was pregnant, and establish a council to advise María until Martí returned.[59] Maria pacified the kingdom and governed until Martí's return a year later and remained active throughout his reign. She served a second term as lieutenant in 1401 while Martí was in Navarre and Valencia and remained one of her husband's ablest advisors. As advocate for the *remença* peasants, Maria de Luna tried unsuccessfully until her death in 1406 to secure a bull from anti-pope Benedict XIII that condemned peasant servitude.[60] His time in Sicily made Martí an innovative ruler and, prompted by the breakdown of public order and warring noble factions during his reign, he experimented with lieutenants, governors, viceroys, and *reformadors* in a mostly successful attempt to impose order and govern new territorial acquisitions—Sardinia, Corsica, and the duchy of Athens.[61] In 1409, Martí, "the Younger," his only son with Maria, died. Elderly and sick, with no legitimate heir, Martí married Margarida of Prades, who was his lieutenant for less than a year.[62]

By Martí's death in 1410, the office of lieutenant general had grown from a single entity in the hands of the eldest son to a multiplicity of offices held by a number of family members.[63] As the office expanded and widened in geographical scope, it became a permanent institution. No longer ad hoc, it had become the highest political office in the realm, superseded only by the king himself. The fact that the lands governed by a lieutenant were not held as apanage nor directly governed by an independent cadet king, made it easy for the Aragonese kings to delegate substantial authority to sons, wives, or brothers.[64] By taking advantage of family loyalty and the

From Queen to Queen-Lieutenant, 1420–35   51

symbolic importance of the ruling dynasty, the lieutenant personified royal power more perfectly than any other office and had a higher dignity than all others. As a form of delegated authority held by a person directly connected to the king, the lieutenancy was fundamental to Aragonese kingship. And, as more queens served as lieutenants, and for longer periods of time, what began as a route to political power for queens had become a key component of Aragonese queenship. The devolution of substantial authority on a hierarchy of queens-lieutenant and the scope of the queen-lieutenant's fully sanctioned de jure and de facto authority had enormous implications for Aragonese theories of monarchy. It is noteworthy that both Elionor of Sicily and Maria de Luna faced little opposition as they assumed substantial public political roles normally exclusively reserved for the king or the eldest son. The instability during Elionor and Maria's lieutenancies, brought on by war with Castile in 1364 and the death of the ruling king without a designated heir increased anxieties, but the proximity of a healthy adult male king was crucial in calming fears of rule by a queen.[65] The need to move quickly and decisively overcame the novelty of a queen convoking a parliamentary assembly, which in both cases were ad hoc and brief. Castilian queens-regent, convoked and presided over the Cortes, so to nobles and municipal elites and their legal advisors, the actions of Elionor and María were not without precedent. María de Molina, wife of Sancho IV (1284–95), was an especially forceful presence in the Cortes of Castile and often worked side by side with Sancho. A skillful negotiator, she worked actively to muster the support of the towns, which she rightly judged to be crucial to Sancho's authority, in the Cortes of Valladolid in 1293 and 1307 and in Medina del Campo in 1305. But of the most part these queens did little more than attend the opening and closing ceremonies. Had the crises faced by Elionor of Sicily and María de Luna persisted, or had either queen remained at the head of regional government longer than was absolutely necessary, some formal protest might have been lodged. The records of 1364 do not state so explicitly, but it is possible that Pere brought in Joan to preside during Christmas to preemptively quell any hints of opposition to his wife's actions.[66] It is safe to say that to their subjects, these politically active queens-lieutenant possessed a status roughly equivalent to that of the kings and were integral to political discourse.

Martí was the last Aragonese king descended from the dynasty created in 1137 through the marriage of Petronila and Ramón Berenguer IV. The tentative political balance created during Martí's reign was upset during, and especially after, the succession crisis, the Compromise of Caspe, and the arrival of the Trastámara dynasty in the Crown of Aragon. Alfonso was his father's lieutenant from 1413 until 1416, and Fernando maintained the political equilibrium as he traveled to each of the constituent realms to convoke the Corts and swear to uphold his subject's privileges and constitutions.[67] Alfonso used numerous lieutenants and viceroys (who were more military leaders than administrators) in Italy, but they possessed both limited jurisdiction and territorial authority and, because the king was close by, were under his strict supervision. The exception is Ferran, duke of Calabria (after 1443, and king of Naples after Alfonso's death), Alfonso's illegitimate son and his lieutenant in various realms.[68] So, when Alfonso decided to add Naples to the Crown, appointing María as his lieutenant was as natural to him as collecting taxes.

María's authority as stipulated in the *privilegios* is, simply stated, constituted power.[69] She had the authority to secure obedience in or conformity to a hierarchical chain of command and derived from a title that stated this. She had substantial power as a result of personal attributes—intelligence, force of personality, will, charisma—and family connections and personal wealth, but without the authority of political status as lieutenant she might not have been able to exercise it. Like so many queens-consort, she occupied a middle ground—although not queen in her own right, she governed forcefully, always with duly sanctioned public authority. Alfonso's *privilegios*, reiterated over the course of her lieutenancy, carefully delineated the boundary between informal power and legitimate authority granted her officially constituted power. Their relationship, predicated on a contractual relationship between political unequals, was never fully reciprocal, but it was a partnership.[70]

The Tools of Government: Consell, Cancillería, Audiència, and Mestre Racional

With the office came a well-educated and professional staff, overwhelmingly composed of lawyers of modest origin, who simply shifted their loyalty from the king to the queen. As lieutenant general of Catalunya, María shared with Alfonso the chief officials of chancery and justice, financial administration, and regional government and her own staff of officials to handle her administrative needs.[71] Alfonso stipulated clearly in the *privile-*

gios that as lieutenant general of Catalunya, María had jurisdiction over the royal council and other high-ranking royal officials:

> Preficiamini insuper et sitis in locum nostrum tanquam maiestatem Nostram regiam representans super Gubernatorem generalem omnium regnorum et terrarum Nostrarum et super omnes gubernatores quorumlibet regnorum et Principatus ac insularum superius expressorum et super omnes Consiliarios Nostros in eis ad Nostra peragenda negocia assignatos et assignandos Cancellarium et Vicecancellarium, Consiliarios Thesaurarium Nostros et racionales Magistros Curie nostre, justicias, merinos, vicarios, Baiulos, suprajunctarios, protarios, procuratores et collectares reddituum et jurium nostrorum et alios quoslibet Officiales Nostros.[72]

Her Consell e Audiència, the royal council and law court, were the heart of government in Catalunya. As both an advisory body and the supreme tribunal in Catalunya, with the queen-lieutenant as its head, it supervised the workings of regional administration, royal finances, and the royal household.[73] The Consell's authority was extensive. Prior lieutenants maintained an extensive administrative court that resembled the king's, notably Joan I (lieutenant from 1360–87), but María was the first queen-lieutenant to maintain a Consell e Audiència separate from the king's with both advisory and judicial functions.[74] Having a separate court and council was important to María's ability to work efficiently and it elevated her status and granted her substantial clout.[75] Her court was a mirror image of Alfonso's in Naples, but they were not equal. Fearing powerful members of the royal council and the temptations posed by his absences, even after decades apart he retained the right to appoint high-ranking clergy. He tried to govern both tightly and loosely at the same time by selecting carefully which tasks and appointments to keep to himself. He controlled who served on her advisory council, what they were to do, and for how long because it freed him to govern more effectively in Naples while reinforcing his own status as superior to hers. He reserved to himself the highest-ranking appointments as a way of demonstrating his supreme authority while personally dispensing favors and rewards for service, but ceded to her the control over lesser appointments, reinforcing María's status as highest in Catalunya but subordinate to that of the king.

The inner circle of political power in Catalunya was firmly in the hands of lawyers and loyal bureaucrats, with chancery, judicial, and fiscal officials forming the nucleus of her Consell e Audiència, represented personally by the chancellor and mestre racional. As president of the Consell and its preeminent member, the chancellor was the king's and queen's closest advisor.[76] Because he was often in Naples, each realm had a vice chancellor, the principal legal officer in the realm, who had a permanent seat on the royal Consell.[77] He was assisted by regent chancellors and a staff of protonotharies (*protonotari*), who prepared and verified the documents, and handled ordinary criminal and civil cases.[78] The chancellor's financial equivalent, the mestre racional was the chief auditor who supervised the accounts of officials of both the royal patrimony and the treasury. The treasurer (*tresorer*), chamberlain, and chief bailiff (*batlle general*) of Catalunya were responsible for managing the royal patrimony in a city, town, or rural locality, and an *advocat fiscal* (a lawyer representing crown patrimony) also had permanent seats on the Consell. Nine representatives of the Corts (three elected from each of three estates, or *braç* of Catalunya) rounded out the Consell membership. Except for the three nobles from the Corts, Consell members were all non-noble and, with two exceptions (the chancellor and the canon from the cathedral of Barcelona), not clerics.[79]

The queen presided over the Consell when it acted in its advisory capacity, but rarely intervened in its work as judicial tribunal.[80] The Audiència had wide jurisdiction over criminal and civil suits, collected fines, and exacted punishment, but it also served an advisory role.[81] The Audiència was scheduled to meet every Friday as a tribunal, with the chancellor (or vice chancellor or regent chancellor, whichever happened to be at court) presiding.[82] Any number of councilors might attend the judicial court, but, as in Naples, the real business was left to the vice chancellor and the jurists. Suits brought before the Audiència in the form of petitions were addressed to the king or queen, the royal lawyers made their decision in a private session, and the judgment was sent on to the queen for her approval. After the queen's sentence was formally written and registered, there was only one avenue of appeal, directly to the king himself. Appeals to the king were rare, but a plaintiff with enough money or influence could do so, or bypass the queen's Audiència altogether and take his or her case directly to Alfonso as a court of first instance.[83] For example, the Consell de Cent of Barcelona wrote to the Catalan ambassadors in Naples in 1450 concerning a sentence María made in favor of one of their members, Felip de Ferrera, in his dispute with the town government of Perpinyà. The representatives of the town, unhappy with the judgment, sought advice from the Consell de Cent on whether to take the case to Alfonso's court or to abide by María's decision.[84] The multiplicity of judicial jurisdictions—royal, ecclesiastical, seigneurial, municipal—overlapped, confusion ensued, and the quality of justice varied widely, depending, as always, on the wealth and status of both plaintiff and defendant.[85] A good example of this is the judicial proceedings concerning the murder of Bernat Senesterra, lord of Monells y Ullastret in northeastern Catalunya. The case was handled in María's Audiència, but because Senesterra was a prominent noble, María consulted with Alfonso at every step of the way. It took nearly a year for a final judgment to be rendered against his murderer, and even longer for the settlement of Senesterra's estate among his widow and sons.[86]

The unprecedented volume of registers and cases in the records of final judgments rendered in royal law courts, more than 168 registers over the course of her lieutenancy, attests to the importance of María's court as a judicial tribunal.[87] No other lieutenant comes close, not even Joan I with sixty-eight. The workload of the chancery office grew so much while Alfonso was in Naples that in 1448 he granted María the authority to add to her secretarial and scribal staff at her discretion, providing her with greater flexibility and control over one of the busiest areas of royal government.[88] There are two plausible explanations for this increase. First, much of the judicial work during Joan's lieutenancy was handled by the king's court, not the lieutenant's. This did not happen during María's lieutenancy because Alfonso was residing in Naples and it was too costly those seeking ordinary justice to travel to his court in Naples. What once would have been referred to the king, or deferred until the king returned to Catalunya, was routinely handled by María's court. This explains why during her first tenure, judicial cases fill only nineteen registers. Second, there could have been a rise in the number of cases overall, in all realms of the Crown of Aragon, not just Catalunya. During the 1440s in Catalunya, feuding noble and patrician families, especially in Girona northeastern Catalunya, took their grievances to the royal court and many of these cases of factional unrest (*bandosidat*) litter the registers. Whatever the cause, the result is clear: The administration of justice was an important part of government. Fees collected for such services as sealing and registering to be paid by the recipients of royal documents constituted an important source of revenue that paid the salaries of the secretaries and chancery staff, half of which went directly to Alfonso in Naples.[89]

Data from scaling fees substantiates documentary evidence for the important role of justice in María's lieutenancy. She possessed and used four silver seals. The great seal of state validated important state documents and letters patent. The common seal authenticated a great variety of documents—minor letters of justice, instructions to royal commissioners, grants of limited duration, provisions concerning salaries of officials, and promissory notes—that carried the status of royal documents but did not have the permanent character that called for the state seal.[90] The secret seal, kept by the protonothary, could only be applied to letters that bore a mark indicating the queen's approval. And the small seal, used to validate letters close, may have been similar to Alfonso's signet seal, which he used as a personal mark of approval for documents to be sealed with the secret seal.[91] What is missing from this collection is as noteworthy as what she possessed. María did not have the authority to use the two most important seals of the Crown—the golden bull, used to validate grants of great distinction, and the small lead seal used for laws, constitutions, grants of baronies, and major grants to towns. These were reserved exclusively for the king's use and documents of that nature were sent to him for final approval. The king's seals indicate the possession of absolute dominion; María's indicated the possession of governmental authority. Her powers, although wide, were limited.

The fact that María did not use the golden bull or the small lead seal could account for the decline in revenue from sealing fees from Aragón, Catalunya, and Valencia during Alfonso's absence. Alan Ryder detected an overall drop in total income from seals, which would, at first glance, seem to indicate that fewer documents were processed by María and Juan from 1432 on, and thus challenges my observation that the Audiència handled a large volume of cases.[92] But the sealing fees were calculated on a progressive basis, the most expensive naturally being those that required the golden bull or the small lead seal, and those official symbols of dominion the king kept with him. Those particular revenues were collected in Naples; therefore, the aggregate totals would be skewed in favor of Naples if they are proportional. At present, Ryder's observation of a drop in the aggregate total is more suggestive than substantive. Until an analysis of the number of cases brought before the queen's Audiència and of the sealing fees for each case, a comparison of that data with prior reigns, and a breakdown of the fees collected from sealing documents is performed, all that can really be said is that María's Audiència rendered more judgments than any prior reign.

Alfonso's careful management of María's Consell and Audiència extended to the office of the mestre racional. When Alfonso first arrived in Naples, he tried to strictly control the finances in all his realms. In the 1420 *privilegio* and all its subsequent emendations, Alfonso gave María leeway in financial administration, but he still preferred to supervise his finances from a central treasury.[93] This worked well up to a point. Transfers of money, goods, and letters of credit were handled efficiently enough when the realm was relatively small and compact, but the addition of Naples strained the system. Even the most efficient treasurer could not be everywhere at once, and financial administration in Catalunya, the wealthiest of the realms of the Crown of Aragon and home of most of the royal demesne lands, was problematic. Because it was more populous than both Valencia and Aragón, and its commerce more extensive, it took more time and effort to collect subsidies, taxes, tolls, and rents. As the seat of María's court, it required a larger staff than in Valencia, and the management of the royal patrimony was more complicated than in Aragón.[94] Although both the mestre racional and the treasurer of Catalunya technically were subordinate to the treasurer general in Naples, they possessed a formidable array of judicial and executive powers and substantial discretionary authority.[95] The mestre racional of each constituent realm was responsible for the collection and disbursal of all royal funds; he controlled allowances in money and in kind given to members of the royal household; and he directed judicial inquiries into allegations of misconduct by officials employed in any financial office.[96] In concert with the queen-lieutenant's chamberlain (*camarlench*) who managed the household finances, María had considerable flexibility and control over expenditures.

María had more autonomy in her dealings with regional and municipal government. In Catalunya, she worked closely with the governor general, the highest ranking regional official responsible for maintaining public order.[97] Alfonso insisted on appointing the governor, but María appointed all the subordinate officials such as regents (*portant veus*), civil lawyers (*advocats*), vicars (*veguers*), and ordinary magistrates.[98] At the intersection of royal, regional, and municipal government were bailiffs, local representatives of crown justice, whose jurisdiction overlapped and conflicted with that of veguers.[99]

The Queen-Lieutenant and Corts of Catalunya: Barcelona and Tortosa, 1419–20 and 1421–23

Before she officially became lieutenant, María stepped into the governmental arena when she worked with the Corts of Barcelona on 11 September 1419. Alfonso had gone to Valencia to prepare for war against Sicily,

Sardinia, and Corsica and summoned the Corts, but had to prorogue it until 11 August. Delays prompted him to order María to take over for him because his brother Juan was in Castile, finalizing his marriage negotiations, but once she stepped in, she kept the chancery busy with the paperwork necessary to raise the money and set in motion the preparations for war.[100] Satisfied with her ability to govern, he issued the *privilegio* that granted her full powers as lieutenant general in April 1420.[101] Her summons to and convocations of the Corts, and the protests over her actions that later followed, defined her lieutenancy. In all, María convoked and presided over twelve parliamentary assemblies in Catalunya: 1421–23 (Tortosa and Barcelona), 1429–30 (Tortosa), 1435–36 (a general Cort at Monzón and regional meetings in Zaragoza, Barcelona, and Valencia), 1439 (Tortosa), 1439–40 (Lleída), 1442–43 (Tortosa), 1446–48 (Barcelona), and 1449–53 (Perpinyà-Barcelona-Vilafranca del Penedès).[102] In Aragón, she presided twice, at Maella in 1423 and Alcañiz-Zaragoza in 1441;[103] and in Valencia twice, in 1437 and 1438.[104] For comparison, Alfonso personally presided over the Corts eight times in the three peninsular realms—twice in Aragón, four times in Catalunya, and probably twice in Valencia—and called eight parliaments in Naples in fourteen years.[105]

Despite Alfonso's clearly stated intentions, and the precedent set by Elionor of Sicily in 1364 and Maria de Luna in 1396, María of Castile faced challenges to her authority each time she convoked and presided over the Catalan Corts. Two issues were crucial—the redress of grievances and the mutual swearing of oaths. The estates—prelates (*braç ecclesiastic*), nobles (*braç militar*), and townspeople (*braç reial*)—presented the king with a list of grievances (*greuges*), complaints of abuse of power by the king or royal officials.[106] The swearing of oaths at the opening of the Corts were, for the Catalans, the heart and soul of their agreement with the kings and their biggest complaint with Alfonso's absence and his use of lieutenants. Whereas the governing elites in Aragón and Valencia had developed a certain amount of political independence and were more amenable to Alfonso's style of ruling, Catalans were seen, and saw themselves, as the natural partner of the king. They insisted that only the king would do, and they were prepared to challenge his legal authority to let his lieutenants stand in for him in the Corts. When the lieutenant in question was María, these challenges could be seen as an attack on a woman with authority, but the Catalans leveled the same complaints against Alfonso's brother Juan. Catalan demands for personal rule by the king and his accountability to them were, in their minds, the critical factors that limited the authority of a lieutenant.

What had changed since 1396? Why did the Catalans resist accepting in 1421 what their predecessors had accepted? The answer is that a profound transformation in the political landscape took place during the interregnum of 1410–12 and after the Compromise of Caspe.[107] Political theories that had been circulating during the fourteenth century came together during the settlement, solidified in the 1420s, and acquired actual power while Alfonso was in Italy.[108] These ideas and practices shaped the political relationship between Catalan constitutional institutions and the monarchy whereby each side agreed to work with the other for the greater good of the realm. It was also, from a neo-Marxist view, a means of subjugating the lower classes to the authority of a ruling class composed of a king and political elites. And finally, it was a *mentalité*, a way of defining Catalunya as a separate political "personality," a convenient shorthand that persisted throughout centuries of rule from Madrid.[109]

Practically speaking, royal authority was counterbalanced by the equal strength of the Corts in each constituent realm.[110] The Corts of Catalunya gained power and prestige when it provided capable governance of the realm during the interregnum of 1410–12.[111] The Catalan estates resisted any royal actions that they interpreted as an attempt to limit their political privileges and economic freedom.[112] These estates were unevenly balanced politically, both among themselves and in relation to royal power. The *braç eclesiàstic*, represented by Archbishop of Tarragona, was not a homogeneous group.[113] Although the Church was the largest landholder in Catalunya, individually its members were neither very rich nor very united, but certain individuals stand out as particularly powerful.[114] Alfonso Borja, later Pope Calixtus III (1455–58), was a canon of Lleída, then bishop of Valencia, then cardinal and one of Alfonso's closest advisors.[115] The *braç militar*, roughly 3 percent of the population, possessed more than 90 percent of the land, but even the most powerful nobles lacked the great territorial estates that made their counterparts in Castile or southern Italy the masters of the state.[116] Their main arena of political action was the Corts, and their main objective was to obstruct royal initiatives, but they were rarely a unified group. Factors such as the size of the family fortune, intermarriage among the noble families of France and Castile, and the strength of familial connections to the royal dynasty splintered the nobility as a bloc. The barons, a relatively closed caste, included the Cabrera

60　　Chapter 3

family, led by the count of Módica; the viscounts of Rocabertí; the viscounts of Illa-Canet; and the counts of Cardona, Montcada, Pallars.[117] Presided over by the Count of Cardona, the *braç militar* numbered about 360 in 1449, substantially more than in the 1360s due to the influx of "new" nobles created by the Trastámaras in the fifteenth century. Many of these nobles descended from parents who once were high-ranking urban citizens (*ciutadans honrats*) granted noble status in return for their support of the Crown.[118] This fusion of urban concerns with knightly status made them the least predictable members, fractious and likely to swing in any direction.[119]

Noble and ecclesiastical power was counterbalanced by the braç reial, representatives of the principal cities and royal towns, led by Barcelona.[120] In the late twelfth or early thirteenth century, the Crown granted town representatives (*sindichs*) full powers to act in the name of the communities (*universitats*) in the Corts. Certain individuals and groups had authority beyond that of the town they represented, some towns challenged Barcelona's pretensions to speak for the braç as a whole, and rural villages in the northeast were sympathetic to Barcelona.[121] The king gained leverage to obtain the legislation and necessary subsidies to keep his government solvent and the merchant patriciates grew rich from the Crown's Mediterranean expansion. The *ciutadans honrats*, known as the *ma major* (literally "upper hand") claimed special privileges over the *ma menor* (lower rank), the majority of the townspeople—poor day laborers and servants—as well as the *ma mitjana* (middle rank), prosperous artisans and merchants, all of whom were left in a subordinate position.[122] The four aldermen (*jurats*, *consuls*, or *pahers*, depending on local usage) and eight elected city counselors (*prohoms*) who formed the executive committee (*consellers de cap*) all were ciutadans honrats. The consellers de cap chose the members of the assembly known as the Consell de Cent, the town council. The consellers de cap were under the nominal jurisdiction of the bailiff, but it was an uneasy relationship. Barcelona's internal affairs were constantly subject to royal intervention, with the consellers de cap meeting twice weekly with the city's royal vicar and bailiff. Tensions often ran high, especially concerning royal fiscal demands.[123] But city government was hardly powerless. Catalunya was the economic backbone of the Crown of Aragon and Barcelona was more than just the seat of government, it was the financial capital of the western Mediterranean. Catalan merchants and financiers had grown wealthy through overseas commerce and by 1400 its textile industry was poised to challenge the markets of England, the Low Countries, and Italy.¹²⁴ And the Consell de Cent of Barcelona was not simply a consultative body.¹²⁵ Its members, especially the consellers de cap, formed an influential patrician oligarchy with formidable financial resources that rivaled the political power of the nobility. They invested their wealth in rural estates and commissioned the major artists of the day to decorate the ceilings and walls and design stained-glass windows of their lavish administrative offices.¹²⁶ Their power grew further with the ascendancy of the Trastámara kings who systematically weakened the political power of the old Catalan nobility by excluding them from participation in the royal council.

The estates did not protest María's first convocation in 1419, but they were vocal when she held her second convocation as lieutenant general in 1421, even though she acted with Alfonso's express command. While fighting the Angevins in Italy, Alfonso told María to summon the Corts of all three realms to request a subsidy to pay for his military expenses.¹²⁷ The members sought to clarify procedural issues when the Corts were convoked by someone other than the king. On 26 May 1421, Marc de Vilalba, abbot of Montserrat, declared that the members of the Corts felt that the king had no right to turn over to anyone his right to convoke the Corts because it was a violation of the laws of Catalunya to do so.¹²⁸ He did not mention the fact that the lieutenant was a woman, nor did he did question María's capabilities. He simply doubted whether any king could transfer this particular regalian right to a lieutenant and added that the king acted without prior consultation.¹²⁹ María presented the *privilegio* of 1420 appointing her lieutenant general, which specifically granted her the power to convoke Corts, and the delegates relented.¹³⁰ In a phrase repeated at every subsequent session over which María presided, Vilalba asserted that they would relent for this one time only ("aquesta vegada tantsolament").¹³¹ María responded that she had full powers ("bastant e plen poder de convocar e celebrar Corts") and swore not to violate any rights or privileges of Catalunya. Her oath echoed the king's oath, itself an echo of feudal oaths of homage and fealty, but it was only a temporary reassurance to the wary Catalans. It is unlikely that María's powers as stipulated in the *privilegio* could have come as a surprise to the assembly. It is more likely that the representatives knew of the provision and that their protest was pro forma, designed to make absolutely certain that the session conformed to all the legal niceties. Throughout the many Corts over which María presided, the estates never accepted without protest her right to do so, even though the royal *privilegios* explicitly stipulated that she (and Juan of Navarre when he was lieutenant) could do so. The Catalan elites, accustomed to having the lion's share of power in the realm, did not like the idea of working without the king and with a lieutenant, regardless of gender. No matter how often Alfonso officially validated all acts of the Corts over which María and Juan presided, the estates contested the king's right to act through lieutenants. Finally, concerned that an absent king would use prorogation, they insisted that Alfonso agree to a stipulation that a Cort could be prorogued only once and for no more than forty days.[132] Prorogation was as a stalling tactic, both expensive and detrimental to the Corts itself. Controlling the number and length of prorogations assured the members of the Corts that the king would not abuse the privilege. The wording is significant, however. It refers only to the king or his successors and not to a lieutenant or other designee, thus leaving open a loophole that gave Alfonso and María ample room to maneuver.[133]

When the Corts was not in session, its interests were advanced by the Diputació del General, a standing committee of the Corts with substantial power. Led by a three-member executive committee (*diputats del general*), the Diputació had its own headquarters in Barcelona outside royal jurisdiction and exempt from the ordinary police.[134] And it had formidable financial resources.[135] It collected taxes, known as *generalidades*, that were levied and spent independent of the king, who relied on it for loans.[136] The diputats, with their constitutional authority and superb financial administration, controlled a network of local collectors who could keep them informed about politics both at home and abroad, and also maintained a squadron of ships to keep them apprised of the military situation.[137] Because the Diputació met when the Corts was not officially in session, it did not depend on royal summons. When delegates to the Corts were weakened by factional disputes, and as the meetings of the Corts became increasingly irregular, the Diputació stepped in. It posed a formidable threat to royal government and was, in Peter Rycraft's estimation, a "parallel executive" to the Crown.[138] An influential oligarchy of Barcelona whose incumbents appointed their successors, it was an effective tool of the political elites. It had the power to legitimize a person or an action, which could work either in favor of or against a lieutenant. For example, in 1396, the Diputació did not challenge Maria de Luna and her provisional assembly gathered in Barcelona to govern while Martí was en route from Sicily, her sister-in-law's claims were rejected and Martí's coronation proceeded along smoothly. Likewise in 1410, the Diputació accepted the nomination of twelve representatives of the Corts to sit with them and provide a provisional government analogous to that of 1396.[139] It was significant, therefore, that in 1421 the diputats did not lodge a formal complaint when María convoked the Corts. They challenged only her rights with respect to the Corts, not the myriad of other rights and responsibilities that she possessed as lieutenant general of Catalunya. The prospect of working not with the king but with a lieutenant, regardless of gender, made them keenly attentive to the fine points of the law.

The Diputació del General reached its institutional maturity during the early fifteenth century and, with the Corts, soon became María's formidable adversary.[140] In 1419 the Diputació exerted its authority against her, and pressed delegates to the Corts of Tortosa to stipulate that a permanent Catalan council be appointed to advise María when Alfonso was absent. The diputats, self-appointed defenders of the privileges of Catalunya and guardians of culture and tradition, argued that this task fell under their purview.[141] The composition of the Consell ultimately respected the Diputació's wishes in spirit without institutionalizing a separate council.

On 23 February 1422, Alfonso sent a letter that formally confirmed the capitols enacted by the Corts with phrase "Plau al senyor rei" ("it pleases the king"), and his signature.[142] In an act both symbolic and tangible, he reiterated that María was within her powers to negotiate with the members.[143] A queen, María had, through the office of the lieutenant, assumed one of the more significant aspects of Aragonese kingship. She affirmed the need for this oath with an act known as "Lo fruyt de las Leys," which stated that the benefit of a law was only found in the observance of it, and, at the same time, granted to the Diputació the authority to investigate all alleged violations of the Usatges, laws, constitutions of Catalunya.[144] This act respected the Catalans' fear that Castilian influence in government might result in a loss of their own political power and endowed the Diputació, as caretaker of Catalan law, with extensive powers that made it an institutional counterweight to royal rule. A summation of decades of incremental change, it legally shaped the relationship between the Crown and their subjects.[145]

María's convocation of the Corts obtained valuable legal support in 1422 with the publication of the *Curiarum Extravagantiorum, rerum summis illustratum*, a closely reasoned study of parliamentary theory, Catalan law, and precedent written by Jaume Callis, a noted canon and civil lawyer and supporter of monarchical privilege.[146] Callis began the *Curiarum*, an important contribution to Catalan jurisprudence, in 1413 while a member of the royal commission revising and codifying the constitutions of the kings, the acts of the Corts, and the Usatges.[147] The *Curiarum* cited the Usatge "Iudicium in curia datum" as precedent and upheld the legality of the royal prerogative to work through lieutenants. Callis admitted the necessity of oaths and confirmations to legitimize the authority of the lieutenant general.[148] Callis's treatise situated the office of the queen-lieutenant at the heart of Aragonese monarchical law and clarified her status within the complex legal relationship between the rulers, both kings and queens, and the ruled. This theory, known as *pactism*, described a form of contractual government that specifically called for a monarchy limited by law and powerful only when united in purpose with the people.

Pactism in theory was a working version of "primus inter pares" in which the status of the king was superior and directing, but not absolute, authority. It finds an eloquent advocate in the Franciscan Francesch Eiximenis (d. 1409), who advocated a limited monarchy that depended on the active participation of all ranks of society to ensure the well-being of all, regardless of rank.[149] In the *Regiment del Princeps* and *Regiment de la Cosa Pública* sections of *Lo Crestià* (also known as *El Dotzé*), he asserted that all men are born free but choose to organize themselves in communities and to elect someone to rule over them, and therefore the nobles (*grans senyors*) should rule over the lesser ranks (the *ma mitjana* and *pobres*). He urged kings to keep their promises, noting that not telling the truth is one of the most prideful and dangerous things for a prince ("Una de les pus vergonyoses e perilloses coses que aparen en príncep, sino servar fe veritat a aquells qui la promet"). His notion of a freely elected ruler permeates pactist ideologies, as does its obverse, the idea that just as kings are made, so too can they be unmade. In the *Regiment de la Cosa Pública*, he stressed the importance of mutual fidelity and loyalty, and considered anyone, king or subject, who broke the political bonds to be a traitor ("E deïen que així és traïdor príncep a son vassall com li trenca la fe, com lo vassall al senyor . . .").[150] He does not specify what he thought should be done to such a tyrant, however, nor does he address the implications of such power in the hands of the community of the realm. Eiximenis's ideas are evident throughout Catalan politics from the interregnum in 1410 to the civil war in 1462.

Eiximenis, who regarded women as inferior to men and advocated educating them so that they could live more pious lives, was not arguing in favor of rule by a woman.[151] In practice, however, royal authority superseded all other forms and his articulation of the Catalan body politic was elastic enough to provide room for the royal prestige of a queen-lieutenant. His argument is a carefully balanced political equilibrium based more on mutual wariness than on trust. The qualities Eiximenis outlined for good government—good faith, mutual respect, and the promise to abide by the agreed-upon terms—are the very things that Catalans complained were violated by Alfonso's absences. Alfonso took advantage of factions and happily played the nobles and patriciates against one another in an attempt to gain leverage.[152] The parliamentary assemblies—Corts and Diputació—formed the pivot of the pactist political and constitutional equilibrium in which the king was recognized as ruler on condition that he respect the laws, liberties, and customs of his subjects. This mutual recognition, "an oath for an oath," in Angus MacKay's apt phrase, was the basis of politics throughout the Crown of Aragon, not just in Catalunya.[153] This contractual agreement was epitomized by the pledge purportedly taken by the Aragonese nobles, "We who are as good as you . . . elect you king on condition that you guard our liberties, and if not, not."[154] The foundation of representative government in the Aragonese realms was the king's recitation of this oath at the opening of each session of the Corts, indicating his willingness to keep his part of the bargain in the negotiations to come. The making of an oath was a deeply personal act. A key component of this constitutional ideology was the belief that the presence of the king—a natural king, not a substitute—was essential to the life of the state and the functioning of its primary function, the administration of justice. Throughout María's lieutenancy, the Catalans continued to insist on the king's return and remained reluctant to accept María as a permanent replacement in the Corts, regardless of precedent and the legitimacy of her authority. The dynamics of this political relationship between the king, his queen-lieutenant, and the Corts-Diputació created the characteristic rough-and-tumble quality of Catalan politics.[155] Callis recognized the potential for royal abuse and strife, and sought to balance and the need to limit royal power to prevent tyranny and promote social harmony. In the *Curiarum*, he argued that a king could not dissolve Corts if there was still business to conduct that he may wish to avoid, considering such actions a violation of the mutual, sworn agreement to work together.[156]

The protests lodged during the Corts of 1421–23 were more than legal niceties but less than hostile challenges. They were important as a way of making certain that the proceedings went completely legitimate. Above all, they signify an abiding respect for the law, and the knowledge that it was in their best interest to conscientiously apply it. The delegates to the Catalan Corts knew the fine points of law and observed it with the utmost seriousness especially when their own rights and privileges were at stake. These petitions and the mutual oath-taking became a common feature of all of María's convocations, and not just in Catalunya.

María probably did not take the initiative in any form in this Corts during Alfonso's first foray into Italy. She no doubt regarded herself as a short-term substitute and had she overstepped her limits, it is certain that the outcry would have been loud and prolonged. But, Alfonso's purpose in calling the assembly was to secure a subsidy, which María complied with. The estates wanted only concessions and guarantees in return. Nevertheless, María swore the oaths, promised to uphold and protect the law, actions that were normally reserved for the king alone. These acts were important symbols of monarchical power, and the substitution of a female body for a male, of a queen for a king, was not yet a routine act. She was a queen, taking the place of a king, in the most important rites of kingship in the Crown of Aragon.

Yet María's convocations have been neglected by most scholars of the period, of monarchy, of political theory, and of representative institutions. Jesús Lalinde Abadía noted that the lieutenant general had the power to convoke the Corts, but did not mention specific instances.[157] Peter Rycraft's otherwise careful and detailed essay mentions María only in passing.[158] Both Lalinde Abadía and Rycraft are typical of most historians who work on the Corts during Alfonso's reign. Because they accept the presumption that the king ruled alone, they assume that María was little more than a passive stand-in, and that in sum, her lieutenancy had no wider impact.[159] I disagree on both counts. Alfonso was the directing authority, but he could not and did not govern alone. María did not rule in her own right, and did not initiate policy, but she was hardly passive. Her lieutenancy influenced political theories of representation and set the stage for later reforms of the office that formalized the lieutenant's right to convoke the Corts and paved the way for the modern viceroyalty.

Reunion and Separation: 1423–35

María presided over the Cortes of Aragón at Maella in 1423 to raise a subsidy for Alfonso's return from Italy. This was the first Aragonese assembly of Alfonso's reign and the bishop of Huesca insisted that she enter into the official records some proof of her right. She reaffirmed her position as lieutenant general in Aragón, appealed to the needs of the kingdom and the king himself to justify the convocation, and swore to uphold the *fueros* and laws of the kingdom.[160] The attitude at this session was favorable, not hostile, and the subsidies were granted without much fuss on the condition that Alfonso would swear the oaths when he returned. Like the Catalan Corts of 1421–23, this meeting was consumed with legislation concerning administration, finance, and commerce.[161] When Alfonso convoked the Aragonese Cortes at Teruel in 1427, he swore the oaths and confirmed the acts passed by the Cortes of Maella.[162]

María stepped down as lieutenant in 1424 when Alfonso returned home. He had a tentative foothold in Italy but his military campaigns in Sardinia and Naples, while not a failure, were not a success either.[163] Events in Catalunya called for his personal attention, and when he arrived in December 1423, he faced two long-standing but hardly pressing disputes—a border dispute in the Pyrenees with the Count of Foix and warring noble families in Girona. More serious issues concerned newly formed factions in the Corts that had brought government to a near standstill and, most problematic of all, the Catalan economy, which was near collapse in 1427 due to the combination of a decline in all types of economic activity and a resultant sharp drop in the collection of taxes.[164]

The most urgent matter facing him was the escalation of hostilities that resulted from Alfonso's and his brothers' meddling in Castilian affairs. The struggle for lands and political power among the Trastámara *infantes*—Juan, Enrique, and Pedro—entangled their wives and nearly came to a violent end in 1429. Enrique provoked both his brother and brother-in-law over control of lordships in Castile. Alfonso summoned the parliamentary assemblies of all three realms to discuss the war between Navarre and Castile that threatened to spill over to the Crown of Aragon.[165] Full-scale war between Juan II of Castile, Juan of Navarre, and Alfonso was narrowly averted in 1429 only by direct and dramatic intervention of María of Castile: She pitched her tent between the opposing armies and refused to budge until her brother, her brother-in-law, and her husband agreed to a peaceful settlement.[166] This is not the action of a passive placeholder. Leaving Joan de Funes, the vice chancellor, and Pere Ram, the prothonotary, in her place, she continued to work with Alfonso to secure peace in all the Aragonese realms.[167] On 19 January 1430, she took over for Alfonso at the Corts of Tortosa, with the support of all three estates and full powers from Alfonso to act in his place.[168]

In a hurry to get the money and return to Italy to fight the war, Alfonso was forceful and intolerant of opposition. He shuttled between

Aragón,[169] Valencia,[170] and Catalunya in the face of widespread protests, not over María's convocation but over the issue of who started the war with Castile and why anyone should have to pay for it.[171] The Aragonese granted him 62,000 florins for the defense of the realm plus 1,000 men on horseback, and 1,000 foot soldiers while the Valencians contributed 28,000 florins. María continued to govern for Alfonso in Catalunya for the duration of the session, where she was questioned relentlessly about the king's motives. The Catalans, especially the barons and prelates, demanded proof that the war was legitimate and not a frivolous waste of their time, money, and manpower. Juan of Navarre was widely blamed for instigating the war, and his involvement cost Alfonso dearly. He asked the Catalan Corts for 60,000 florins, but had to settle for 30,000.[172] A serious illness kept her out of the public eye for much of 1429, but María took over for her husband frequently after that and before his final departure for Naples in 1432.[173] This long session (two and one-half years) resulted in a reform of the judiciary, a statute concerning creditors, a promise to void all proceedings arising from the 1429 war with Castile, new stipulations on the jurisdiction of royal officials, and "Commemorants," a statute that obliged peasants fleeing servile tenure to sell the land to an approved successor within one year or risk it falling forfeit to the lord.[174] Alfonso was relatively close at hand, which may explain the lack of real opposition from the Catalans to María's convocations. The Catalans may have felt that, with Alfonso nearby, their traditional privileges would not be abused, or perhaps they felt could request a prorogation if they felt things were not going well.

This sense of a return to a status quo did not last long, however. After nearly ten years in Spain, Alfonso had grown weary of intrigues and infighting. In 1432 he seized the chance to try once again to conquer the kingdom of Naples for the Crown of Aragon.[175] When he left for Naples in the spring of 1432, Alfonso also left behind unfinished business in the Corts of Catalunya, which he had convoked on 16 August 1431 and María finished on 15 January 1434.[176] As he did so, the secretary of the Corts noted, because Alfonso "found it necessary to leave at once from the Corts, and once again left and went, God willing, away from his realms and lands . . . constituting and creating as Lieutenant General in the said principality of Catalunya and president of the Cort, to continue it [Corts] in his absence, the Queen, his wife, giving and authorizing full authority to the said Queen." Alfonso literally took the money and ran. Having extracted the sum of 50,000 florins, he immediately left Barcelona to begin to provision his fleet.[177]

This time he intended to grant the lieutenancy not to María but to Juan of Navarre, who remained heir to the Aragonese throne and thus was constitutionally qualified to act for the king. Relations with Castile were calm but still tense, and Alfonso wanted to have a strong soldier fully empowered to act should Juan II take advantage of Alfonso's absence. But on 13 May 1432, the day that he was about to turn over the lieutenancy to Juan, the Catalan Corts asked that María be placed in charge.[178] An abiding personal animosity had developed between Juan and the Catalans that threatened to impede government at all levels. They feared, and rightly so, that Juan would drag them into further conflict with Castile. Alan Ryder suggests that they thought, but did not state outright, that María would not be nearly as difficult to deal with as Juan and that they could more easily get their way. Alfonso relented and named María lieutenant general in Catalunya and Majorca:

Ex certa nostra scientia et consulte, ampliantes vobis illustri Regine Marie, consorti nostre carrissime, potestatem quam vos cum alia carta nostra data Barchinone externa die, locumtenentem generalem nostram in Principatu Cathalonie et regno Maioracarum constituimus, vt in ipsa carta plenius continetur ac dicionem regnorum quibus presidere, nobis absente vos volumus, Tenore presentis vos eandem Reginam Mariam nedum in dictis Principatu et regno, ymo etiam in regnis nostris Aragonum et Valentie et omnium subditorum nostrorum in eis presentium et forum sortiendum preficimus, et in omnibus et singulis regnis et Principatu predictis generalem locumtenentem nostram constituimus, facimus, creamus ac etiam ordinamus cum latissima potestate ea omnia regendi et gubernandi quamdiu nos abesse contigerit ab eisdem meroque et mixto imperio, alta et bassa jurisdiccione et plenissima gladii potestate vtendi.[179]

On 29 May 1432, he set sail from Alfachs for Sicily with ten galleys.[180] María's governmental authority was essentially the same in 1432 as in 1420, and included all of Alfonso's Iberian realms. There was, however, one key difference: Juan of Navarre appears to have governed Aragón and Valencia until July 1434 by virtue of his status as heir and not through any official appointment.[181] This multiplicity of offices and frequent overlap of lieutenants was a characteristic practice of Alfonso.[182] He left little to chance and defined each lieutenant's powers and duties according to need, not theory.[183] The co-lieutenancy arrangement was not a perfect solution, and may have been intended all along as a temporary solution.

It is clear from the documents and the disposition of powers that Alfonso valued Juan's military expertise more than his administrative skills, and certainly more than his diplomacy. In 1426, when Alfonso planned to transfer the prisoner Jaume of Urgell, a dangerous noble who was one of the contestants for the throne in 1410, to another location, he told the official in charge of the transfer not to divulge so secret a matter to Juan of Navarre.[184] He knew that the bellicose temperament of his brother clashed with the Catalans' sensitivity to any royal heavy-handedness, so he made certain that Juan was never lieutenant of Catalunya unless María was co-lieutenant. There was little difference between María's or Juan's authority in terms of jurisdiction or authority from 1432 to 1453, except that presumably Juan was expected to take seriously the phrase "plenissima gladii potestate." Alfonso relied on María to keep the administration running smoothly and used her as a buffer between Juan and the Catalans. They never governed together at the same time: María was in charge when Juan was away, and vice versa.[185]

No amount of careful planning could have prepared María for what came next. In 1435, Juan of Navarre, still officially lieutenant general of Aragón and Valencia, joined Alfonso in Italy. He arrived just in time to take part in the disastrous defeat of the Aragonese navy near Ponza on 5 August 1435.[186] Alfonso, his brothers Juan and Enrique, and a host of his nobles were captured. News of the defeat at Ponza traveled quickly and tensions were extraordinarily high. Juan's capture meant that his powers as lieutenant general of Aragón and Valencia automatically devolved to María, who was suddenly thrust into a precarious and dangerous situation. On 29 August the Consell de Cent of Barcelona wrote to María, assuring her that they would meet with her as soon as possible to discuss terms of the king's release.[187] In early September, the Catalan ambassadors who were present in Italy at the time conveyed news of the king's safety.[188] María, communicating with Alfonso through his protonothary, personally issued the summons to Corts on 15 October 1435, citing the obvious inability of the king to do so as justification for her unprecedented action.[189] She summoned a Cortes Generales of the three realms to meet in Monzón to request a subsidy of 100,000 gold florins to pay for his ransom, to organize a fleet of twenty-two galleys and eight sailing ships to come to his rescue, and to negotiate with the Genoese. All the training—with her mother, her mother-in-law, her councilors and trusted aides—and her own personal talents and skills would be tested in what ultimately would become the pivotal moment of her reign.

Chapter 4
A Permanent Lieutenancy, 1436–48

BEFORE 1436 María was a novice lieutenant. Although she was working alongside Alfonso, there is little indication of her own will or judgment in her actions. Alfonso's capture at Ponza changed everything. Without her husband or his brothers to rely on, María stepped into the public sphere on her own and demonstrated her talent for governance. After his release from captivity, Alfonso stayed in Italy to pacify the kingdom. He moved the main offices of royal government—the chancellor, the keeper of the seals, and the chief financial officer—to Italy and governed from there. By 1442, Naples was secure and by 1448 he had a permanent court in Naples based on Aragonese institutions. But governing became a balancing act. Adding unruly Naples to the diverse and complex but well-ruled Crown of Aragon was complicated by rapidly changing economic, social, and political conditions. Catalan prelates, nobles, and urban patricians had lost easy access to the king, and were not entirely happy that they were at the margins of political life. They understood that they would benefit from the commercial potential of an Aragonese possession in Italy, but quickly estimated the political costs of their displacement from the political center of gravity. They admitted the legality of a queen-lieutenant acting in place of the king, but found it difficult to accept Alfonso's preference of Naples to Barcelona, and worse, that he seriously considered abandoning Barcelona by having María join him there.[1]

Regular embassies between the two royal courts started as early as February 1435 when Antoni Vinyes, a royal notary, was sent to Italy to discuss the office of the mestre racional. In 1437 Alfonso instituted a regular monthly mail service between Naples and Barcelona, a trip that by boat took an average of four weeks, weather and travel conditions permitting.[2] Ambassadors and royal couriers shuttled back and forth across the western

Mediterranean bearing letters and documents too important to be trusted to ship captains. In addition to these official embassies, the members of the Barcelona town council frequently sent their own emissaries at their own expense, and barons and prelates traveled back and forth when need dictated.[3] Letters were posted from all parts of the western Mediterranean, including Genoa,[4] Palma de Mallorca,[5] Nice,[6] Gaeta,[7] and Castillo de Archi, near Naples.[8]

But María stayed in Barcelona. From 1432 until her resignation in 1453, she handled the routine business of government in Catalunya—administration of ordinary civil and criminal justice; supervision of the financial offices; governance of all subordinate comital, regional, and municipal officials; and maintenance of public order. She handed over to Alfonso all matters dealing with military affairs, diplomacy, the higher nobility, and the church. She wrote detailed letters describing the issues and outlining her proposed plans, suggested candidates for vacant offices, referred judicial cases that fell outside her jurisdiction, and reported to him the deliberations of her own council and court.[9]

This arrangement worked well up to a point. María's convocation of the Corts per se remained problematic for the Catalan ruling elites, but the issue took on greater significance during the mid-1440s when the Corts of Catalunya and the Cortes of Aragón were almost continuously in session from 1435 to 1458. The issues under discussion were as contentious as the constitutional issues raised by María's convocations. Alfonso's need for money to fund his Italian campaigns collided with an economic downturn that caused social and political upheaval in Barcelona. He looked everywhere for money. He began a systematic recuperation of alienated royal patrimonial lands, demanded extraordinary taxes, and finally agreed to grant the manumission of the *remença* peasants in exchange for a fee. These issues galvanized Catalan society, and María and Alfonso worked together through the Corts itself and its various committees and deputations.[10] This mountain of work for the king and queen is an archival bounty for the historian. Thousands of documents—royal letters both public and private, memoranda, charters, records of the Consell de Cent and the Diputació del General, the *procesos* of the Corts, diplomatic and commercial correspondence—do more than simply describe what happened. This circular correspondence testifies to a dynamic political culture, a vibrant literate public sphere where the queen-lieutenant was situated in the center, actively engaged in the circulation of ideas and the ongoing construction of a distinctive ruling partnership.

The Cortes of Monzón: 1435–36

With Alfonso held hostage, María was in a dangerous position. Before she would leave for Monzón to meet with the delegates to the Cortes Generales of the three realms, she asked for and received two extraordinary guarantees. The first was an official order of safeguard from the Diputació del General, the Cortes, and the local authorities to protect her and her royal officials. The second permitted six or more algutzirs, or municipal officials, to exercise royal jurisdiction in Monzón, which was not included in the *privilegio* of 1432 and thus outside her jurisdiction.[11] She was not exaggerating the threat: In December 1436 there were rumblings of unrest in Barcelona.[12] She dealt quickly with the troublemakers, but the possibility of widespread civil insurrection could not have been far from her thoughts.

The first session was scheduled to begin on 15 November but was prorogued until 25 November because the three realms, as before, protested her "illegal" convocation, despite the force of precedent and the obvious need to work together to aid the king.[13] These protests were nearly identical in substance and tone to those from earlier sessions and, as before, María included a copy of the *privilegio* of 1432 in her plenary address. She reiterated that she possessed "full and sufficient power, generally and specifically, to call, convoke, celebrate, convoke or serve at the Corts in each one of the aforementioned kingdoms and lands . . . and ordered the aforementioned *cedula* and the letter (*respuesta*) with those powers from the king to the queen authorized and given there be inserted in the *proceso* of the aforementioned Cort."[14] To bolster his wife's position, the captive Alfonso sent the Corts three letters of support, one each to the Catalans, Aragonese, and Valencians. Given the gravity of the situation, the estates, at the urging of the Abbot of Montearagon, consented to the proceedings. As before, María agreed to abide by the laws and all rights and privileges of each realm.

María's personal pleas were instrumental in obtaining 4,500 florins from the Consell de Cent needed to free the Catalan ambassadors, and she continued to press the Cortes for the money needed to ransom the king.¹⁵ On 15 December she formally addressed the Cortes and ordered the representatives to work with her to secure the king's speedy release and discuss negotiations for a settlement with the Genoese and payment of the ransom for the other prisoners.¹⁶ What María and none of the delegates knew at that time, due to delays in mail delivery, was that in mid-September, Alfonso, although still technically a prisoner of war, had been released from the Genoese into the comfortable custody of Filippo Maria Visconti, the duke of Milan.¹⁷ In October, Juan of Navarre and some of the barons and prelates were set free.¹⁸ On 6 January 1436, María, unaware that Alfonso and his brothers had been released on 1 December, granted permission to a delegation from the Consell de Cent to negotiate directly with the Genoese for his release.¹⁹ On that same day, Alfonso ordered Bernat Corbera, Andreu de Biure, and the Consell de Cent of Barcelona to keep María informed of their actions at all times.²⁰ She worked closely with them and with the Diputació during the winter of 1436, meeting often with councillors and deputies to negotiate the terms of the agreement with Genoa and the status of Catalan merchants in Italy.²¹ When she finally realized that Alfonso was free, and that Visconti had personally loaned Alfonso 30,000 ducats to cover his expenses while in the duke's custody, she questioned the need for the Cortes. María pushed ahead anyway, but it is unclear whether she did so because she felt that Alfonso would still need the money because the Crown was still officially at war with Genoa, or because she was waiting for explicit orders from Alfonso himself.²²

This confusion slowed the work of the Cortes at Monzón, prompting Alfonso to send Juan of Navarre to assist. María admonished Aragonese knights and nobles who claimed that they should not have to serve at sea, conveyed the king's intention to continue the war with Genoa, and ordered the estates to discuss the king's demands for six armed ships and three hundred men to assist him in Italy.²³ On 20 March, she reminded the delegates of the seriousness of the situation and directed them to stop wasting time.²⁴ But her arguments fell on deaf ears. On 31 March 1436, backed by Alfonso, she suspended the Cortes General, left Monzón, and told each realm to meet separately and vote a subsidy independent of the others. In a surprising turnabout, the Catalans responded favorably at first, while the Aragonese proved surprisingly difficult for María to handle. The representatives greeted her with coldness ("fredament"), blocked her every move, and were unwilling to work with her at all.²⁵ Alfonso decided to compromise, and he substituted her with Juan of Navarre, who presided over the regional Cortes of Aragón at Alcañiz while María continued to meet with the Corts in Barcelona and Valencia.[26] By then, the Catalans had toughened their stance and now they, too, refused to provide money to Alfonso unless he came to preside personally over the Corts. Both Juan and María faced tremendous resistance to their attempts to negotiate. María made a personal appearance before the plenary session of the Consell de Cent, and successfully persuaded them to agree to work with her.[27]

Alfonso's two-lieutenant strategy underscored his seriousness and reinforced the legality of both María and Juan as lieutenants. But the Aragonese never stopped pushing back. After they knew of Alfonso's release, their promises of money and arms came attached with a demand that he return immediately to his Spanish realms. They wanted the king, not a stand-in, male or female. Even Juan of Navarre, as lieutenant general in Aragón, was not a fully acceptable substitute. Later, at the Cortes of Alcañiz in 1436, Juan was obliged to swear an oath approving the fueros, promise that his royal officials would observe them, and agree to expand the powers of the Diputación.[28]

Angel Canellas López attributed María's failure with the Aragonese at Monzón to personal weakness, arguing that Alfonso substituted Juan for María in Aragón because she had not succeeded in dominating the Cortes.[29] But his answer says more about modern attitudes toward women in power than the medieval ones do. It was not a question of feminine weakness or tough masculine arm-twisting. Luisa María Sánchez Aragonés, who makes vaulable comparisons of the actions of María and Juan of Navarre in the Corts, argues that Aragonese intransigence was a symptom of a constitutional crisis. She believes that the Cortes of Monzón were part of an Aragonese attempt to impose on the king a pactist policy much like that of the Catalans. While recognizing that María was fully empowered to act in the place of the king, the Aragonese estates saw themselves as a legally constituted executive body.[30] And, unlike her convocations in 1429–30, the king was far away and the kingdom imperiled. Yes, Juan was able to convince the Aragonese to relent, but María had already worn them down.

María left Aragón and opened the Corts in Barcelona on 15 May 1436, where the Catalan clergy and nobles, who also resented having to pay for Alfonso's Italian ventures, were as combative as the Aragonese. María, neither meek nor weak, expelled dissenters from the session and imprisoned them.[31] The estates vehemently argued that her actions were in violation of their privileges, but she argued that she acted under the peace and truce statutes. While the estates stiffened their resolve, Alfonso began preparations for an attack on Genoa. The plans were well along as early as May 1436, when he wrote to the Diputació del General that his armada was nearly ready.[32] He continued to press María to move quickly to get the money he needed to arm his ships, pay his soldiers, and maintain his court in Italy. Recognizing the difficulty of her situation and the need to act in concert, he wrote to the Corts once again making clear his support for her ("ab creença a vos comanada") as his legitimate representative.[33] By the time the session ended on 12 June 1437, the issues at hand were less important than the discord within the Corts itself.[34] The real problem concerned the two competing executive institutions in the realms—the Corts and the Diputació del General on the one hand, and María, the lieutenant general, on the other—both wanting to dominate the other.

The Aragonese ultimately agreed to contribute 220,000 florins and a fleet of galleys, and the Valencians 50,000.[35] As it turned out, Alfonso needed the money more than he did the fleet. By Christmas 1436, in a move that took everyone by surprise, he was free and his former captor, Filippo Maria Visconti, the duke of Milan, was now his closest ally. Shared love of hunting aside, the duke and the king recognized mutual diplomatic interests in keeping the Genoese at bay. Alfonso convinced Visconti that an Aragonese Naples was less a threat than a Genoese Naples backed by Angevin French troops.[36] Thus armed with friends and cash, Alfonso decided to stay in Italy to complete the conquest of Naples. Recognizing the problems he faced in long-distance rulership, wanting to protetct himself should something happen to either Juan or María, and fearing that war with Milan and Genoa would spill over into Catalunya, Alfonso named Juan co-lieutenant in Catalunya with María. Juan made it clear that his interests lay elsewhere, so Alfonso blocked any hostile moves his brothers might make toward Castile by making peace with his brother-in-law, Juan II of Castile. To further strengthen Juan of Navarre's ties to the Crown of Aragon, Alfonso formally designated his brother Juan as his heir until he had a legitimate son to succeed him.[37] These moves were only temporarily successful. Once the threat from Genoa and Pisa subsided, Juan devoted more attention to his own kingdom of Navarre, necessitating yet another modification in the lieutenancy. On 24 November 1438, Alfonso asserted María's ability to govern alone, revoked the co-lieutenancy arrangement of 1436, and in a *privilegio* nearly identical to that of 1432, granted her full powers as lieutenant in Aragón, Valencia, and Majorca as well as Catalunya.³⁸ Once the threat of plague subsided, she resumed her work in Valencia while Juan acted in her place in Aragón.

Juan's tough stance worked at Monzón in 1436, but it could only carry him so far. Often preoccupied by affairs in his own kingdom of Navarre and a troublemaker in Castile, he often left Aragón to its own devices. The representatives at the Cortes of Zaragoza, summoned in 1439 to deal with the defense of the kingdom against French invasion, objected to Juan's presiding, demanded to see his credentials, rebuffed his requests for a subsidy to cover his personal expenses, and asked Alfonso to return because the situation was grave.³⁹ María took over at the next Aragonese convocation, in 1441 at Alcañiz and Zaragoza, and the mood was much calmer. The demands for her credentials took the tone of pro forma requests, not hostile challenges.⁴⁰ In return for reform of the judiciary and legislation designed to bolster the Aragonese economy, Alfonso received his much-needed money, and the Cortes loaned María 17,000 florins, only half the amount he requested.⁴¹ The tense hostility between Juan and the Aragonese reappeared in 1446 when he convoked the Cortes of Zaragoza to deal with the war with Castile. When the Cortes repeatedly demanded that Juan produce evidence of his power to convoke, he responded with hostile intransigence. In their letters to Alfonso, representatives of the Cortes accused Juan of starting the war. The only business conducted came at the specific, personal request of Alfonso, whose obvious conciliatory tone was not lost on the Aragonese.⁴² Juan was absent from many of the sessions and the Cortes retaliated by rebuffing all his requests. Because María was able to modulate her stance to match the circumstance she was more successful than Juan, whose tough-guy stance worked against him. She could be tough or conciliatory, assertive or dominating, and the longer she served as lieutenant, the more adept she became at discerning which tone would work best.

Refining Long-Distance Government

By 1440, Alfonso recognized that what had worked well for three contiguous realms was less effective when stretched to include Naples. He discovered that it was easier to govern the outlying realms from the efficiently bureaucratized Barcelona than from Naples, an administrative nightmare after decades of chaotic rulership. Even though the administration functioned smoothly while the king was in Italy, the Catalanes repeatedly petitioned María to persuade Alfonso to return to Catalunya. The longer Alfonso was away, the more these groups declared that their particular problem was something that only the king could resolve.[43] They began to go over María's head, and those who could afford the expense of the journey took their case directly to the king. Not only did this undermine her effectiveness, it clogged the Neapolitan court. Alfonso, never fond of administrative detail, could no longer escape the fact that tinkering with embassies and regular mail service was no substitute for real reform.[44]

As an indication of his increased trust in his wife and his preoccupation with the war in Italy, Alfonso refined and amplified her powers as lieutenant, giving her greater control over finances. In October 1440, admitting that it was a difficult decision for him to make (it was "arduorem negociorum"), he bowed to reality and extended María's local control over financial matters, including expenditures. He continued, noting that because María was part of his body ("de altera a parte nostri corporis")—a striking use of the royal body metaphor—and was his lieutenant ("vices gerentis"), he would entrust her with money collected in Catalunya that pertained to the royal fisc. She could receive, recover, and hold ("recepere recuperare et habere") all receipts, fines, and redemptions ("apochas fines quitancias"); make and sign orders for subsidies, including death taxes and criminal fines ("remissiones mortis et altius cuiuscumque criminis"); and she could collect any moneys collected by the administration of justice ("tribunus omnimodem et comiteribus plenarie"). Above all, she was free to spend any money not earmarked for Naples ("cum libera et generali administratio").[45]

His reforms attempted to eliminate, or at least minimize, the overlap of central and regional authority. The distinctions between the treasurer general in Naples and each mestre racional, particularly with respect to tax collection, were not clearly delineated and were complicated by antiquated accounting and auditing methods. Such an arrangement left plenty of room for ingenuity and fraud. An audit conducted in 1448 after the death of the Treasurer General Mateu Pujades revealed not only that he had never rendered any proper account, but also that he owed very large sums of money to the Crown. Pujades's estate was seized and his family ordered to pay the debt. To Alfonso, the lesson was clear. He stipulated that all officials who handled royal funds would be subject to a periodic audit by the mestre racional and personally held accountable for all sums.[46] The Pujades scandal increased Alfonso's discomfort with granting María rather wide discretionary powers in the financial department. But his reforms were too restrictive. In 1449, María pleaded poverty and complained to him that she needed more control over her finances because her officials were not getting paid regularly. She sent Berenguer de Montpalau to argue her case directly to Alfonso, who claimed to need more money to pay the costs of war in Italy. It took almost a year of pleading with "paraules molt dolses e gracioses" for her to once again receive funds from Alfonso and retain local control over expenditures in Catalunya.[47]

This dispute between Alfonso and María was more than just a struggle for control of money. It was indicative of a wider problem that afflicted the Crown of Aragon during Alfonso's reign. Improved accounting practices and centralized control could not solve the persistent problem of insufficient income. The economy of all the Crown realms prospered in general during Alfonso's reign, but the prosperity was by no means uniform. The Catalan economy had been in a slump since the mid-1420s, and was showing only feeble signs of recovery. This sluggishness limited its competitive strength, resulted in a decrease in the volume of trade, which in turn led to a decline in the taxable wealth. Extending the mercantile basis of the realm to include Naples may have been beneficial to the king, but it was disadvantageous to Catalan merchants. Claude Carrère attributes the downturn to structural defects such as the inflexibility of maritime enterprise and the high cost of money relative to that of the Catalun merchants' trading partners, but Mario del Treppo argues otherwise.[48] Del Treppo has asserted, I believe correctly, that there was a political component to the sluggish economy because the Catalan economy was closely connected to Alfonso's military and political maneuvers in Italy. In particular, he has observed that the flow of "monetary current" was always directed toward the capital city, so that when Naples displaced Barcelona, a negative cash flow in Barcelona resulted. As the costs of business rose and currency was devalued, ordinary revenues did not yield a substantial surplus over the sums necessary for ordinary government. Alan Ryder agrees with del Treppo's argument for the role of politics in economics: Alfonso tried to use economic links among the various realms as a way of creating an artificial bond to hold together the Crown. As Alfonso's political fortunes surged, so did the economy, and vice versa. Business with the Crown, especially in the traffic of the products of war, could be especially lucrative but depended on continued skirmishing, which was unpredictable, unstable, and, in the end, counterproductive. Alfonso tried to support local commerce by buying Catalan cloth and Sicilian grain to support his army, a scheme that worked for a few years but quickly fell apart when his opponents signed the Peace of

Lodi in 1453. The bottom fell out of the artificially high cloth and grain markets, and the economy as a whole suffered.[49]

Routine subsidies and forced loans from the Iberian realms were not enough to support the cost of routine trans-Mediterranean government plus the burden of protracted warfare in Italy, the Mediterranean, and Castile. A six-month campaign in Ancona cost Alfonso 80,000 ducats; entertaining the Emperor Frederick III for ten days cost more than 100,000 ducats. Alfonso fought ceaseless skirmishes with Castile and battled pirates along the Catalan, Valencian, and Mallorcan coastlines. Ryder estimated that in a state of war, which was common throughout the 1440s and early 1450s, Alfonso's revenues fell short of his needs by between 200,000 and 300,000 ducats a year. This sum had to be raised in Spain and Italy by customary aids, grants from the Corts, clerical subsidies, indirect taxation, sale of offices and privileges, fines, and loans.[50] Alfonso's initial response was to appeal to his subjects for more money, more often. He had little difficulty with the parliamentary assemblies of Aragón and Valencia whose economies were stable, even prosperous at times, but the Catalans felt they had borne the brunt of taxation and military expenditures and they made demands that he was unwilling to grant. In return for their money, they wanted more power. They insisted that the king's council be chosen with the consent of the Corts, that the Audiència should render judgments independently of the king, and that royal orders that violated the Constitutions or Usatges of Catalunya were to be nullified.[51]

No matter how clearly Alfonso delineated the parameters of the lieutenancy itself, events often forced him to change who goverened where. Juan and Enrique continued to meddle in Castile, hostilities became war, they were defeated at the battle of Olmedo on 19 May 1445, and Enrique died shortly thereafter. This catastrophe may have quelled Juan's appetite for intrigue, at least temporarily, but it created an unstable situation along the Aragonese and Valencian border with Castile. Juan continued to neglect his duties in Aragón and his relationship with Alfonso worsened. The king relied on María to provide not only good government but also accurate accounts of Juan's behavior.[52] In October 1445, Alfonso reinstated Juan as lieutenant general in Aragón and Valencia but he made clear his awareness that the frequent switching of one lieutenant for another would weaken the status and prestige of the office. He sternly warned Juan that if he relinquished the office to intervene in Castile it would be given to María permanently, and that he would not treat his wife "as a child does a toy on a string."[53] The metaphor is telling: Juan's capricious and self-serving behavior infantilized María and threatened the stability of the Crown. Alfonso's threat was clear, and Juan paid attention to it. In the future, Alfonso brought Juan in when a military crisis threatened and he needed a soldier-lieutenant not a queen-lieutenant, and let him go as soon as the military threat subsided. Juan's preoccupation with events in Navarre and Castile interefered with his responsibilities in Aragón and Valencia.[54] Even when the military situation was calm, Juan could not be trusted to focus on his duties as lieutenant. In 1438 Alfonso wanted to force the Justicia of Aragón from office but he doubted that Juan would carry out his orders ("because he [Juan] does not wish to face the unpleasantness"), so he arranged for María to take over the task, and he had a notary keep a complete record of all Juan's council proceedings.[55] Juan's ambitions had been curbed by Alfonso's warning in 1445, but after the debacle at Olmedo, Alfonso still did not trust his brother to stay out of Castilian affairs. He wrote privately to the commissioners of the Aragonese Cortes in 1453 that they should ignore Juan if he tried to block an extension of the truce with Castile.[56] Lacking a legitimate heir, Alfonso had no choice but to rely on Juan, in spite of his faults, or risk losing control of Naples.[57] Unlike Juan of Navarre, María respected the office and took her responsibilities seriously. During her tenure as lieutenant, there were no attacks on her character or her ability to govern, and Alfonso never scolded her. Alfonso's preference for María could not have been lost on the Catalans themselves, who were instructed to report on the proceedings of the Barcelona town council and parliamentary assemblies to both Alfonso and María.[58]

Alfonso had another good reason to switch lieutenants from time to time—the fragile state of María's health.[59] She suffered from a chronic ailment, perhaps epilepsy, and was prone to fevers and other debilitating viral or bacterial illness. María's medical history is difficult to interpret because of the vague descriptions of symptoms and diagnoses.[60] Her poor health may have been the cause of her infertility, but Alfonso's long absences certainly clouds the issue. He was reluctant to appoint a substitute for María when she fell ill and typically preferred to assume a "wait and see" approach. Until she recovered, the king trusted the well-organized, highly efficient Catalan bureaucrats to handle routine matters of tax collection and processing of judicial petitions.

This configuration—María as lieutenant general of Catalunya and Majorca, and Juan of Aragón and Valencia—would last until 1453. On only a handful of occasions in 1453 do their documents appear simultaneously, and there is no other direct evidence of joint governance.[61] Alfonso gave both Juan and María a greater leeway than he did to his lieutenants and viceroys in Italy, partly because the political situation in Italy was not yet stable, and partly because Juan and María were more trusted family members. And there was no civil war, no coup d'état, no serious threat of foreign invasion. The relative calmness testified to the general acceptance of lieutenants in general and a woman in particular, as well as to the stability of the kingdom as a whole. Still, no matter how stable it was, long-distance government was frustrating for everyone.[62] In 1441, Alfonso told María that he would not approve new *fueros* (municipal laws) in the kingdom of Aragón that would reform justice and prohibit all officials from selling royal offices. After the letter was sent to María, Alfonso's scribes realized the mistaken phrasing and sent a second letter with corrections. María was baffled by the first letter but began working out a deal with the Cortes, while stalling for time to clarify. When she got the revised letter, she was forced to go back to the committee of the Cortes and tell them that, after all, Alfonso would approve their request.[63] Bisson and Suárez Fernández consider Alfonso's long absences catastrophic for the Aragonese monarchy, but I disagree. Ryder argues convincingly that the Crown was saved from catastrophe because Alfonso relied on sound institutions as he also devised new administrative procedures to handle long-distance government.[64] The Crown of Aragon as a whole remained stable throughout Alfonso's reign and María proved herself to be a prudent, fair, and effective proxy for her husband.[65]

The Cost of War: The Corts of Lleída (1439–40) and Tortosa (1442–43)

After 1436, the confrontations over María's right to preside over the Corts of Catalunya became more frequent and the hostility more obvious. Alfonso's continued absence and María's convocations were a persistent theme in letters from the Consell de Cent to their Catalan ambassadors resident in Naples, who tried to use these issues as leverage in the ongoing negotiations for money to support the king's military campaigns in Italy. The Consell de Cent consellers complained vehemently of the delays and dissolutions of the Corts. In a very rare mention of their distress at the lack of a legitimate heir, the consellers even suggested that the ambassadors appeal to Alfonso's marital duty ("lo gran deute de matrimoni") in order to get him to leave Italy, reunite with María, and produce an heir, not specifying their preference for a son or a daughter.[66] This is a remarkable admission of their unease with Alfonso's absence, two years after his release from captivity. He seemed unconcerned about the succession and was perfectly comfortable with María governing in his stead. To the Catalan ruling elites, Alfonso neglected both his Spanish realms and the traditional duties of a king, but he felt obliged to stay in Italy and complete the task he had begun.

In 1439 he asked María to summon a Corts to request a subsidy to fund his fight against the Genoese.[67] She became so ill, "more dead than alive," that her opening speech to the Corts was read for her.[68] She urged Alfonso to appoint someone to take over for her, but he wrote back saying that he preferred her and no other, suggesting that she prorogue the Corts and recuperate in Valencia. But Alfonso was not about to take chances. Because Juan and the Infante Enrique were engrossed in Castilian affairs, he drew up documents appointing his nephew, Carlos of Viana, the nineteen-year-old son of Juan of Navarre, as lieutenant general. Carlos, a royal prince who was the son of Alfonso's formally designated heir, was young and inexperienced. To complicate matters, Carlos and his father were not on good terms and Alfonso had serious legitimate concerns about how the two would get along. María's health improved, Carlos of Viana was not needed, and she once again faced protests over her right to preside.[69] At the opening session in Lleída on 23 February 1440, Simon Salvador, the bishop of Barcelona, speaking on behalf of the all the members ("nomine totius dicte Curie"), told María that before they could consider any requests from the king, they needed verification that she had the authority to convoke and preside.[70] As before, María submitted a copy of the *privilegio* of 1432.[71] Then, in a ritual strikingly similar to that of the ceremony of the king swearing an oath to th Corts, she agreed to observe the privileges, constitutions, and laws of Catalunya and "with her own hands touching, [she agreed] to abide by and not violate, to observe and make known and to hold to the prelates, religious people, clerics, high-ranking people, nobles, barons, knights, landholders . . . and the citizens, burgesses, and inhabitants of the cities, towns, and places, all the Usatges of Barcelona, constitutions and capitols of the Corts of Catalunya, liberties, privileges, uses and customs."[72] Her "own hands touching" may indicate that she was in the pose of a Christian at prayer, but also recalls vassalage rituals of oath-taking, symbolism that could not have been lost on the viewers. Satisfied that the queen would abide by the same rules as the king would, Bishop Salvador recognized her right to preside. His affirmation is followed by similar ones from each estate, and a final declaration of satisfaction that all the legal requirements have been met.[73] Unlike the king's oaths and the implication of full sovereignty, the delegates' consent was limited to this instance ("Consenten per aquesta vegada tant solament conuocacio, congregacio e celebracio de la present Cort") and for the specific reasons given by Alfonso, provided they did not violate the liberties and customs of Catalunya.[74] In the exchange of oaths, María repeated her earlier promise to uphold the rights and privileges, and she emphasized that it was not her intention to cause any prejudice to any person or group.[75]

The queen and the estates then settled down to business, but very little was accomplished. Delays, prorogations, and changes of venue prompted the estates to ask Alfonso to come home to preside personally. To counter the Diputació's legal assault while the Corts were prorogued, Alfonso sent two jurists, Luis de Castell and Francesch Torres to provide juridical opinions to María's Consell and Audiència on the legality of all sorts of actions.[76]

The complaint that Alfonso violated the laws and customs became a legalistic litany in all procesos of the Corts held in the fifteenth century, many of the letters to María or Alfonso and among the representatives of the Corts.[77] The Corts of Tortosa in 1442 sums up the mood of the Catalans and their strong desire to work directly with the king. The genesis of this Corts was unique and an indication of the growing influence of the Diputació del General. In the summer of 1442, just after Alfonso's final conquest of Naples on 4 June,[78] the diputats del general met with a group of Catalan nobles who then went to María to ask her to summon the Corts.[79] This act violated no statutes, it neither usurped royal authority to call the Corts nor the Corts' own authority to negotiate with her. The reason for the Corts, the diputats told María, was simply to remind the king of his obligation to come to Catalunya and personally swear to uphold the laws and constitutions before the three estates of the realm. If he did so, they would happily grant him a large subsidy. In August, Alfonso hinted that because Naples was safely in his control he might consider a trip to Catalunya.[80]

In preparation for the king's return, María summoned the estates to meet in Ulldecona on 7 September 1442 but, because she still had to close the Aragonese Cortes at Zaragoza, the opening session was prorogued until 19 October.[81] Again, she faced protests over her convocation by the representatives at the Corts who doubted that the king would keep his word. Their distrust was fueled by their fear that the king was not only physically but also financially beyond their reach. They were generous in the wake of the defeat at Ponza, but now they found themselves far from the king's ear but close enough to see his hand in their coin purses. During a year in Naples (29 July 1442 to 20 August 1443), Antoni Vinyes, the Consell de Cent's ambassador, complained at length that he was granted only two personal meetings with Alfonso, both of them short and fruitless.[82] If the Catalans thought that their support of Alfonso in the aftermath of Ponza would buy them influence, they were wrong. Barcelona broke with both the other estates as well as other towns in the braç reial and decided not to recognize the sessions of the Corts or to accept responsibility for the king's Italian campaigns.[83] Alfonso kept them at bay for months, sending Galceran de Requesens, the next governor general of Catalunya, to Barcelona with personal letters assuring them that María's convocation was temporary and promising to return as soon as possible. By December, however, Alfonso, well aware that he was being bribed, told María in a letter that "As for the suggestion that they [the Catalan Corts] might agree to offer us some amount of money provided we consent to go there, we tell you it is not our intention to sell them our coming at any price. . . . Without any price or money that may be offered for that purpose we intend to do it with God's help, and we wish to be always at total liberty to go and come as we will."[84] She was to work with them, as before, but he argued that Naples was too newly conquered and his presence there was far more urgent than in Barcelona.

Alfonso toyed with the Corts, telling them, as he did in 1440, that a generous subsidy would hasten his victory and thus his return home. Each side had the other pegged. The Corts knew that Alfonso needed their money, and Alfonso was told that without the king, the Corts was, in the words of Bishop Margarit in 1454, "like a widow."[85] Alfonso, as king, had the upper hand, of course. He had two lieutenants covering for him, his wife in Catalunya, Mallorca, and Valencia, and his brother in Aragón. He reiterated his staunch support for them as they governed his Spanish realms and he ruled Naples. And while he was in Naples, he grew to prefer a more authoritarian hand than the Catalans, or even the Aragonese, would have permitted him. He did not see, nor did he care to see, that by staying in Naples not only was he avoiding face-to-face meetings with the unruly and contentious Catalans, but he was also refusing to face the increasingly difficult situation in which he had placed his wife.[86]

In 1446, just as María was increasingly beleaguered with procedural and constitutional challenges to her authority in the Corts, she received

86   Chapter 4

juridical support from Tomás Mieres, a prominent jurist and member of
the king's council.[87] Mieres, who may well have written this work on Alfonso's request, discussed the issue of a lieutenant's convocation at great
length in *Apparatus super Constitutionibus Curiarum Generalium Cathalonie*. Mieres was attempting to harmonize older native customary laws
that emphasized monarchical aspirations of control with demands by the
urban ruling elites for greater liberty and political control. Mieres ruled
that the authority to convoke the Corts did not rest entirely with the king,
but that it could be delegated by him and thus could fall to representatives such as ambassadors, papal nuncios, or *sindichs*. He disagreed with
commentators, notably Callís, who felt that the approval of the estates was
needed for any and all royal designates, and felt that the task of convocation could legally fall under the jurisdiction of the governor general, who
was not even a member of the royal family.

Mieres's clear-headed thinking became contradictory when he tack-
led the issue of women and the rights of queens to convoke the Corts.
He cited the precedent of Elionor of Sicily, wife of Pere IV, as a fully
empowered lieutenant whose Corts were ratified by the king. He qualified his argument, however, by noting that he felt that the queen, as a
woman, could not exercise ordinary jurisdiction because women were, by
nature, weak, changeable, and unstable and legally unreliable because they
were unable to give truthful witness. He noted that some women were
superior to others, and made it clear that he found María to be "pruden-
tissima" and "sapientissima" and that when she interpreted the Usatges
and other laws, she was as thoughtful as the king. He concluded with the
contradiction that even though queens should not convoke Corts, out of
necessity he would make an exception in the case of María.[88] Mieres shares
with John of Salisbury the belief that women were unfit to rule, except
when that woman was the Empress Matilda or the wife of his employer.
While the opinions of both Callís and Mieres resolved certain points of law
with regard to representation of the king before the Corts, their misogynist sidestepping muddied the legal waters. His assumption about gender
added a new dimension to the discussion. By presuming that women were
untruthful witnesses and unable to render justice, thereby excluding them
from ruleship, Mieres transformed an office that was gender-neutral to one
slanted in favor of men. His argument for María as an exception would
become a familiar phrase, still used to defend an ancient prejudice. This is
as, as far as I can determine, the pivotal moment in the gender assignment
of the office of the lieutenant. Unlike Mieres, jurists working on behalf of

the Corts and the Diputació chose not to make gender an issue. In all their protests and petitions read before the Corts or written directly to the king they put aside their personal sentiments. They adhered to a strict interpretation of Catalan law and argued that the king himself had to convoke the Corts, swear the oaths, and approve all legislation. Nowhere in the extant records is there a trace of the misogynist language of Mieres.

As for María, she knew well that she was not ruling in her own right but was acting in the place of a fully competent adult king who happened to be elsewhere, and who could presumably be called on in an emergency. Despite the protests and challenges to her authority with respect to the Corts, there were no calls for her recall or demotion. This may be due in part to a respect for the royal family, partly to the undeniable legality of her authority, and partly to Alfonso's ardent defense of her. Juan of Navarre faced similar challenges with the complaints against his lieutenancy in Aragón, phrased in the same language as those directed against María. This is not to say that María was treated exactly the same as Juan of Navarre but the documents, even when one reads between the lines, do not support any charge of misogyny in challenges to María's authority to govern. The issue was strictly constitutional. Whatever the nobles and prelates and townspeople may have felt about rule by a queen-lieutenant, they were careful to keep any personal sentiments to themselves and their protests focused strictly on legal issues. I have not found a single example of an ad feminam attack on María as lieutenant, and even jurists such as Tomás Mieres, who bent over backward to exclude women from political life, defended María as a capable lieutenant. It was clear to all that María worked hard and lived a circumspect life. It was also clear that she never intended to supplant her husband's rule, so that the debate never focused on whether a woman could or should rule, but rather on the fine points of the legality of a lieutenant's authority in the Corts.

Moreover, she respected the seriousness with which the Catalans took the formal oaths the king swore before the Corts to uphold and defend their laws and privileges. In her dealings with the Corts, more than anywhere else, she was particularly careful to adhere closely to Alfonso's explicit intentions. Her actions in the Corts were prudent, carefully measured, and diplomatic. But she could be very tough-minded when necessary, and was an expert at stalling to buy time.[89] The Catalans may have believed her easier to manipulate than Juan, but she managed to extract money and to make deals with an extraordinarily contentious populace during very trying times.

It could be argued that the protests never led to her demotion because she was merely a figurehead, but I believe that is an incorrect assessment of her lieutenancy.[90] First, the very strength of the Corts that caused her so much trouble may have actually worked in her favor at the same time. Because all laws were enacted in the Corts, the ruling elites must have felt that they had some measure of control over her actions. As long as she stayed within the agreed-upon parameters by swearing the oaths and providing the appropriate letters of credential, and as long as Alfonso approved in writing all the acts and constitutions of the Corts, the estates were willing to accept her as Alfonso's legitimate representative. Furthermore, Alfonso worked with her, not around her, and insisted that everyone else do the same. His letters and instructions expressed his intentions but left her with considerable leeway in the actual implementation.

Institutional Maturity

María grew more competent in governance during the 1440s. The longer Alfonso was away, the more tensions mounted and tempers flared. The Catalans resented not only his absence but also the costs they incurred in their embassies back and forth to Naples. By the late 1440s relations between the king and the Corts were strained. The Catalans felt that by setting up his court in Naples and breaking all of his promises to return, Alfonso had violated his part of the bargain. This sentiment is clearly evident in a group of letters from Antoni Vinyes, Barcelona's representative to the Corts held in Perpinyà in 1449, filled with complaints about delays and claims that the convocation itself was a violation of the Usatges and other Catalan laws.[91]

Relations between Alfonso and María were increasingly strained, too. Perfunctory salutations such as "Amada muller" and "Carissima reyna" aside, the correspondence between Alfonso and María was strictly business. Long before the 1440s, she must have resigned herself to her marriage to an absentee husband, and only after 1450 did she give up on the thought of his return to Spain.[92] Duty-bound and well trained, she devoted herself to the task at hand, to govern Catalunya in his stead. Most of the time the couple was in accord, but one disagreement stands out from the rest, perhaps because it is such a personal statement in a sea of businesslike instructions and reports. In 1448 Alfonso needed money to pay for the weddings of his illegitimate son, Ferran, and two daughters,

María and Leonor.⁹³ He asked María to petition the Corts for a *maridatge* tax.⁹⁴ She objected to his request, dragged her feet for more than a year, and delayed the transfer of the money for the children Alfonso called "nostre filles illustres" but whom she referred to as "bastardes filles."⁹⁵ In her reluctance, there are umistakable echoes of the 1420s when his mistresses and the birth of Ferran underscored her own childlessness. The dispute over payment for the marriage festivities continued until 1450, when it was mentioned in a letter from the ambassadors of the Consell de Cent to the representatives at the Corts in Perpinyá.⁹⁶ Her own reluctance to collect the subsidy no doubt had a negative effect on Valencians and Aragonese, and especially the Catalan nobles and townspeople, who were reluctant to part with money even when it directly affected them. Pleading poverty ("penuriament" and "gran pobresa"), the Catalan towns of Lleída and Tortosa allied with Barcelona to try to convince Alfonso to change his mind.⁹⁷ She complained to her treasurer, Galceran Oliver, that they were doing a great disservice ("gran desseruey") to the Crown by their failure to pay up promptly. She finally gave in to her "molt alt e molt illustre senyor," but not without snapping at him about raising for money for his "bastardes filles."⁹⁸ The Aragonese Cortes did not happily part with the money, either. In the Cortes of Zaragoza (1446–50), the estates lodged a formal protest against the *maridatges* as excessive taxation.⁹⁹ In the end, Alfonso had to be content with only one-third of the customary rate. Her promptness and diligence in collecting other subsidies of all sorts leads me to conclude that she was able to tolerate his mistresses and their children, but she would not endure willingly or without complaint the humiliation of having to publicly request money for their wedding festivities.

The Recuperation of Royal Patrimony

By the mid-1440s, needing still more money to support two courts, Alfonso turned to forced loans from courtiers, nobles, and merchants, and even pawned his jewels. Then he began to tap the resources of the royal demesne. He said he wanted to improve management of the estates pertaining to the royal patrimony, and to stop the erosion of Crown rights and revenues, but he really wanted to regain the lands and lordships that had been alienated from the Crown since the reign of Martí in the late fourteenth and early fifteenth centuries.¹⁰⁰ Alfonso had taken steps in this direction earlier in his reign, in 1416, but his actions were limited in scope compared to this initiative. He named Pere de Besalú, a former chancery secretary, as his *procurador reial de patrimonio reial*, in charge of royal interests in the peninsular realms and the Balearics. Although the ultimate responsibility for the conservation of the royal demesne lay in the office of the chamberlain, over time it devolved upon the overburdened mestre racional. Besalú became the official guardian of royal patrimony, responsible for the administration of all accounts connected with the royal demesne and the rights and revenues of the Crown. Although Besalú owed his appointment to Alfonso, in Catalunya he was directly responsible to María. Besalú himself possessed wide-ranging authority that extended to include a supervisory role over the operations of the treasurer and mestre racional.[101] Any document involving the financial interest of the Crown had to be approved, registered, and countersigned by him; the mestre racional was to submit to him regular summaries of accounts; the treasurer general was to register with him all records of accounts received and expenditures; all receipts for money, bullion, or goods was to be sent to his office before being forwarded to the treasurer's office; and payments made were to be compiled in a detailed schedule on the day of or the day after they were made.[102]

Besalú arrived in Valencia in 1446, assisted by local financial officers (*procuradors fiscal*) and crown administrators (*procuradors reial*) whose jurisdiction was restricted to various locales such as the county of Pallars and Empúries.[103] Alfonso ordered that anyone who alienated royal property without receiving royal assent had to obtain official approval through Besalú's office. This order applied to anyone currently holding land without relevant documents, regardless of when the original alienation was made. Landholders had to present Besalú with the relevant documents, obtain from him the king's assent, take a new oath of fealty, and, of course, pay a fee for the privilege of holding these lands. If relevant documents could not be produced, the landholder risked forfeiture to the Crown; anyone caught forging documents in order to circumvent the process was threatened with the same fate.[104] Besalú began in Valencia, and encountered no serious opposition there. By the spring of 1447, he had finished his work there and was ready to move to Catalunya.[105]

The Catalan lords had been paying close attention to what Besalú was doing in Valencia, and feared that royal actions would truncate their lands, curtail their jurisdiction, diminish their wealth, compromise their status, and place many of their peasants, free or servile, under royal jurisdiction. Besalú's actions stirred up hostilities ("grans vexacios"), and the outcry was loud, articulate, and widespread.[106] The landlords considered Besalú a trespasser who violated their jurisdiction, and they argued that these actions contravened the privileges and constitutions of Catalunya. The Diputació del General, wary of royal agents in general, became especially touchy when Besalú began to investigate landholding and the royal patrimony in 1446. The Diputació argued that Besalú and his staff wrongfully overstepped their jurisdiction concerning financial matters and violated traditional Catalan rights and privileges. In June 1447 the Catalan lords took their case before the Corts, then meeting in Barcelona, to condemn Besalú's actions.[107] They claimed that the very presence of Besalú was a violation of the constitutions of Catalunya, particularly "Dels commisaris," which prohibited royal officials from interfering with the privileges and laws of Catalunya.[108] The lords flooded María's *Audièencia* with litigation concerning disputed property titles (*pro luïcione*).[109]

The simmer came to a boil when Jaume Ferrer, prominent jurist and royal procurador, arrived in the county of Pallars to assist Besalú. Ferrer was a strong advocate of royal authority and it was widely known that he was no friend of the nobles.[110] Pallars, situated northwest of Barcelona in the Pyrenees, close to both the Aragonese and French borders, had large tracts of property alienated from the royal demesne during the reign of Martí. The Count of Pallars, Arnau Roger IV, a nephew of the bishop of Urgell and a member of one of the oldest noble Catalan families, was generally, but not unequivocally a strong supporter of the crown. His strong pactist views and leadership in the Corts brought him into conflict with the Crown on several occasions. He had been dutifully loyal since 1432 after María brought him before the royal court in violation of the peace and threatened to seize his goods and lands.[111]

On 1 January 1448, Alfonso sent Joan de Gallach, regent-chancellor in Naples, to María to discuss with her in person the host of problems related to the royal patrimony, both in Valencia and Catalunya.[112] He made it clear that he wanted Ferrer and Joan de Montbuy, the regent governor of Catalunya who was assisting Besalú, to continue. He wanted her to continue to supervise their work, but the letter did not specify, even in the most general of terms, how she was to do this. His vagueness indicates that he did not care if she used diplomacy, threats, fines, imprisonment, confiscation, or personal charm—his only concern was that the work should proceed unimpeded. The reports of Ferrer and Montbuy's findings were to be turned over to her and she would verify these documents, but beyond that he seemed uninterested in them.[113] He wanted to recuperate patrimonial lands and replenish his treasury, but he left the methods, timing, and almost all other details to María.

But the Count Pallars had no intention of surrendering one inch of his territory. He invited French troops under the banner of his kinsman, the count of Foix, to cross the border and protect his landholdings.[114] The Consell de Cent of Barcelona, calling them "armed soldiers" ("gent darmes de Cathalunya") of the king, came to his defense.[115] The Consell de Cent of Barcelona complained in a letter to Alfonso that actions against Pallars contradicted the laws and customs of Catalunya and asked the king to revoke the act and return all property to its former state.[116] On 26 October 1448 María ordered the count to appear at her court in Perpinyà to explain his actions.[117] In his defense, the count reminded Alfonso and María that he was only defending his lordly jurisdiction and the privileges granted by the Corts. He ordered his men to harass Ferrer and impede his work while he mobilized the support of his fellow barons.[118] Pallars's actions had a ripple effect, eventually involving the bishop of Perpinyà, ambassadors of the queen of France who happened to be in Pallars en route to Barcelona, and finally, Arnau Roger, bishop of Urgell and the count's kinsman.[119]

Alfonso recalled Besalú but the situation remained tense. The nobles, in defense of Pallars but also knowing their own lands were at risk, disputed the legal status of Besalú and Ferrer. They asserted that a letter of justice not signed by the king without being executed personally by the queen as well, had no value. They argued that the constitutions of Catalunya prohibited any official without title of viceroy, lieutenant, or protector, whether called procurador, or delegate, or any other name or title, from being sent to Catalunya, and asserted that they would have considered such a person to be a private person who could have been resisted without incurring any fine.[120] Implicit in this tortuous legal argument challenging the authority of the royal agents is a formal recognition of María's. Their demand for the signatures of both king and queen on a document to attest to its legality signified that they acknowledged the importance and status of María as lieutenant general in Catalunya. The nobles aimed to weaken the king and ended up strengthening the queen.

María took another approach, telling the Consell de Cent of Barcelona that the count was guilty of poor administration and mistreatment of the peasants of his county ("mala e pessima administracio" and "maltractant"). She claimed that returning his lands to Crown control, they would bring the land back to safety, security, and better government ("es util e necessary sien constuits e posats en seguretat e stament e repos tranquille e los homens e vassals de aquell en bo e saludable regiment e gouernacio"). She threatened anyone allying with the count with a fine of 5,000 florins.[121] This letter, a lengthy diatribe against the count, presents the count in the worst possible light with continued references to scandals and perils, destruction and shame. Pallars was not the only lord who objected to Alfonso's and María's attempts to repatriate Crown lands, but Pallars was the only one to flirt with treason. García Aznar de Añon, the bishop of Lleída, and Joan Ramón Folc II, count of Cardona, both called on the legal expertise of the Diputació del General to defend them, but they never resorted to threats or violence.[122] The count of Pallars proved a formidable adversary, forcing María to apply pressure from all sides. She called to the bishop of Urgell to persuade his nephew to cooperate with her and ordered the Diputació del General to give up its support of the count or risk reprisals.[123] She sent the governor of Catalunya, Galceran de Requesens, and the vicar of Lleída, to Pallars to seize the count's lands and property.[124] In November 1448, violence among the knights and the queen's officers erupted in the regions in and around the county of Pallars. The Diputació del General reported related violence in Tremp as early as October 1448.[125] The Consell de Cent sent reports of the violence ("bandosidad") in Valles to María.[126] Violence continued in the Bergueda, near the French border, well into 1449.[127]

While trying to prevent further unrest, she defended her royal officials. She argued that Montbuy held his office on the orders of the king and herself ("per manament per ordinacio del Senyor Rey e nostre"), and that actions against him by the lords in Girona were prejudicial and an insult to the king's honor ("preiudicial e carregos al dit Senyor e sa jurisdiccio, preheminencia, e superioritat").[128] In this action, she was well within her jurisdiction as lieutenant. The *privegios* specified not only that she should be accorded the same dignity as the king and but also that she had similar authority over subjects who owed homage and service to the king.[129]

Recognizing that Pallars was near treason and not wanting the situation to get out of control, the Consell de Cent sent Pere Dusay and Jacme Ros to María to deliver a letter and personally plead for clemency. On 12 December 1448, the Consell de Cent tried a humble tone, signing their letter as "your humble servants and vassals who humbly kiss your hands."[130] This last statement, unique among all the documents that I examined, is strikingly obsequious for the normally haughty Consell de

Cent. Deferential behavior on the part of the patricians of Barcelona was rare, and this seems excessive, as though the writers have taken their humility too far or are being insolent in their arrogance. It was clear to them that although Alfonso was hundreds of miles away, forceful royal authority remained close at hand in the person of María. They knew that Alfonso and María corresponded regularly and frequently, and this letter makes clear their recognition that the king and queen governed as one. Alfonso sent his chancellor, Arnau Roger, bishop of Urgell and kinsman of the count, to mediate the dispute. Having lost the support of both his kinsman and the Consell de Cent, Pallars backed down. On 19 May 1449 the count began to relent.[131]

Although María may not have initiated the policy or contributed much to its genesis, she had considerable leeway in how and when to implement it and what punitive measures to impose. She built alliances with the Consell de Cent and the Diputació del General by weakening their ties with Pallars with charges of treason. The Consell's fawning letter of December 1448 signaled a begrudging acceptance of the limits of their power with María as lieutenant. The intervention of the bishop of Urgell was crucial in bringing the dispute to a close, but he brought to the table a strong suit: he was a kinsman, a high-ranking prelate, and the chancellor of the Crown of Aragon. His status and prestige combined with María's royal lieutenancy to break the will of the count of Pallars.

María issued letters, both patent and close, to the royal officials in and near the county of Pallars—the vicars of Girona, Vic, Osona, and Lleída—as well as the bishop of Urgell, the count of Cardona, the municipal authorities of towns in Pallars, Consell de Cent, and the Diputació del General.[132] These letters spelled out the credentials of the royal agents, stipulated fines of up to 1,000 florins for anyone engaging in violence against her officials, and informed them of the action she was planning to take against violators. Her principal concern throughout was to prevent the unrest in Pallars from spreading, especially in light of the French soldiers allied with the count. She wrote frequently to Besalú, Ferrer, and Montbuy in Pallars to keep them informed of any news from Alfonso.[133] As events unfolded, she informed Alfonso when she issued the order to confiscate the count's land and moveable goods, and her plans for the disposition of the property.[134]

It is not entirely clear how much revenue was eventually generated by Alfonso's attempts to recover and reorganize the royal patrimony, but the incident reveals as much about royal government in Catalunya as it does about royal finances. María worked closely with Alfonso—there are more than fifty letters between them concerning Pallars—and tried to prevent the crisis from escalating.[135] The incident raises the important and difficult issue of jurisdiction, especially the question of where a lieutenant fit within royal, comital, episcopal, municipal bailiwicks. This was a very difficult matter to resolve. Governed and governors alike had to cope with complications caused by the overlapping and conflicting jurisdictions of a lieutenant. The confusion over who was in charge of whom, and what impeded government, slowed collection of subsidies, and hindered the administration of justice. Such problems are familiar to any student of medieval institutions, but in the Crown of Aragon the lieutenancy posed a new set of jurisdictional conflicts. The Catalans carefully guarded their privileges and sought the advice of jurists and lawyers to resolve their disputes and did not hesitate to challenge the lieutenant or the king when they felt aggrieved. The issue of jurisdiction—whether seigneurial, ecclesiastical, regional, or municipal—was one that the Catalans considered with absolute seriousness. It became the centerpiece of the conflict over the *remença* peasants and the issue that clearly delineated the boundaries of María's authority as lieutenant.

Social, Economic, and Political Unrest in Barcelona

The Crown's financial woes worsened in the late 1440s, revealing structural weaknesses in the economy. Catalan commerce, especially the cloth trade, faced external challenges from coastal piracy, increased competition from Italy and Germany, and a contraction of international markets as the Turkish empire expanded and threatened Mediterranean shipping in the east.[136] In this volatile environment two rival groups formed. The Biga ("roof beam"), an association of ciutadans honrats, merchant financiers, lesser urban nobles, and wealthy guild merchants possessed vast wealth and wielded political authority through the executive council of the Consell de Cent.[137] The Biga was opposed by the Busca ("fragment"), composed of lesser guild masters and artisans who had both numerical superiority and the economic potential to augment greatly the wealth and prestige of Catalunya, not to mention the Crown's taxes and customs duties. They were politically disadvantaged by their disproportionate representation in municipal government. The Busca was stymied by the protectionist measures of the patrician oligarchy that controlled the

Consell de Cent, and they demanded reforms in municipal government that would permit more equitable representation.[138] Behind the Busca stood Galceran de Requesens, lord of Molins de Rei and Santa Creu d'Olorda, *batlle general* of Catalunya in 1435, and governor of Catalunya since 1442. He worked tirelessly on their behalf to undermine the Biga.[139] For him, reform in Barcelona went beyond loyalty to the Crown; it took on the character of a personal mission, and his enemies worked zealously to destroy him.[140]

The behavior of these two groups was not entirely predictable, however. There was considerable fluidity among the membership of each group that depended as much on wealth and rural landholdings as on social rank. Alfonso disliked the strength of the Catalan oligarchy and saw this as an opportunity to weaken them. Both Alfonso and María recognized the political advantages of breaking their political dominance, but Alfonso was reluctant to alienate the patriciate altogether. They mandated a modest increase in political representation of the social groups from the middling ranks of merchants and artisans and played newly formed factions against one another to weaken the traditional oligarchical affiliations.[141] Neither party was happy with this compromise, but the situation was sensitive and Alfonso was slow in coming to a decision.

While he pondered, embassies from both sides went to Naples to present their cases to the king.[142] Alfonso told Antoni Vinyes, the Biga envoy and prominent ciutadan honrat, not to worry about the situation because he loved the city and would treat it well.[143] Meanwhile, Alfonso made similarly appeasing remarks to the Busca delegate. Members of both royal courts found themselves in the uncomfortable position of taking sides against their friends. Even Arnau Fonolleda, Alfonso's most trusted secretary, was excluded from confidences he would normally have shared because Alfonso entrusted all Barcelona business to another secretary allied with the Busca.[144] María's position was especially difficult. She had just emerged from the bruising battles with the count of Pallars with her office and her dignity intact, but now she found herself poised between two more or less balanced powers whose animosity threatened to tear apart the principality. Although not entirely excluded from an active role in the dispute, when both sides took their case directly to Naples María was left with the exquisitely delicate task of sorting through the compromises. In a familiar line of appeal, the Busca first took their case for reforms in municipal representation to the Consell de Cent for approval; when their proposals were rejected they put the pressure on María. When she hesitated, waiting for news from Naples, they grew impatient and took their case directly to Alfonso, who grew exasperated at the tactics used to gain his approval and decided that henceforth he would receive all his information only from María.[145]

The problem was that the mood in Naples changed often. Alfonso was careful, shrewd and, at times, very slippery. He may not have transmitted sensitive information in a letter of instruction but relied on a trusted official to convey the message in person, verbally. Many letters sent to María via royal officials told her to "listen well" to the messenger, thus implying that some important items on the agenda may not have been written down.[146] To mask his intentions, he commonly sent bogus letters or instructions to Spain, and then sent couriers flying off with a countermand drafted in such a way that those in his confidence would understand to disobey the second letter.[147] The vagaries of the mail service (*correu volant*) made this an extremely risky practice, and may well have led María to hesitate, even when a letter looked authentic rather than risk a misstep. Indeed, perhaps the most difficult part of her job during this period was determining when to act and when to stall, as her thirty-four prorogations of the Corts demonstrate.[148] She formed the buffer between Biga and Busca and waited for Alfonso to decide.[149]

The situation worsened in January 1449 when María summoned the Corts to request a financial subsidy to support Alfonso's continued military campaigns in Italy, a source of persistent irritation for both the king and the Catalans.[150] In the ensuing standoff the delegates from Barcelona to the Corts demanded that Alfonso return and personally preside while María insisted on her rights as lieutenant to convoke and preside over the Corts.[151] The work of government was delayed, the Corts was prorogued thirty-four times, and in the end it required Alfonso's personal intervention—but not his presence—to break the stalemate.[152] He ordered the Corts to meet in his absence with María presiding and promised that he would return to confirm the privileges, constitutions, and laws of Catalunya.[153]

The showdown between the Biga and Busca was temporarily resolved, but negotiations among the two parties, María, and Alfonso dragged on. Each side gained and lost a little until María's resignation in 1453.[154] Galceran de Requesens fared no better than the queen as lieutenant. His support of the Busca party guaranteed that his tenure would be short and

98 Chapter 4

he was brought down by the still-powerful Biga party and the ciutadans honrats of Barcelona. The ten-year civil war eventually settled the question of representation.

The Queen, the King, and Political Discourse in the *Res Publica*

But the events of the 1440s and early 1450s indicate much more than this. María had become Alfonso's indispensable partner in government. Letters, memorials, and official acts and charters circulated among the king, queen, nobles, municipal elites, and peasants. Although often couched in dense official rhetoric, these vivid and sometimes personal statements are daily testaments to the seriousness of the growing crisis in the towns and the countryside. Beyond the bare facts, these documents expose María's and Alfonso's will and temperament in ways rarely seen in official correspondence and permit a careful analysis of the couple's working relationship. Their letters, royal directives, as well as private letters, were exchanged among merchants who plied the Mediterranean trade routes, delegates to the Corts, the Consell de Cent of Barcelona, lawyers and prelates. The *procesos* of the Corts—containing attendance lists, speeches given before the assembly by the king, queen, *infante*, or anyone speaking on behalf of an estate—fill in important details and rarely heard voices.

A vivid visual testimony of this complex political relationship can be seen in the only image of her painted during her lifetime. This large, half-page manuscript illumination (see Frontispiece to this volume), painted in 1448 by Bernat Martorell (d. 1452), shows the queen presiding over a session of the Consell de Cent.[155] Catalan jurist Jaume Marquilles formally presents to the queen and the members of the town council (consellers) his commentaries on the Usatges, the fundamental law code of the city of Barcelona.[156] To emphasize her royal distinction, María is drawn larger in scale and she sits alone, above the others on a gold-colored throne. The gold baldichin creates a special regal space for her that draws the viewer's eye to the central action of the picture, reinforce her power and status, and set her apart from the consellers and members of the clergy. She wears a crown and a turban, an allusion to the fashion of the Castilian court of her childhood that favored Moorish styles, to cover her hair.[157] Her loose-fitting rich royal blue robe covers a gold gown; both are trimmed with fur. Were it not for the exoticism of the turban, the luxury of the fur, and the richness of the colors, María's appearance suggests a modesty bordering on the monastic. She tilts her head slightly toward the conssellers, in a gesture both feminine and respectful. The sheathed sword of justice, a regalian object traditionally reserved exclusively for the king, rests in her lap.

This portrait is not a false idealization of queenship.[158] It contains a wealth of unexpected iconographic details that represent the historical reality of María as queen and clearly indicates her vital role in the political life and governance of the realm. It is a very tightly composed image: All eyes are focused on the ceremony, even the two hovering figures on the balcony and the crowd gathered outside are active observers. The setting is most likely the outdoor patio (*llotja*) of the Trentenari, a hall in Barcelona often used for formal celebrations. The five principal conssellers—Bernat Sapila, Pere Romeu, Pere Serra, Berenguer Llull, and Felip de Ferrera—seated directly on her right, are dressed in their official *gramalla*, the distinctive red, fur-trimmed robes of their office, and seated on a gold bench. Marquilles himself, dressed in an ecclesiastic blue gown, offers the book to the first conseller.[159] María sits alone on the throne in a position of authority, without any other member of the royal family—no heir, no father, no husband. By arming her with the sword of justice, Martorell has violated conventional royal iconography because he was painting what he saw, not what theorists imagined the body politic to resemble.

The viewer's eye oscillates between three points in the picture: the queen, the donor, and the five conssellers, emphasizing the discursive character of their political relationship. The queen's downward gaze and the inclination of her head direct our eye to the conssellers, whose red gowns blend and merge, rendering them an almost amorphous physical mass made distinctive only by the artist's very personal rendering of their facial features. The tilt of María's head implies participation, a circular connection between her and the conssellers. Furthermore, María looks directly at the conssellers; her gaze is not downcast, but neither is it sexual or angry or challenging. She is a mild, serene witness to the formal donation of the manuscript and the dialogue between Marquilles and the conssellers. In the painting, as in real life, María has taken the place of her husband and has become his alter ego (*alter nos*, in Catalan). What is particularly striking is how undisturbed the conssellers are. They take for granted that a queen has literally displaced a king. For everyone present, this represents just another day at the office.

This image illustrates the mechanisms of a *res publica*, a literate, bourgeois public that engaged in lively debate about the political life of the realm.[160] For medievalists, it may seem anachronistic to regard people in the Middle Ages in terms Jürgen Habermas would use.[161] When I say public political sphere I mean not simply the "high politics" of governments and states, but also the power relationships and conflictual processes that constitute political discourse. The narrowness of Habermas's definition of modernity and "public political discourse . . . in the world of letters" has been a stumbling block for anyone studying premodern societies. He defines "public" not as merely the flip side of "private," but in its political sense, as a *res publica*, a literate, bourgeois public that engaged in lively debate about the political life of the realm. But Habermas's definition of a bourgeois public as a fully realized "public sphere in the world of letters" of the royal court and "co-extensive with public authority" can encompass the political public sphere in the Middle Ages. The key is to carefully consider the broader implications of Habermas's work.

In the late medieval Crown of Aragon a literate (and even a functionally literate) elite urban public did engage in lively debate about politics. Instead of doing so in coffeehouses or with newspapers, they participated in the parliamentary assemblies, argued their cases before civil magistrates, and, at times, corresponded directly with the king or queen. They were situated in a "public sphere in the political realm" and the topics under consideration were concerned with the *res publica*.[162]

Reading the documents in this way has important implications for the role of the queen in the institution of monarchy. The voice of the queen is suppressed, often absent, unless she speaks the language of charters and public pronouncements.[163] But discourse takes many shapes, and because of the very public political nature of life at court, queenship is a discursive practice. Even when denied full access to the traditional avenues of political power, the queen had just enough status and proximity to the center of power to engage in the public political sphere. The interaction between María and Alfonso and their literate elite and bourgeois subjects was indeed discursive. True, this particular public sphere was limited to a small elite group, and the exchange of ideas and policies in this particular context does not share a one-to-one correspondence with Habermas's schema. But this epistolary exchange was indeed public discourse in the medieval Crown of Aragon. It was public, co-extensive with public authority, the royal court was an integral component, and the topics under consideration were concerned with the *res publica*.[164] This sphere and these ideas were public political discourse and María was a full participant

A Permanent Lieutenancy, 1436–48

in the political culture. Each party in this protracted struggle—the queen, the king, the landlords, and the peasants—operated within a set of implicit rules and patterns of thought that comprise contractual monarchy. As they participated in the parliamentary assemblies, argued their cases before civil magistrates, and, at times, corresponded directly with the king or queen—even if she did not explicitly govern—they were engaged in an exchange of ideas that served to both define and redefine rulership as it moved among the participants.

Describing the discursive character of María's practice of rulership reveals monarchy as a complex entity, a multiplicity of power relations that are not separate entities, but rather elements contained within a network whose power circulates, or functions as a chain, or as Foucault notes, "never localised here or there, never in anybody's hands, never appropriated as a commodity or a piece of wealth. And not only do individuals circulate between its threads; they are always in the position of simultaneously undergoing and exercising this power."[165]

The operations of this discursive political relationship are particularly evident in the controversial decision by Alfonso and María to free a group of semiservile peasants known as the *remences*, tied to the land in an archaic quasi-feudal agrarian system. As the king, the queen, and their subjects exchange hundreds of letters, political ideas circulate and proposals were debated and refined. In the records of this struggle, which is the subject of the next chapter, it is possible to hear the voice of a queen working in the public political sphere and to gauge her impact on Aragonese political culture.

Chapter 5

The Struggle to Liberate the *Remença* Peasants, 1448–53

THE REMENCES, peasants of northeast Catalunya who were tied to the land in onerous serf-like conditions, were the last vestiges of a quasi-feudal landholding system that was antiquated long before its institutional demise in the late fifteenth century. Their name is derived from the Catalan term *remença* (redemption), the monetary payment required to purchase their freedom from a secular or ecclesiastical lord.[1] What began as a contractual arrangement in the tenth century had become a codified system of both landholding and social hierarchy by the fifteenth century. The *remences* had been agitating for their freedom since the reign of Martí, but they were opposed by nobles and wealthy urban landlords who controlled the town council of Barcelona.

María of Castile strongly supported the peasants' efforts and did not hesitate to say so. She met personally with delegated peasant representatives and forcefully implemented royal decrees ordering their manumission. Nobles and landlords resisted. They tried to go over María's head to Alfonso, to bypass her authority by stalling, and threatened her with armed resistance. In response, she punished secular and ecclesiastical lords who ignored her orders. The crisis polarized Catalan society, dominated political discourse, and nearly halted government from 1447 to 1453. Ultimately, the issue became not just peasant manumission, but who was to decide the issue itself. The king? The lieutenant general? The Corts? The *remença* dispute thus became emblematic of the wider theoretical issues of authoritarian rule, contractual kingship, the scope of the office of the lieutenant general, and representative government. Through it all, María recognized Alfonso's authority as superior to hers and carried out his or-

The Struggle to Liberate the *Remença* Peasants, 1448–53   103

ders until the summer of 1453 when, frustrated by his decision to revoke the manumission decrees, she resigned her lieutenancy. Her tact, tenacity, and shrewd political skills, coupled with Alfonso's adamant support of her, ultimately weakened their opponents. Her handling of this controversial question—indeed, the fact that she handled it at all—demonstrates a genuine monarchical partnership between María and Alfonso.

Each party in this protracted struggle—María, Alfonso, the landlords, and the peasants—operated within a set of implicit rules and patterns of thought characteristic of the political culture of the medieval Crown of Aragon. This culture was pragmatic and open to the public political activities of queens. María's authority, officially mandated yet clearly held at the king's pleasure, was constrained by the fact that she worked within a culture that accepted her power and authority as lieutenant but that clearly preferred to work with the king. Nevertheless, her actions in the *remença* dispute reveals that the Crown of Aragon operated as a truly discursive practice.

Historiography

The body of scholarly work on the *remences* during the reign of Alfonso and María, like that of their reign as whole, is surprisingly thin. In his pioneering study of the *remences* during the reign of Alfonso V, Santiago Sobrequés i Vidal called attention to the "vast unknown period" between the death of Maria de Luna in 1406 until 1448. He criticized scholars, known collectively as the "Girona school," named for the city that was the epicenter of the *remença* crisis, for creating and perpetuating the myth of quiescence in the Catalan countryside in the 1440s. It was not, he said, a time of "legislative calm, of silent and underground agitation" among the *remença* peasants that foreshadowed the Catalan civil war, but his work remains one of the few examinations of the period.[2]

The origins of peasant servitude in the Crown of Aragon have been discussed most recently by Paul Freedman, who builds on the works of Pierre Bonnassie and Archibald Lewis on social groupings, and Josep Salrach on the formation of a "national" identity in early Catalan society.[3] Freedman's work, both a synthesis of current historiography concerning medieval agrarian life and an analysis of the particular legal, social, and economic conditions in Catalunya, is an essential text on the *remences*. But

104   Chapter 5

he gives short shrift to Alfonso's reign, and nowhere does he mention the
actions of María of Castile.[4] On the other end of the timeline are those
scholars who pick up the story after 1448.[5] Jaime Vicens Vives was interested in Fernando II and the *Sentencia Arbitral de Guadalupe* of 1486
that legally freed the *remences*. He regarded 1486 as a pivotal date in Catalan history, much as 1789 signaled the end of the *ancien régime* in France
and devoted just over twenty pages to an analysis of the decades between
1388 and 1462.[6] Some of the best recent works are modest regional studies written to commemorate the quincentennary of the Sentencia Arbitral.[7] The aftermath of the civil war and 1486 and the problem of the
remences, is of interest to historians of modern Spain.[8] Eva Serra i Puig, in
her ground-breaking book on the social and economic conditions of the
peasants in the Sentmenat in the seventeenth century, argues instead that,
although the legal status of the peasants changed in 1486, agricultural life
remained grindingly poor, and real social and economic change did not
occur until nearly two hundred years later.[9]

Works that do encompass a wider temporal span tend to focus narrowly on a specific point. Francisco Monsalvatje y Fossas studied the county
of Besalú and Julián de Chía on the Girona countryside.[10] Both works
contain valuable transcriptions of primary sources but little analysis of the
wider political situation. Eduardo de Hinojosa y Naveros was interested
in the legal aspects of peasant servitude while José Coroleu also looked
at servitude from a mostly legal standpoint, but he looked at the reign of
Juan II and the civil war.[11] José Pella i Forgas discussed the *remences* in the
county of Empúries (the region is known as the Empordà) in the heart of
upland northeast Catalunya, often referred to *Catalunya vella* (ancient
Catalunya).[12] They briefly discussed María's role but did not analyze in
detail much of the period of the 1440s. More regional studies pick up
where Hinojosa, Chía, Monsalvatje y Fossa and Pella y Forgas left off but
continue to ignore the 1440s.[13] Alan Ryder has written probably the most
comprehensive narrative study in English, but is particularly interested in
the civil war itself.[14] Teresa Vinyoles Vidal, in an entirely different and
decidedly welcome approach, has examined the struggle from the point of
view of the elite women whose families held land on which the *remences*
lived.[15] These works are tremendously important, but I am not interested
in the origins or conditions of peasants' servitude. I am interested in the
actions of both Alfonso and María in this stuggle, and particularly Maria's
political support of the rememces' efforts to gain manumission from the

Crown in the 1440s and early 1450s when both the Crown and the peasants came painfully close to resolving the matter.

Peasant Servitude in Catalunya Until 1416

The most sweeping and harshest laws concerning the peasants, enacted as early as 1202, left most peasants outside royal protection. Peasants were more clearly defined as subordinate to lords and the *mals usos* (evil customs) were used to define their legal status.[16] Two mals usos were routine levies: *arsina*, a fine for deliberate or accidental burning of a peasant's house or other property; and *firma di spoli forçada*, a payment in return for the lord's guarantee of agreements concerning dowry. But the most universally despised customs not only restricted a peasant's freedom but humiliated the peasant as well. For example, a lord could arbitrarily demand labor services, force a nursing woman to serve as wet nurse, and subject the peasant to unwarranted physical abuse. Three mals usos were especially severe: *intestia*, the lord's right to a considerable portion of the moveable goods left by a peasant who died intestate; *exorquia*, a similar levy exacted when a peasant died without legitimate heirs; and *cugucia*, the seizure of a peasant's property if his wife had been adulterous. The redemption payment itself should be considered a sixth mal uso. The legislation of 1202 further recognized the *ius maletractandi* that permitted not only physical coercion but also seizure of their property without justification or explanation.[17]

Implementation and enforcement of statutes concerning peasant tenure were not uniform throughout the thirteenth century. Conditions varied widely and cases involving peasants and lords suggest that there was no universal index of servitude and that the lords themselves were not strong enough to enforce the legislation. Economic improvement in the thirteenth century provided the lords with greater wealth and stability.[18] The strength of the lords is evident in the statute "En les terres o llocs," enacted in the Corts of 1283, which prohibited tenants who customarily made redemption payments from seeking protection on royal lands.[19] The payment of redemption became the key element of servile tenure and bound the peasant closely to the land.[20] Until the mid-fourteenth century, the king and his lay and ecclesiastical lords were the most lenient and less likely to use violence to enforce their lordship. The price of redemption varied widely, according to personal status (age, marital status, or gender) and from place to place (most *remences* were concentrated in the upland northeast near Girona and Vic, and lands to the west of Barcelona).[21] The Black Death changed dramatically the conditions of tenure under both ecclesiastical and lay lords.[22]

After 1348 Catalunya experienced profound demographic decline, the desertion of villages (*masos ronecs*), wide economic fluctuations, rising wages, unstable currency, and massive social disruption accompanied by a realignment of the social, political, and economic forces of the realm.[23] The decades immediately after the plague favored the peasantry, and until the 1380s, the lords were forced to offer more favorable terms in order to attract tenants. When the lords tried to remedy their situation by insisting on exactions based on their old rights, they discovered that the old social and economic patterns had altered. A handful of families affiliated with the royal family remained after 1400, but they no longer controlled the largest lands. While the economic fortunes of the nobles declined, the elites of Barcelona were able to maintain, and later, extend their holdings in the countryside. By the turn of the fifteenth century, the elites of Barcelona controlled substantial rural lordships.[24]

All peasants felt the pinch, but the most violent and widespread peasant unrest was confined to *Catalunya vella* in the northeast, especially the region near Girona and Vic, where lordships were small and seigneurial power was mostly local and the crisis was most acute. Alongside the *remences* were numerous peasant freeholders, and this juxtaposition of free and servile tenures stimulated unrest, while in areas where freeholders were lacking (for example, west of the Llobregat river), peasant unrest was minimal. In the south and west, serfdom was rare and peasants worked the land within a structure of great lordships, especially ecclesiastical. After 1348, the social and economic distinctions among peasants accelerated, with some able to take advantage of the deserted holdings and wage increases, while others sank even deeper.[25] Rural unrest often arose from attempts by the lords to make relatively prosperous peasants pay extra seigneurial dues for the deserted farmsteads that they had acquired in the aftermath of the plague.[26]

Although all varieties of unrest collided in the mid-fifteenth century, it is my purpose to examine only the problem of the *remences*. Alfonso commingled the recuperation of alienated royal patrimony with peasant servitude when he proposed to place the *remences* under royal protection by claiming that all alienated lands without valid title would revert to the

The Struggle to Liberate the *Remença* Peasants, 1448–53   107

Crown. The lands he seized in Catalunya *vella* or near Barcelona had substantial numbers of *remences* living on them. When the nobles protested Crown actions concerning the *remences*, they were also protesting Crown attempts to repatriate their lands. But it is doubtful that a return of lands to royal control meant an abolition of the mals usos on that land.[27] Alfonso saw that he could make money two ways, first by collecting a fee for the manumission, and then by reaping the benefits of the land itself and the servile labor of the peasants.

For the *remences* the issue was not entirely economic, it was more a question of a fundamental change in their legal status. They believed that the abolition of the mals usos would remove the most humiliating mistreatment, and that their improved legal standing would naturally bring with it the freedom to make a better life. There were, in fact, two wings of the *remença* movement. One group was relatively affluent, conservative, and willing to pay the seigneurial dues and rents, and they wanted above all to suppress the mals usos and obtain a confirmation of their free status. The other group was poor, and they proposed a more radical reform of landholding that not only guaranteed them their legal freedom but also granted them full and free ownership of their lands and an abolition of all seigneurial dues.[28]

In some ways, the *remença* wars bear a strong resemblance to other social revolts of the later Middles Ages such as the Ciompi in Florence, the Jacquerie in France, and the English rising of 1381. The *remença* risings became entwined with urban unrest on the part of artisans and lesser guild masters.[29] Like the Ciompi, the Jacquerie, and the English rising of 1381, the immediate outcome of the *remença* uprisings was violence and bloodshed. But the *remença* struggle continued for generations, prompting Pierre Vilar to call the years between 1348 and 1486 as "the Hundred Years' War of the Catalan countryside."[30] The *remença* struggles differed from these other European revolts, however, in that the most important allies the *remences* had were the Aragonese kings and their lieutenants. The English kings effectively suppressed the risings of 1381, which were not confined to the countryside but included urban centers, too. But these revolts are not entirely dissimilar.[31] In France, the king violently quashed the revolt of the Jacquerie in 1358. In Florence, the Ciompi overthrew the ruling oligarchy in 1378, only to be themselves brutally thrown out within weeks. In spite of intense pressure from the barons and landlords, the Aragonese kings since the 1390s had attempted to abolish servile tenure. They were not always consistent in their policies, nor were they acting out of purely philanthropic motives. For Kings Joan I and Martí, the most pressing cause for their pro-*remença* policy was the rise of peasant agitation. The *remença* revolt thus can be seen as a kind of active petition directed at the king, whom the peasants perceived as an idealized arbiter between the peasants and the lords.

The earliest serious negotiations to reform laws concerning the *remences* date to the reign of Joan I. In 1388 the king, citing moral justification and legal precedents, questioned whether servitude and the mals usos had outlived their supposed value. From the Avignonese pope, Clement VII, he sought a bull that would order the release of the *remences* held by ecclesiastical lords from liability to the mals usos in return for the payment of an unspecified amount of money. The peasants would compensate the lords in return for an end to the most degrading aspects of servile tenure, but the institutions of rent and tenancy would not change. Nothing substantial happened immediately, but his proposition later became the basis for all settlements.[32]

Conditions in the countryside worsened after the anti-Jewish riots of 1391 extended beyond towns into rural areas. The peasants' violent actions against both secular and ecclesiastical lords—systematic destruction of land and goods, threats against lords carried out by bands of peasants—and the widespread refusal to remit customary services and payments, demonstrated that they were not only angry, but also well organized.[33] It had become clear that the Crown needed to find a permanent solution to the problem, and rather than suppress the peasants' protests, Joan acted in their behalf. He permitted the peasants to hold assemblies, and in 1395 he renewed his request for a formal admonition of the harsh treatment of the peasants by the ecclesiastical lords, this time to the new Avignonese pope, Benedict XIII.[34] Joan offered to collect four florins per year from each peasant household, with half earmarked for the pope and half for the Crown in return for the peasants' manumission. He died that year, however, before he could fully implement any reform programs.

During the reign of Martí, the Crown continued its support of the *remences*. In 1402, Martí's wife, Maria de Luna, appealed to Pope Benedict, her kinsman, to order the condemnation of servitude on church lands. In her letter to Benedict, she denounced servitude as unjust, detestable, against God and imperiling the souls of those who hold peasants under such abominable conditions. Benedict issued a bull to the cardinal-bishop of Girona condemning the landlords' most serious abusive practices against the peasants, but the queen's intention was to abolish servitude not just

The Struggle to Liberate the *Remença* Peasants, 1448–53   109

on ecclesiastical lands but secular ones as well. Maria preferred that the next steps be taken from within Catalunya, and a commission was established, but she died in 1406, before anything of substance resulted. Some money had been collected and these assets were frozen in an account, but it is not known exactly what became of it.[35] Mark Meyerson and Nuria Silleras-Fernández credit Maria with acting out of conviction, not political expediency.[36] Indeed, her work on behalf of the *remences* proved to be one of her most enduring of her many accomplishments. Her actions served as precedent for all later settlements because they extended the discussion beyond purely political motivations to see the issue's moral and ethical dimensions.

María of Castile followed in the footsteps of her predecessor and may have felt that Benedict XIII's opinion on the *remences* justified her passionate defense of them in the 1450s. María worked closely with Jaume Ferrer, a notary and jurist whose family had worked on behalf of the *remences* with Martí and Maria de Luna; his expertise in the issue and opinions must have had an effect on María of Castile's own views. Ferrer's knowledge of his father's and grandfather's writings may well have been the basis of María's argument to Alfonso, and the weight of papal opinion must surely have bolstered her in the fight. This may have been an especially potent weapon against recalcitrant ecclesiastical lords, as when in 1449 she reminded Pere de Urrea, the archbishop of Tarragona, of Benedict's ruling on the *remença* peasants.[37] Moreover, the information was widely known among the educated ruling elites. In a letter of 19 October 1450, the Consell de Cent wrote to Joan Marimon and Bernat Sapila, their representatives in Naples, outlining Benedict's opinion and the actions of Martí and Maria de Luna. They urged Marimon and Sapila, in their upcoming discussions with Alfonso, to argue very carefully, protest only Alfonso's "novel" actions that not only freed the peasants but also placed them under Crown jurisdiction, and not to tread on those areas in Benedict's bull limited to treatment of the peasants.[38]

Seen in this light, María of Castile appears to be the inheritor of a line of reasoning rather than its inventor. Still, she forcefully advocated the manumission of the *remences* in one venue where Maria de Luna, due to her early death, did not—in the Corts. Where Maria de Luna worked behind the scenes to obtain Benedict's support, María of Castile worked in the full light of public scrutiny. By refusing to give in, despite ferocious protests and the threat of violence in the countryside, and by maintaining a high profile throughout the debates, she changed the terms of the debate over servile tenure as well as the character of the lieutenancy and Aragonese queenship.

The Crown's Early Initiatives in Favor of the *Remences*: 1416–46

A brief economic upsurge in Catalunya in the first decades of the fifteenth century eased the relations between lords and tenants, and the outbreaks of violence in the countryside subsided temporarily.[39] It would be misleading, however, to interpret this as a sign that harsh tenure had disappeared or that the problem had disappeared. The nobles may have been weakened economically by the havoc of the plague, but as a group they remained a formidable political bloc. Newly emboldened by their governance of the realm through the Corts during the interregnum and their role as king-maker in the Compromise of Caspe, they still could force the king to make concessions in return for either money, or political advantages, or both. The *remences* suffered a setback in the Corts of Barcelona in 1413 when Fernando consented to legislation ("Com a molts") that strengthened the power of landlords by enforcing existing peace statutes against anyone whose land had been confiscated but who continued to make threats against new tenants.[40]

When Alfonso succeeded his father in 1416, he inherited a combination of frustrated peasants and infuriated noble, ecclesiastical, and urban landlords. Like his father, he wanted to placate both the nobles and the peasants, and his policies for the duration of his reign were no doubt as infuriating to his subjects as they are to anyone today. Instead of equilibrium, he achieved only a perpetual state of imbalance. The issues of *remença* manumission and the king's right to decide the issue without first taking counsel from the Catalans, were handed off to María to settle in the Corts, which, as we have seen, was on the verge of a constitutional crisis and the site of numerous challenges to María's authority. Of course, this prelude to civil war, seen so clearly from the distance of five hundred years, developed slowly and incrementally from the first Corts over which María presided in 1420.

At the Corts of Tortosa in 1420, María (no doubt acting on Alfonso's expressed intention) approved the right of peasants to pay a fee to transfer tenure from one lord to another in seven parishes in vall d'Hostoles and la Muntanya and authorized peasants from the regions of La Selva

(Vilobí d'Onyar) and the Baix Empordà (Pedrinyà, Caça de Pelràs, and la Pera) the right to form groups led by official representatives (sindichs).[41] After 1420, however, Alfonso became increasingly occupied with affairs in Italy and Castile, and between 1420 and 1432 he made some concessions to the peasants and some revocations of permission to form sindichs. In 1431, the *remences* of Olot were granted permission to meet and form sindichs, only to have it rescinded later.[42] It was a time in which high rents created a reactionary mood, especially among the ecclesiastical lords from Muntanya, Empordà, and Girona, who were guided by the obstinate bishop Bernat Pau.

This group used the Corts of Tortosa in 1432 to pressure the Crown to act in their favor and not make any changes in the legal status of peasants. The delegates requested and Alfonso granted them jurisdictional concessions over peasants, ignoring Benedict XIII's prior opinion. Alfonso agreed to stipulate that certain peasants were bound to the land under the laws of the realm. Using the peace and truce statutes as a model, he allowed landlords to seize the lands of any peasant regardless of status who deserted his lands and abolished any rights of freedom for fleeing peasants.[43] The power of custom in the hands of the lords was still too strong for the king to supersede with a "novetat," no matter how many papal opinions he could muster.

The next decade was dominated by the successes and failures of Alfonso's military campaigns in Italy. Whatever was happening in the countryside remains, to us at this time, a mystery. Given later events, it is unlikely that the *remença* peasants were silent or inactive. They were not, however, actively seeking Crown support or taking arms against their lords, and by the same token, the Crown took no action either in favor of or against the peasants. In 1442, María conceded to the peasants of Corça, Sant Sadurni, and Cruïlles the privileges and freedoms of Barcelona, but a year later required them to pay a higher price for their freedoms.[44] In 1444 she halted altogether the process of redemption of the peasants of Begur and Peratallada, probably due to opposition from nobles.[45] This halting, zigzag course of action bears María's name but Alfonso's hallmark. As later events demonstrate, she felt a strong obligation to stand by her decisions, but Alfonso was a little more willing to sell his policy to the highest bidder.

There is truth to Vicens Vives's claim that the Aragonese kings used the peasants as leverage to weaken the nobles, but Alan Ryder has pinpointed the larger issue.[46] He attributes the Crown's pro-*remença* policy to economic self-interest rather than to a simple power play, ethics, or morality. Ryder argues that Alfonso wanted to use the redemption payments to make up his chronic financial shortfalls. He recognized the futility of collaboration with the Corts because many lords who resisted changes in the legality of the *remences* were either themselves members of the urban patriciate of Barcelona or close allies among the higher clergy and nobility, and they had tremendous influence in both the Corts and the Diputació del General. It was at precisely this moment in 1442 that the Diputacío del General petitioned María to summon a Corts with the underlying motive of offering Alfonso money in exchange for his return to Barcelona. Unwilling to accept a subsidy with such strings attached, Alfonso sought another way to obtain much-needed money.[47] His advisers, mostly canon and civil lawyers, investigated the possibility of recovering the alienated royal patrimony to undermine feudal types of jurisdiction and alleviate the Crown's fiscal problems. His advisers also suggested that he assist the *remences* in their struggle to obtain their freedom.

Alfonso's financial situation was dire. He had devised a complex financial strategy whereby wealthy cloth merchants and financiers received bills of exchange drawn on a variety of royal funds throughout the Aragonese domains, usually Barcelona, Valencia, or Perpinyà. Like the Italian *imprestanza*, this system permitted the Crown to purchase Catalan cloth using bills of credit. The cloth was used as a payment-in-kind for three months' wages for a soldier in the army. The Crown's bills of exchange were backed by estimated collections of the hearth tax in Naples and tax revenues from the cloth trade, and these in turn were used by the merchants and financiers as letters of credit for international investments. Alfonso's innovative solution worked wonders for the Catalan cloth trade and paid for his army, but inflated estimates in the collections of the Neapolitan hearth tax nearly ruined the fragile scheme.[48] The Aragonese treasury had a perennial problem with cash flow, and could seldom cover routine disbursements. The amounts owed to the merchant-bankers were far from routine. In 1444 the Aragonese treasury owed Jacme Casasaia of Barcelona 50,000 ducats; in 1448, it owed Bertran Crexells of Perpinyà 41,500 ducats. Payment in cash was out of the question, and quasi-barter solutions were unacceptable to the merchants.[49]

María spent much of her time in the late 1440s and early 1450s haggling with the Catalan Corts about getting and spending money, but even revenue from the bills of exchange fell short of the king's needs.[50] As his bills of exchange came due, Alfonso looked around again and decided to let the *remença* peasants purchase their legal freedom. In this matter he could afford to be generous—the vast majority of *remences* did not live on crown lands.⁵¹ María of Castile, like Maria de Luna fifty years earlier, took the side of the peasants. Subsequent events demonstrate that she vigorously implemented Alfonso's decrees and imposed fines and censures on any landholder who physically threatened her royal agents as they enforced the collection of the tall, the *remença* redemption payment. When a bidding war between the landowners and the *remences* ensued, Alfonso played one side off the other in an attempt to extract the most money while ruffling the fewest feathers.

Tentative Royal Actions and the Corts of Barcelona, 1446–48

On 30 June 1446, María summoned a Corts to meet on 27 July in Barcelona at the Priory of Natzaret to discuss Alfonso's request for money.⁵² The diputats del general and the estates reiterated their now-familiar petitions for the king to return to Barcelona, to meet personally with them, and to swear the oaths before the Corts. But Alfonso, who would not be coerced into returning to Catalunya against his will, told María that "the Catalans can keep their money to spend some other time."⁵³ He was burdened with the complexity of Italian politics, and even though Juan of Navarre was once again dangerously enmeshed in Castilian intrigue, he had to stay in Naples to safeguard his still-fragile kingdom there.⁵⁴ Even though María was ill, the diputats and their advisers came to her bedside to tell her that they would grant a subsidy of 104,000 florins after their grievances were resolved. Among those grievances was the problem of the king's absence, but Alfonso would not budge. He insisted that they continue to work with María in his absence.⁵⁵ The payment was delayed, and the king froze all Crown expenditures and ordered all embassies to stay put.⁵⁶ As both sides began to stiffen in their resolve, the Corts, for the first time, began to take up the issues of landholding and the *remences*.

Earlier that year Pere de Besalú, the conservador reial, and Jaume Ferrer, the procurador reial for the county of Pallars known to be sympathetic to the *remences* began their inventory of alienated royal patrimony.⁵⁷ Pallars had no *remences* but a lot of alienated royal property and the presence of Besalú and Ferrer in the vicinity agitated the local lords, who began to harass and physically threaten Ferrer.⁵⁸

Meanwhile, in February 1447 peasants in the Empordà were granted royal permission to hold meetings. Little is known of these meetings except the bare outlines.[59] The origins and outcome remain a mystery, and it is not certain that these peasants were *remences* alone or joined with other, free tenants. They had been agitating for some relief from their onerous status for decades, but the timing of the grant may have been in response to isolated reports of *remença* peasants abandoning farmsteads under secular or ecclesiastical lords or those of the diputats del general and settling on royal lands.[60] More ominous reports from the period indicating that peasants in scattered locales had been threatening their lords in a variety of ways, such as erecting crosses and digging large pits on the lords' lands.[61]

On 4 August 1447, the secular and ecclesiastical lords presented a petition to Joan Marimon, Alfonso's personal envoy, conveying their concern over the peasant unrest, and their annoyance ("gran vexació") with the actions of Besalú and Ferrer. They minced no words.[62] In their opinion, Besalú was "un home scandalós, gran inventor de novitats, scelerat, detestable," and they referred to him as the "so-called royal secretary." They blamed Ferrer personally for the destruction of much of Pallars, not only the lands of the count but other lands as well.[63] They took their petition to the Corts, demanding the recall of Jaume Ferrer and Besalú. The Consell de Cent of Barcelona soon followed suit, complaining at length about prorogations of the Corts and how María's royal council was giving her bad advice.[64]

Alfonso took his time responding, and when he did it was evident that he did not want to break completely with the lords. In January 1448 he backed down. He promised to make public the information gathered by Jaume Ferrer, and to establish a commission composed of the Maestre Racional Pere de Santcliment, his assistant, Barthomeu Scayó, and the prothonotary Pere Ram to mediate the dispute.[65] And, in a gesture of conciliation, he recalled Besalú to Naples.[66] But he made it clear in a letter read before the Corts that, for the moment at least, he did not intend to return to Catalunya. In April 1448 María granted the Corts a three-month period of suspension from all royal investigations into landholding and closed the assembly on 11 May.[67] Alfonso turned down an offer of 30,000 florins from the Corts rather than cede to them the right to decide on the *remences* and landholding, but urged María to keep working with the Corts and the diputats del general to reach a settlement agreeable to all parties.[68]

During this respite from the Corts, María met with four peasant representatives from Girona on 2 June 1448 near Vilafranca del Penedès.

The details of this meeting, unprecedented both for what was done and for its symbolic importance, are not known. The information is reported obliquely, after the fact, in letters between Alfonso and María in which they discuss strategy and implementation. I have found no record of the event itself—no notarial record, no crown document, no instruction from Alfonso ordering the meeting—but the registers are filled with letters describing the angry reactions of the lords who refer to the meeting.[69]

We know very little about the peasants themselves and even less about the sindichs who represented them. The names of individual peasants appeared in various letters, but, to date, little else can be said of them. For example, we know of a *remença* sindich named Pere Amay ("sindich del negoci de les *remences*") and a peasant named Ramon Seriat ("home de rehemença"), because María intervened on the latter's behalf to the vicar (*veguer*) of Rosselló-Cerdanyà, to whose court he had been summoned for his role in fomenting unrest. María ordered Seriat's release on the grounds that he had been unlawfully detained, and warned the veguer that further harassment would result in fines or imprisonment.[70] Although we know very little about the communities or localities they represented and how they were selected, we do know the identity of a few of the notaries—Joan Bacaller, Pere Morera, and Jacme Coma—who worked on their behalf only because they were mentioned in letters kept in either crown or municipal archives.

These second-hand sources do agree on certain key pieces of information. In the name of all the communities subject to the *remença*, the representatives of the *remences* offered the Crown a combined payment of 64,000 florins for the intervention in the Corts securing their redemption. Apparently there is no mention of their legal status nor of any measures concerning landholding of existing tenancies.[71] Alfonso took the decisive step on 1 July 1448.[72] In a letter patent he ordered that representatives of the peasants could meet, provided that groups were no larger than fifty, would meet in the presence of a royal official, and set a combined price for their redemption of 100,000 florins. On September 1448 Alfonso notified his prothonotary, Arnau Fonolleda, that the *remences* had his approval to meet under the terms of the 1 July letter patent, and he authorized María to collect the redemption (*tall*, meaning "cut").[73] He instructed María to apply the tall collected directly to his debt to Bertran Crexells, the merchant banker from Perpinyà who held some of the Crown's bills of exchange.[74] Alfonso's actions in 1448 may well have been the first serious attempt by an Aragonese monarch to resolve the problem peacefully. It is not clear whether his timing was a direct response to María's meeting with the peasant representatives the month before, the result of the increasing tension in the countryside, or the poverty of his treasury. In its details, his plan was not a new idea but rather a confirmation of preexisting conditions.

The *remença* sindichs elected by the members of the community subject to the redemption first met on 13 October 1448 near Girona.[75] The landlords were outraged. The bishop of Girona, on the pretext that the *remences* had instigated unrest and therefore broke their side of the bargain, claimed that he had the rightful jurisdiction as their feudal lord and opposed their meetings.[76] In the late fall and winter of 1448, the Diputació del General, stepping into the fray because the Corts had been suspended, joined forces with the Consell de Cent of Barcelona and opposed the publication of the royal provision of 1 July 1448. Lords from Barcelona who controlled large tracts of land in Sabadell, Terrassa, and Montcada (with many *remences* under Barcelona's jurisdiction) agreed to detain royal officials who tried to work with the *remences*.[77] This alignment of forces anticipated almost exactly the alliances of the civil war fourteen years later, and at times, especially in their defiance of royal orders and subsequent actions toward royal officials, they were openly treasonous.

The diputats ordered that any official who tried to implement the order would be arrested and fined. They asked a jurist, Joffre d'Ortigues, to determine the validity of the letter patent that was sent not under Alfonso's autograph signature but that of his chancellor, the bishop of Urgell, and to ascertain whether such a letter had to be obeyed.[78] And, they wrote directly to María in Perpinyà, telling her that they considered the letter patent to be in violation of the constitutions of Catalunya and therefore, they were unable to comply.[79] They gave Bernat Aybrí, an oïdor de comptes for the Diputació and a prominent citizen of Perpinyà, the power to act in their name.[80] Then, under the signature of the archbishop of Tarragona, they wrote to the estates and other cities and towns to muster their support in a unified action to fight royal actions that were prejudicial to their lands, lordship, and status in the realm.[81] Letters were sent to all the vicars throughout Catalunya, with individual requests sent to Pere Deztorrent, procurador from Barcelona whose jurisdiction included the Ampurdán. They notified all royal officials in Rosselló and Cerdanya that they considered the royal decree a violation of the constitutions and privileges of Catalunya, specifically the act of the Corts approved by Pere IV at the Corts of Monzón, the statutes of Pere III in 1283, and those of Jaume II at the Corts of Girona.[82]

María was undaunted. She continued implementation of Alfonso's letter patent, sent royal officials into the field to begin collection of the tall, and ordered three Crown lawyers, Francesch Castelló, Johan de Foxa, and Francesch Giganta, to discuss the matter with the Diputació's lawyers.[83] She sent Jacme Coma to Naples to relay news and give a report directly to Alfonso, who gave a blanket approval of the actions she had taken.[84] Feeling the pressure of all this royal activity on behalf of the *remences*, the Consell de Cent and diputats del general met on 16 December to discuss how to respond.[85] They agreed that María was not to be easily persuaded, and sent the viscount of Illa-Canet, who represented the *braç militar* in the Diputació and had substantial landholdings in the baronies of Pinós and Mataplana (in the Alt Berguedà) and Illa i Canet (in Rosselló), all with large numbers of *remença* peasants, to meet with María personally.[86] In his strongly worded instructions to Illa-Canet, the archbishop of Tarragona outlined why the *remences* should not be freed: they do not pay any extraordinary taxes ("seruituts" or "drets de generalitats"), they are defiant of authority ("traydors"), and to free them would lead to the destruction of Catalunya.[87]

On 29 December, the diputats del general wrote directly to the twelve *remença* sindichs "electes per lo fet vulgarment dit de les remençes," telling them in no uncertain terms that they opposed the royal decrees.[88] The danger from such an organized opposition was palpable, and it worked: The peasants abandoned their meetings in February 1449.[89]

The 1449 Decree Granting *Remença* Manumission

Unmoved by the opposition, on January 16 1449 María ordered all cities, towns, villages, and other locales throughout the realm to publish openly a copy of Alfonso's intention to collect a tall of three florins from each *remença* household in return for abolition of the mals usos. This decree contains the three essential elements that later appear in the Sentencia Arbitral of 1486: the right to elect representatives, the right to assemble openly and freely, and the payment of a tall. On the same day she wrote a similar letter to Francesch Castelló, Francesch Giganta, and Johan de Foxa, her chancery officials who handled materials concerning the *remença*, informing them of the decision.[90] Within the year, nearly one-third of the tall was collected from close to 20,000 peasant households, which even María admitted was almost a miracle.[91] This indicates either that the tall was a reasonable amount to expect a peasant household to pay (for comparison, the Consell de Cent paid three florins to the messengers who delivered their letters), or that most peasants anticipated some sort of royal bargain for their legal freedom.[92]

In an act of open defiance, the lords of Barcelona, Vilafranca del Penedès, Sabadell, Terrassa, Montcada, and other neighboring lands impeded collection of the tall by refusing to grant royal officials access to their lands. The archbishop of Tarragona, in a letter to Arnau d'Orta, diputat local in Manresa, said that the clergy and knights of Eparraguera, near Barcelona, were opposed to the remença decrees and, with money from the Diputació, they were willing to go to war.[93] The Diputació declared that the counties of Empuriès (once part of the royal demesne) and Pallars, the viscounty of Illa-Canet, and the bishopric of Girona were not royal territories, despite the findings of the procurador reial.[94]

Alfonso tried to defuse the situation and agreed to turn the matter over to the Corts for open discussion. On 30 January, with Alfonso's letters of support in hand insisting that María possessed full authority to convoke, preside, prorogue, and negotiate in his place, María issued a summons to the three estates to meet in Barcelona on 15 March.[95] This session did not officially open until a year later, on 11 March 1450. Beset by countless delays and prorogations, the assembly moved twice, first from Perpinyà to Barcelona, because the estates complained about having to meet in the royal palace, which they considered filled with unhospitable royal agents, and finally to Vilafranca del Penedès, because of an outbreak of pestilence in Barcelona. These many prorogations bred distrust.[96] In May 1449, the Consell de Cent reported María's comment that Alfonso was serious about continuing the Corts, but in their opinion she said that because she wanted to buy time while waiting for explicit instructions from Alfonso.[97]

For the next year, in the interim before the Corts officially opened, however, the Diputació functioned as the permanent representative body of Catalunya. During 1449, these two groups stirred up much unrest among the estates, causing María to complain that they considered themselves omnipotent.[98] The ruling elites of Barcelona led the offensive as the diputats del general allied with the Consell de Cent. On 15 May 1450, the consellers wrote to their representatives to the Corts in Perpinyà, telling them to insist that the remença issue be handled in the Corts, where they could control it, rather than in either María's or Alfonso's royal council.[99] This coalition was joined by two prominent and influential barons—

Bernat Joan de Corbera, the count of Módica and Arnau de Vilademany i de Blanes. Vilademany was a particularly harsh lord who forced his peasants to formally recognize their obligations, a practice that María later outlawed.[100]

The Diputació tried again to convince María to change her mind, no doubt hoping to change Alfonso's as well. A twelve-member commission (four from each estate) elected by the diputats del general, led by Galceran de Pinós i Fenollet, the viscount of Illa-Canet, went directly to her to demand that she issue an order to stay ("sobreseiment") the *remença* decrees. If she would not, the viscount threatened to take the matter over her head and travel to Naples to request that Alfonso return to deal with the matter directly.[101] The commission had little influence over María, however, and she proved that she could be just as obstinate as they were. When her messengers Jacme Coma and Joan de Montbui reported that Bernat de Pau, the bishop of Girona, failed to comply with the collection of the tall, she alerted Alfonso and, most probably with his support if not his explicit instruction, ordered the seizure of the temporalities of the contumacious bishop and the cathedral chapter of Girona if he did not comply immediately with the royal decrees. The bishop retaliated by threatening her officials with excommunication, but she continued collection in spite of it.[102]

At Alfonso's urging, she promoted Joan de Montbui, a knight who strongly supported the *remença* decrees, to the post of regent governor of Catalunya and sent him to Girona.[103] The lords' reaction to Montbui was reminiscent of the outcry against Pere de Besalú.[104] The lords were particularly virulent in their attitude toward Montbui, even though Galceran de Requesens, whom Alfonso personally assigned to work with Montbui, was doing practically the same thing but took very little abuse for it until later.[105] The answer may lie in the fact that Requesens, a wealthy landholder and governor of Catalunya, outranked Montbui, a knight ("cavaller") and regent governor, on both counts. It may also be that Montbui was the agent most often present, whereas Requesens was more often in Barcelona than Girona. To calm the furor and appease his lords, Alfonso suggested that Montbui be removed, but María wrote him a strong letter supporting all of her officials.[106] No matter who bore the brunt of the baronial oppositions, because of the sensitivity of the matter and the sums of money involved, María was forced to devote more of her staff to collect the tall and to keep order in the countryside. And she had them keep an eye on one another's work, as when she ordered Pere Roig, a lieutenant treasurer, to report on García Boran, a procurador fiscal in Girona. Her actions indicate that she was acutely aware of the need to adhere as closely as possible to the precise letter of the law and to avoid the appearance of overstepping legal boundaries.[107]

The behavior of the high-ranking prelates, which ranged from the bishop of Girona's open hostility to the moderate passivity of prelates outside the fray, was despicable. The archbishop of Tarragona was, admittedly, in a very difficult position. As spokesman of the Corts and the ecclesiastical representative for the Diputació, he had an obligation to speak on behalf of the clerical estate. As a landlord, he controlled extensive properties, but there were no *remença* peasants on his lands, nor were there any allegations of the mistreatment of anyone under his jurisdiction. It is not surprising, therefore, that María would try to convince him to abandon his opposition. She wrote to him in February 1449, reminded him of Benedict XIII's opinion on the matter, and in a placating tone, she appealed to him as one of the Crown's most loyal supporters. Even though the decree did not pertain to him directly, she implied that his support, as a member of the diputats del general, was crucial.[108] Alfonso added his own very influential voice and sent Galceran de Requesens to speak with the archbishop on his behalf. He urged Requesens to argue in favor of the moral and ethical issues, that all men, rich and poor, should be treated alike ("principalment . . . axi en aquella egualment tractar lo chich com lo gran e lo pobre com lo rich car aquella en si no admet accepcio, o distinccio de persones alguna").[109] He then wrote directly to the Diputació, accusing them of usurping royal jurisdiction, and repeating his comment about equal treatment.[110] Alfonso's emphasis on treatment was, in itself, a compromise no matter how noble and egalitarian the phrasing. He was not advocating a radical restructuring of the social hierarchy, simply insisting on decent treatment for everyone subject to his law. María reiterated the point when she read a letter from Alfonso to the Consell de Cent on 29 March 1449.[111]

Finding María so steadfast, the Diputació changed tactics.[112] The viscount of Illa-Canet convoked a meeting of prelates, nobles, and townspeople to elect nine ambassadors to go over María's head and confer personally with Alfonso in Naples. After months of seemingly intractable negotiations, each side gave a little bit. Alfonso softened his stance and offered a compromise. If the lords would immediately stop mistreating their peasants, he would suspend all royal orders concerning the *remences*. Many small proprietors signed this compromise, but the barons and ecclesiastical lords remained fiercely opposed to all royal orders as an unnecessary humiliation.[113] On 30 April, María issued a stinging letter to all the disobedient lords, telling them in no uncertain words that their actions had placed the land in such turmoil as had never been seen, and that only God could pardon them.[114] The Diputació gave in, probably because their embassy to Naples was fruitless, and on 5 May 1449, ordered comital officials to comply with the collection of the tall. Nevertheless, the issue was far from fully resolved. The collection of the tall proceeded very slowly, royal officials and peasants faced widespread routine harassment, and María's Audiència began to fill up with cases involving unrest in the countryside.[115]

These lords, with the Diputació and the Consell de Cent as their mouthpiece, simply changed their tactics. They flooded María's Consell with protests. They raised jurisdictional issues: The count of Pallars argued that Joan de Montbui, whom he considered a private person, did not have the proper authority to act in the Empordà and refused to honor his royal letter of credential.[116] In addition to claiming that the decrees violated the constitutions and privileges of Catalunya,[117] they deliberately dragged their feet concerning publication or compliance,[118] or simply refused to publish the decrees,[119] or refused to comply with them,[120] or considered the decrees illegal because they lacked the king's or queen's autograph signature,[121] or complained of fraud in the collection.[122] They argued that the king was not the *remences*' immediate overlord and therefore had no right to alter their legal status in any way.[123] Some lords, the count of Cardona for example, claimed that they had no *remences* on their lands and therefore were exempt.[124] In defense of the Crown, María asserted that as king and queen, they were the natural overlords of all subjects regardless of intermediate jurisdiction and that she would regard all actions against the peasants as a dishonor to the king, subject to punishment and fines.[125] Treason would not be part of the vocabulary until 1462, but dishonorable actions against the king amounted to tacit treason nevertheless.

Legal disputes, protests, and negotiations notwithstanding, María still struggled to collect the tall and maintain public order, and in the summer of 1449 she sent her treasurer Galceran Oliver, to meet personally with Alfonso and give an account of the state of the realm. She asked him to come to Catalunya, stressing the seriousness of the situation. She then outlined the major problems she faced: her jurists had doubts about Alfonso's legal right to collect the luïcions; French troops summoned by the Count of Pallars were massing at the border; she had been having difficulty collecting the *maridatge* subsidy. On the bright side, she had collected 28,000 of the 36,000 florins from the *remences*.[126] Before Oliver could respond, she fell ill, further delaying the opening of the Corts.[127] Her illness prevented her from speaking in person at the plenary session and she sent Jaume Vila, her secretary, to read her letters to the Consell de Cent. She scolded the estates for their unreasonable tardiness in collecting the tall and gave them twelve days to do so or risk fines of 5,000 florins.[128] She remained firm in her support of the *remences*, as she stated in a letter to Alfonso written on 18 February 1450.[129] She may have sensed that Alfonso was wavering, or perhaps had heard from her emissaries that he was leaning in favor of the lords. Whatever her underlying motives may have been, she described the threats against the peasants and urged him not to change his mind.

Alfonso responded on 1 March that he would consider her advice. She responded quickly, reminding him that the *remences* had acted in good faith and that he should not be fooled or led on by the embassy from the Consell de Cent and Diputació, and she denounced his willingness to play one side off the other.[130] Whether or not Alfonso had yet made up his mind to abandon the peasants, he knew it was risky to convoke the Corts in an atmosphere where passions ran high on all sides. But he would not abide the effrontery of contumacious subjects. In February 1450 he ordered María to seize the lands of lords in Sabadell, Terrassa, and Montcada, an action met with an unsurprising flood of protests by the Consell de Cent, within whose jurisdiction these localities fell.[131] María fully supported this decision despite the ardent outcry against it, and when he wavered, she told him that to restore them would be a mistake and then, in an appeal to his regal pride, she predicted that the Crown would suffer a loss of reputation.[132]

María continued to collect the tall as though nothing extraordinary had happened. She wrote to the *remença* sindichs approving their twelve *pagadors* who were to handle the administrative fees incurred in the collection.[133] She even sent out a letter patent to all lords with *remença* peasants reiterating the 1 July 1448 decree.[134] The Consell de Cent and the Diputació were enraged, and demanded that the issue be adjudicated in the Corts.[135] The problem with this solution was that the estates were pitted against the Crown and there was no impartial jurist or judge on whom everyone could agree. The most respected jurists were Arnau de Vilademany i de Blanes, who was staunchly in favor of the lords, and Tomás Mieres, who was just as staunchly royalist. Mieres, in fact, had represented the king in the Corts of 1449–53 as "legum doctores, consiliarii domini Regis" and had denounced the mals usos as early as 1438 in the *Appara-*

tus super Constitutionibus curiarum generalium Catahlonie.[136] One month later, when the Corts finally opened on March, both sides were well armed with familiar arguments, strategies, and tactics.[137]

The Corts of 1449–53 and the Queen's Resignation

As soon as the Corts met in Perpinyà, the Diputació del General disbanded and the Consell de Cent stepped forward as the driving force behind the opposition to the *remença* decrees. As strong a political force as the oligarchy of Barcelona was, it could be outflanked by upland towns and villages who resented its dominance. The peasants of Catalunya could neither tolerate nor afford a political system that subsidized, economically as well as politically, the elites at the expense of the middling and lesser ranks of society.[138]

The estates protested the delays and the choice of the queen's palace in Perpinyà, where they felt they could not speak freely. The selection of the place to hold the meeting was, in principal, the prerogative of the king and depended largely on royal needs, but in theory it required the consent of the Corts. For María, the venue often depended on such variables as her health, outbreaks of epidemics, the weather (she preferred southern locales, if possible), and convenience to most members.[139] They were, however, much less agitated than before over the absence of the king. They acknowledged that María had special authority from Alfonso, a sign either that his earlier letter had preempted any challenges, or that they had simply given up hope that Alfonso would appear and decided to concentrate on the matters at hand.[140] Their first concern was that the assembly proceed quickly, without further delays and without suspension of the meetings before all the business was concluded.[141] They wanted the matter settled in the Corts, where they had more control, and they clearly did not want a repeat of the hamstrung and aborted Corts of 1448.[142]

Barcelona's influence was evident from the start, as seen in a series of letters from their representatives at Corts—Antoni Vinyes, Joan Ros, Pere Deztorrent, and Felip de Ferrera. They exchanged detailed regular reports of the proceedings in Perpinyà and in Barcelona.[143] On 20 April the consellers wrote to their sindichs telling them to block any action until they were satisfied with the outcome of negotiations over the *remences*.[144] They complained of the delays due to the late arrival of various representatives (the Corts was prorogued thirty-four times between 22 March 1449 and

14 March 1450).[145] Joan Ros and Felip de Ferrara complained that Alfonso and María always consulted with each other and used mail delays as a ploy to stall. Ferrara questioned María's legal capacity to convoke the Corts and asked the consellers to obtain legal advice on the matter.[146] Before the Corts officially opened, the Diputacío del General had already allied with the Consell de Cent and mustered the support of the nobility.[147] A split in the noble estate appeared, however, when a dispute arose between the viscounts of Illa-Canet and Vilademany over the selection of a nine-member commission responsible for advising the Corts on the *remences*.[148] The nobles were not alone in their factional rifts, and their problems were quickly mended. The truly serious split was taking place in the braç reial, as expected with Barcelona acting against Perpinyà and Lleída.[149] María tried to resolve one of the principal grievances of the Corts and to placate the nobility by ordering the *remences* to pay the ususal "censos, rendes, e altres drets" while the tall was being collected but before any final decision was made concerning their legal status, but her order to the lords to stop harassing the peasants did little to pacify their temper.[150]

During the summer of 1450, María began to have doubts about a mutually satisfactory outcome, even as she reassured her own officials and received reassurances in return from Alfonso. María confessed to Pere de Besalú that she thought Alfonso would be diligent with the latest embassy from the Corts in Naples and would resist their demands, if the price was right, and that if Alfonso were to change his mind it would prejudice royal rights and prestige in Catalunya.[151] The slow pace of collection of the last of the tall began to take its toll on her patience. On 30 April 1450 she snapped at her royal officials. She gave them six days to force the lords' compliance or risk forfeiture of their own jurisdictions and possessions. They would also be held responsible for payment of all expenses incurred by the Crown in their prosecution.[152] Some of her letters reveal how terribly alone she must have felt that summer. On 1 July 1450, she wrote to Jaume Vila of Jaume Ferrer's impending arrival from Naples and told Vila to stay for a few days so they could all meet together, because there is such a scarcity ("gran fretura") of intelligent people at her court.[153] Bowing to pressure from the nobles, Alfonso asked María to demote her close and loyal assistant, Joan de Montbui, but she insisted that to do so would impair the negotiations with the *remences* and make all the other royal officials vulnerable to harassment and threats. María asked Jaume Vila, then on his way to Naples, to plead with Alfonso on Montbui's behalf using "paraules molt dolses e gracioses."[154]

As the tensions mounted and the stakes rose, the personalities of both Alfonso and María come into clearer view than before, when the correspondence was routine and formulaic. Alfonso appears more hardheaded and determined to win his point at all costs, while María seems to have a clearer sense of her non-negotiable dignity as a queen and lieutenant. As she came to realize that her husband was willing to use the peasants as bargaining chips, or perhaps that he never really bargained in good faith at all, she began to doubt his intentions and her letters to Alfonso revealed a novel, more passionate tone. On 20 July 1450, in a letter to Jaume Vila, she considered the entire matter of the *remences* in peril of collapse ("E lo negoci per ço sta en bassat e en gran perill") because the peasants had lost hope ("sindichs e pagesos començer a perdre cor e sperança'), all because of Alfonso's bad faith negotiation and double-dealing.[155] Shortly thereafter, she begged Alfonso not to change his mind and revoke his support, or risk serious unrest among the peasants ("qualsevol sinistre o perill que de aço pugues insurge lo que deu no vulla").[156] She was not exaggerating the seriousness of the situation. That summer, the countryside, quiet for more than a year, came alive again with threats of unrest. María reported to Jaume Vila that she had news from Jaume Ferrer and Pere Prats that the *remença* sindichs were nervous.[157] In September, there were reports of unrest in Cruïlles, and in November more localities in and around Girona reported peasant unrest.[158]

The Corts—impeded by factional disputes, procedural debates, and ineffectual commissions—stalled, and little was accomplished until the fall of 1451. The events of 1451 and 1452 were mostly filled with watching and waiting and with embassies to and from Naples, marked by Alfonso's periodic changes of heart. On 20 July 1451, María met personally with the Consell de Cent of Barcelona and the diputats del general to request that the Corts provide 400,000 florins in exchange for Alfonso's return to Catalunya so he could deal personally with the *remença* issue and the recovery of patrimonio reial. The importance of the queen's rare appearance at the Casa de la Ciutat was signified not only by the ceremonial rituals, which are similar in many respects to the ceremony depicted in Martorell's frontispiece miniature, but by the prominent barons who accompanied her: Joan Ruiz de Corella, the governor of Valencia; Andreu de Biure, the count of Cocentayna; and Ramon Gilabert, a knight who served as lawyer in María's court. The account of the meeting, written by the secretary of the town council, suggests that María was carrying out Alfonso's wishes rather than acting on her own initiative: "She made it known that the king needed 400,000 florins to be used to leave Naples and recover his patrimony [in Catalunya]."[159] The councillors and deputats del general agreed to consider the king's request, and two months later, on 15 September, the Corts agreed to the subsidy.[160] On 22 November 1451, María wrote directly to the homens de *remença* explaining that because the manumission decrees would be prejudicial to the lords, she and Alfonso were seriously considering a revocation of the original decrees of 1 July 1448 and ordering a return to the status quo ante.[161] A "gran clamor" among the peasants resulted,[162] but in March of 1452, notwithstanding the threat of violence and rebellion, Alfonso tentatively accepted the offer from the Corts while delaying public announcement until May.[163]

The couple's working relationship was transformed by Alfonso's revocation of the *remença* decrees. After decades of letters filled with calm, measured, carefully phrased, and sometimes bland statements, the correspondence after 1452 is markedly personal. María's frustration and annoyance spilled over in her letters to him. Alfonso had decided to abandon the *remences* against her advice, in effect over her head, and she insisted that he tell her precisely why he had changed his mind. As if to emphasize that he now wanted her to simply carry out intentions without listening to her, she wanted to know explicitly what he wanted her to do and when.[164] She had lost all credibility within the Corts, she wrote, and no one will work with her directly. As for the *remences*, they were most aggrieved ("gransissimament agreujiats") at the turn of events. The *remença* sindichs were afraid to return home. If they came back without the deal they were promised, they would face 400,000 very angry peasants.[165]

María's pleas fell on deaf ears. In May 1452 Alfonso reinstated the *remença* obligations to their lords and suspended collection of the tall. He made no serious attempt to return, and grew annoyed at the Corts' insistence that his subsidy was predicated on his return. His economic problems mounted and he grew impatient with the lords. On 30 March 1453, he changed his mind once more.[166] He revoked the obligation he had ordered in May 1452, and reordered the collection of the tall. The peasant unrest grew intolerable, and by the spring of 1453 Alfonso must have realized that he could ignore it no longer.[167] In a final about-face, on 15 July 1453, Alfonso reestablished peasant obligations to their lords.[168]

An exhausted María continued to work through the summer of 1453. In her letters to Alfonso she described seemingly endless wrangling in the Corts and frustration with petty demands. Her health began to decline, but her anger did not abate. On 25 July 1453 she wrote another angry letter to Alfonso about the *remences*, this time telling him that the *remences* were very angry at having spent much for nothing, and that the burden of this decision—she foresaw great quarrels with the *remences*—was on both their consciences.[169] But her patience with and tolerance for Alfonso's maneuvers had run out. At the end of August she notified Alfonso that she intended to resign as lieutenant general of Catalunya on the pretext that she was needed in Castile to broker another peace between her ever-sparring brother-in-law and brother. She then notified her closest advisers and members of her staff in September that she would be resigning as lieutenant general.[170]

María's extraordinary resignation defied royal traditions and legal precedents. Queens may be banished or sent into seclusion, as Eleanor of Aquitaine was by Henry II of England when she plotted against him with their sons. Queens would relinquish their rights to rule in favor of their sons, most notably in Spain when Queen Berenguela of León passed the throne to her son, Fernando III. As regents, queens technically are obliged to step down when their sons are old enough to rule on their own. As dowagers, queens retire. But no Aragonese queen-lieutenant had ever resigned.[171] Her move was the result of several, undoubtedly linked causes. First, and most important, it is a clear statement of her frustration with Alfonso's policies. She could not have sent a more powerful signal of her disapproval of his actions. He could prevaricate or procrastinate when he read her letters containing protests and warnings, but the message that arrived with this letter to Alfonso was unambiguous—and it left him alone with his decisions about the *remences*. In her letter of resignation, María expressed her sadness at spending five years negotiating fruitlessly in the Corts ("non ha sortit algun fruyt ni algun util"), and predicted that the quarrels over Corts and peasants would continue.[172] Second, her decision may have been prompted by concerns about her health, which had been stable for some time, but had always been a problem. She was fifty-two, still active and vibrant mentally but old enough that the prospect of more years of wrangling with both her husband and the *remença* peasants could not have been appealing. Finally, and most important for the institution of the queen-lieutenant, her decision underscores the limits of her power. She could disagree with Alfonso, she could harangue and plead and send embassy after embassy to him to try to get him to change his mind. But she had gone as far as she could go. She could not overstep her authority. She was the king's lieutenant, and powerful as that office was, it was always held at her husband's pleasure. It is just as extraordinary that her

128   Chapter 5

resignation prompted no serious outcry from any of their Catalan subjects. The lieutenancy had changed hands often enough during Alfonso's
reign to make them accustomed to such moves and, coupled with what by
then was a finely tuned bureaucracy suited to his style of govenance, they
waited to see what the king would do next.

Alfonso's next move was a mistake. He appointed Galceran de Requesens, a knight without any connections at all to the royal family, to take
her place.[173] The financial strength of the Requesens family placed them
in the service of the Crown, first as magistrates and then as governors of
Catalunya, a post that had taken on an almost hereditary quality.[174] As
governor of Catalunya, Galceran de Requesens's pro*remença* connections
and antibaronial alliances alienated almost all entrenched noble and patrician factions and very nearly united all the warring factions in the Corts
in opposition to him. Before María left, she warned Alfonso that the new
government might not run so smoothly. The government of Barcelona
was torn over electoral reform that would weaken the ruling elites in favor
of the middle and lower social ranks. Requesens's lieutenancy was opposed
by many who knew him to be an advocate of the *remences* and the reform
program in Barcelona, and she thought things would go badly.[175]

Her predictions proved accurate. Requesens took office on 19 October 1453 and remained in office for one year, driven out by the nobles in
northeast Catalunya who opposed the *remença* decrees and by the patriciates in Barcelona who opposed electoral reform.[176] Requesens's position
was difficult from the start. He wrote to Alfonso on 20 October to report
the protests to his lieutenancy.[177] In a letter to María a week later he asked
her to intervene on his behalf with the Consell de Cent, who were opposing his actions. The second letter is a remarkable admission of his difficult
position. He asked María to return to Barcelona and resume as lieutenant
in his place.[178]

Alfonso recognized his mistake and did not repeat it. In July 1454
he replaced Requesens with his brother Juan of Navarre who, for all his
shortcomings, was at least a member of the royal family and likely to be
more palatable to the Catalans.[179] Juan continued to have difficulties with
the Corts, particularly over his support of the Busca party in Barcelona and
the *remença* peasants.[180] For some, in a telling expression of their attitude
toward the sex of the lieutenant, only the king would do. Joan Moles de
Margarit, bishop of Perpinyà, lamented that Catalunya was "totally ruined
and lost" without the king.[181] The issue for him was not whether the per-

son in charge was a queen-lieutenant or the brother of the king—the crux of the matter was that Alfonso had a sworn obligation to come to Catalunya and rule personally. But Alfonso ignored his words, and once again, those of his wife. He later reversed his policy toward the peasants, when on 5 October 1455 he issued a letter patent that ordered a provisional suspension of the mals usos and *remença* obligations.[182] This provided a temporary respite from the wrangling, but one that would not last long.

María left Catalunya on 9 October 1453 and spent the rest of that year and most of 1454 in negotiations with her brother and brother-in-law concerning the Castilian succession.[183] As in 1429, she took a leading role in reconciling the two sides, and her diplomatic skills enabled her nephew Enrique peacefully to succeed Juan II as king of Castile in July 1454.[184] Her last years, from 1454 to 1458, were spent mostly in Valencia and mostly quietly, where she governed as lieutenant general and only occasionally took part in events in Catalunya.[185] It is unclear whether she was aware that in the fall of 1457 Alfonso, with a young new mistress in his life who might bear him a legitimate son and who had her own eye set on a crown, had tried unsuccessfully to annul their marriage.[186] She had been seriously ill since August 1457, and for a few weeks late that summer she hovered between life and death. She was well enough later, and on 16 March 1458 met with Barthomeu Sellent, who was sent by the Diputació to Valencia to discuss with her events of the Corts.[187]

The lives of María and Alfonso ended in 1458 much as they had been lived since 1432, apart and with little emotion or sentiment toward each other. Alfonso died on 27 June, but María had no knowledge of the seriousness of his illness, and did not hear of his death until 15 July. She mourned him publicly and privately in ways that betray an emotion or affection toward him, or at the least, a recognition of his importance in her life. She ordered the palace in Valencia into mourning and made no secret of her grief.[188] Alfonso did not mention his wife and partner in governance in his will, although he made provisions for every other family member.[189]

Less than two months later, on 4 September, María of Castile died in Valencia.[190] The things that mattered most to her in life are clearly reflected in her will, dated 21 February 1457. She had designated Alfonso as her heir, but because he predeceased her, on 31 August 1458 she had added a codicil to her will transferring the rights to her brother-in-law, Juan II. She made customary provisions to her natal family members and was generous to all the women in her court, including her donation of her collection of more than seventy books to her closest attendant, Yolada de Monpalau.[191] María was buried 7 September in the Monasterio de Sant Trinitat in Valencia, dressed as a Clarissan nun.[192] Alfonso was buried in Naples until his remains were reburied at Poblet, with the other kings of the Crown of Aragon.[193]

Chapter 6
Queenship, Kingship, and the Dynamics of Monarchy

A CASTILIAN PRINCESS BY BIRTH and an Aragonese queen by marriage, María was born and raised to be queen but not necessarily to rule. In many ways she fit the conventional image of a medieval queen: She made substantial charitable donations, endowed a number of religious institutions, was a patron of the arts, and acted as peacemaker between her husband, her brother, and her brothers-in-law. But she was also unconventional, at least from the wider European perspective, because she governed Catalunya for more than two decades as her husband's legitimate representative. As the sixth Aragonese queen who was also lieutenant general of Catalunya, she followed local legal norms and political traditions, but the scope of her official authority and the length of her tenure in office set her apart. Her royal council and court of justice were the supreme royal institutions in Catalunya, superseded only by Alfonso's government in Naples. Her royal officials administered routine justice, financial accounting, and supervised regional and municipal officials. She punished wrongdoers and rewarded those who served the Crown. She was integral to the day-to-day governance of the principality during times of calm and crisis.

As queen, María was the less dominant partner in the relationship and this made her own practice of queenship particularly sensitive to subtle shifts in medieval notions of kingship theory and practice. Alfonso's absence and the remença crisis of the 1450s disrupted immediate and local power relations and redefined the relationship, creating what Louise Fradenburg calls "queenly time."[1] As queen-lieutenant she held office because Alfonso appointed her to do so but, as she made clear in her opposition to his policies and in her resignation, she was not a figurehead. María became a queen by living as a queen, changing the category as she lived it and inspired it. Her reign illustrates that queenship, an integral component of monarchy, is discursive and discourse is generative. It is an incessant project, a daily act of reconstruction and interpretation situated in a zone of multiple and overlapping cultures, in which personality and temperament have some degree of influence over a queen's expression of her own unique practice of queenship. When Alfonso went away to conquer and govern Naples, he inasmuch provided the essential space, the "queenly time," for María to perform the functional political role of queenship.

As queen-lieutenant, she also affected the practice of kingship. Alfonso's reliance on lieutenants to rule his constituent realms for extended periods, coupled with María's degree of involvement on all levels in government, transformed both the institution and the political landscape. In all other lieutenancies, whether a prince's or a queen's, the king worked directly with his subjects as he took council with his magnates and clerics, met with town councils, and convoked sessions of the Corts. With such wide jurisdiction, it would have been surprising if she had faced no challenges, and the events of the late 1440s and early 1450s clearly demonstrate the practical limits of her authority. The fact that the ruling elites tried to go over María's head and negotiate directly with Alfonso suggests that they knew that policy did not originate with her. At times she even used the Catalans' awareness of this as a way to buy time or to avoid making a difficult decision. She worked with Alfonso, in his place and always on his behalf, but this did not diminish her prestige nor did it undercut the Catalans' recognition of her authority. It was simply a clear statement of the limits of her office, and these limits assuaged any lingering fears that she would try to rule in her own right while preserving the overarching power of the king. She was a hard-working queen, driven by a sense of duty and obligation to both the Catalan people and her husband to remain in an increasingly untenable position. She recognized that her authority stemmed not from her own right to rule as heir to the kingdom but rather from her husband's will, and in general she deferred to Alfonso's judgment. She did not hesitate to express her opinions or to suggest alternative solutions, but she never initiated new policy or acted against his will, and thus the basic parameters of kingship remained intact.

Although María was careful not to supplant completely the king's authority, she did not simply carry out orders. Alfonso granted María considerable freedom to implement his expressed intentions. This is most striking in the day-to-day administration of justice, an area traditionally associated with kingship. Except for a handful of prominent cases, María did not consult with Alfonso concerning the cases that came before her in the

Audiéncia. She supervised financial administration and territorial governance with the merest involvement from Alfonso. She wrote to him about what she planned to do, or had done, and he approved it in substance. He reserved to himself the prerogative to approve only the highest-ranking official appointments, but in all others María acted without his prior approval. When wealthy urban and rural landlords did go directly to Alfonso in Naples, their actions say more about the Catalan elite's notions of rulership than it does about María's political skills. Their political bargain was with the king, and in their minds only the king himself would suffice. No lieutenant, regardless of status or legal mandate, neither the queen nor the king's brother, was acceptable when it came to an issue as divisive as the *remences*.

Her actions at the center of power made her a focal point for contemporary juridical attitudes concerning delegation and representation. As Catalan jurists refined the notion of what precisely constituted kingship, and as they revised the customs and laws that made a king, by extension, they redefined what made a queen. The heart of the dispute was the constitutional and jurisdictional definition of the legal boundaries of the authority of the king and his lieutenants. The legal treatises that addressed the issue of the limits of María's power as queen-lieutenant were also eloquent statements of the limits of kingly power and the rightful place of the ruler in society. But the struggle between María and the estates in the Corts was not simply about rule by a woman. There is no evidence of overt misogyny directed against María, suggesting that the Catalans were not overly troubled by rule by a woman. This does not mean that the Catalans would have embraced María as a ruling queen, but neither does it mean that they would have rejected her. It simply means that a queen as lieutenant general was acceptable, and that the presence of a fully competent adult king reassured the Catalan elites that the social order would not be disrupted.

Gender was an issue, but one so deeply imbedded in culture and society that its presence is not apparent in the words preserved in registers. Her childlessness was perhaps more acutely painful to her, her husband, and her mother-in-law than to her subjects, although they were concerned enough to remind Alfonso that he had marital matters to attend to. But in all other respects, she fit comfortably within the accepted gender norms of fifteenth-century Catalunya. It is clear that when given a choice, the estates in the Corts preferred to work with María rather than Juan of Navarre. His difficult lieutenancy in Aragón is ample evidence that María was not singled out for attack because she was a woman. The political issues were the same no matter who the lieutenant was. The problem was not whom the king left in charge, but that he preferred to govern his Iberian realms through lieutenants. The crux of the problem Alfonso and María faced was resistance to long-term rule by delegated authority and strongly held medieval ideas on governance that depended on a king's oaths to govern in person, if not continually at least periodically. In the end, the dynamic interplay between queenship and kingship affected the ideology, structures, and practice of Aragonese monarchy. María was ensnared in an ideological clash between older, feudal notions of a personal contract between the king and his subjects, and Renaissance forms of impersonal, bureaucratic rulership. It is impossible to separate her work as queen-lieutenant from that of Alfonso as king. They united Aragonese queenship and kingship in a way that underscores gender as a potent and fundamental force in the theory and practice of medieval monarchy.

In many ways, Catalan notions of contractual kingship in the fifteenth century were archaic and ill-suited to the needs of a monarchy with vast territorial possessions. Contractual kingship demanded the personal presence of the prince to seal the bargain between governed and governor, but it became increasingly difficult to do this as the Crown expanded eastward into the Mediterranean. Alfonso stretched it to the limit when he conquered Naples. He was comfortable delegating authority to lieutenants, and Valencia and Aragón were accustomed to rule by lieutenants, but the Catalan barons and prelates resisted. They found contractual kingship congenial, clung to their older ideas of oaths and contracts, resented having to work with the king's delegate instead of the king himself, and were especially hostile to his assertions of supreme royal authority. By forgoing a coronation, he made it clear that he considered himself king by right of birth, not by approval of the estates of the realm. His relations with the Catalans were, in many ways, a fight to limit constitutional restraints on royal power. He fought for the principal of royal prerogative when the nobles and ecclesiastical lords argued that he was violating their jurisdiction when he granted manumission to the *remences*. His preference for Italy, where he encountered forms of rulership that differed with contractual notions, worsened matters. The Catalan nobles and prelates united with the Diputació to do whatever it would take to get Alfonso to change his mind, even if it meant lengthy procedural squabbles over who signed a letter and obvious tactics for buying time. He carefully guarded his royal prerogatives and was not averse to institutional experimentation, which the diputats and the members of the Consell de Cent dismissed as "novelties." Alfonso asserted that as king, his authority was superior and that his interests above all were for the well-being of his subjects of all ranks. In the end, his need for money overruled his desire to weaken the nobles, or maybe he just realized that he did not have the clout—militarily, especially—to stick to his original intentions.

Because kingship and queenship work in dynamic tension, when Alfonso weakened contractual kingship he strengthened the office of the queen-lieutenant. He was guided by pragmatism, not theory, and his working relationship with María developed out of geographic necessity. When his views on rulership collided with those of the Catalans, the result was not a lessening of tension, but rather the transfer of the burden of coping with that tension from himself to María. Alfonso simply did not have the stomach for prolonged conflict with the Catalans. Thomas Bisson and Luis Suárez Fernández argue convincingly that Alfonso stayed in Italy because he so disliked this contentious public sphere.[2] In retrospect, it is clear that once he was happily settled in Naples, he had no serious intention of ever leaving, and he left it to María to haggle with the Catalans, which strengthened her position in routine matters. María was not naturally contentious and she was willing to work with the Catalans, who directed their anger toward Alfonso, and their goodwill toward María gave her considerable leeway. He relented on the manumission of the *remences*, knowing that the peasants were militarily less threatening than the nobles and mindful of the fact that he did not have to face them himself. By 1453 it was clear that both king and the Corts had very nearly run out of the two most important elements in contractual kingship—mutual respect and a willingness to compromise. This breakdown in the monarchy, in turn, signaled the end of María's lieutenancy in Catalunya.

The clash over the *remences* is a sensitive indicator of the dynamic relationship of María and Alfonso. By situating her as both queen and queen-lieutenant within a broader context of monarchy, she is restored to her to her natural place as a vital component of Aragonese rulership. In a more general sense, situating a queen within monarchy broadens the scope and range of the study of medieval politics by problematizing and historicizing the sex-gender hierarchy of monarchy. This, in turn, provides a richer understanding of medieval government, and offers a more adequate definition of monarchy. Analyzing rulership as a partnership, as it was for María and Alfonso, reveals it to be a malleable, permeable, elastic, and multivocal political institution that can be envisioned, metaphorically speaking, as a flexible sack. It accommodated both the king and the queen—their personalities, circumstances, and a fairly wide variety of political theories and attitudes toward women in governance—without rupture. When empty, it returned to its original patriarchal shape. Its potential to expand explains the variation in practice. This metaphor permits an examination of both kingship and queenship together to discern not only their distinct shape but also the distinct configuration that they take on together.

The mechanics of this institutional flexibility is clearly detected in the ideological clashes over the repeated and protracted challenges to María's authority to convoke and preside over the Corts. Alfonso stretched the institution, María accommodated to the changes, the Catalan nobles took note, necessitating some fine-tuning from Naples, and the cycle continued. The noble and ecclesiastical estates framed their argument as a defense of traditional privileges against what they believed was an authoritarian monarch's abuse of power, as stretching the institution beyond tolerable limits. Alfonso expanded the scope of the office when he argued that he was acting well within the law when he appointed María as his fully empowered lieutenant. The barons, prelates, and the Consell de Cent of Barcelona had a valid point when they complained that the king had a responsibility to meet personally with the Corts, and sought to bring the office back to an earlier configuration. They were correct when they argued that this personal contact was fundamental to the pact at the heart of Catalan government and was, indeed, integral to contractual kingship. But Alfonso saw nothing wrong in substituting what he regarded as an outmoded and unworkable ideology with one more in line with his needs, and presumably, those of his realms. To him, there was ample room in the institution of monarchy to accommodate the king, his lieutenants, and their subjects.

It is important to remember, however, that the dispute was cultural and personal as well as political and institutional. Alfonso, personally inclined more toward the more forceful Castilian monarchy, had an authoritarian streak that went against the grain of Catalan politics. Like his father, his relations with the Catalans had always been stormy. In a letter to the Corts in 1450, he blamed obstruction of justice not on his own unwillingness to work with the Corts but to the "impertinent so-called Customs of Barcelona, Constitutions of the Corts of Catalunya, privileges, alleged Usatges, and liberties."[3] He used Naples as a refuge from their contentiousness and the more important the decision, the more likely he was to vacillate and procrastinate. He complained about the problematic Catalans, but he always paid attention to their petitions for they were his fiscal mainstay. Until her departure in 1453, María stood between her husband and her subjects. She implemented Alfonso's expressed intentions as forcefully as she could, moderated the tone on both sides, and maintained the public order in an environment filled with anxiety, hostility, compromise, demands, counterdemands, retaliation, and more compromise.

As for the *remences*, they had fought a revolution brought on by rising expectations. They had kept their side of the bargain and came very close to realizing their goals, only to have them snatched away at the last minute. Time and again, they came close to achieving some measure of change, only to witness a return to the status quo ante. María knew well the strength and fervor of the *remences*, but Alfonso underestimated them and did not live to see the consequences of his mutable policies. The fundamental issue at stake for the Corts and Diputació and the Crown may have been economic—the legal status of the enserfed peasantry enriched the lords. For the peasants, however, the issue was legal status as well as economics—it was about securing an abolition of the mals usos to free them to do work to enrich themselves. They understood that status mattered and they made the removal of legal impediments an essential component of their demands. They knew that they held a legal and moral position favorable to their own social setting, that they could muster royal support, and that they were favored by jurists reluctant to bolster servile tenure, but their efforts were doomed in 1453 by the potent forces of custom and the entrenched power of the lords. The next generation of *remences* differed greatly from earlier generations in that they were able to organize themselves financially, politically, and, as they demonstrated in 1462, militarily, too.

The disastrous civil war from 1462 to 1472 overshadowed the reign of his brother and successor, Juan of Navarre.[4] Juan was a complex and contradictory man, even more authoritarian than his elder brother. His overbearing, often bullying, personality made him more enemies than friends. He was still engaged in fruitless skirmishes with Castile and he had a tense relationship with France. He had governed the kingdom of Navarre since the death of his first wife, Blanca, in 1441, in the name of their son Carlos of Viana. But Carlos and Juan had a deeply problematic relationship owing to the father's unwillingness to relinquish his claim to Navarre in favor of Carlos; he then disinherited him in favor of his daughter Leonor, wife of Gaston de Foix. Tensions between father and son worsened when Juan married again in 1444, and many of the later political problems in the Crown of Aragon can be traced to personal problems in the royal family.⁵ The troubled relationship of Juan and Carlos deteriorated further in 1451 when he appointed his second wife, Juana Enríquez, governor of Navarre with Carlos; the next year she gave birth to Fernando, who would succeed his father as king in 1479. The family drama worsened in 1458 when Juan appointed Carlos, then thirty-three years old, as lieutenant general in Catalunya, where he proved to be enormously popular. Juan later imprisoned him on trumped up charges of treason, and when he died of tuberculosis in September 1461, accusations of foul play surfaced, with detractors accusing not only Juan but also Juana of plotting against Carlos in favor of Fernando.⁶

Given this troubled history, it is fascinating to note how easily Juan delegated authority to his second wife, Juana Enríquez, and later, Fernando. Apparently, two centuries of rule through lieutenancies chosen from the royal family and his own experience of governing with María of Castile had fostered a habit of co-rulership. He used the flexible institutional framework for a corporate rulership to his advantage. But by 1458 he had learned to be careful. He preferred Spain to Italy and his absences were generally due to military engagements with Castile, so he was close at hand and chose to use lieutenants when the need arose, not regularly or continuously as Alfonso did. The kingdom of Naples had devolved to Alfonso's son Ferran, which shortened the distances among the various realms and lessened his need for lieutenants for long periods of time. Because of his proximity, Juana and Fernando convened or presided infrequently over sessions of Corts, and thus she encountered few of the difficulties that María faced.

Juan endowed Juana with powers very similar to those possessed by María of Castile, and in many ways she was truly co-ruler with Juan. Their marriage was certainly more successful as a personal relationship and in dynastic terms, which made them a closer couple than Alfonso and María ever had been. Throughout her marriage to Juan, Juana was one of his closest advisers and most valuable allies, traveling with him throughout Navarre and the Aragonese realms. Juan relied on her intelligence and discretion, her prodigious familial, financial, and political connections in Castile, and her tenacious and formidable negotiating skills. Juana was nothing if not intrepid and, no newcomer to politics, she shrugged off the personal attacks after the death of Carlos and succeeded him as lieutenant general.⁷ She took full advantage of the office of queen-lieuenant that was in no way diminished by María's resignation.

Like Maria, Juana maintained an extensive court with separate chancery and treasurer, but without the judicial and legislative offices that María of Castile had possessed in parallel with Alfonso's Neapolitan court.[8] Amid the turbulence and widespread civil unrest that erupted in the wake of Carlos's death, she suppressed opposition in the towns and countryside and secured support for her husband and Fernando. In June 1461, she negotiated on behalf of the Crown to moderate the anti-royalist Capitulations of Vilafranca del Penedès. Like her sister-in-law before her, Juana sided with the *remences*, a position that made her highly unpopular with the city magistrates of Barcelona and the landlords. Unlike the six Aragonese queen-lieutenants who preceded her, Juana is noted for her active military involvement, notably the early campaigns of the ten-year civil war. In June 1462, she and Fernando fled from forces led by the rebellious Count of Pallars and took refuge in a royal castle in Girona only to find themselves besieged for a month. She organized the defense of the castle and held the rebels at bay until Juan and Louis XI of France arrived with military support. Although not personally at the head of an army, she was a tough negotiator who rallied and helped organize and provision an array of forces in defense of the Crown in the Ampurdán, accompanied forces to Barcelona and into Aragón.[9]

Juana was a key negotiator in the treaties of Sauveterre and Bayonne in May 1462 that settled the succession of Navarre and allowed the French to occupy the territories of Rousillon and Cerdanya to France in return for military support. She was virtually prisoner, with her daughter Juana, in the castle of Lárraga in 1463. Hostilities worsened, the French, Castilians, and Portuguese intervened, and periodically the Catalans "deposed" (most notably in 1462) Juan, Fernando (occasionally), and Juana. Her deposition, although a dubious honor, is a clear indication of her power and importance in the political sphere.[10] After her release from Lárraga and as the civil war intensified, she turned her attentions to governing Crown realms as lieutenant general from 1464 until her death in 1468.[11] With Fernando at her side, and seeking to pacify the warring factions, she presided over the Cortes of Aragón that met in Zaragoza from 1466 to 1468. During this period, she traveled extensively throughout the realms in the midst of civil war, gathering troops and supplies, negotiating with military leaders while personally attending to the business of governing—collecting taxes, holding courts of justice, dealing with the church, and managing Crown lands and her own patrimony.[12] The war outlived her by four years, but it is fitting that her indefatigable work as co-ruler with her husband and as tutor to her son mark her as the last queen-lieutenant of the Crown of Aragon.

The marriage of Fernando of Aragón and Isabel of Castile in 1469 and their succession in 1479 to the united realms of the Crown of Aragon and Castile dramatically altered the institutions of government. The situation was unique in many ways largely because Isabel was queen of Castile in her own right.[13] To her, the lieutenancy was superfluous. But Fernando recognized that he would be spending significant amounts of time away from his Aragonese realms, and in 1479 he named Enrique, count of Empúries and Segorbe, his lieutenant general.[14] With this act, the lieutenancy lost forever its association with queenship. In the Corts of 1480–82, Fernando stipulated that the lieutenant general had complete authority to convoke the Corts regardless of the mental or physical condition of the king. In addition, he passed this model for territorial administration on to lands governed by Castile. The office was the model for the viceroyalty, which proved so valuable to later Spanish kings. Without the power to convoke parliamentary assemblies, the viceroy's power would have been seriously curtailed and the king would have to personally travel to various realms or rely on the centralized enactment of legislation and adjudication of lawsuits. Such an arrangement would have been cumbersome at best for the European possessions and nearly impossible in the case of the territories of the New World, which were months away by sea voyage. It is ironic that what began as an attempt to protect the ancient privileges and customs, and an assertion of the contractual nature of medieval kingship, ended up instead as the impetus for political change. The modern form of monarchy relied heavily on delegated authority within a centralized institutional structure, one that better suited the needs of kings ruling vast maritime empires.

It is significant that the last two queen-lieutenants, María of Castile and Juana Enríquez, were Fernando's aunt and mother, respectively. The degree of political engagement of these two women, as well as the partnership forged by them with their husbands, was not lost on him as he governed alongside his wife and sought solutions to absentee rulership in a widely dispersed collection of realms that included Castile, the Crown of Aragon, his Habsburg inheritance in central Europe, and the Americas.[15] He was well trained in a monarchy that takes full advantage of the entire royal family. In 1535, his grandson Carlos V transformed the lieutenancy, renamed it the viceroyalty, and used it to rule the vast Spanish empire in the New World.[16] When he needed someone to govern one of his European realms when he was absent, which was often, Carlos turned instead to the regency and appointed his wife, Isabel of Portugal as well as his aunt Margaret of Austria and his sister Mary of Hungary. These were formidable women. Isabel, regent of Spain for Carlos at several key points in the reign, was very much her husband's political partner. Margaret was regent of the Netherlands for her father, the emperor Maximilian, from 1507 until 1514, and then from 1519 until 1530 for Carlos.[17] Mary was regent in Hungary after the death of her husband, Louis, and then succeeded Margaret as regent in the Netherlands from 1531 until 1555, where she was important to Carlos late in his reign as he confronted the Protestants.[18]

The year 1555, when Philip succeeded his father as king of Spain, signals an important shift in Spanish political life. The pragmatic and, in the Crown of Aragon, contractual, political culture of medieval monarchy transformed into an increasingly absolutist and bureaucratic form. The legitimate, officially sanctioned office of political authority of the Aragonese queen-lieutenant was curtailed sharply as Castilian institutional forms dominated the resulting Habsburg monarchy. Queen-lieutenants were replaced by powerful viceroys, secretaries and ministers, educated in universities and trained professionally, who governed for kings when they were absent, either physically or mentally.[19] As a result, a once dynamic relationship of monarchy that relied on both king and queen for its functioning became fixed in a position where the king was the superior authority and the queen relegated to a subordinate status. Monarchy in Spain ceased to be a working political partnership shared by a king and queen.[20] This is not to say that early modern Habsburg queens were powerless, for indeed they were influential women.[21] But their power was less likely to be official, legitimate authority and more likely to be unofficial, exercised privately. No matter how powerful any single Habsburg queen may have been, once the institutional linkage of queenship with the Aragonese lieutenancy was broken, the nature and location of a queen's power changed fundamentally and profoundly from that of her medieval predecessors. Monarchy became increasingly masculinized in the early modern era with the growth of ministers and secretaries and the exclusion of women from the public political aspects of monarchy, and was abetted by authoritarian and absolutist tendencies across western Europe.[22]

Conclusion

At their deaths in 1458, Alfonso and María left behind a distinctive form of monarchy, a co-rulership based on the tried-and-true institution, the queen-lieutenant, made newly powerful after decades of success. Their political partnership began out of necessity and succeeded in part because their marriage was a personal failure but also because they were pragmatic, practical, and open to innovation. Not bound by ideology or tradition, they tweaked the mechanisms of governance and were opportunistic, taking advantage when they could of local legal and political customs. These strategies and practices were embedded in the institution of monarchy that operated within the public political sphere where both king and queen were capable of exercising both political power and authority through official and unofficial channels. Alfonso took full advantage of the relational character of monarchy that allowed him to select the office of the lieutenancy from a particular social repertoire while remaining attentive, to the extent that it suited his immediate needs, to the demands of a particular situation and limits set by the culture.[23] He practiced what Foucault termed a "double conditioning of a strategy by the specificity of possible tactics, and of tactics by the strategic envelope that makes them work."[24] Alfonso and María and their immediate successors were co-operators in an institution that was contradictory, contested, subject to constant change, and weakly bounded, thus inherently ad hoc.[25] Their dynamic set of practices in a particular cultural zone, what Marshall Sahlins terms "hot zones" that "creatively and pragmatically construed and reconfigured ongoing values."[26] In similar fashion, the ruling elites in Catalunya were fully aware of the tactics and strategies characteristic of Aragonese monarchy and they, too, tried to exploit the ambiguous nuances of the office of the queen-lieutenant. Regarding monarchy as the dynamic relationship of kingship and queenship permits a better understanding of how theory, agency, and gender—coupled with economy, geography, warfare, or demography—affect rulership.

It is a remarkable sign of the strength of the office of the queen-lieutenant that royal government could work so well under such enormous pressure. For a medieval monarchy ruled by an absentee king and his queen-lieutenant to remain intact in the face of serious threat of rebellion was more the exception than the rule. The Catalan nobles and the Corts played an important role in making a king in 1412, but they had no intention of unmaking him in 1453. The Catalans wanted a king, but on their own terms, or at least a return to past kings who had more respect for their traditional liberties and privileges. Both Alfonso and the members of the Corts and the Diputació pushed Catalunya's distinctive contractual kingship to the practical limits of its theoretical boundaries.

The roots of the problem are deeper than the clash of old and new, or Castilian and Catalan, or Catalan and Italian culture, or personality. A lieutenant who was also a queen was a double inversion of the political order, and the significance was not lost on the Catalans. The problems María encountered went beyond simple notions of gender and moved into the highly subjective realm of personality that is deeply influenced by prevailing notions of gender. But even in this regard María confounds our expectations. She remains elusive to us in many aspects of her personality, but her diplomacy and trustworthiness contributed to her success just as Juan of Navarre's heavy-handed and reactionary political style led to his difficulties. Intelligence, diplomatic skills, tact, shrewdness, even tenacity are hard to measure and vitally important to the success of a monarchical partnership, especially to Aragonese pactist monarchy. They are traits more often gendered as masculine. Her active role in the Corts and in the efforts to liberate the remença peasants shows her as a shrewd negotiator and savvy diplomat. Everyone, from the loftiest baron to the lowliest peasant sindich, took her seriously. They may not have liked the idea of a lieutenant, and they may not have liked her, but they understood that her signature on a letter was as good as the king's. It is impressive that she was able to maneuver skillfully to obtain great sums of money in exchange for few political concessions, and to support the remença peasants despite bitter opposition from the Corts, the Consell de Cent of Barcelona, the barons, and the high-ranking ecclesiastical lords. It says a great deal about mutual respect that, while Alfonso was alive, the Catalans fought not with weapons but with jurists. There seems to have been a shared determination to find a way to make long-distance government succeed. No doubt, each side was convinced that the other would eventually relent. When Alfonso would not come to Catalunya, Catalan emissaries went to him. Alfonso, by his prolonged absence from his Iberian realms, risked civil insurrection by granting manumission to the *remences* and he must have known it. The king never wavered in his belief that María had *plena potestas* to act in his place. Her calm and reasonable temperament, her quiet diplomacy and tact, and her skill at pacifying bellicose tempers contributed to her success. Her strength of character reduced the risks of Alfonso's absence, but as subsequent events demonstrated, character and diplomacy were no substitute for a workable solution.

By the time of María's resignation in the fall of 1453, the Corts, once the site of reasonably amicable disputation, had been transformed into a warren of partisan demands for participation in government, animosity, and wariness. During his years in Italy, where he had far more room to maneuver without the legalistic obstacles the Catalans placed in his way, Alfonso had crafted a form of kingship that differed dramatically from that of his predecessors. He took to heart the literal meaning of *alter nos* like no other king had done before or has done since. By doing so, he reshaped Aragonese kingship into a genuine political partnership and made it clear that, for him, this partnership included his queen. The marriage of María and Alfonso, while not conventionally happy by any standard, was an enormously successful political partnership. Ultimately, their ruling partnership faltered on the fundamental question of who should be the ultimate authority. That question, however, would not be fully answered during Alfonso's lifetime.

The political partnership of Alfonso V and María of Castile is captured visually in Martorell's painting of María receiving the legal treatise in 1448. In the painting as in real life, she has taken the place of her husband. She has become his alter ego (*alter nos*). Martorell employed attributes traditionally associated with kingship iconography to portray a queen governing as king, or more accurately, as monarch, as ruler. This painting, rich with the images of governance and leadership and the administration of justice, would signify the same political realities if it were a painting of Alfonso instead of María. By placing a queen on the throne and depicting her as a ruler, Martorell has put a new face on monarchy. This painting is a form of aesthetic empowerment of women via representational codes and conventions. It testifies to the existence of the vital working partnership between a king and a queen by substituting María for Alfonso and situating her serenely at the center of the body politic of the medieval Crown of Aragon.

Genealogy
The Trastámara Family
in the Crown of Aragon

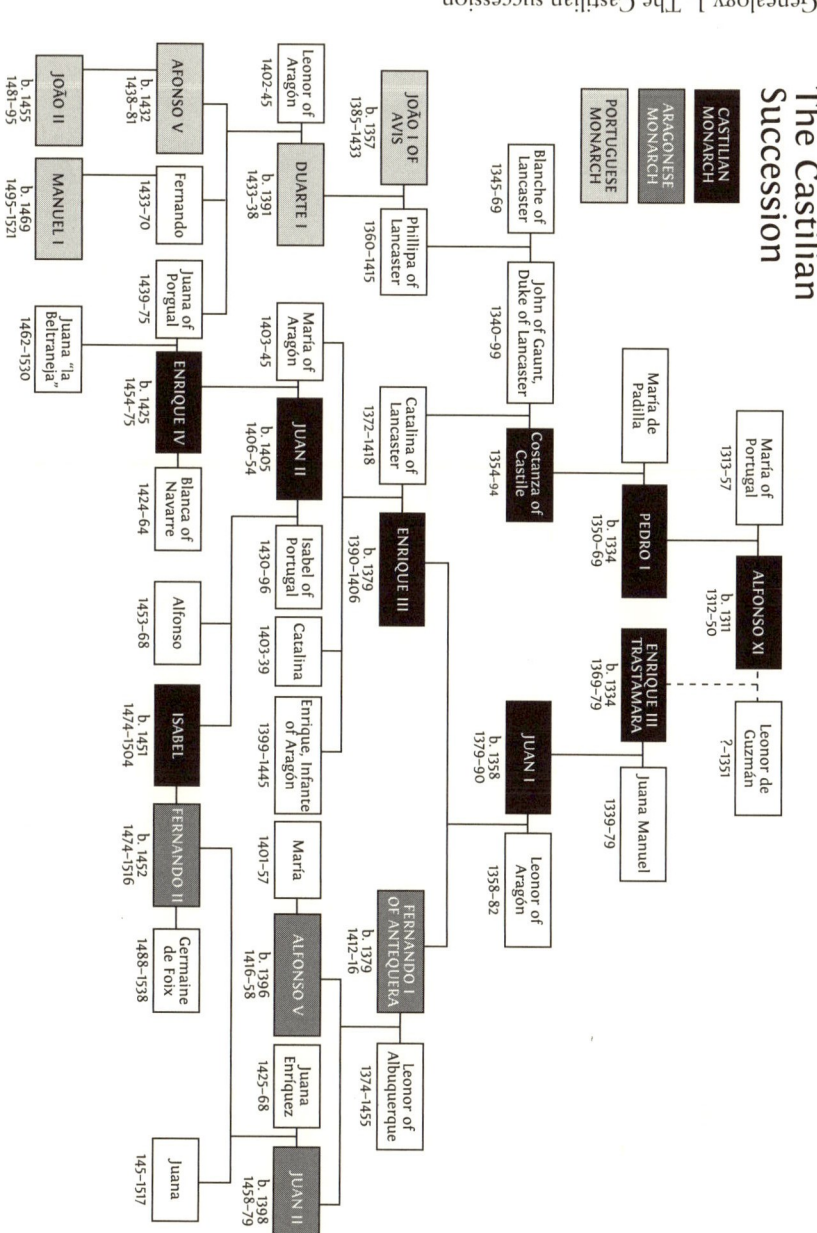

Genealogy 1. The Castilian succession.

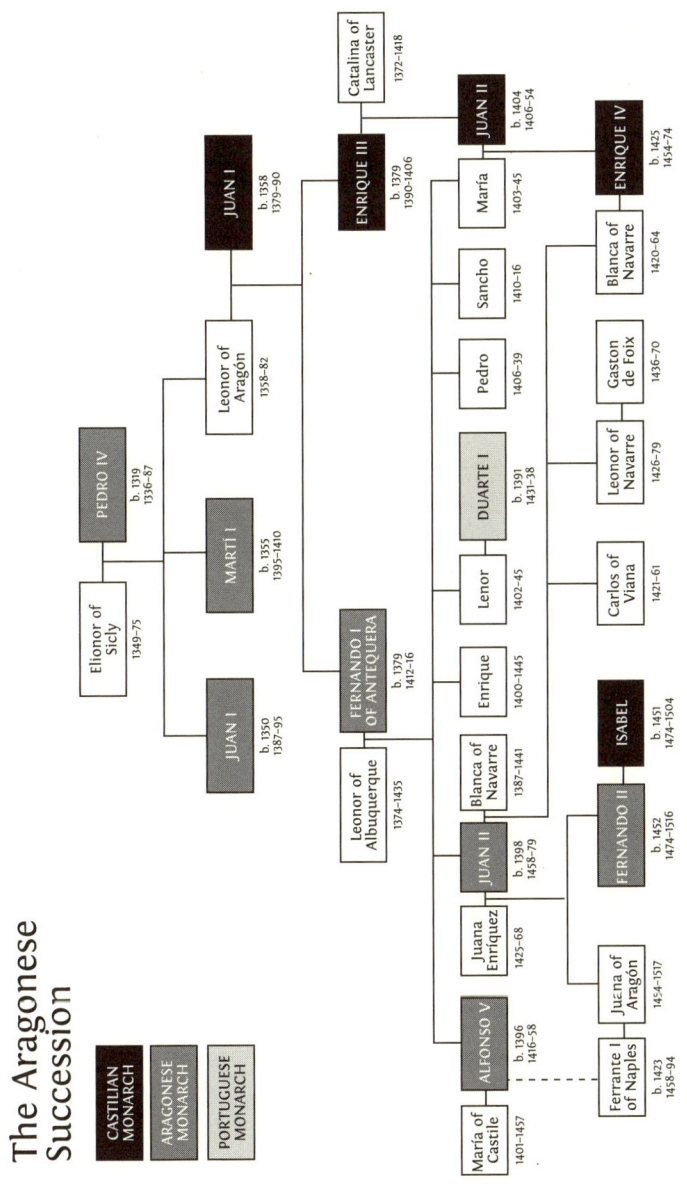

Genealogy 2. The Aragonese succession.

Abbreviations

Archival Sources

ACA: C	Barcelona: Arxiu de la Corona d'Aragó, Cancillería	
	Com	Comune
	ComSS	Comune Sigilli Secreti
	Cur	Curia
	CSS	Curiae Sigilli Secreti
	Div	Diversorum
	DR	Domine Regine
	Grat	Gratiarum
	Itin	Itinerum
	Litt	Litterarum et albaranorum
	Ofi	Oficialum
	Pec	Pecuniae
	PCC	Promiscuum Curie et Comune
	Sec	Secretorum
	Sent	Sententiarum
	Var	Varia
ACA: CR	Barcelona: Arxiu de la Corona d'Aragó, Cartes reales	
ACA: G	Barcelona: Arxiu de la Corona d'Aragó, Generalitat registers, "N" Serie	
ACA: Leg	Barcelona: Arxiu de la Corona d'Aragó, Legislació	
AHCB	Barcelona: Arxiu Historíc de la Ciutat de Barcelona, Consell de Cent registers	
	Del	Deliberations
	LRO-A	Lletres Reials Originales, Serie A
	LRO-B	Llettres Reials Originales, Serie B
	LC	Lletres Closes
	LCO	Lletres Comunes Originales
ARV: MR	Valencia: Arxiu Reial de Valencia, Mestre Racional register	

Published Sources

Alfonso the Magnanimous   Alan Ryder. *Alfonso the Magnanimous: King of Aragon, Naples, and Sicily, 1396–1458*. Oxford: Clarendon Press, 1990.

Anales   Geronimo Zurita. *Anales de la Corona de Aragón.*

150   Abbreviations

[1562–82] Ed. Angel Canellas López. 8 vols.
Zaragoza: 1967–77.

Cortes   *Cortes de los antiguos reinos de Aragón y de Valencia
                            y principado de Cataluña.* 23 vols. Vols. 12–13:
                            1416–58. Madrid: Real Academia de la Historia,
                            1915.

Doña María de Castilla   Francisca Hernández-León de Sánchez. *Doña
                            María de Castilla, Esposa de Alfonso el Magnánimo.*
                            Valencia: Universidad de Valencia, 1959.

España cristiana   Suárez Fernández, Luis, and Juan Regla Campisto.
                            *España cristiana, crisis de la reconquista, luchas
                            civiles: Pedro I, Enrique II, Juan I y Enrique III de
                            Castilla (1350–1406); Pedro IV el ceremoioso, Juan
                            I y Martín de Humano de Aragon (1336–1410);
                            Carlos II el malo (1332–1387); y Carlos el noble
                            de Navarra (1361–1425).* Vol. 14 of *Historia de
                            España.* Ed. Ramón Menéndez Pidal. Madrid:
                            Espasa-Calpe, 1966.

Història de Catalunya   Ferran Soldevila. *Història de Catalunya.* 3 vols.
                            Barcelona: Editorial Alpha, 1934.

History of Medieval Spain Joseph F. O'Callaghan. *A History of Medieval
                            Spain.* Ithaca, N.Y.: Cornell University Press,
                            1975.

Kingdom of Naples   Alan Ryder. *The Kingdom of Naples Under Alfonso
                            the Magnanimous.* Oxford: Clarendon Press, 1976.

Medieval Crown of Aragon Thomas N. Bisson. *The Medieval Crown of
                            Aragon.* Oxford: Clarendon Press, 1984.

Spanish Kingdoms   Jocelyn N. Hillgarth. *The Spanish Kingdoms, 1250–
                            1516.* 2 vols. Oxford: Clarendon Press, 1976–78.

Los Trastámaras   Luis Suárez Fernández, Angel Canellas López, and
                            Jaime Vicens Vives. *Los Trastámaras de Castilla
                            y de Aragón en el siglo XV: Juan II y Enrique IV
                            de Castilla (1407–1474), El compromiso de Caspe,
                            Fernando I, Alfonso V, y Juan II de Aragón (1410–
                            1479).* Vol.15 of *Historia de España.* Ed. Ramón
                            Menéndez Pidal. Madrid: Espasa-Calpe, 1964.

Notes

Chapter 1. Alter Nos: The Lieutenancy of María of Castile

1. María's designation, "of Castile," refers to the place of her birth, not the kingdom she ruled. *Doña María de Castilla*, 59–61.
2. The medieval Crown of Aragon consisted of several distinct political entities gathered together under a single ruler. The crown originated in 1137 with the marriage of Petronila of Aragón and Ramón Berenguer IV, count of Barcelona. The rest of the crown realms were added by conquest: the kingdom of Mallorca and the Balearic islands between 1229 and 1235; Valencia, 1238; Sicily, 1282; and Sardinia, 1322. At various other times and with varying degrees of success, the Aragonese kings controlled Corsica and the duchy of Athens. To keep matters simple when referring to this federative polity, I will refer to the Crown of Aragon when discussing it as a whole and, when otherwise necessary, specify individual regional kingdoms or counties. *Medieval Crown of Aragon*, 27–31, 64–67, 87–89, 95–96, 93, 111.
3. Alfonso's reign is explored in detail in *Kingdom of Naples* and *Alfonso the Magnanimous*. For a concise survey of the reign, see *Medieval Crown of Aragon*, 140–47; *História de Catalunya* 2: 41–80.
4. ACA: C registers 2948–3280.
5. Jesús Lalinde Abadía, *La institución virreinal en Cataluña (1471–1716)* (Barcelona: Instituto de Estudios Mediterráneos, 1964), 47–49, 53–60, 78–81, 85–86, 159–64; idem, "Virreys y lugartenientes medievales en la Corona de Aragón," *Cuadernos de Historia de España* 31 (1960): 98–172; and Antonio García Gallo, "Los orígenes de la administración territorial de las Indias," *Anuario de Estudios del Derecho Español* 15 (1944): 16–100. See also Luis G. de Valdeavellano, *Curso de História de las instituciones Españolas: de los origines al final de la Edad Media*, 2nd ed. (Madrid: Editorial Revista de Occidente, 1970), 436–38.
6. Medieval Spain encompassed several realms that spoke distinct languages and this creates confusion for many readers. When the realm in question is the federative realm of the Crown of Aragon, the confusion is compounded by the fact that a key constituent realm—the kingdom of Aragón—is rendered in Catalan as Aragó and in English as Aragon. For clarity, when referring to the federative entity that encompassed more than the kingdom of Aragón, I call it the Crown of Aragon and the word Aragon does not get an accent. But when I refer to the medieval kingdom of Aragón, I use an accent to distinguish it from the Crown as a whole.
7. Theresa Earenfight, "Absent Kings: Queens as Political Partners in the Medieval Crown of Aragon," in *Queenship and Political Power in Medieval and Early Modern Spain*, ed. Earenfight (Aldershot: Ashgate, 2005), 33–51.

152 Notes to Pages 1–3

8. Lalinde Abadía, *La institución virreinal*, 78–81.

9. On a queen's patronage networks, see Rita Costa Gomes, *The Making of Court Society: Kings and Nobles in Late Medieval Portugal*, trans. Alison Aiken (Cambridge: Cambridge University Press, 2003), 57–78; Bethany Aram, *Juana the Mad: Sovereignty and Dynasty in Renaissance Europe* (Baltimore: Johns Hopkins University Press, 2005), 7–9.

10. Rafael Conde, Ana Hernández, Sebastiá Riera, and Manuel Rovira, "Fonts per a l'estudi de les Parlaments de Catalunya: Catáleg dels processos de Corts i Parlaments," in *Les Corts a Catalunya*, ed. Direcció General del Patrimoni Cultural (Barcelona: Generalitat de Catalunya, 1991), 25–61; Luis González Antón, *Las Cortes de Aragón* (Zaragoza: Librería General, 1978).

11. Luisa María Sánchez Aragones, *Cortes, monarquía y ciudades en Aragón durante el reinado de Alfonso el Magnánimo (1416–1458)* (Zaragoza: Institución Fernando el Católico, 1994), 222, 420–23.

12. María Rosa Muñoz Pomer and María José Carbonell Boria, "Las Cortes Valencianas medievales: aproximación a la historiografía y fuentes para su estudio," in *Les Corts a Catalunya*, 270–81.

13. For Catalunya, see Jesús Lalinde Abadía, "Los Parlamentos y demas instituciónes representativas," in *La Corona d'Aragona e il Mediterraneo: aspetti e problemi comuni, da Alfonso il Magnanimo a Ferdinando il Cattolico (1416-1516), IX Congreso de Historia de la Corona de Aragón*, 4 vols. (Naples: Società Napoletana di Storia Patria, 1978), 2: 103-79; Donald J. Kagay, "The Development of the Corts in the Crown of Aragón, 1064–1327" (Ph.D. dissertation, Fordham University, 1981); Peter Rycraft, "The Role of the Catalan 'Corts' in the Late Middle Ages," *English Historical Review* 89 (1974): 241–69.

14. Bernard Reilly, *The Kingdom of León-Castilla Under Queen Urraca, 1109–1126* (Princeton, N.J.: Princeton University Press, 1982); Peggy Liss, *Isabel the Queen*, 1992; 2nd ed. (Philadelphia: University of Pennsylvania Press, 2004); and Aram, *Juana the Mad*.

15. John Carmi Parsons, "Family, Sex, and Power: The Rhythms of Medieval Queenship," in *Medieval Queenship*, ed. John Carmi Parsons (New York: St. Martin's Press, 1993), 1–11; Jo Ann McNamara and Suzanne Wemple, "The Power of Women Through the Family in Medieval Europe, 500–1100," in *Women and Power in the Middle Ages*, ed. Mary Erler and Maryanne Kowaleski (Athens: University of Georgia Press, 1988), 83–101.

16. Dawn Bratsch-Prince, "A Queen's Task: Violant de Bar and the Experience of Royal Motherhood in Fourteenth-Century Aragon," *La Corónica* 27, 1 (1998): 21–34; Carla Freccero, "Marguerite de Navarre and the Politics of Maternal Sovereignty," in *Women and Sovereignty*, ed. Louise Olga Fradenburg (Edinburgh: University of Edinburgh Press, 1991), 133–49; Pauline Stafford, "Sons and Mothers: Family Politics in the Early Middle Ages," in *Medieval Women: Essays Presented to R. M. T. Hill*, ed. Derek Baker (Oxford: Clarendon Press, 1978), 79–100; and three essays in *Medieval Mothering*, ed. John Carmi Parsons and Bonnie Wheeler (New York: Garland, 1996): Marjorie Chibnall, "The Empress Matilda and her Sons," 279–94; Kimberley LoPrete, "Adela of Blois as Mother and

Countess," 313–33; and John Carmi Parsons, "The Pregnant Queen as Counsellor and the Medieval Construction of Motherhood," 39–61.

17. Heather J. Tanner, "Queenship: Office, Custom, or Ad Hoc? The Case of Queen Matilda III," in *Eleanor of Aquitaine, Lord and Lady*, ed. Bonnie Wheeler and John Carmi Parsons (New York: Palgrave, 2003), 133–58.

18. Ana Echevarría Arsuaga, *Catalina de Lancaster: reina regente de Castilla, 1372–1418* (Hondarribia: Nerea, 2002); idem, "Catalina of Lancaster, the Castilian Monarchy, and Coexistence," in *Medieval Spain: Culture, Conflict, and Coexistence: Studies in Honour of Angus McKay*, ed. Roger Collins and Anthony Goodman (Basingstoke: Palgrave, 2002), 79–122; idem, "The Queen and the Master: Catalina of Lancaster and the Military Orders," in Earenfight, *Queenship and Political Power in Medieval and Early Modern Spain*, 91–105. Older studies give the year of Catalina's birth as 1373, but Echevarría Arsuaga has corrected this to 1372.

19. Her sister, Philippa, married João I of Portugal (1385–1433). For a full account of the Anglo-Castilian alliance, see Peter E. Russell, *The English Intervention in Spain and Portugal in the Time of Edward III and Richard II* (Oxford: Oxford University Press, 1955). For an overview, see *History of Medieval Spain*, 419–27, 523–48; *España cristiana*, 99–378.

20. They are María, Leonor, and Ferran, duke of Calabria and King of Naples after Alfonso's death. *Alfonso the Magnanimous*, 123–24, 184; *Doña María de Castilla*, 80.

21. See Teresa Vinyoles Vidal, *Història de les dones a la Catalunya medieval* (Lleída: Pagès, 2005), 16–23, 83–90, 140–45; David J. Viera and Jordi Piqué-Angordans, *La dona en Francesc Eiximenis* (Barcelona: Curial, 1987).

22. Earenfight, "María of Castile, Ruler or Figurehead? A Preliminary Study in Aragonese Queenship," *Mediterranean Studies* 4 (1994): 45–61.

23. Pere Tomich, *Histories e conquestes dels reys d'Aragó e comtes de Catalunya* (Valencia: Anubar, 1970; facsimile printing of the 1534 edition).

24. Gabriel Turell, *Recort: obra feta per Gabriel Turell de la ciutat de Barcelona en l'any 1476* (Barcelona: Biblioteca "L'Avenç," 1894).

25. *Anales de la Corona de Aragón*, 5: 433–34 (marriage); 6: 102–5, 123–33 (parliament of 1435); 6: 246–50 (Corts of 1441); 7: 63–68 (departure for Castile); and 7: 206–7 (death).

26. Lorenzo Valla accompanied Alfonso in Italy after 1435 as his unofficial secretary. His *Gesta Ferdinandi regis Aragonum*, ed. Ottavio Besomi (1445; Padua: In aedibus Antenoreis, 1973) was intended as an introduction to Alfonso's reign, but the storm of controversy that surrounded Valla and his quarrel with his master, poet and orator Antonio Beccadelli (Panormita), doomed the project. Beccadelli's *De dictis et factis Alphonsi regis Aragonum et Neapolis* (Pisa: Gregorius de Gentis, 1485) is the fullest account of Alfonso's military campaigns in Italy.

27. *Alfonso the Magnanimous*, 306–57.

28. Ibid., 358–92.

29. Alan Ryder, *The Wreck of Catalonia: Civil War in the Fifteenth Century* (Oxford: Oxford University Press, 2007).

154 Notes to Pages 7–9

30. Pierre Vilar, "Le déclin catalan de Bas Moyen-Âge," *Estudios de Historia Moderna* 6 (1956–59): 3–68.

31. Jaime Vicens Vives, *An Economic History of Spain*, trans. F. M. López-Morillas (Princeton, N.J.: Princeton University Press, 1969), chaps. 14–19.

32. Claude Carrère, *Barcelone: centre économique a l'epoque des difficultés, 1380–1462*, 2 vols. (Paris: Mouton, 1967).

33. Carme Batlle i Gallart, *La crisis social y económica de Barcelona a mediados del siglo XV*, 2 vols. (Barcelona: Consejo Superior de Investigaciones Científicas, 1973).

34. Mario del Treppo, "The 'Crown of Aragon' and the Mediterranean," *Journal of European Economic History* 2 (1973): 161–85; and idem, *Els mercaders catalans i l'expansió de la corona catalano-aragonesa al segle XV*, trans. Jaume Riera i Sans (Barcelona: Curial, 1976; originally published as *I mercanti catalani e l'expansione della Corona d'Aragona nel secolo XV* (Naples: Arte Tipografica Napoli, 1972).

35. *Los Trastámaras*, 373–75, 726–28.

36. *Medieval Crown of Aragon*, 145.

37. *Kingdom of Naples*, 431.

38. *Història de Catalunya*, 2: 65–66, 71–75.

39. *Kingdom of Naples*, 229–35; *Alfonso the Magnanimous*, 358–92.

40. *Medieval Crown of Aragon*, 140.

41. Luis Suárez Fernández, in *Los Trastámaras*, discussed the politics of the period in broad terms while Batlle i Gallart and Claude Carrère were concerned principally with the social and economic conditions in Barcelona. See also Batlle i Gallart, *La crisis social y económica de Barcelona*; idem, *L'expansió baixmedieval (segles XIII–XV)*, vol. 3 of *Història de Catalunya*; and Carrère, *Barcelone*.

42. Andrés Giménez-Soler, "Retrato histórico de la reina doña María," *Boletín de la Real Academia de Buenas Letras de Barcelona* 1 (1901–2): 71–81.

43. Ferran Soldevila, "La reyna María, muller del Magnánim," *Memorias de la Real Academia de Buenas Letras de Barcelona* 10 (1923): 213–345.

44. Augustí Duràn i Sanpere, *Barcelona i la seva història*, 3 vols. (Barcelona: Editorial Curial, 1972–5), 1: 201, 700; *Doña María de Castilla*, 47–53.

45. Sant Trinitat was an established male monastery but María got papal bulls from Eugene IV to expand the monastery and convert it into a Clarissan convent in 1445. For Isabel de Villena, see Joan Fuster, "Jaume Roig i Sor Isabel de Villena," *Revista Valenciana de Filologia* 5 (1955–58): 227–60; Albert G. Hauf, *D'Eiximenis a Sor Isabel de Villena: Aportació a l'estudi de la nonstra cultura medieval* (Valencia: Institut de Filologia Valenciana, 1990, 307–9) and Rosanna Cantavella, "Introduction" to *Protagonistas femenines a la "Vita Christi"*, ed. Rosanna Cantavella and Lluïsa Parra (Barcelona: La Sal, 1987), vii–xxxi., esp, vii–ix. See also *Alfonso the Magnanimous*, 312.

46. For Maria as a patron of literature, see Soldevila, "La reyna Maria, muller del Magnánim." For particular authors, see Martí de Riquer, *Aproximació al Tirant lo Blanc* (Barcelona: Quaderns Crema, 1990); Fuster, "Jaume Roig i Sor Isabel de Villena," 227–60; Cantavella, "Introduction" to *Protagonistas femenines a la "Vita Christi"*, xix–xxvii. Other works composed or published under her pa-

tronage are *Curial e Güelfa*, a chivalric novel by an anonymous author; the poetry of Ausiàs Marc; and theological treatises by Joan Roís de Corella, considered the last great Catalan writer of the Middle Ages.

47. Beatrice Canellas and Alberto Torra, *Los Registros de la Cancillería de Alfonso el Magnánimo* (Madrid: Ministerio de Educación, Cultura y Deporte, Centro de Publicaciones, 2000).

48. The royal registers in the Arxiu de la Corona d'Aragó alone that cover the period 1416 to 1458 number nearly 900 volumes, with 332 chancery registers for her reign. The material in the ACA can appear confusing because the lieutenancy rotated at times between María and Juan of Navarre between 1419–58, but María's registers run continuously. See ACA: C 2948–3280. For the period after 1453, when registers document María's lieutenancy in Valencia as well as her replacements, Galceran de Requesens and Juan of Navarre, see ACA: C 3319–23 (1453–56).

49. The king's registers that pertained to Catalunya were moved from Naples to the Arxiu de la Corona d'Aragó in Barcelona shortly after his death in 1458, and have been organized to conform to ACA practices. The principal sources used in this study were found in the *Secretorum, Varia,* and *Curiae* registers.

50. She governed Valencia as queen-lieutenant at various times during the 1430s and continuously after her retirement from the lieutenancy in Catalunya in 1453 until her death in 1458.

51. The three-member executive board of the Diputació del General met regularly when the Corts was not in session. Their letters fill seven registers covering the period 1446 to 1452.

52. Additional printed sources for municipal government include *Llibre de les solemnitats de Barcelona*, 1: 1424–1546, ed. Agustí Duran i Sanpere and Josep Sanabre (Barcelona: Institució Patxot, 1930); *Manual de Novells Ardits, vulgarment apellant Dietari del Antich Consell Barceloní*, vol. 2, 1446–77, ed. D. Frederich Schwartz y Luna and Francesch Carreras y Candi (Barcelona: Henrich, 1893); Ignacio Rubio y Cambronero, *La Deputació del General de Catalunya en los siglos XV y XVI*, 2 vols. (Barcelona: Diputació Provincial, 1950); *Rubriques de Bruniquer: Ceremonial dels Magnífichs Consellers y Regiment de la Ciutat de Barcelona*, 5 vols. (Barcelona: Henrich y Campanýia, 1912–16).

53. *Cortes de los antiguos reinos de Aragón y de Valencia y principado de Cataluña; Dietari de la Diputació del General de Cathalunya*, ed. Arxui de la Corona d'Aragó, vol. 1, 1411–1458 (Barcelona: Diputación Provincial de Barcelona, 1974); *Parlaments a les Corts Catalans*, ed. Ricard Albert and Joan Gassiot, vols. 19–20 of *Els Nostre Classics* (Barcelona: Imprenta Varia, 1928).

54. José María Madurell Marimón, *Mensajeros Barceloneses en la Corte de Nápoles de Alfonso V de Aragón, 1435–1458* (Barcelona: Consejo Superior de Investigaciones Científicas, 1963).

55. ACA: C Var 3276, fols. 2r–61v, 6 August 1416 until 6 April 1420.

56. Alfonso refers to her as lieutenant general before the official *privilegio* is issued. ACA: C Var 3276, fols. 70v–71r, 5 March 1420.

57. Cary J. Nederman and N. Elaine Lawson, "The Frivolities of Courtiers Follow the Footprints of Women: Public Women and the Crisis of Virility in

156 Notes to Pages 12–13

John of Salisbury," in *Ambiguous Realities: Women in the Middle Ages and Renaissance*, ed. Carole Levin and Jeanie Watson (Detroit: Wayne State University Press, 1987), 82–98; Joseph F. O'Callaghan, "The Many Roles of the Medieval Queen," in Earenfight, *Queenship and Political Power in Medieval and Early Modern Spain*, 21–32. More work has been done for the early modern period. See Constance Jordan, "Woman's Rule in Sixteenth-Century British Political Thought," *Renaissance Quarterly* 40, 3 (1987): 421–51; Carole Levin, "John Foxe and the Responsibilities of Queenship," in *Women in the Middle Ages and Renaissance*, ed. Mary Beth Rose (Syracuse, N.Y.: Syracuse University Press, 1986), 113–33; A. N. McLaren, *Political Culture in the Reign of Elizabeth I: Queen and Commonwealth, 1558–1585* (Cambridge: Cambridge University Press, 1999).

58. Francis Oakley, *Kingship: The Politics of Enchantment* (Malden, Mass.: Blackwell, 2006); Reinhard Bendix, *Kings or People: Power and the Mandate to Rule* (Berkeley: University of California Press, 1979); Fritz Kern, *Kingship and Law in the Middle Ages* (Oxford: Oxford University Press, 1956); Henry Myers, *Medieval Kingship* (Chicago: Nelson-Hall, 1982); Walter Ullmann, *A History of Political Thought: The Middle Ages* (Harmondsworth: Penguin, 1975); Mary Douglas, *How Institutions Think* (Syracuse, N.Y.: Syracuse University Press, 1986); Clifford Geertz, "Centers, Kings, and Charisma: Reflections on the Symbolics of Power," in Geertz, *Local Knowledge* (New York: Basic Books, 1983, 121–46; Jack Goody, *Succession to High Office* (Cambridge: Cambridge University Press, 1966).

59. Ernst Kantorowicz , *The King's Two Bodies: A Study in Mediaeval Political Theology* (Princeton, N.J.: Princeton University Press, 1967).

60. This valorization and privileging of the male ruler has deep roots in Greek, Roman, and Christian Patristic thought and are intricately linked to attitudes toward the human body. See Joan Cadden, *Meanings of Sex Difference in the Middle Ages: Medicine, Science, and Culture* (Cambridge: Cambridge University Press, 1993).

61. Kantorowicz, *King's Two Bodies*, 80.

62. Theresa Earenfight, "Without the Persona of the Prince: Kings, Queens and the Idea of Monarchy in Late Medieval Europe," *Gender & History* 19, 1 (April 2007): 1–21.

63. Kari Borreson, *Subordination and Equivalence: The Nature and Role of Women in Augustine and Thomas Aquinas*, trans. C. H. Talbot (Washington, D.C.: Catholic University of America Press, 1981); Vern Bullough, *The Subordinate Sex* (Urbana: University of Illinois Press, 1973); Barbara Garlick, Suzanne Dixon, and Pauline Allen, eds., *Stereotypes of Women in Power: Historical Perspectives and Revisionist Views* (Westport, Conn.: Greenwood, 1992); Susan Moller Okin, *Women in Western Political Thought* (Princeton, N.J.: Princeton University Press, 1976); Maureen Quilligan, *The Allegory of Female Authority: Christine de Pizan's "Cité des dames"* (Ithaca, N.Y.: Cornell University Press, 1991); Arlene Saxonhouse, *Women in the History of Political Thought: Ancient Greece to Machiavelli* (New York: Praeger, 1985); Joan Wallach Scott, *Gender and the Politics of History* (New York: Columbia University Press, 1988).

64. Elizabeth A. Lehfeldt, "Ruling Sexuality: The Political Legitimacy of Isabel of Castile," *Renaissance Quarterly* 53 (2000): 31–56; Peggy McCracken, *The*

Romance of Adultery: Queenship and Sexual Transgression in Old French Literature (Philadelphia: University of Pennsylvania Press, 1998); and John Carmi Parsons, "Violence, the Queen's Body, and the Medieval Body Politic," in *"A Great Effusion of Blood"? Interpreting Medieval Violence*, ed. Mark Meyerson, Daniel Thiery, and Oren Falk (Toronto: University of Toronto Press, 2004), 241–67.

65. Núria Silleras-Fernández, "Spirit and Force: Politics, Public and Private, in the Reign of Maria de Luna (1396–1406)," in Earenfight, *Queenship and Political Power in Medieval and Early Modern Spain*, 78–90; idem, *Power, Piety, and Patronage in Late Medieval Queenship: Maria de Luna* (New York: Palgrave Macmillan, 2008); Kimberly A. LoPrete, "Adela of Blois and Ivo of Chartres: Piety, Politics, and the Peace in the Diocese of Chartres," *Anglo-Norman Studies* 14 (1991): 131–52; John Carmi Parsons, "Piety, Power, and the Reputations of Two Thirteenth-Century English Queens," in *Queens, Regents, and Potentates*, ed. Theresa M. Vann (Denton, Tex.: Academia, 1993), 107–23.

66. See two essays in *Power of the Weak: Essays in the History of Medieval Women*, ed. Jennifer Carpenter and Sally-Beth MacLean (Urbana: University of Illinois Press, 1995): Lois Huneycutt, "Intercession and the High Medieval Queen: The Esther Topos," 126–46, and John Carmi Parsons, "The Queen's Intercession in Thirteenth-Century England," 147–77; and Paul Strohm, "Queens as Intercessors," in *Hochon's Arrow: The Social Imagination of Fourteenth-Century Texts*, ed. Paul Strohm (Princeton, N. J.: Princeton University Press, 1992), 95–120.

67. Pauline Stafford, *Queen Emma and Queen Edith: Queenship and Women's Power in Eleventh-Century England* (Oxford: Blackwell, 1997); idem, *Queens, Concubines, and Dowagers: The King's Wife in the Early Middle Ages* (Athens: University of Georgia Press, 1983).

68. Kimberley LoPrete, *Adela of Blois, Countess and Lord (ca. 1067–1137)* (Dublin: Four Courts Press, 2007).

69. Marjorie Chibnall, *The Empress Matilda: Queen Consort, Queen Mother, and Lady of the English* (Oxford: Blackwell, 1991).

70. Laura Gathagan, "Embodying Power: Gender and Authority in the Queenship of Mathilda of Flanders" (Ph.D. dissertation, City University of New York, 2002).

71. Wheeler and Parsons, eds., *Eleanor of Aquitaine, Lord and Lady*.

72. Marion Facinger, "A Study of Medieval Queenship: Capetian France, 987–1237," *Studies in Medieval and Renaissance History* 5 (1968): 3–47; Miraim T. Shadis, "Motherhood, Lineage, and Royal Power in Medieval Castile and France: Berenguela de León and Blanche de Castille" (Ph.D. dissertation, Duke University, 1994).

73. Echevarria Arsuaga, *Catalina de Lancaster*.

74. Helen E. Maurer, *Margaret of Anjou: Queenship and Power in Late Medieval England* (Woodbridge: Boydell, 2003).

75. "It is in this sphere of force relations that we must try to analyze the mechanisms of power. In this way we will escape from the system of Law-and-Sovereign which has captivated political thought for such a long time. . . . [P]erhaps we need to go one step further, do without the persona of the Prince, and decipher power mechanisms on the basis of a strategy that is immanent in force

158   Notes to Pages 14–20

relations." Michel Foucault, *The History of Sexuality*, vol. 1, *An Introduction* (New York: Random House, 1978; original French edition, 1976), 97.

76. *Alfonso the Magnanimous*, 306–57.

77. "La qual dita reyna fonch dotada de perfeccio, de seny e de virtut, molt honesta tot lo temps de la sua vida, tement Deu e amant justicia e ministrar aquella," in *Dietari del capella d'Alfons V el Magnànim*, ed. María Desamparados Cabanes Pecourt (Zaragoza: Anubar Ediciones, 1991), 57.

78. *Spanish Kingdoms*, 2: 203; Francesch Eiximenis, *Regiment de la cosa Pública*, ed. Daniel de Molins de Rei (Barcelona: Editorial Barcino, 1927); and Jill Webster, *Francesc Eiximenis: La societat Catalana al segle XIV*, 2nd ed. (1967; Barcelona: Edicions 62, 1980).

79. *Alfonso the Magnanimous*, 116–74; *Història de Catalunya*, 2: 46–47, 50–56, 81–82.

80. *Alfonso the Magnanimous*, 360-69; *Kingdom of Naples*, 32–53.

81. *Història de Catalunya*, 2: 54–55, 65, 69.

82. *Alfonso the Magnanimous*, 388–91; *Història de Catalunya*, 2: 76–77.

83. José Nieto Soria, "Del rey oculto al rey exhibido: Un síntoma de las transformaciones políticas en la Castilla bajomedieval," *Medievalismo* 2, 2 (1992): 5–27; John Huxtable Elliott, "A Europe of Composite Monarchies," *Past & Present* 137 (November 1992): 48–71.

Chapter 2. From Castilian Princess to Aragonese Queen

1. *España cristiana*, 276–79; *History of Medieval Spain*, 419–27, 523–77; *Spanish Kingdoms*, 1: 385–408.

2. Recent research on women's participation in warfare may well contradict even this, however. See James M. Blythe, "Women in the Military: Scholastic Arguments and Medieval Images of Female Warriors," *History of Political Thought* 22, 2 (Summer 2001): 242–69; Karen Caspi-Reisfeld, "Women Warriors During the Crusades, 1095–1254," in *Gendering the Crusades*, ed. Sarah B. Edgington and Sarah Lambert (New York: Columbia University Press, 2002), 94–107.

3. Henry Myers, *Medieval Kingship* (Chicago: Nelson-Hall, 1982), 99–148; William Chaney, *The Cult of Kingship in Anglo-Saxon England* (Berkeley: University of California Press, 1970), 174–220; Fritz Kern, *Kingship and Law in the Middle Ages* (Oxford: Oxford University Press, 1956), 5–27; J. M. Wallace-Hadrill, *The Long-Haired Kings* (London: Methuen, 1962), 148–248.

4. Ana Echevarría Arsuaga, *Catalina de Lancaster: reina regente de Castilla, 1372–1418* (Hondarribia: Nerea, 2002); idem, "Catalina of Lancaster, the Castilian Monarchy, and Coextistence," in *Medieval Spain: Culture, Conflict, and Coexistence. Studies in Honour of Angus McKay*, ed. Roger Collins and Anthony Goodman (Basingstoke: Palgrave, 2002), 79–122; Joseph F. O'Callaghan, "The Many Roles of the Medieval Queen," in *Queenship and Political Power in Medieval and Early Modern Spain*, ed. Theresa Earenfight (Aldershot: Ashgate, 2005), 21–32; Theresa M. Vann, "The Theory and Practice of Medieval Castilian Queen-

Notes to Pages 20–21   159

ship," in *Queens, Regents, and Potentates*, ed. Theresa M. Vann (Denton, Tex.: Academia Press, 1993), 125–47.

5. The earliest representative assemblies in Spain were held in León in 1188, thus predating the English Magna Carta by twenty-seven years. Joseph F. O'Callaghan, *The Cortes of Castile-León, 1188–1350* (Philadelphia: University of Pennsylvania Press, 1989), 9–19. See also Peter Linehan, "The Politics of Piety: Aspects of the Castilian Monarchy from Alfonso X to Alfonso XI," *Revista Canadiense de Estudios Hispánicos* 9, 3 (Spring 1985): 385–404; idem, "Frontier Kingship: Castile, 1250–1350," in *La Royaute sacrée dans le monde chrétien*, ed. Alain Boureau and Claudio Sergio Ingerflom (Paris: École des Hautes Études en Sciences Sociales, 1992), 71–79; José Manuel Nieto Soria, *Fundamentos ideológicos del poder real en Castilla, siglos XIII al XVI* (Madrid: Ediciones de la Universidad Complutense, 1988); Adeline Rucquoi, "De los reyes que no son taumaturgos: los fundamentos de la realeza en España," *Relationes* 51 (1992): 54–100; Teofilo Ruiz, "Unsacred Monarchy: The Kings of Castile in the Late Middle Ages," in *Rites of Power: Symbolism, Ritual, and Politics Since the Middle Ages*, ed. Sean Wilentz (Philadelphia: University of Pennsylvania Press, 1985), 109–44.

6. For Eleanor of Aquitaine, see two collections of essays: *Eleanor of Aquitaine, Lord and Lady*, ed. Bonnie Wheeler and John Carmi Parsons (New York: Palgrave Macmillan, 2003) and *Eleanor of Aquitaine: Patron and Politician*, ed. William W. Kibler (Austin: University of Texas Press, 1976). See also Margaret Howell, *Eleanor of Provence: Queenship in Thirteenth-Century England* (Oxford: Blackwell, 1998); John Carmi Parsons, *Eleanor of Castile: Queen and Society in Thirteenth-Century England* (New York: St. Martin's Press, 1995).

7. David Carpenter, *The Minority of Henry III* (Berkeley: University of California Press, 1990); Helen E. Maurer, *Margaret of Anjou: Queenship and Power in Late Medieval England* (Woodbridge: Boydell, 2003); Sophia Menache, "Isabelle of France, Queen of England: A Reconsideration," *Journal of Medieval History* 10 (1984): 107–24; and Charles T. Wood, "The First Two Queens Elizabeth, 1464–1503," in *Women and Sovereignty*, ed. Louise Fradenburg (Edinburgh: University of Edinburgh Press, 1991), 121–31.

8. On the duty of kings to seek counsel, see Myers, *Medieval Kingship*, chapters 4 and 5. There was a range of options within the institutional structure of monarchy. For instance, co-rulership occurs when the incumbent and successor hold the office simultaneously (as in the case of Charlemagne and Louis the Pious); dual paramountcy is a doubling up of the supreme office (Fernando of Aragon and Isabel of Castile); corporate dynasties essentially duplicate the supreme office with different names (the mayors of the Palace under Merovingian kings); and stand-ins and stake-holders such as lieutenants, regents, protectors, and queens-dowager assume temporary duties of governance. Jack Goody, *Succession to High Office* (Cambridge: Cambridge University Press, 1966), 1–66.

9. Myers, *Medieval Kingship*, 276.

10. Echevarría Arsuaga, *Catalina de Lancaster*, 46–47; idem, "Catalina of Lancaster," 79, 83.

11. She may have attended the coronation of Richard II in 1377, and may

160   Notes to Page 22

have accompanied her mother northward in the wake of the Peasants' Revolt of
1381 that destroyed her father's London Savoy Palace. Echevarría Arsuaga, *Catalina de Lancaster*, 26–31.

12. Echevarría Arsuaga, *Catalina de Lancaster*, 49–50; idem, "Catalina of
Lancaster," 89; Josè Manuel Nieto Soria, *Ceremonias de la realeza: Propaganda y
legitimación en la Castilla Trastámara* (Madrid: Nerea, 1993), 29.

13. Echevarría Arsuaga, "Catalina of Lancaster," 83; idem, *Catalina de Lancaster*, 46–47.

14. Laws pertaining to a queen's right to inherit and succeed varied widely
and changed over time. On dowries in general, see Goody, *Succession to High Office*, 26; and Thomas Kuehn, *Law, Family, and Women: Toward a Legal Anthropology of Renaissance Italy* (Chicago: University of Chicago Press, 1991), 129–42,
197–257. For classic studies, see Diane Owen Hughes, "From Brideprice to
Dowry in Mediterranean Europe," *Journal of Family History* 3 (1978): 262–96;
and Stanley Chojnacki, "Dowries and Kinsmen in Early Renaissance Venice," *Journal of Interdisciplinary History* 5 (1975): 572–600. For royal women in England, France, and Germany, see Jane Martindale, "Succession and Politics in the
Romance-Speaking World," in *England and Her Neighbors 1066–1453*, ed. Michael
Jones and Malcolm Vale (London: Hambledon Press, 1989), 19–41, especially
27, 34–36; Suzanne Fonay Wemple, *Women in Frankish Society: Marriage and the
Cloister, 500–900* (Philadelphia: University of Pennsylvania Press, 1981), 44–50;
Karl Leyser, *Rule and Conflict in an Early Medieval Society* (London: Blackwell,
1989), 49–73; Eleanor Searle, "Women and the Legitimisation of Succession at
the Norman Conquest," *Anglo-Norman Studies* 3 (1980): 159–70.

15. Alfonso VI of León named Urraca, Alfonso VIII of Castile named Be-
renguela, and Alfonso IX of León named Sancha and Dulce as their successors.
Bernard Reilly, *The Kingdom of León-Castilla Under Queen Urraca, 1109–1126*
(Princeton, N.J.: Princeton University Press, 1982), 51–53; Miriam Shadis,
"Motherhood, Lineage, and Royal Power in Medieval Castile and France: Be-
renguela de León and Blanche of Castille" (Ph.D. dissertation, Duke Univer-
sity, 1994), 50–57, 188–9. See also O'Callaghan, "Many Roles of the Medieval
Queen," 21–32; and Vann, "The Theory and Practice of Medieval Castilian
Queenship," 125–47.

16. Heath Dillard, *Daughters of the Reconquest: Women in Castillian Town
Society, 1100–1300* (Cambridge: Cambridge University Press, 1984), 28, 64, 77;
María Isabel López Díaz, "Arras y dote en España. Resumen histórico," in *Nuevas
perspectivas sobre la mujer*, ed. María Angeles Durán, 2 vols. (Madrid: Universidad
Autónoma de Madrid, 1982), 1: 83–106; and three essays in Vann, *Queens, Regents, and Potentates*: Patricia Humphrey, "Ermessenda of Barcelona: The Status
of Her Authority," 15–35; Donald Kagay, "Countess Almodis of Barcelona: 'Illustrious and Distinguished Queen' or 'Woman of Sad, Unbridled Lewdness,'"
37–47; and William Clay Stalls, "Queenship and the Royal Patrimony in Twelfth-
Century Iberia: The Example of Petronila of Aragón," 49–61.

17. Reilly, *Kingdom of León-Castilla Under Queen Urraca*, 51–53; Vann,
"Medieval Castilian Queenship," 125–47; *History of Medieval Spain*, 213–14.

18. Peggy Liss, *Isabel the Queen: Life and Times*, 2nd ed. (Philadelphia: Uni-

Notes to Pages 22–24   161

versity of Pennsylvania Press, 2004; first edition, 1992), 113–18; *Spanish Kingdoms* 2: 351–54.

19. Recent research on England suggests that rather than being always subordinate, queens were, or could be, on a more equal footing with men. Janet Nelson has found that early coronation *ordos* for queens and empresses gave them a status roughly equal to that of kings. This "partnership of [the king's] realm" was, of course, not one of equals, but neither was it one in which the queen was entirely subordinate and without political power of any sort. Nelson, "Early Medieval Rites of Queen-Making and the Shaping of Medieval Queenship," in *Queens and Queenship in Medieval Europe*, ed. Anne J. Duggan (Woodbridge: Boydell, 1997), 301–15; idem, "Gendering Courts in the Early Medieval West," in *Gender in the Early Medieval World*, ed. Leslie Brubaker and Julia M. H. Smith (Cambridge: Cambridge University Press, 2004), 185–97.

20. O'Callaghan, "Many Roles of the Medieval Queen," 21–26.

21. Joseph F. O'Callaghan, *The Learned King: The Reign of Alfonso X of Castile* (Philadelphia: University of Pennsylvania Press, 1993), 93, 185, 220, 224–26, 228.

22. Harriet Lightman, "Political Power and the Queen of France: Pierre DuPuy's Treatise on Regency Government," *Canadian Journal of History* 21 (1986): 299–312; André Poulet, "Capetian Women and the Regency: The Genesis of a Vocation," in *Medieval Queenship*, ed. John Carmi Parsons (New York: St. Martin's Press, 1993), 93–116. For a discussion of medieval and early modern regency theory, see Katherine Crawford, *Perilous Performances: Gender and Regency in Early Modern France* (Cambridge, Mass.: Harvard University Press, 2004), 13–23.

23. María Antonio Carmona Ruiz, *María de Molina* (Barcelona: Plaza Janés, 2005); Mercedes Gaibrois de Ballasteros, *María de Molina, tres veces reina* (Madrid: Espasa-Calpe, 1936).

24. Miriam T. Shadis, "Berenguela of Castile's Political Motherhood: The Management of Sexuality, Marriage, and Succession," in *Medieval Mothering*, ed. John Carmi Parsons and Bonnie Wheeler (New York: Garland, 1996), 335–58; idem, "Motherhood, Lineage, and Royal Power," 50–57, 188–89; Vann, "Medieval Castilian Queenship," 125–47; and *History of Medieval Spain*, 335–36.

25. Roger Collins, "Queens-Dowager and Queens-Regent in Tenth-Century León and Navarre," in Parsons, *Medieval Queenship*, 79–92.

26. Echevarría Arsuaga, "Catalina of Lancaster," 85, 91; idem, *Catalina de Lancaster*, 51–65.

27. There is no full modern treatment of the reign of Enrique III and the chronicle of his reign needs a new critical edition. *Crónica de Enrique III de Castilla*, in *Biblioteca de Autores Españoles*, vol. 68, ed. Cayatano Rosell (Madrid: Real Academia Española, 1953). For an overview of his reign, see *España cristiana*, 303–78; *History of Medieval Spain*, 534–41; and *Spanish Kingdoms*, 1: 400–405. Echevarría Arsuaga discusses Enrique from Catalina's perspective in *Catalina de Lancaster*, 51–91.

28. For the interregnum, see *Història de Catalunya*, 1: 422–70, 2: 1–20; *Los Trastámaras*, ix–cxxix. On the co-regency, see Ana Echevarría Arsuaga, "The Queen and the Master: Catalina of Lancaster and the Military Orders," in Earen-

162 Notes to Pages 24–25

fight, *Queenship and Political Power*, 91–105, esp. 97-99; idem, *Catalina de Lancaster*, 157–58; Manuel Dualde and José Camarena, *El Compromiso de Caspe* (Zaragoza: Institución "Fernando el Católico," Diputación Provincial de Zaragoza, 1971); *Historia de España*, 81–86; *Spanish Kingdoms*, 1: 215–38. On Fernando's reign, see *Història de Catalunya*, 2: 20–40.

29. Echevarría Arsuaga, "Catalina of Lancaster," 92–94, 97–102; *History of Medieval Spain*, 534, 541, 546, 550.

30. Myers, *Medieval Kingship*, 1.

31. Ernst Kantorowicz, *The King's Two Bodies: A Study in Mediaeval Political Theology* (Princeton, N.J.: Princeton University Press, 1957), 381.

32. Echevarría Arsuaga, *Catalina de Lancaster*, 49–50; idem, "Catalina of Lancaster," 89; Nieto Soria, *Ceremonias de la realeza*, 29. Enrique reiterated this in his will, noting that if Juan were to die before Maria without legitimate heirs, she would inherit and rule the realms; if María died, then his daughter Catalina would inherit and rule. He also made provisions for a regency council. *Crónica de Enrique III de Castilla*, 266.

33. Inheritance is inextricably linked to the transmission of land and lordship, from which follows a similar entitlement and succession to office. But clear, straightforward rules indicating a single individual as the true heir are rare throughout the world, and in Europe were not clearly defined until well into the central Middle Ages. See Goody, *Succession to High Office*, 25–26, and the following essays in *Family and Inheritance*, ed. Jack Goody, Joan Thirsk, and E. P. Thompson (Cambridge: Cambridge University Press, 1976): Jack Goody, "Inheritance, Property, and Women: Some Comparative Considerations," 10–36; Joan Thirsk, "The European Debate on Customs of Inheritance, 1500–1700," 177–91; and E. P. Thompson, "The Grid of Inheritance: A Comment," 328–60.

34. The precedent for naming a royal daughter a *primogenita* goes back at least to Berenguela, who was designated as such in the Treaty of Seligenstadt that formalized her betrothal to Conrad, son of Frederick Barbarossa. The proposed marriage never happened and Berenguela never ruled directly, although she was regent throughout the minority of her brother, Enrique I (r. 1214–17). But her designation as *primogénita* remained juridically significant and she remained an important politically active figure throughout her son's reign. Shadis, "Berenguela de León and Blanche de Castille," 50–57, 182–89, 207–13.

35. O'Callaghan, "Many Roles of the Medieval Queen," 21–32.

36. Alfonso García Gallo, "El derecho de sucesión del trono en la Corona de Aragón," *Anuario de Historia del Derecho Español* 36 (1966): 5–187, especially 67–71; Próspero de Bofarull y Mascaró, *Los condes de Barcelona vindicados*, 2 vols. (Barcelona: Monmany, 1836), 2: 205; Stalls, *History of Medieval Spain*, 224, 257–58; *Medieval Crown of Aragon*, 27–31.

37. Succession crises loomed three times since 1164 and none were resolved in favor of a female claimant. The Crown did pass from brother to brother twice: first from Alfons III (1285–91) to Jaume II (1291–1327), and then from Joan I (1387–95) to Martí (1395–1410). *Medieval Crown of Aragon*, 100–101, 124–25; García Gallo, "El derecho de sucesión"; María Valentina Gómez Mampaso, "La mujer y la sucesión al Trono," in *Nuevas perspectivas sobre la mujer*, ed. María

Notes to Page 26   163

Angeles Durán, 2 vols. (Madrid: Universidad Autónoma de Madrid, 1982), 1: 127–35; Federico Udina Martorell, "La organización político-administrativa de la Corona de Aragón (1416–1516)," in *La Corona d'Aragona e il Mediterraneo: aspetti e problemi comuni, da Alfonso il Magnanimo a Ferdinando il Cattolico (1416–1516)*, 4 vols., IX Congreso de Historia de la Corona de Aragón (Naples: Societá Napoletana di Storia Patria, 1978), 1: 49–83; *Medieval Crown of Aragón*, 107, 125–26, 133–36.

38. Pedro IV, King of Aragon (Pere III of Aragon), *Chronicle*, trans. Mary Hillgarth, intro. and notes by J. N. Hillgarth, 2 vols. (Toronto: Pontifical Institute of Mediaeval Studies, 1980), 2: 392–93; *Anales de la Corona de Aragón*, 8: 5; *España cristiana*, 468–70.

39. A 1328 legal determination in favor of Charles of Valois, later supported by the fraudulent application of Salic Law, barred women from both inheriting the crown and transmitting the right to rule to both male and female heirs. Colette Beaune, *The Birth of an Ideology: Myths and Symbols of Nation in Late-Medieval France*, trans. Susan Ross Huston (Berkeley: University of California Press, 1991; original French edition, 1985), 245–65; Fanny Cosandey, *La Reine de France: symbole et pouvoir, XVe–XVIIIe siècle* (Paris: Gallimard, 2000), 19–54; Sarah Hanley, "Identity Politics and Rulership in France: Female Political Place and the Fraudulent Salic Law in Christine de Pisan," in *Changing Identities in Early Modern France*, ed. Michael Wolfe (Durham, N.C.: Duke University Press, 1997), 78–94; Craig Taylor, "The Salic Law and the Valois Succession to the French Crown," *French History* 15, 4 (2001): 358–77; *History of Medieval Spain*, 416; *Medieval Crown of Aragon*, 109.

40. Castile experienced serious upheaval in the thirteenth century with the minorities of Enrique I (1214–17) and Fernando III (1217–52) and a century later when Pedro the Cruel (1350–69) was challenged by his illegitimate brother, Enrique of Trastámara (ruled as Enrique II, 1369–79). Clara Estow, *Pedro the Cruel of Castile, 1350–1369* (Leiden: Brill, 1995), 180–269.

41. Elizabeth A. R. Brown, "The Ceremonial of Royal Succession in Capetian France: The Double Funeral of Louis X," *Traditio* 34 (1978): 227–71; Ralph E. Giesey, *The Juridic Basis of Dynastic Right to the French Throne* Transactions of the American Philosophical Society n.s. 51, 5 (Philadelphia: American Philosophical Society, 1961), 5–8, 11; Andrew W. Lewis, *Royal Succession in Capetian France: Studies in Familial Order and the State* (Cambridge, Mass.: Harvard University Press, 1981), 24–32, 51–61, 155–56, 194–95; Charles T. Wood, *The French Apanages and the Capetian Monarchy, 1124–1328* (Cambridge, Mass.: Harvard University Press, 1966), 3–7, 23–26, 147.

42. The distinction between public and private space, which varies across time and depends on social rank and gender, is particularly problematic when speaking of queens. In this context, I follow Harald Kleinschmidt, who regards the public/private as three zones—spaces of daily experience (domestic or family environment, an emotionally charged private space), spaces of regular communication (wider local environment, public politically charged space), and spaces of the world. See Kleinschmidt, *Understanding the Middle Ages: The Transformation of Ideas and Attitudes in the Medieval World* (Woodbridge: Boydell, 2000), 33–61.

164   Notes to Pages 27–28

43. Marta VanLandingham, "Royal Portraits: Representations of Queenship in the Thirteenth-Century Catalan Chronicles," in Earenfight, *Queenship and Political Power in Medieval and Early Modern Spain*, 109–19. For comparison to Alfonso X, see O'Callaghan, "Many Roles of the Medieval Queen," 21–32.

44. Anne J. Cruz, "The Female Figure as Political Propaganda in the 'Pedro el Cruel' Romancero," in *Spanish Women in the Golden Age: Images and Realities*, ed. Magdalena S. Sánchez and Alain Saint-Saens (Westport, Conn.: Greenwood, 1996), 69–89.

45. Echevarría Arsuaga, "Catalina of Lancaster," 89; idem, *Catalina de Lancaster*, 84–88, 138; *Doña María de Castilla*, 30–42, 57–59.

46. She suffered from a variety of maladies—mostly fevers and something the queen herself calls "accidents"—as did both her mother and father, but it is extremely difficult to know for certain what was ailing her. As far as I know, there is no first-hand account of her "accidents," although most scholars conclude that she was infertile and prone to a number of chronic ailments. They call her "accidents" epilepsy, which presumably, afflicted her mother, too. The most balanced account based on archival sources is Lluís Comenge i Ferrer, who concluded that she suffered from "passion hipocondríca" and "sofocación de la matriz" (suffocation of the womb) and problaby epilepsy. *La medicina en el reinado de Alfonso V de Aragón* (Barcelona: Espasa, 1903). Much of the subsequent scholarship on María's health is often riddled with misogyny and a retrospective Freudian analysis. For example, J. Garcia Llauradó claimed that her lieutenancy was a compensation for her unsatisfying marriage: "Nueva interpretación de la enfermedad de la Reina Doña María de Castilla, esposa del Magnánimo," *Medicina clínica* 19 (1952): 192–98. I am especially grateful to Monica Green for her insights on women and medicine in the Middle Ages who notes that the presence of both fevers and "accidents" complicate matters and cautions against making retrospective diagnoses. On women's health, with a description of suffocation of the womb, epilepsy, and other maladies that afflicted women, see Monica H. Green, editor and translator, *The "Trotula": A Medieval Compendium of Women's Medicine* (Philadelphia: University of Pennsylvania Press, 2001), 21–33.

47. Her letters to her mother, more than one hundred in all, are contained in ACA: C DR 3108, 3162.

48. Alfonso sent his brother, *infante* Juan, as the official Aragonese representative. Luis Corell Ruiz, *Una copia del testamento de Catalina de Lancaster* (Valencia: Instituto Valenciano de Estudios Historicos, 1952), 78; *Alfonso the Magnanimous*, 61–62.

49. ACA: C Pec 2412, 120r–v; *Crónica de Juan II de Castilla*, ed. Juan de Mata Carriazo y Arroquia (Madrid: Real Academia de la Historia, 1982), cap. 132, 286–88; *Ensayo de una Bibliografía de Libros de Fiestas celebradas en Valencia y su antiguo reino*, 2 vols., ed. Salvador Carreres Zacarés (Valencia: Hijo de F. Vives Mora, 1926), 2: 92–97; Echevarría Arsuaga, *Catalina de Lancaster*, 164–67; *Doña María de Castilla*, 59–61; *Alfonso the Magnanimous*, 35–37; *Història de Catalunya*, 49–50.

50. Ryder speculates that the formal betrothal and approval of her dowry

took place at Tordesillas in April 1408. *Alfonso the Magnanimous*, 13. See Echevarría Arsuaga, *Catalina de Lancaster*, 100, 106, 136.

51. Echevarría Arsuaga, "Catalina of Lancaster," 97. The marital politics of the Trastámara and Antequera families continued for two more generations. Juan II and María of Aragon's son, Enrique IV, ruled Castile (1454–74). When María of Aragón died in 1445, Juan married Isabel of Portugal; their daughter, Isabel, "la Católica," married Fernando of Aragón, uniting the two dynasties and the peninsula, except for Portugal and Navarre; both were later incorporated into the Spanish crown and then broke free. *History of Medieval Spain*, 547–77; Liss, *Isabel the Queen*, 56–69; William D. Phillips, *Enrique IV and the Crisis of Fifteenth-Century Castile (1425–1480)* (Cambridge, Mass.: Medieval Academy of America, 1978); *Spanish Kingdoms* 2: 300–347.

52. *Alfonso the Magnanimous*, 53, 63–64.

53. A fourth brother, Sancho, died in 1417. For a full discussion of this political-familial history, see *Los Trastámaras*. For the impact on the Crown of Aragon, see *Alfonso the Magnanimous*, chapters 2, 4–7; for the wider importance for Castile and European history, see *History of Medieval Spain*, 551–55, 562–66, 580; *Spanish Kingdoms* 2: 301–14.

54. Echevarría Arsuaga, *Catalina de Lancaster*, 136.

55. *Alfonso the Magnanimous*, 13.

56. The dowry that Sancha, daughter of Alfonso V of Asturias-León (999–1028), brought to her marriage to Fernando I of Castile (1035–65) enabled them to reunite briefly the two realms and initiate the reconquest. *History of Medieval Spain*, 194. Marie of Montpellier's marriage to Pedro II of Aragon (1196–1213) opened the door to Aragonese influence north of Pyrenees and set the stage for the conquests of their son, Jaime I (1213–76). Elizabeth Haluska-Rausch, "Unwilling Partners: Conflict and Ambition in the Marriage of Peter II of Aragon and Marie de Montpellier," in Earenfight, *Queenship and Political Power in Medieval and Early Modern Spain*, 3–20. Teresa of Portugal, illegitimate daughter of Alfonso VI of León (1065–1109), married Henry of Burgundy, and together they governed the nascent kingdom of Portugal from 1109 to 1128. López Díaz, "Arras y dote in España," 1: 83–106; *History of Medieval Spain*, 213–17, 221. See also Ana Rodríguez López, "Dotes y arras en la politica territorial de la monarchía feudal castellan, siglos XII–XIII," *Arenal: Revista de Historia de las Mujeres* 2, 2 (1995)· 271–93.

57. María Teresa Ferrer i Mallol, "El patrimoni reial i la recuperació dels senyorius jurisdiccionals en els estats catalano-aragoneses a la fi del segle XIV," *Anuario de Estudios Medievales* 7 (1970–71): 351–491.

58. ACA: C Grat 1685: 122r–126v; Atanasio Sinués Ruiz and Antonio Ubieto Arteta, eds., *El Patrimonio Real en Aragón durante la edad media* (Zaragoza: Anubar, 1986), 98.

59. The copious correspondence concerning collection of María's dowry is in ACA: C Var 3276: fols. 2r–61v, 6 August 1416–6 April 1420. It was resolved, more or less to everyone's satisfaction, by 6–7 March 1421, ACA: C Var 3276: 69r–72r. *Doña María de Castilla*, 61–72; Andrés Giménez-Soler, "Retrato his-

tórico de la reina doña María," *Boletín de la Real Academia de Buenas Letras de Barcelona* 1 (1901–2): 71–81; *Alfonso the Magnanimous*, 37.

60. On the symbolism of Fernando of Antequera's coronation, see Angus MacKay, "Signs Deciphered: The Language of Court Displays in Late Medieval Spain," in *Kings and Kingship in Medieval Europe*, ed. Anne J. Duggan (London: Centre for Late Antique and Medieval Studies, 1993), 287–304.

61. Roser Salicrú i Lluch, "La coronación de Ferran d'Antequera: l'organització i els preparatius de la festa," *Anuario de Estudios Medievales* 25, 2 (1995): 699–759; idem, "Las demandas de la coronación de Fernando I en el reino de Aragón," in *Aragón en la Edad Media: Homenaje a la profesora Carmen Orcástegui Gros* (Zaragoza: Universidad de Zaragoza, 1999), 1409–27. For earlier coronations in the Crown of Aragon, see Prim Bertrán Roigé, "La pretendida coronación de Juan I y el estamento nobiliario de Aragón," *Hidalguía* 240 (1993): 691–703; Antonio Durán Gudiol, "El rito de la coronación del rey en Aragón," *Argensola: Revista de Ciencias Sociales del Instituto de Estudios Altoaragoneses* 103 (1989): 17–39; and Bonifacio Palacios Martín, *La coronación de los reyes de Aragón, 1204–1410* (Valencia: Anubar, 1975).

62. *Alfonso the Magnanimous*, 117, 254.

63. Salicrú i Lluch, "La coronación de Ferran d'Antequera," 703–5; Palacios Martín, *La coronación de los reyes de Aragón*, 21–26, 91–93, 201–8, 240–46, 269–76; Bertrán Roigé, "La pretendida coronación de Juan I," 691–93.

64. I am grateful to Joseph F. O'Callaghan for his insights on coronations. See also Ruiz, "Unsacred Monarchy," 109–44; Linehan, "Frontier Kingship," 71–79.

65. *Alfonso the Magnanimous*, 42, 49, 360.

66. José María Font i Rius, "Las instituciones de la corona de Aragón en la primera mitad del siglo XV," *Ponencias del IV Congreso de la História de la Corona de Aragón* (Barcelona: Comisión Permanente de los Congresos de la Corona de Aragón, 1976), 209–23, esp. 216–19; and Carme Batlle i Gallart, *La Crisis social y económica a mediados del siglo XV*, 2 vols. (Barcelona: Consejo Superior de Investigaciones Científicas, 1973), 1: 133–64.

67. Francisco Elías de Tejada, *Las doctrinas políticas en la Cataluña medieval* (Barcelona: Ayma, 1950), 180–209; Jaume Sobriqués i Callicó, *El pactisme a Catalunya: una praxi política en la història del pais* (Barcelona: Edicions 62, 1982), 7–34.

68. *História de Catalunya*, 1: 398–400, 406–7.

69. Mark Meyerson, "Defending Their Jewish Subjects: Elionor of Sicily, Maria de Luna, and the Jews of Morvedre," in Earenfight, *Queenship and Political Power in Medieval and Early Modenr Spain*, 55–77; Dawn Bratsch-Prince, "A Reappraisal of the Correspondence of Violant de Bar (1365–1431)," *Catalan Review* 8 (1994): 295–312; idem, "A Queen's Task: Violant de Bar and the Experience of Royal Motherhood in Fourteenth-Century Aragon," *La corónica* 27, 1 (1998): 21–34; Nuria Coll Juliá, *Doña Juana Enríquez, lugarteniente real en Cataluña, 1461–68*, 2 vols. (Madrid: Consejo Superior de Investigaciones Científicas, 1953).

70. Marta VanLandingham, "The Hohenstaufen Heritage of Costanza of

Sicily and the Mediterranean Expansion of the Crown of Aragon in the Later Thirteenth Century," in *Across the Mediterranean Frontiers*, ed. Dionisius Agius and Ian Richard Netton (Turnhout: Brepols, 1997), 87–104.

71. Roger Sablonier, "The Aragonese Royal Family Around 1300," in *Interest and Emotion: Essays on the Study of Family and Kinship*, ed. Hans Medick and D. W. Sabean (Cambridge: Cambridge University Press, 1984), 210–39.

72. *Medieval Crown of Aragon*, 116. For documentation on her reign (1377–86), see ACA: C 1586–90.

73. Núria Silleras-Fernández, "Spirit and Force: Politics, Public and Private, in the Reign of Maria de Luna (1396–1406)," in Earenfight, *Queenship and Political Power in Medieval and Early Modern Spain*, 78–90, esp. 82–84; idem, *Power, Piety, and Patronage in Late Medieval Queenship: Maria de Luna* (New York: Palgrave Macmillan, 2008); Aurea Lucinda Javierre Mur, *María de Luna, reina de Aragón* (Madrid: Consejo Superior de Investigaciones Científicas, 1942), 52–84. My thanks to Robert Berkhofer, III, for his insightful comments on the queens' coronation.

74. *Alfonso the Magnanimous*, 3.

75. ACA C: CR Caja 2 (1416): #191, 1 July; #302, 12 September; #329, 27 October; Caja 3 (1416): #302, 12 September; Caja 4 (1417): #409, 22 February; #419, 4 March; #440, 9 March; #515, 14 May; Caja 5 (1417): #566, ca. 15 June; #567, 30 June; #622, 624, 14 September; #635, 23 October; Caja 6 (1417–18): #671, 8 November; #690, 3 December; #707, 5 January; Caja 7 (1418): 861: 15 June; #880: ca. 20 June; #885, 2 July; #897, 13 July; #903, 14 July; Caja 8 (1418): #945, 11 August; #955, 20 August; #972, 8 September; #975, ca. 10 September; #993, 27 September; #1052 & 1053, 20 November; Caja 9 (1418–19): #109, 11 December; #1137, 13 January; #1180, 16 February; #1222, 27 (?) March. See *Alfonso the Magnanimous*, 18–44.

76. *Alfonso the Magnanimous*, 47–48, 53, 55–56, 61, 63–64, Echevarría Arsuaga, "The Queen and the Master," 97–105.

77. *Alfonso the Magnanimous*, 56, 59, 62–64

78. Rita Costa Gomes, *The Making of Court Society: Kings and Nobles in Late Medieval Portugal*, trans. Alison Aiken (Cambridge: Cambridge University Press, 2003), 9-55, 57–78; quote on 34. For a useful comparison to the early Middle Ages, see Nelson, "Gendering Courts," 185–97.

79. *Doña María de Castilla*, 129–44. For the queen's household in general, see Marta VanLandingham, *Transforming the State: King, Court and Political Culture in the Realms of Aragon, 1213–1387* (Leiden: Brill, 2002), 173–94.

80. Pere's organization was the first systematic bureaucratization of the finances of royal government. The document outlining these reforms is known as *Ordenaciones fetes per lo molt alt senyor en Pere terç, re d'Aragó, sobra lo regiment de tots officials de la su cort*, issued in 1344, is based on the *Leges* Palatinae of Mallorca. This system of household organization would endure, with some modifications, notably of the office of the Maestre Racional in 1419, until the reign of Fernando II (1479–1516). VanLandingham, *Transforming the State*, 27–30; Francesch Carreras y Candi, "Redreç de la reyal casa. Ordenamements de Pere 'Lo Gran' e Anfós 'Lo Lliberal,'" *Boletín de la Real Academia de Buenas Letras de Barcelona* 39, 3

(1909): 97–108; Luis G. Valdeavellano, *Curso de história de las instituciones Españolas: de los origines al final de la Edad Media*, 2nd ed. (Madrid: Editorial Revista de Occidente, 1970), 490–91, 495–96.

81. José Trenchs Odena and Antonio María Aragó, José Trenchs Odena and Antonio María Aragó, *Cancillerías de la Corona de Aragón desde Jaime I a la muerte de Juan II*, vol. 1 of *Folia Parisiensia* (Zaragoza: Institución "Fernando el Católico," 1982), 50–52; José María Font i Rius, "Las instituciones de la corona de Aragón," 209–23.

82. There were three majordomos, one each for Aragón, Catalunya, and Valencia-Mallorca. The office was similar to the older seneschal, which was the hereditary domain of the Montcada family until it was abolished in 1344. VanLandingham, *Transforming the State*, 25–27, 142–45, 160–66; John Shideler, *A Medieval Catalan Family: The Montcadas, 1000–1230* (Berkeley: University of California Press, 1983), 20–29, 61–62, 118.

83. VanLandingham, *Transforming the State*, 101–14.

84. *Kingdom of Naples*, 19–20, 57–61, 65–68, 73–75, 87; *Doña María de Castilla*, 130–31.

85. *Kingdom of Naples*, 57–58; *Doña María de Castilla*, 130–31.

86. Corts of Barcelona, 1422, caps. 8, 24 in *Constitucions e altres drets de Catalunya*, 3 vols. (Barcelona: 1588, 1704; facsimile edition, Barcelona: Romargraf, 1973), 112.

87. A particularly vivid case of this is that of Juana I. Bethany Aram, *Juana the Mad: Sovereignty and Dynasty in Renaissance Europe* (Baltimore: Johns Hopkins University Press, 2005), 7–9, 34–64.

88. *Alfonso the Magnanimous*, 367–69. Of course, when he moved to Naples in the 1430s, he added Italians to his retinue.

89. ACA: C Cur 3203, 172r, 25 June 1450.

90. The *Cambra* originated during the reign of Jaume I, when he gave Teresa Gil Vidaure half the tithes for the castles of Jérica and Toro. This was a lease, but a permanent one, and a custom that would solidify into a right over the next three hundred years. Robert I. Burns, *The Crusader Kingdom of Valencia: Reconstruction on a Thirteenth-Century Frontier*, 2 vols. (Cambridge, Mass.: Harvard University Press, 1967), 1: 165.

91. The Cambra de al Reyna became an important institution in the fourteenth century. Pere IV had been obliged by his marriage contract to provide Elionor of Sicily with a minimum source of revenues, and began granting her, in 1359, with various *aljamas* (properties set aside for the Muslim subject). ACA: C 1534: 137 (5 Oct 1359); 1536: 45 (20 Feb 1360); 1536: 62 (20 Feb 1360); 1537: 48 (15 June 1361). The Muslims of Eslida asked to be given to the queen. ACA: C 1205: 60 (31 March 1365). John Boswell, *The Royal Treasure: Muslim Communities Under the Crown of Aragon in the Fourteenth Century* (New Haven, Conn.: Yale University Press, 1977), 205–7.

92. When Elionor took over the major Aragonese *aljamas*, she regulated their finances minutely and prohibited the taking of loans that were not in the best interests of the *aljamas*. ACA: C 1570, fol. 87, 6 March 1361; Boswell, *Royal Treasure*, 205–7. The queen's zeal prompted Pere to tighten up his procedures,

but the Aragonese *aljamas'* financial state worsened and in 1413-14 Leonor of Albuquerque had to point out to the creditors of her hard-pressed *aljama* in Zaragoza that "all of the goods of the *aljama* are not sufficient to pay its debts." ACA: C 2422: 60 (1413); C 2423: 273 (1414) in Francisco Macho y Ortega, "Documentos relativos a la condición social y jurídica de los mudéjars aragonese," *Revista de Ciencias Jurídicas y Sociales* 5 (1922): 143-60, 444-64, esp. 158-59.

93. In Valencia the queen had income from some of the sheep flocks. Burns, *Crusader Kingdom of Valencia*, 1: 167.

94. ACA: C Sec 3227, 53r–55v, 9 June 1449; 57r–58v, 30 June 1449; 75r–76r, 24 July 1449.

95. ACA: C Sec 3227, 43v–44v, 22 April 1449; 75r–76r, 24 July 1449; 93r–v, 21 October 1449; 99v–100v, 6 December 1449; 104r–105r, 24 January 1450; 121r–123v, 6 May 1450; 134v–136v, 3 September 1450.

96. ACA: C Sec 3227, 42r–43v, 22 April 1449.

97. ACA: C Sec 3227, 29v–31v, 14 October 1448; 42r–43v, 22 April 1449; 44v–48v, 30 April 1449; 53r–55v, 9 June 1449; 55v–56r, 25 June 1449; 57r–58v, 30 June 1449; 64r–65v, 12 July 1449; 70r–v and 73v–74v, 8 July 1449; 75r–76r, 24 July.

98. *Doña María de Castilla*, 72–74.

99. ". . . hoy miercoles 18 del presente mes, ha venido lo que a las mulleres, por disposicion natural, cada mes acostumbrada de venir, el cual nunqua habia havido." ACA: C DR 3162: 80v, 18 August 1417; Comenge i Ferrer, *La medicina en el reinado de Alfonso V*, 19–32; *Doña María de Castilla*, 34.

100. *Alfonso the Magnanimous*, 123–24, 184, 358–60.

101. *Alfonso the Magnanimous*, 121–23.

102. Comenge i Ferrer, *La medicina en el reinado de Alfonso V*, 27.

103. Zurita reports that the identity of the mother was unknown and reports the rumors of three possibilities—Guerladona Carlina Reverit, Margarita de Hijar, one of María's personal attendants, or María's sister Catalina. *Anales de la Corona de Aragón*, 6: 132–33. Ryder argues that Carlina Reverit is the most likely the child's mother. *Alfonso the Magnanimous*, 123.

104. *Llibre de les solemnitats de Barcelona*, ed. Agustí Durán i Sanpere and Josep Sanabre, 2 vols., vol. 1, 1424–1546 (Barcelona: Institució Patxot, 1930), 1: 30. Leonor lived another decade, dying on 16 December 1435. *Alfonso the Magnanimous*, 221.

105. *Alfonso the Magnanimous*, 123–24.

106. *Anales de la Corona de Aragón*, 6: 133; Comenge i Ferrer, *La medicina en el reinado de Alfonso V*, 26–27.

107. *Alfonso the Magnanimous*, 184; Soldevila, "La reyna María," 243–44.

108. For Ferran (known to the Italians as Ferrante, see *Alfonso the Magnanimous*, 221, 230–31, 239–40, 268, 350–57, 304–11, 400–430; for María and Leonor, *Alfonso the Magnanimous*, 184, 268, 274, 309, 421.

109. The implications of the Compromise of Caspe still reverberate. Many Catalans, then and now, consider it to be the end of Catalan sovereignty and the beginning of Castilian hegemony. On the events surrounding the interregnum and the Compromise, see Santiago Sobrequés i Vidal, *Els barons de Catalunya i*

170 Notes to Pages 38–40

el Compromis de Casp (Barcelona: Rafael Damau, 1966); idem, *El compromís de Casp e la noblesa catalana* (Barcelona: Curial, 1973). For the political and social context, see *Los Trastámaras*, 345–50. On Fernando I, see Jaime Vicens Vives, *Els Trastámares, el segle XV* (Barcelona: Editorial Teide, 1956), 69–102. See also José Angel Sesma Muñoz, "El sentimiento nacionalista en la Corona de Aragón y el nacimiento del la España moderna," in *Realidad e imagines del poder: España a fines de le Edad Media*, ed. Adeline Rucquoi (Valladolid: Ambito, 1987), 215–31.

110. *Alfonso the Magnanimous*, 358–70.

111. Santiago Sobrequés i Vidal, *Els barons de Catalunya* (Barcelona: Editorial Teide, 1957), 139–42, 174–79, 176–89, 196–201, 203–5.

112. *Los Trastámaras*, 373–77.

113. *Alfonso the Magnanimous*, 65.

114. "Quod Nos cuius incumbit humeris tam pro recuperacione et reduccione ad Coronam nostram regiam nonnullarum civitatum, villarum et castrorum nostrorum regni Sardinie que a perfidis sardis domus Nostre regie rebellibus tam diu occupata tirranice detinentur, quam pro domando regaliter cornua superborum ipsorum cervices ad sauve fidelitatis nostre jugum viriliter reducendo, allisque justis et racionalibus causis Nobis recurrentibus, versus dictum regnum Sardinie velut partem hereditatis Nostre preciose paratam classem et signa nostra victricia ad presens." *Cortes* 13: 83.

115. On the Italian campaigns, see *Alfonso the Magnanimous*, 45–115.

116. A three-year truce with the Genoese had expired in January 1420, and neither side had made any attempts to negotiate a renewal. *Alfonso the Magnanimous*, 74.

117. *Alfonso the Magnanimous*, 24–44, 382.

118. *Alfonso the Magnanimous*, 147–58.

119. This order of succession was stipulated in Ferndando I's will. *Alfonso the Magnanimous*, 69, 220.

120. *Los Trastámaras*, 373–83.

121. *Alfonso the Magnanimous*, 73.

122. He was referring to her as *locumtenens generalis* in documents issued in both their names as early as 5 March 1420, but the *privilegio* officially granted her the authority. ACA: C Var 3276: 70v–71r.

123. *Cortes*, 13: 83 and 20: 432–35; ARV: MR 9050, 3v–4v; *Doña María de Castilla*, 87. On 7 April 1420 he announced her appointment as Lieutenant General in a letter patent. ACA: C Var 3276: 68r–69.

124. Signed by the king, it was witnessed by his secretary Francesch Davinyó; a magnate, Federico de Luna; and two knights, Joan Vilaragut and Ramón Xatmar (Alfonso's *mayordomo*). *Cortes*, 13: 83–88.

125. For example, Alfonso's *privilegio* granting the lieutenancy of Catalunya to Juan of Navarre on 20 January 1436 is nearly identical in all respects except details concerning jurisdiction and geographic scope. ARV: MR, 9050, fol. 5r–7v.

126. Hernández-León de Sánchez argued that Alfonso withdrew completely from the governance of his peninsular realms, but I find that very hard to believe, given the exchange of letters among all parties involved in governing the realms. *Doña María de Castilla*, 87. It is true, however, that when he leaves in 1420, she

literally replaces him in the registers as the originator of the chancery documents. There is no break in flow of letters when he leaves and she takes over. Alfonso's chancery went with him and from this point, until his return in 1423, when he takes over and then they sign documents together. See, for example, ACA: C Varia 3276: 69r, 6 March 1420 and 105v–106v, 15 May 1424.

127. Giménez-Soler, "Retrato histórico," 71–81; Soldevila, "La reyna María," 235–39; *Los Trastámaras*, 374–75.

Chapter 3. From Queen to Queen-Lieutenant, 1420-35

1. Theresa Earenfight, "Absent Kings: Queens as Political Partners in the Medieval Crown of Aragon," in *Queenship and Political Power in Medieval and Early Modern Spain*, ed. Theresa Earenfight (Aldershot: Ashgate, 2005), 33–51. On lieutenants in general, see Jésus Lalinde Abadía, *La institución virreinal en Cataluña (1471–1716)* (Barcelona, 1964); idem, "Virreyes y lugartenientes medievales en la Corona de Aragón," *Cuadernos de Historia de España* (Buenos Aires) 31 (1960): 98–172.

2. For her documents, see ACA: C 289–290. Roger Sablonier, "The Aragonese Royal Family Around 1300," in *Interest and Emotion: Essays on the Study of Family and Kinship*, ed. Hans Medick and D. W. Sabean (Cambridge: Cambridge University Press, 1984), 210–39.

3. ACA: C 426–427; *Medieval Crown of Aragon*, 101.

4. These dates correspond to the material contained in the registers, not the actual dates of her lieutenancy. She was queen until Joan's death (1395), but the registers for her lieutenancy run from 1379 to 1430 and are mingled with personal household and private documents. ACA: C 1807 and 1815–1824 (1379–1410); 2029–2062 (1388–1430). *Medieval Crown of Aragon*, 121–26.

5. Maria de Luna served two separate terms as lieutenant, 1396–97 and 1401. She was not lieutenant for the entire span covered by the registers but she was active in Martí's government, and the registers run continuously and can be misleading. ACA: C 2105–2110 (1372–97); 2327–2354 (1396–1407). Núria Silleras-Fernández, *Power, Piety, and Patronage in Late Medieval Queenship: Maria de Luna* (New York: Palgrave Macmillan, 2008), 37–64; Aurea Lucinda Javierre Mur, *María de Luna, reina de Aragón* (Madrid: Consejo Superior de Investigaciones Científicas, 1942), 52–84.

6. She was lieutenant for one year, 1412, but the registers of her documents cover her life span. ACA: C 2355 (1412–21). *Medieval Crown of Aragon*, 130.

7. For the documents of the co-lieutenancy of Juana with her son, Fernando, see ACA: C 3495–3501 (1461–77). For Juana's lieutenancy without Fernando, see ACA: C 3503–4 (1461–7). Nuria Coll Juliá, *Doña Juana Enríquez, lugarteniente real en Cataluña (1461–68)*, 2 vols. (Madrid, Consejo Superior de Investigaciones Científicas, 1953).

8. *Doña María de Castilla*, 87.

9. Alan Ryder, "The Evolution of Imperial Government in Naples Under Alfonso V of Aragon," in *Europe in the Late Middle Ages*, ed. John Rigby Hale,

John Roger Loxdale Highfield, and Beryl Smalley (Evanston, Ill.: Northwestern University Press, 1965), 332–57. Although Ryder is primarily interested in Italian government, his work is pertinent to Catalunya because Alfonso patterned his institutions in Naples after the Catalan-Aragonese model, and Ryder makes frequent comparisons to government in both places.

10. The governmental lieutenancy did not exist officially in Castile and Navarre. The office there was strictly military, but the regency was common there. In Navarre, Toda Asnúrez, was regent for her son García I Sánchez (926–70); Urraca Fernández and Jimena González, grandmother and mother, respectively, were regents for Sancho III Garcés, el Mayor (1000–35). María de Molina, wife of Sancho IV of Castile, was regent for both her son, Fernando IV (1295–1312), and grandson, Alfonso XI (1312–50) during a period of anarchy and warfare. Berenguela of León was regent for her younger brother, Enrique III (1214–17), and succeeded him after his death. María Antonia Carmona Ruiz, *María de Molina* (Barcelona: Plaza Janés, 2005), 131–274; Mercedes Gaibrois de Ballesteros, *María de Molina, tres veces reina* (Madrid, Espasa-Calpe, 1936), 43–46; Miriam Shadis, "Motherhood, Lineage, and Royal Power in Medieval Castile and France: Berenguela de León and Blanche de Castille" (Ph.D. dissertation, Duke University, 1994), 50–57, 182–89, 207–13; *History of Medieval Spain*, 335–36, 401, 403, 432.

11. Lalinde Abadía, "Virreyes y lugartenientes," 99–100. On papal legates, see Mario Oliveri, *The Representatives: The Real Nature and Function of Papal Legates* (Gerrards Cross: Van Duren, 1980); and Gino Paro, *The Right of Papal Legation* (Washington, D.C.: Catholic University of America Press, 1948).

12. Ernst Kantorowicz, *The King's Two Bodies: A Study in Mediaeval Political Theology* (Princeton, N.J.: Princeton University Press, 1957), 336–83.

13. I hesitate to use the term "empire" when referring to both the Plantagenet realms and the Crown of Aragon. Some scholars, notably John Gillingham and Martin Aurell, use the term freely. John Gillingham, *The Angevin Empire*, 2nd ed. (New York: Oxford University Press, 2001); Martin Aurell, *L'empire des Plantagenêt: 1154–1224* (Paris: Perrin, 2003). But it is a problematic term when referring to the Crown of Aragon. It was a Mediterranean power, a conglomeration of cultures in the Mediterranean, one overlayed on another and each interacting with the others. The problem is that "empire" often connotes an ideology of conquest that may have been part of the Angevin conquests of France, but it debatable when speaking of the Crown of Aragon. Alan Ryder calls the Crown an empire but does not, to my mind, clarify what he means. I agree with Jocelyn Hillgarth who argues against a "Catalan Mediterranean empire," noting that there were three distinct phases of expansion, each with its own purposes and methods and that the federative nature of the Crown mitigated any imperial tendencies. See "The Problem of a Catalan Mediterranean Empire 1229–1327," *English Historical Review* Supplement 8 (1975).

14. W. L. Warren, *Henry II* (Berkeley: University of California Press, 1973), 204, 228–30, 560–64.

15. Corsica was only nominally a Crown realm. The Crown also had a short-

lived toehold in France in Montpellier and Provence, and a tenuous claim to the Duchy of Athens. *Medieval Crown of Aragon*, 38, 67–69, 93, 111.

16. John W. Baldwin, *The Government of Philip Augustus: Foundations of French Royal Power in the Middle Ages* (Berkeley: University of California Press, 1986).

17. And it persisted as a distinct entity within the larger Castilian crown well into the early modern period. See John Huxtable Elliott, *The Revolt of the Catalans: A Study in the Decline of Spain (1598–1640)* (Cambridge: Cambridge University Press, 1963).

18. Lalinde Abadía, *La institución virreinal*, 47–49; idem, "Virreyes y lugartenientes," 100–10.

19. Alfonso García Gallo, "El derecho de sucesión al trono en la corona de Aragón," *Anuario de historia del derecho español* 36 (1966): 5–187, esp. 31–45; Ralph Giesey, *The Juridic Basis of Dynastic Right to the French Throne*, Transactions of the American Philosophical Society n.s. 51, part 5 (Philadelphia: American Philosophical Society, 1961), 5–8, 11.

20. Andrew W. Lewis, "Anticipatory Association of the Heir in Early Capetian France," *American Historical Review* 83 (1978): 906–29; idem, *Royal Succession in Capetian France: Studies in Familial Order and the State* (Cambridge, Mass.: Harvard University Press, 1981), 24–32, 51–61, 155–56, 194–95; and Charles T. Wood, *The French Apanages and the Capetian Monarchy, 1124–1328* (Cambridge, Mass,: Harvard University Press, 1966), 3–7, 23–26, 147.

21. Elizabeth McCartney, "Ceremonies and Privileges of Office: Queenship in Late Medieval France," in *Power of the Weak: Studies on Medieval Women*, ed. Jennifer Carpenter and Sally-Beth MacLean (Urbana: University of Illinois Press, 1995), 178–219, esp. 178–81.

22. Lalinde Abadía, *La institución virreinal*, 47–49, 263.

23. English Protectors, for all practical purposes, functioned as regents without the formality or the strictures of a regency council but with limited jurisdiction. J. R. Lander, *Government and Community: England, 1450–1509* (Cambridge, Mass,: Harvard University Press, 1980), 179–94.

24. J. R. Lander, "Henry VI and the Duke of York's Second Protectorate, 1455–56," in *Crown and Nobility, 1450–1509*, ed. J. R. Lander (Montreal: McGill-Queen's University Press, 1976), 74–93; T. B. Pugh, "Richard Plantagenet (1411-60), Duke of York, as the King's Lieutenant in France and Ireland," in *Aspects of Late Medieval Government and Society*, ed. J. G. Rowe (Toronto: University of Toronto Press, 1986), 107–41.

25. Baldwin, *Government of Philip Augustus*, 102–4; Kimberly A. LoPrete, "Adela of Blois and Ivo of Chartres: Piety, Politics, and the Peace in the Diocese of Chartres," in *Anglo-Norman Studies* 14 (1991): 131–52; and André Poulet, "Capetian Women and the Regency: The Genesis of a Vocation," in *Medieval Queenship*, ed. John Carmi Parsons (New York: St. Martin's Press, 1993), 93–116, esp. 108.

26. Only two nonroyal family members were lieutenants in the Crown of Aragon: Hug de Angelsola, lieutenant in Mallorca (1397–1403) and Galceran de

174 Notes to Pages 45–47

Requesens, lieutenant in Catalunya (1453–6). See ACA: C 2356–2358 for Angelsola, and ACA: C 3319–3332 for Requesens. Lalinde Abadía, "Virreyes y lugartenientes," 112, 129–31; García Gallo, 'El derecho de sucesión al trono," 31–45.

27. French kings used the apanage to placate younger sons while discouraging them from extending their reach. Wood, *The French Apanages*, 7–12, 39–99, 304–10, 441–65.

28. Evelyn Jamison, "The Administration of the County of Molise in the Twelfth and Thirteenth Centuries," *English Historical Review* 176 (1929): 529–59, and 177 (1930); 1–34; David Carpenter, *The Minority of Henry III* (Berkeley: University of California Press, 1990), 21–22.

29. Henry I's wife, Matilda, had viceregal authority during the king's frequent absences in Normandy, but little is known of her actions. Henry G. Richardson and G. O. Sayles, *The Governance of Mediaeval England from the Conquest to the Magna Carta* (Edinburgh: Edinburgh University Press, 1963), 32–33, 154–69; idem, *The Administration of Ireland, 1172–1377* (Dublin: Dublin Stationery Office for Irish Manuscripts Commission, 1963), 9; Warren, *Henry II*, 204, 228–30, 560–64; C. Warren Hollister and John W. Baldwin, "The Rise of Administrative Kingship: Henry I and Philip Augustus," *American Historical Review* 83 (1978): 867–905.

30. Baldwin, *Government of Philip Augustus*, 220–25; Joseph Reese Strayer, "Normandy and Languedoc," in *Medieval Statecraft and the Perspectives of History* (Princeton. N.J.: Princeton University Press, 1971), 49.

31. P. S. Lewis, *Later Medieval France: The Polity* (London: Macmillan, 1968), 139, 159–63, 198, 228; Warren, *Henry II*, 204, 228–30, 560–64; Carpenter, *Henry III*, 21–2; Baldwin, *Government of Philip Augustus*, 220–25.

32. The Capetian kings did much the same thing but, unofficially. Louis VIII (1223–26) played a limited role in government only after 1220, when he was thirty-three years old. Baldwin, *The Government of Philip of Augustus*, 102–4, 220–25, 340; Strayer, "Normandy and Languedoc," 49.

33. He set a precedent for the later lieutenancies of Charles VI (1380–1422) and Charles VII (1422–61). Richard Barber, *Edward, Prince of Wales and Aquitaine* (New York: Scribners, 1978), 151; James Henderson Burns, *Lordship, Kingship, and Empire: The Idea of Monarchy, 1400–1525* (Oxford: Clarendon Press, 1992), 43; Lewis, *Later Medieval France*, 139–63, 198–228.

34. Barber, *Edward, Prince of Wales*, 115, 175–77.

35. On Aragonese kingship, see Suzanne F. Cawsey, *Kingship and Propaganda: Royal Eloquence and the Crown of Aragon, c. 1200–1450* (Oxford: Oxford University Press, 2002); *Medieval Crown of Aragon*, 13, 72, 155.

36. Lalinde Abadía, *La institución virreinal*, 78-81; *Història de Catalunya*, 1: 342–76.

37. Hillgarth, "The Problem of a Catalan Mediterranean Empire;" Mario del Treppo, "The 'Crown of Aragon' and the Mediterranean," *Journal of European Economic History* 2 (1973): 161–85.

38. Jesús Lalinde Abadía, "Las instituciones de la Corona de Aragón en el siglo XIV," *VIII Congreso de Historia de la Corona de Aragón*, 3 vols. (Valencia: 1970), 2, part 2: 9–52; Francisco Sevillano Colom, "Apuntes para el estudio de

la cancillería de Pedro IV el Ceremonioso," *Anuario de la Historia del Derecho Español* 20 (1950): 137–241; idem, "De la Cancillería de la Corona de Aragón," in *Martínez Ferrando, archivero: miscelánea de estudios dedicados a su memória* (Barcelona: Atenas, 1968), 451–81; idem, "Las cancillerías de Fernando I de Antequera y de Alfonso el Magnánimo," *Anuario de la História del Derecho Español* 35 (1965): 169–216; José Trenchs and Antonio María Aragó, *Cancillerías de la Corona de Aragón y Mallorca desde Jaime I a la muerte de Juan II, Folia Parisiensia*, vol. 1 (Zaragoza: Institución "Fernando el Católica," 1982), 51–52; and Luis G. de Valdeavellano, *Curso de história de las instituciones españolas: de los origines al final de la Edad Media*, 2nd ed. (Madrid: Editorial Revista de Occidente, 1970), 447–49.

39. On Jaume's reign, see *Història de Catalunya*, 1: 194–255; *Medieval Crown of Aragon*, 58–85.

40. *Medieval Crown of Aragon*, 86–94; *Història de Catalunya*, 1: 255–85.

41. Lalinde Abadía, "Virreyes y lugartenientes," 100–111.

42. Various princes served as lieutenants during this period. Alfons (later Alfons II, 1285–91), served 1282–85 (ACA: C 59–62). The lieutenancy of Pere, brother of Alfons II, from 1290 to 1296 overlapped with the reign of their brother, Jaume II (ACA: C 85–89). Alfons III (r. 1327–36) was lieutenant for his father from 1317 to 1327 (ACA: C 363–425). Sicily was the source of many new administrative practices in the Crown of Aragon. See Marta Vanlandingham, *Transforming the State: King, Court and Political Culture in the Realms of Aragon, 1213–1387* (Leiden: Brill, 2002), 10.

43. ACA: C 351–362 (1309–13); *História de Catalunya*, 1: 296–332.

44. Sablonier, "Aragonese Royal Family," 210–39.

45. *Medieval Crown of Aragon*, 101.

46. Lalinde Abadía, "Virreyes y lugartenientes," 108–12.

47. Oriol Oleart i Piquet, "Organització i atribucions de la Cort General," in *Les Corts a Catalunya*, 15–24; Josep María Gay Escoda, "La creació del dret a Corts i el control institicional de la seva observança," in *Les Corts a Catalunya*, 86–96.

48. The *procesos* of the Corts list attendees, the records of legislation, and speeches given before the assembly by the king, queen, *infante, infanta*, or anyone speaking on behalf of an estate. The *procesos* have survived in manuscript form, and many have now been edited and published. The most complete edited records are for Catalunya, collected in the *Cortes*. Rafael Conde, Ana Hernández, Sebastiá Riera, and Manuel Rovira. "Fonts per a l'estudi de les Parlaments de Catalunya. Catáleg dels processos de Corts i Parlaments," in *Les Corts a Catalunya*, 25–61. For the records of the Catalan Corts, see *Constitucions e altres drets de Catalunya*, 3 vols. (Barcelona: 1588, 1704; facsimile edition, Barcelona: Romargraf, 1973). For speeches made by the kings, queens, and other dignitaries, see *Parlaments a les Corts Catalans*, ed. Ricard Albert and Joan Gassiot, Els Nostre Classics 19, 20 (Barcelona: Imprenta Varia, 1928). For Aragón, see the *Cortes del Reino de Aragón, 1357–1451: Extractos y fragmentos de procesos desaparecidos*, ed. Angel Sesma Muñoz and Esteban Sarasa Sánchez (Valencia: Anubar, 1976). The Corts of Valencia have not been edited. See María Rosa Muñoz Pomer and María José Car-

bonell Boria, "Las Cortes Valencianas medievales: aproximación a la historiografía y fuentes para su estudio," in *Les Corts a Catalunya*, 270–81.

49. His father, Pere III, served as lieutenant for his father from 1329 to 1356 (ACA: C 565–584). 202 registers document Joan's long and busy lieutenancy. Although first named lieutenant in 1358, Joan's registers begin in 1361 and end with his coronation in 1387. ACA: C 1390 (one folio in a register devoted to war) and 1607–1808.

50. The parliamentary assemblies are known as the Corts in Catalunya and Valencia, and Cortes in the kingdom of Aragón. *Medieval Crown of Aragon*, 156–58. On medieval parliaments in general, see Antonio Marongiu, *Medieval Parliaments: A Comparative Study*, trans. S. J. Woolf (London: Eyre and Spottiswiide, 1968). On the parliamentary assemblies in Spain in general, see *History of Medieval Spain*, 435–45, 584–91; and Valdeavellano, *Curso de história de las Instituciónes Españolas*, 463–84.

51. *Cortes del Reino de Aragón*, 155.

52. *Doña María de Castilla*, 112.

53. The ACA registers for her reign, dated 1347–75, call her "consort," not lieutenant. ACA: C 1562–1585. Her work with the Catalan Corts is documented in *Cortes*, 2: 135–452. See also Luis González Antón, "Primeras resistancias contra el lugarteniente general-virey en Aragón," *Aragón en la Edad Media* 8 (1984): 303–14, esp. 304–6.

54. For the records of her convocation of the Corts in 1364 and 1365, see *Cortes*, 2: 135–448, and 15: 446–52. See also Mark Meyerson, "Defending Their Jewish Subjects: Elionor of Sicily, Maria de Luna, and the Jews of Morvedre," in Earenfight, *Queenship and Political Power in Medieval and Early Modern Spain*, 55–77; González Antón, "Primeras resistancias," 304–6; *Història de Catalunya*, 1: 370–74.

55. González Antón, "Primeras resistancias," 307; *Història de Catalunya*, 1: 346–9.

56. Dawn Bratsch-Prince, *Violante de Bar (1365–1431)*, trans. María Morrás (Madrid: Ediclás, 2002), 29–35; *Medieval Crown of Aragon*, 121–26.

57. Because Maria was active in Martí's government, the registers run continuously and are misleading—she was not lieutenant for the entire span covered by the registers. Martí was lieutenant for his father (ACA: C 2063–2104, 1372–1402; some registers overlap with those of his personal reign). Silleras-Fernández, "Maria de Luna;" Javierre Mur, *María de Luna*, 52–84; *Medieval Crown of Aragon*, 125–31, 148; *Història de Catalunya*, 1: 397–98, 400, 406–7.

58. Bratsch-Prince, *Violante de Bar*, 35–36; Javierre Mur, *María de Luna*, 52–84; Lalinde Abadía, "Virreyes y lugartenientes," 114; Núria Silleras-Fernández, "Queenship en la Corona de Aragón en la Baja Edad Media: estudio y propuesta terminológica," *La corónica* 32, 1 (Fall 2003): 119–33; idem, "Widowhood and Deception: Ambiguities of Queenship in Late Medieval Crown of Aragon," in *Shell Games: Scams, Frauds and Deceits (1300–1650)*, ed. M. Crane, M. Reeves, and Richard Raiswell (Toronto: Centre for Renaissance and Reformation Studies, 2004), 187–205.

59. *Cortes* 4: 248–400 (Barcelona, 1396); 4: 301–67 (Barcelona, 1396–97).

60. Núria Silleras-Fernández, "Spirit and Force: Politics, Public and Private, in the Reign of Maria de Luna (1396–1406)," in Earenfight, *Queenship and Political Power in Medieval and Early Modern Spain*, 78–90; Javierre Mur, *María de Luna*, 52–84; and González Antón, "Primeras resistancias," 307–8. See ACA: C 2327–2351 for documents on her lieutenancy, and *Cortes* 4: 248 et passim for her convocation of the Corts in 1396.

61. Lalinde Abadía, *La institución virreinal*, 47–49; *Medieval Crown of Aragon*, 127–28.

62. Little is known of her short reign. ACA: C 2355; *Medieval Crown of Aragon*, 130.

63. Most remained lieutenants while some, notably in Sicily between 1291 and 1391, became cadet princes. In 1291, the kingdom of Sicily passed to Jaume II's brother Frederick, who governed first as viceroy and then as king in his own right. After a century as a cadet kingdom, in 1391 it passed once more into direct rule by the Aragonese kingdom when Martí inherited the crown after the death of his brother, Joan I. *Medieval Crown of Aragon*, 90–94.

64. Sicily is the exception to this statement. It was ruled as a cadet kingdom from 1291 until 1391. *Medieval Crown of Aragon*, 87–88, 90–94, 98, 123–27.

65. Harriet Lightman makes a similar point in "Sons and Mothers: Queens and Minor Kings in French Constitutional Law" (Ph.D. dissertation, Bryn Mawr College, 1981), 62–63.

66. Joseph F. O'Callaghan, *The Cortes of Castile-León, 1188–1350* (Philadelphia: University of Pennsylvania Press, 1989), 28–31, 35, 61–62, 73–75, 80, 89–93, 98, 105–6, 123–24, 138–40, 147, 153–54, 196–98.

67. Alfonso was his father's lieutenant from 1413 until his own accession in 1416 (ACA: C 2443–2444). Lalinde Abadía, *La institución virreinal*, 47–49.

68. Ryder, "Evolution of Imperial Government," 332–37.

69. Michelle Zimabist Rosaldo and Louise Lamphere, eds., *Women, Culture, and Society* (Stanford, Calif.: Stanford University Press, 1974), 99–100; Leonard Krieger, "The Idea of Authority in the West," *American Historical Review* 82, 2 (1977): 249–70.

70. Theresa Earenfight, "Political Culture and Political Discourse in the Letters of Queen María of Castile," *La corónica* 32, 1 (Fall 2003): 135–52.

71. On royal administration in general see Valdeavellano, *Curso de história de las instituciones Españolas*, 485–90. On the Aragonese court in general, see Vanlandingham, *Transforming the State*, 23–154; for Naples, see *Kingdom of Naples*, 1–26.

72. *Cortes*, 13: 83–84.

73. The advisory functions are better understood than the judicial ones, partly because the nomenclature is inconsistent and partly because of the poverty of studies on royal justice in Catalunya. The terms Sacrum Consilium, Consell, and Audiència are used rather loosely and it is unclear whether the functions remained the same over time. There is, moreover, no systematic collection of pertinent documents. José María Font y Rius, "Las instituciones de la corona de Aragón en la primera mitad del siglo XV," *Ponencias del IV Congreso de la História de la Corona de Aragón* (Barcelona: Comisión Permanente de los Congresos de la Corona de

Aragón, 1976), 209–23; Ryder, "Evolution of Imperial Government," 345–51; *Kingdom of Naples*, 104; Valdeavellano, *Curso de história de las instituciones Españolas*, 450–59.

74. Before 1439 it may not have been called specifically an *Audiència*, but after that it can be identified as such in most Aragonese realms. It is not clear whether the functions remained the same over time. Ryder, "Evolution of Imperial Government," 345–46.

75. For María's official appointments from 1442 through 1456, see ACA: C Ofi 3114 and 3115.

76. Corts of Barcelona, 1422 (caps. 1, 5), in *Constitucions*, 77, 97; Vanlandingham, *Transforming the State*, 29–38, 55–58, 68–83.

77. *Kingdom of Naples*, 142.

78. Corts of Barcelona, 1422 (caps. 6, 9), *Constitucions*, 73, 98; Sevillano Colom, "Cancillerías de Fernando I," 186–88; Valdeavellano, *Curso de história de las instituciones Españolas*, 603–4; *Spanish Kingdoms*, 2: 282; *Kingdom of Naples*, 18–20.

79. On the mestre racional, see VanLandingham, *Transforming the State*, 120–30, 142–46, 150–54; Angeles Masia de Ros, "El maestre racional en la Corona de Aragón: una pragmatica de Juan II sobre dicho cargo," *Hispania* 10 (1950): 25–60; *Kingdom of Naples*, 18–20, 26.

80. *Alfonso the Magnanimous*, 360–61.

81. *Cortes*, 13: 84.

82. *Constitucions*, 94; Vanlandingham, *Transforming the State*, 83–87.

83. *Kingdom of Naples*, 107.

84. AHCB: LC VI–15, 78r–v, 15 June 1450; doc. 227 in José María Madurell Marimón, *Mensajeros Barceloneses en la Corte de Napoles de Alfonso V de Aragón, 1435–1458* (Barcelona: Consejo Superior de Investigaciones Científicas, 1963), 293.

85. Valdeavellano, *Curso de história de las instituciones Españolas*, 556–58, 576.

86. The case consumed dozens of folios during 1448 and 1449, starting with ACA: C Sec 3227, 4r–5r, 13 May 1448 and passim.

87. See ACA: C Com 2948–3113. Register 2948 covers just the brief period in 1419 when María was lieutenant but before he left for Naples. There are sixteen registers for the lieutenancy from 1420–23, and ninety-nine for the period 1432–53. The rest pertain to the period of her lieutenancy in Valencia or to María's work as queen alone, not queen-lieutenant from 1420 to 1448. Beatrice Canellas and Alberto Torra, *Los Registros de la Cancillería de Alfonso el Magnánimo* (Madrid: Ministerio de Educación, Cultura y Deporte, Centro de Publicaciones, 2000), 51.

88. ACA: C Cur 2657, fol. 50r, 8 April 1448.

89. *Kingdom of Naples*, 243–49.

90. The great seal measured 84 mm in diameter, the common seal was 48 mm, and the small seal 30 mm. All surviving impressions in red wax are preserved in the Arxiu de la Corona d'Aragó and illustrated in Santiago Sobrequés i Vidal and Jaume Sobrequés i Callicó, *La guerra civil Catalana del segle XV*, 2 vols. (Barcelona, Edicions 62, 1973), 48; *Doña María de Castilla*, 97.

91. These official seals of the lieutenant general of Catalunya, used by María in her capacity as lieutenant general of Catalunya, bear the eight vertical bands that represent the coat of arms of the principality in a lozenge surrounded by a foliate design. Her personal seals included a gold seal emblazoned with her arms and a circular seal also used by the king that bore the shield of Crown of Aragon. Her personal seals were destroyed at her death. *Doña María de Castilla*, 96–98; *Kingdom of Naples*, 243–49. On women and seals in general, see Brigitte Bedos Rezak, "Women, Seals, and Power in Medieval France," in *Women and Power in the Middle Ages*, ed. Mary Erler and Maryanne Kowaleski (Athens: University of Georgia Press, 1988), 61–82.

92. *Kingdom of Naples*, 243–49.

93. Masia de Ros, "El maestre racional," 35–36.

94. *Kingdom of Naples*, 191.

95. Ryder, "Evolution of Imperial Government," 351–54; *Medieval Crown of Aragon*, 156.

96. *Kingdom of Naples*, 18–20, 57, 170, 191; Valdeavellano, *Curso de história de las instituciones Españolas*, 491–92; Font i Rius, "Las instituciones de la corona de Aragón," 209–11.

97. *Cortes*, 13: 84. Valdeavellano, *Curso de história de las instituciones Españolas*, 514–17, 547, 550–52. Corts of Barcelona, 1422 (cap. 2, 19), *Constitucions*, 156, 187.

98. For María's official appointments, see ACA: C Off, 3114 (1442–58) and 3115 (1446–56). See also Jesús Lalinde Abadía, *La gobernación general en la Corona de Aragón* (Madrid and Zaragoza: Consejo Superior de Investigaciones Científicas, 1963), 234, 301–63; idem, *La jurisdicción real inferior en Cataluña ("Corts, veguers, batlles")* (Barcelona: Ayuntamiento de Barcelona, 1966), 123, 179–209; Font i Rius, "Las instituciones de la corona de Aragón," 216–19.

99. Corts of Barcelona, 1422 (caps. 2 and 23), *Constitucions*, 107, 187; Lalinde Abadía, *Gobernación general*, 18, 69, 89, 152–53, 179–81.

100. The documentation for her first lieutenancy can be found in ACA: C CR, Caja 10 (1419–20), letters 1230–1367; ACA: C DR 3109 (1418–19), 3162 (1416–18); ACA: C Com 2948–2966 (1419–27); ACA: C ComSS 3110–3111 (1416–33); ACA: C Div 3116–3122 (1420–23); ACA: C Cur 3163–3169 (1420–24); ACA: C CSS 3218–3219 (1422–4); ACA: C Sec 3222–3224 (1420–23); ACA: C Sent 3237–3240 (1420–23); ACA: C Itin 3260–3261 (1420–3); ACA: C Var 3276 (1416–46); *Cortes*, 12: 55–351; and 16: 50–115; Conde et al., "Fonts per a l'estudi," 25–61.

101. *Alfonso the Magnanimous*, 67–72.

102. Conde et al., "Fonts per a l'estudi," 25–61. Records of individual sessions, are edited in *Cortes*: 13: 1–616 (1421–23); 14: 1–355 (1429–30); 19: 1–453 (1436); 20: 312–37 (1439); 20: 349–443 (1440); 21: 1–133 (1442–43); 21: 191–380 (1446–48); 22: 1–304 (1449–53).

103. Luisa María Sánchez Aragones, *Cortes, monarquía y ciudades en Aragón durante el reinado de Alfonso el Magnánimo (1416-1458)* (Zaragoza: Institución Fernando el Católico, 1994), 222–23, 420–23. The Aragonese nobility was split into an upper (*ricoshombres*) and lower (*caballeros*) estate, giving that assembly four

separate estates, not three. Luis González Anton, *Las Cortes de Aragón* (Zaragoza: Librería General, 1978), 86–88.

104. María may not have been present at the 1438 Cortes because at the time she and Juan of Navarre were co-lieutenants. Muñoz Pomer and Carbonell Boria, "Las Cortes Valencianas medievales," 270–81.

105. *Kingdom of Naples*, 125; Lalinde Abadía, "Los Parlamentos," 153–59.

106. Gay Escoda, "La creació del dret a Corts," 93; Coral Cuadrada, "El greuges del Sagramental en les Corts catalanes (segles XIV–XV)," in *Les Corts a Catalunya*, 208–16. For Aragón, see Sánchez Aragonés, *Cortes, monarquía y ciudades en Aragón*, 191.

107. Jaume Sobrequés i Callicó and Santiago Sobrequés i Vidal regard the Compromise and the introduction of a Castilian dynasty, accompanied by distinctly different attitudes toward rulership, as the first step in the loss of Catalan independence. Sobrequés i Callicó, *El pactisme a Catalunya: una praxi política en la història del pais* (Barcelona: Edicions 62, 198), 212–23; idem, "El pactisme en l'origen de la crisi política catalana: les Corts de Barcelona de 1413," in *Les Corts a Catalunya*, 79–85; Santiago Sobrequés i Vidal, "La petita noblesa catalana i l'interregne de 1410–1412," *Estudis d'Historia Medieval* 3 (extract) (Barcelona: Institut d'Estudis Catalans, 1970). For a slightly less jaundiced view, see Manuel Dualde and José Camarena, *El Compromiso de Caspe* (Zaragoza: Institución Fernando el Católico, Diputación Provincial de Zaragoza, 1971); and Valdeavellano, *Curso de história de las instituciónes españolas*, 425–26.

108. Santiago Sobrequés i Vidal, *La alta nobleza del norte en la Guerra Civil Catalana de 1462–1472* (Zaragoza: Institución "Fernando el Católico," 1966), 11–43; and idem, *Els barons de Catalunya i el Compromís de Casp* (Barcelona: Rafael Damau, 1966).

109. The term "pactism" is a modern coinage. Sobrequés i Callicó, *El pactisme a Catalunya*, 8–10.

110. For comparison, see Castile, see O'Callaghan, *Cortes of Castile-León*, 1–40; and Evelyn Procter, *Curia and Cortes in León and Castile, 1072–1295* (Cambridge: Cambridge University Press, 1980), 1–93. For France, see Lewis, *Later Medieval France*, 328–74; J. Russell Major, *Representative Institutions in Renaissance France, 1421–1559* (Madison: University of Wisconsin Press, 1960), 50–116; and Marongiu, *Medieval Parliaments*, 95–105. For England, see two essays in *The English Parliament in the Middle Ages*, ed. R. G. Davies and J. H. Denton (Philadelphia: University of Pennsylvania Press, 1982): A. L. Brown, "Parliament, c. 1377–1422," 109–40, and A. R. Myers, "Parliament, 1422–1509," 141–84; Marongiu, *Medieval Parliaments*, 76–94.

111. Peter Rycraft, "The Role of the Catalan 'Corts' in the Late Middle Ages," *English Historical Review* 89 (1974): 241–69, esp. 242; Donald Kagay, ed. and trans., *The Usatges of Barcelona: The Fundamental Law of Catalonia* (Philadelphia: University of Pennsylvania Press, 1994), 49.

112. Font i Rius, "Las instituciones de la corona de Aragón," 216–19; and Carme Batlle i Gallart, *La crisis social y económica a mediados del siglo XV*, 2 vols. (Barcelona: Consejo Superior de Investigaciones Científicas, 1973), 1: 133–64.

113. The coronation of the Aragonse kings, if there was one, also fell to the archbishop of Tarragona. Rycraft, "The Role of the Catalan 'Corts,'" 258.

114. Donald Kagay, "The Development of the Corts in the Crown of Aragon, 1064–1327" (Ph.D. dissertation, Fordham University, 1981), 13–15.

115. *Alfonso the Magnanimous*, 59, 255, 259, 261, 313, 367–68, 407–17, 420–21; *Kingdom of Naples*, 38–41, 97–98.

116. *Kingdom of Naples*, 18–19.

117. Carme Batlle y Gallart, "El bisbe Arnau Roger de Pallars i la seu d'Urgell (1437–61)," *Estudios Históricos y Documentos de los Archivos de Protologos* VI (1978): 219–28; Santiago Sobrequés i Vidal, *Els barons de Catalunya* (Barcelona: Editorial Teide, 1957), 189–91, 203–205, 256–57; idem, "Una illustre família banyolina: els Samasó," in *Societat i estructura política de la Girona medieval*, ed. Santiago Sobrequés i Vidal (Barcelona: Curial, 1975), 285–300, esp. 285–93.

118. *Cortes*, 22: 5–16.

119. Sobrequés i Vidal, *La alta nobleza*, 14–15, 24, 39–40; Jesús Lalinde Abadía, "Los Parlamentos y demas instituciones representatives," in *La Corona d'Aragona e il Mediterraneo: aspetti e problemi comuni, da Alfonso il Magnanimo a Ferdinando il Cattolico (1416–1516): IX Congreso de Historia de la Corona de Aragón*, 4 vols. (Naples: Societá Napoletana di Storia Patria, 1978) 2: 103–79, esp. 128.

120. Towns had taken part in Catalan assemblies since 1214 and the number of towns represented gradually became fixed at eighteen in Catalunya and thirteen in Valencia. José María Font i Rius, "Origines del regimen municipal de Cataluña," *Anuario de Historia del Derecho Español* 16 (1945): 388–529; 17 (1946): 229–585, esp. 558, 562–65; Lalinde Abadía, "Los Parlamentos," 124–29; Kagay, "Development of the Corts," 67–71; *Medieval Crown of Aragon*, 13, 72, 80–81, 155; and Rycraft, "The Role of the Catalan 'Corts,'" 254–55.

121. Batlle y Gallart, *La Crisis social y económica de Barcelona*, 1: 137–64; Rycraft, "The Role of the Catalan 'Corts,'" 254–7.

122. James Amelang, *Honored Citizens of Barcelona: Patrician Culture and Class Relations, 1490–1714* (Princeton, N.J.: Princeton University Press, 1986), 25–8; Augustí Durán i Sanpere, *Barcelona i la seva història*, 3 vols. (Barcelona: Editorial Curiel, 1972–75), 1: 141–43; Batlle i Gallart, *La crisis social y económica*, 1: 144–55, 168–71.

123. Durán i Sanpere, *Barcelona i la seva història*, 1: 141–43, 282–95; Font i Rius, "Origines del regimen municipal de Cataluña," 418–48; Francesc Carreras Candi, *Barcelona*, vols. 3 and 4 of *Geografía general de Catalunya*, 11 vols. (reprint of original, undated nineteenth-century edition (Barcelona: Edicions Catalanes, 1980); idem, "Hegemonía de Barcelona en Cataluña durante el siglo XV," *Discursos leídos ante la Real Academia de Buenas Letras de Barcelona* (Barcelona: Jesús Roviralta, 1898).

124. Alan Ryder, "Cloth and Credit: Aragonese War Finance in the Mid-Fifteenth Century," *War and Society* 2, 1 (May 1984): 1–21, esp. 2–4; and del Treppo, "The 'Crown of Aragon' and the Mediterranean," 166–69.

125. *Constitucions*, 156.

182 Notes to Pages 61–62

126. Carme Batlle i Gallart, "Una famlilia barcelonesa: les Deztorrent," *Anuario de Estudios Medievales* 1 (1964): 471–88; idem, "La oligarquía de Barcelona a fines del siglo XV: el partido de Deztorrent," *Acta historica et archaeologia mediaevalia* 7–8 (1986–87): 321–35; Judith Berg Sobré, *Behind the Altar Table: The Development of the Painted Retable in Spain, 1350–1500* (Columbia: University of Missouri Press, 1989), 288–97; Durán i Sanpere, *Barcelona i la seva història*, 1: 282–95.

127. The summonses were issued 18 March, 1421. The first session took place 26 May in Tortosa, moved to Barcelona on 23 June 1421, and concluded 20 July 1423. *Cortes*, 13: 1–11. Conde, et al., "Fonts per a l'estudi," 39; *Doña María de Castilla*, 113–14; *Alfonso the Magnanimous*, 103.

128. The abbots of Montserrat, the holiest religious place in Catalunya, and of Poblet, the royal burial site, generally spoke on behalf of the prelates. Nine bishops represented the sees of Barcelona, Elna (Perpinyà), Girona, Lleída, Mallorca, Vic, Tarazona, Tortosa, Urgell. Abbots from the monasteries of Montserrat, Poblet, Santes Creus, Scala Dei, and Sant Jeroni, sat in their own right, joined by senior officers of the military orders. Batlle i Gallart, "El bisbe Arnau Roger de Pallars" 218–22; Rycraft, "The Role of the Catalan 'Corts,'" 257–59.

129. "Jatsia dupten que lo cas de conuocacio de Cort puxa esser comunicat per lo dit Senyor Rey a nenguna persona de qualseuol dignitat o condicio situ." *Cortes*, 13: 40; *Parlaments a les Corts Catalans*, 140–50.

130. "Possitis ulterius Curias aut Parlamentum celebrare et tenere regnicolis cuiuslibet dictorum regnorum, et Principatus pro Curiis sive Parlamento ut volueritis congregare, et in ipsis Curiis Parlamento aut congregationibus foros, constiticiones sive capita edere, concedere aut facere et omnia alia facere et exercere que Nos facere possemus, si personaliter existeremus in eis." *Cortes*, 13: 86.

131. "Protesten e retenen empero ab deguda e humil reverencia los dits convocats que, per aquest consentiment, aquesta vegada tantsolament fet e donat per los sguarts dessus dits, no sia fet preiudici algu en esdevenidor tacitament ne expressa, directament ni indirecta al dit Principat ni als Usatges de Barchinona, constitucions, actes o capitols de Cort de Cathalunya libertats, franqueses, usos of costumes en general o en particular a aquelles en universal als prelats ecclesiastiques persones, magnats, barons, militars e homens de ciutats e viles Reyals. . . . Encara protesten es retenen, que la present Cort convocacio, celebracio e finament daquella no sien ne puxen esser tretes a consequencia en algun temps en semblant cars maior o menor ne puscha esser engendrat preiudici algu en proprietat o possessio vel quasi al dit Principat or Braços daquell de les protestacions e retencions nos entenen a departir per algun acte contrari subsequent." *Cortes*, 13: 40–42.

132. "Ab aquesta present Constitucio statuim, e ordenam, que de aci avant, com lo dit Senyor, o successors seus hauran convocada Cort, o Parlament en alguna Ciutat, Vila, o Loc del Principat de Cathalunya, e lo dit Senyor Rey, o successors seus no seran personalment en la Ciutat, Vila, o Los assignada, o asignat, la dita Cort, o Parlament no pugan esser prorogada, o porrogat en una vegada, o en moltas sino per quaranta dies: e si dins aquells lo dit Senyor, o altre successor seu no sera vingut personalment a la dita Ciutat, Vila, o Loc, la dita convocacio

e unjuntcio de la Cort, o Parlament sien reipsa circunducta, e absolta." *Constitucions*, 41.

133. This session also established criteria for royal officials in the Audiència, chancery, treasury and finance office. *Cortes*, 13: 73, 77, 97–98, 112, 153, 156, 160, 164–65, 187, 411–12; *Constitucions*, 73, 77, 93–94, 97–98, 107, 109, 112, 144, 153, 156, 160, 187, 288, 292, 400, 411–12, 508–9.

134. Antonio de la Torre y del Cerro, "Orígenes de la Deputació del General de Catalunya," *Discursos Leídos en la Real Academia de Buenas Letras de Barcelona* (Barcelona: Atlas Geográfico, 1923), 1–52, esp. 25–28. On the Diputación del Reino, a similar institution in Aragón, see González Anton, *Las Cortes de Aragón*, 129–33.

135. María Teresa Ferrer i Mallol, "Origen i evolució de la Diputació del General," in *Les Corts a Catalunya*, 152–59; Ignacio Rubio y Cambronero, *La Deputació del General de Catalunya en los siglos XV y XVI*, 2 vols. (Barcelona: Diputació Provincial, 1950, 1: 149–55, 165–69; 2: 209–14; and Josep María Sans i Travé and Consepció Ballart i Marsol, "El catàleg de Diputats i Oidors de Comptes de la Generalitat de Catalunya (1359–1710) de Pere Serra i Postius," *Estudis Històrcs i Documents dels Arxius de Protocols* 8 (1980): 63–118; Federico Udina i Martorell, "Importància i influència de la Cort General i la Diputació del General a Catalunya," in *Les Corts a Catalunya*, 129–41, esp. 138–39.

136. Durán i Sanpere, *Barcelona i la seva història*, 1: 232–34; *Medieval Crown of Aragon*, 174, 180.

137. They exercised an executive authority unmatched even by the Florentine Monte di Pietat or the Genoese Casa di San Giorgio. Rycraft, "The Role of the Catalan 'Corts,'" 249.

138. Ferrer i Mallol, "Origen i evolució de la Diputació del General," 152–59; Rycraft, "The Role of the Catalan 'Corts,'" 253; Udina i Martorell, "Importància i influència de la Cort General i la Diputació del General," 129–41; Valdeavellano, *Curso de história de las Institucónes Españolas*, 481–83; Jaime Vicens Vives, "La transformació de la generalitat medieval," in *Obra Dispersa*, 2 vols. (Barcelona: Editorial Vicens-Vives, 1967; originally published, 1936), 1: 30–43.

139. Javierre Mur, *María de Luna*, 52–84; Rycraft, "The Role of the Catalan 'Corts,'" 251–52; Udina i Martorell, "Importància i influència de la Cort General," 138–39.

140. Font i Rius, "Las Institucónes de la corona de Aragón," 212–14; Rycraft, "The Role of the Catalan 'Corts,'" 247.

141. "Entes hauem que denant vosaltres hauets carrech en virtut de Constitucio de Cathalunya de mantenir e deffendre los Usatges, Constitucions e capitols de Cort comuns a tots los tres Braces . . . ," *Cortes*, 14: 200. For precedent, see *Cortes*, 12: 92, 192, 199, 277–80.

142. The Corts enacted measures pertaining to minters and moneylender, inheritance, lawyers, and notaries; nineteen personal petitions were granted. *Constitucions*, 128, 136, 164–65, 172–73, 285–86; *Cortes*, 13: 41, 136, 172, 288–89, 357, 455–63; José Coroleu and José Pella y Forgas, *Las Cortes Catalanas* (Barcelona: Revista Historica Latina, 1876), 65–68, 239–43.

184   Notes to Pages 63–65

143. *Cortes*, 13: 521–25; Ana Hernández Calleja, "Tipología de los procesos de Cortes," in *Les Corts a Catalunya*, 62–70; Gay Escoda, "La creació del dret a Corts," 93; *Constitucions*, 44–45.

144. "Lo fruyt de las Leys es observança de aquellas, en altra manera en va son ordenadas: en per amor de aço, desijants, los Usatges de Barcelona, Constitucions, e Capitols de Cort de Cathalunya, e altras leys de la Terra, e encara los Privilegis Generals, e Communs a tots los tres Braços atorgats, esser observats, de assentiment, e approbatio de la dita Cort donam facultat, e statuim, e ordinam, que si sera cas, que lo Senyor Rey, o nos. . . ." *Constitucions*, 45–46; reprinted in Antonio García Gallo, *Manual de Historia de Derecho Español*, 2nd ed., 2 vols. (Madrid: 1964), 2: 967–68.

145. Kagay, *Usatges*, 49; *Los Trasámaras*, 707–11.

146. Also known as the *Curiale* or *de Curiis*, the work is collected with Callis's other works in *Antiquiories Barchinomensium Leges, quas vulgas usaticos appellat cum commentariis supremorum Juris Consultorum Jacobi Calicii* (Barcelona: 1594). Juan Beneyto-Perez, "Jaime Callís y su 'Tratado de las Cortes,'" *Recueil de Travaux d'Histoire et de Philologie* 3, 34 (1952): 55–65; Francisco Elías de Tejada, *Las doctrinas políticas en la Cataluña medieval* (Barcelona: Ayma, 1950), 181–86; Kagay, *Usatges*, 48; and Lalinde Abadía, "Los Parlamentos," 162.

147. The Catalans commissioned Jaume Callís and another jurist, Narcís de Sant Dionís, to compile all the laws, rights, privileges, constitutions, and capitols of the Corts and translate them into Catalan. This compilation, known as the *Constitucions e altres drets de Catalunya*, was also completed in 1422. Later editions in 1495, 1588–89, and 1704 incorporated parliamentary laws and royal decrees. Beneyto-Perez, "Jaime Callís y su 'Tratado de las Cortes,'" 55–65.

148. For the text of this *Usatge*, see *Constitucions*, 37; Kagay, *Usatges*, 48–49.

149. Francesch Eiximenis, *Regiment de la Cosa Publica*, ed. Daniel de Molins de Rei (Barcelona: Editorial Barcino, 1928). See also Jill Webster, *Francesc Eixemenis: la societat catalana al segle XIV* (Barcelona: Edicions 62, 1967), 11–19; Elías de Tejada, *Las doctrinas políticas en la Cataluña medieval*, 138–63.

150. Eiximenis, *Regiment de la Cosa Pública*, cap. 15, in Webster, *Francesc Eixemenis*, 14–15.

151. He dedicated the *Regiment de la Cosa Pública* to the *jurats* of Valencia and a copy was kept in the town hall in Valencia for public consultation. Carme Battle i Gallart, *L'expansió baixmedieval (segles XIII–XV)*, vol. 3 of *Història de Catalunya*, ed. Pierre Vilar (Barcelona: Edicions 62, 1988), 335–38.

152. Alfonso was a master practitioner of divide and rule who intervened regularly in urban government and manipulated elections. Jaime Vicens Vives, "Alfonso el Magnánimo y Barcelona," in *Obra Dispersa de Jaume Vicens Vives*, 2 vols. (Barcelona: Editorial Vicens-Vives, 1967), 1: 251–60; *Kingdom of Naples*, 18–19; Sánchez Aragonés, *Cortes, monarquía y ciudades en Aragón*, 155, 393–95.

153. Angus MacKay, *Spain in the Middle Ages: From Frontier to Empire, 1000–1500* (London: Macmillan, 1977), 105.

154. For a translation of the pledge, see *History of Medieval Spain*, 581–82. See also González Anton, *Las Cortes de Aragón*, 23–30; Ralph Giesey, *If Not,*

Not: The Oath of the Aragonese and the Legendary Laws of Sobrarbe (Princeton, NJ: Princeton University Press, 1968). Kagay notes that this oath had less force in Valencia; see "The Development of the Corts," 179.

155. Font y Rius, "Las instituciones de la corona de Aragón," 209-23.

156. Lalinde Abadía, *La institución virreinal*, 53-60; Sobriqués i Callicó, *El pactisme a Catalunya*; 7-34; Elías de Tejada, *Doctrinas políticas*, 180-209.

157. Lalinde Abadía, "Los Parlamentos," 2: 113-22. See Valdeavellano, *Curso de história de las* Instituciónes *Españolas*, 478-81.

158. Rycraft, "The Role of the Catalan 'Corts,'" 253.

159. *Kingdom of Naples*, 229-35; *Alfonso the Magnanimous*, 358-92; *Medieval Crown of Aragon*, 140.

160. A copy of her oath is in García Gallo, *Manual de Historia de Derecho Español*, 2: 803-4.

161. González Anton, *Las Cortes de Aragón*, 112; Sánchez Aragonés, *Cortes, monarquía y ciudades en Aragón*, 137, 420-26; *Cortes del Reino de Aragón*, 89-95.

162. Sánchez Aragonés, *Cortes, monarquía y ciudades en Aragón*, 420; *Los Trasámaras*, 379-80.

163. *Alfonso the Magnanimous*, 72, 114-15.

164. On the Catalan economic crisis in 1427, see Jaime Vicens Vives, Luís Suárez Fernández, and Claude Carrére, "La economía de los paises de la Corona de Aragón en la baja Edad Media," in *VI Congres d'historia de la Corona d'Arago* (Cagliari: Artes Graficas Arges, 1957), rept. in *Obra dispersa de Jaume Vicens Vives*, ed. M. Battloni and E. Giralt, 2 vols. (Barcelona: Editorial Vicens-Vives, 1967), 2: 220-37; and Claude Carrére, *Barcelone: centre économique a l'époque des difficultés, 1380-1462*, 2 vols. (Paris: Mouton, 1967), 718-52.

165. *Medieval Crown of Aragon*, 143; *Alfonso the Magnanimous*, 153-74; *Los Trastámaras*, 385-92, 711-15.

166. *Alfonso the Magnanimous*, 158-60; *Los Trastámaras*, 385-92; *Medieval Crown of Aragon*, 143; *Història de Catalunya*, 2: 81-82.

167. Sánchez Aragonés, *Cortes, monarquía y ciudades en Aragón*, 219-21, 421; *Cortes del Reino de Aragón*, 107-30.

168. The summons was issued on 19 September 1429, the first session was held on 19 November, and the assembly concluded on 11 May 1430. *Cortes*, 14: 1-355; 15: 1-130; Conde et al., "Fonts per a l'estudi," 39; Coroleu and Pella y Forgas, *Las Cortes Catalanas*, 245-46.

169. González Anton, *Las Cortes de Aragón*, 112; Sánchez Aragonés, *Cortes, monarquía y ciudades en Aragón*, 219-21, 421; *Cortes del Reino de Aragón*, 107-30; Esteban Sarasa Sánchez, "Las Cortes de Aragón en la edad media (estado de la cuestión y planteamiento general)," in *Les Corts a Catalunya*, 299-301.

170. Muñoz Pomer and Carbonell Boria, "Las Cortes Valencianas medievales" 279. For Alfonso's whereabouts, see Andrés Giménez-Soler, *Itinerario del rey don Alfonso de Aragón i de Nápoles* (Zaragoza: Maríano Escar, 1909), 97-106.

171. *Los Trastámaras*, 385-91.

172. *Cortes*, 14: 81-82, 118, 221-23, 315.

173. Coroleu and Pella y Forgas, *Las Cortes Catalanas*, 244.

186   Notes to Pages 68–70

174. *Cortes*, 17: 180–83.

175. *Alfonso the Magnanimous*, 175–95; *Los Trastámaras*, 697–706, 719–24; *Medieval Crown of Aragon*, 143–44.

176. *Cortes* 17: 1–328; 18: 329–444.

177. *Cortes*, 17: 215: "E per ço com al dit Senyor cove de necessitat partirse de present de la dita Cort e encara exit e anar, Deus volent, fors sos regnes e terres . . . constituheix e crea loctinent sua general en lo dit Principat de Catalunya e president en la Cort, per continuar aquella, en absencia del dit Senyor, la Reyna sa muller, e dona e atorga plen poder a la dita Reyna." For the details of Alfonso's trip, see *Alfonso the Magnanimous*, 179–83.

178. *Alfonso the Magnanimous*, 183–84; *Doña María de Castilla*, 87.

179. ARV: MR 9050, fol. 3v–4v; *Cortes*, 20: 432–5. This was announced in a letter patent dated 14 May 1432. ACA: C Var 3276: fols. 139v–142r.

180. ARV: MR 9050, fol. 3v–4v; *Cortes*, 20: 432–35.

181. The Crown archives do not include any registers for Juan during this period, and Jaime Vicens Vives does not mention any governmental actions taken by Juan until 1454. Jaime Vicens Vives, *Juan II de Aragón (1398–1479): monarquía y revolución en la España del siglo XV* (Barcelona: Editorial Teide, 1953); *Alfonso the Magnanimous*, 194.

182. Ryder notes that Alfonso was especially diligent in supervising his Italian lieutenants and viceroys. "Evolution of Imperial Government," 338.

183. Lalinde Abadía, *La institución virreinal*, 60.

184. *Alfonso the Magnanimous*, 130–31.

185. Even the joint lieutenancy of Juan and María in Catalunya lasted only two years, from November 1438 to October 1440. This Corts is discussed further in Chapter 5.

186. Jaume Safont was present at the scene and wrote a first-hand description of the battle. ACA: G 4, fol. 23, 5 August 1435; doc. 29, Madurell Marimon, *Mensajeros Barceloneses*, 101–103. The Diputació included a lengthy account of the king's capture. *Dietari de la Diputació del General de Cathalunya*, ed. the Arxui de la Corona d'Aragó, vol. 1: 1411–58 (Barcelona: Diputación Provincial de Barcelona, 1974), 102–4. See also *Alfonso the Magnanimous*, 203–209; *Història de Catalunya*, 2: 54–56.

187. AHCB: LC VI-4, 107, doc. 39 in *Mensajeros Barceloneses*, 109–10.

188. The ambassadors—Joan Llull, Joan Bussot, and Francesch Castelló—were in Naples from 2 June 1435 to 12 June 1436. The letters list the prisoners, the conditions of their imprisonment, and suggestions for their release. Madurell Marimon, *Mensajeros Barceloneses*, 10–24, docs. 24–103. See, for example, letters from Castelló to the Consell de Cent: 6 September (doc. 47, pp. 115–18), 7–8 September (doc. 48, pp. 118–21); 9 September (doc. 50, pp. 122–23); 9 September (doc. 51, pp. 123–24); 12 September (doc. 52, pp. 124–25); from Castelló and Bussot, 16 September (doc. 53, pp. 125–26); from Castelló and Bussot, 23 September (doc. 54, pp. 127–28).

189. *Doña María de Castilla*, 115–20; *Los Trastámaras*, 393–96.

Chapter 4. A Permanent Lieutenancy, 1436–48

1. Alan Ryder, "The Evolution of Imperial Government in Naples Under Alfonso V of Aragon," in *Europe in the Late Middle Ages*, ed. John Rigby Hale, John Roger Loxdale Highfield, and Beryl Smalley (Evanston, Ill.: Northwestern University Press, 1965), 332–57, esp. 333–35; Jesús Lalinde Abadía, *La gobernación general en la Corona de Aragón* (Madrid and Zaragoza: Consejo Superior de Investigaciones Científicas, 1963), 162–63; idem, *La institución virreinal en Cataluña (1471–1716)* (Barcelona: Instituto de Estudios Mediterráneos, 1964), 305–6; idem, "Los Parlamentos y demas institucións representativas," in *La Corona d'Aragona e il Mediterraneo: aspetti e problemi comuni, da Alfonso il Magnanimo a Ferdinando il Cattolico (1416–1516): IX Congreso de Historia de la Corona de Aragón*, 4 vols. (Naples: Societá Napoletana di Storia Patria, 1978), 2: 103–79, 160–64; Federico Udina i Martorell, "La organización político-administrativa de la Corona de Aragón (1416–1516)," in *La Corona d'Aragona e il Mediterraneo: aspetti e problemi comuni, da Alfonso il Magnanimo a Ferdinando il Cattolico (1416–1516)*, 4 vols. (Naples: Societá Napoletana di Storia Patria, 1978), 2: 74.

2. ACA: C Sec 2695, fol. 61r–v.

3. José María Madurell Marimón, *Mensajeros Barceloneses en la Corte de Nápoles de Alfonso V de Aragón, 1435–1458* (Barcelona: Consejo Superior de Investigaciones Científicas, 1963), 7–72.

4. Francesch Castelló to the Barcelona town council, 12 September 1435, AHCB: LCO X-7, 144r–v, doc. 52 in Madurell Marimón, *Mensajeros Barceloneses*, 124–25.

5. Francesch Despla and Guillem Deztorrent to the Barcelona town council, 9 March 1444, AHCB: LC VI-10, 15r–16v, doc. 184 in Madurell Marimón, *Mensajeros Barceloneses*, 240–42.

6. Antoni Vinyes to the Barcelona town council, 18 August 1442, AHCB: LCO X-12, 88r–v, doc. 159 in Madurell Marimón, *Mensajeros Barceloneses*, 213–14.

7. Mateu Pujades to the town council of Barcelona, 4 June 1442, AHCB: LCO X-12, 61r–v, doc. 154 in Madurell Marimón, *Mensajeros Barceloneses*, 211.

8. Bernat Fivaller and Pere Joan de Santcliment to the town council of Barcelona. AHCB: LCO X-23, 97r–v, doc. 436 in Madurell Marimón, *Mensajeros Barceloneses*, 475–76.

9. *Doña María de Castilla*, 98–104.

10. For Aragón see Luisa María Sánchez Aragonés, *Cortes, monarquía y ciudades en Aragón durante el reinado de Alfonso el Magnánimo (1416–1458)* (Zaragoza: Institución Fernando el Católico, 1994); and Esteban Sarasa Sánchez, "Las Cortes de Aragón en la edad media (estado de la cuestión y planteamiento general)," in *Les Corts a Catalunya*, 296–303. For Valencia see María Rosa Muñoz Pomer and María José Carbonell Boria, "Las Cortes Valencianas medievales: aproximación a la historiografía y fuentes para su estudio," in *Les Corts a Catalunya*, 270–81; and José Trenchs Odena and Vicente Pons Alós, "La nobleza valenciana a través de las convocatorias a Cortes (siglos XV–XVI)," in *Les Corts a Catalunya*, 368–83.

11. *Los Trastámaras*, 393.

12. Carme Batlle i Gallart, *La Crisis social y económica de Barcelona a mediados del siglo XV*, 2 vols. (Barcelona: Consejo Superior de Investigaciones Científicas, 1973), 2: 398-99.

13. The sessions of these important meetings are poorly understood because the *procesos* have not been edited. Chronicles, letters, and other narrative sources report its occurrence, and some of the proceedings were included in the records of the Consell de Cent and the Diputació del General. See Madurell Marimón, *Mensajeros Barceloneses* and the *Llibre de les solemnitats de Barcelona*, vol. 1, *1424-1546*, ed. Agustí Duran i Sanpere and Josep Sanabre (Barcelona: Institució Patxot, 1930). For the Diputació, see *Dietari de la Deputació del General*, ed. the Arxui de la Corona d'Aragó, vol. 1: 1411-58 (Barcelona: Diputación Provincial de Barcelona, 1974). See also Rafael Conde, Ana Hernández, Sebastiá Riera, and Manuel Rovira, "Fonts per a l'estudi de les Parlaments de Catalunya. Catáleg dels processos de Corts i Parlaments," in *Les Corts a Catalunya*, 25-61, esp. 41; and José Coroleu and José Pella y Forgas, *Las Cortes Catalanas* (Barcelona: Revista Historica Latina, 1876), 246-9.

14. "... el qual notoriament es absent de sus regnos e terras la ha constituhido, creado su lugarteniente en todos sus regnos e tierras e le ha dado pleno e bastant poder general e encara special para poder clamar, convocar, celebrar, convocar o servar cortes en cada uno de los ditos sus regnos e tierras.... E mandada la dita scedula e la present respuesta con el poder por el senyor Rey a la dita Reyna atorgado e dado eyeer insertades en el processo de la dita Cort." Extract from Cortes of Monzón-Alcañiz, 1436-36, ACA General Procesos de las Cortes, no. 976, fols. 42v-43, quoted in Sánchez Aragonés, *Cortes, monarquía y ciudades en Aragón*, 141, n. 23.

15. AHCB: Del 1433-37, fols. 157v-158v, 12-15 November 1435, cited in Madurell Marimón, *Mensajeros Barceloneses*, 23-24.

16. "... per la dita raho, aquell consell favor e ajuda, que lo dit senyor rey e nos speram de vosaltres, e de gran naturalesa e amor que de vosaltres se pertany ... en manera que a la total deliurança de la persona del dit senyor, e a la presta recuperació de aquella." AHCB: Procesos de las Cortes Generales de Monzón (1435-36), doc. 78, Madurell Marimón, *Mensajeros Barceloneses*, 150-51.

17. *Anales de la Corona de Aragón*, 6: 98; Madurell Marimón, *Mensajeros Barceloneses*, 17-18; *Alfonso the Magnanimous*, 205-7.

18. AHCB: LCO X-7, 170, 23 October 1435; doc. 66 in Madurell Marimón, *Mensajeros Barceloneses*, 140-41. Juan arrived in Barcelona on 29 December 1436. *Dietari de la Diputació del General*, 106.

19. AHCB: LCO X-8, 7, 6 January 1436; 21, 26 January, cited in Madurell Marimón, *Mensajeros Barceloneses*, 17-18; *Alfonso the Magnanimous*, 209.

20. AHCB: Procesos de las Cortes Generales de Monzón (1435-36), 116r-v, 6 January 1436, doc. 83 in Madurell Marimón, *Mensajeros Barceloneses*, 155-56.

21. AHCB: LCO X-8, 7r-v, 6 January 1436; 25r-26v, 6 February 1436; 26v, 7 February 1436; and ACA: C Div 3129, 69v, 6 March 1436; docs. 84, 87, 95 and 98 in Madurell Marimón, *Mensajeros Barceloneses*, 155-58, 160-61, 162-64, 169-70, 172.

22. *Alfonso the Magnanimous*, 208.
23. Madurell Marimón, *Mensajeros Barceloneses*, 18–19.
24. Madurell Marimón, *Mensajeros Barceloneses*, 18, n. 32; Sánchez Aragonés, *Cortes, monarquía y ciudades en Aragón*, 141–42, 421.
25. "E com la senyora reyna veheés los affers de la present General Cort ésser tant fredament. . . ." Madurell Marimón, *Mensajeros Barceloneses*, 18, n. 32.
26. Muñoz Pomer and Carbonell Boria, "Las Cortes Valencianas medievales" in *Les Corts a Catalunya*, 279; *Los Trastámaras*, 395–96.
27. Consell de Cent, 15 March 1437, *Llibre de les Solemnitats*, 1: 82–84.
28. Luis González Anton, *Las Cortes de Aragón* (Zaragoza: Librería General, 1978), 112; idem, "Primeras resistencias contra el lugarteniente general-virrey en Aragón," *Aragón en la Edad Media* 8 (1984): 303–14, esp. 308–14; Sánchez Aragonés, *Cortes, monarquía y ciudades en Aragón*, 144, 422.
29. Angel Canellas López, "Alfonso el Magnánimo e Aragón," *Estudios sobre Alfonso el Magnánimo* (Barcelona: Universidad de Barcelona,1960), 7–24.
30. Sánchez Aragonés, *Cortes, monarquía y ciudades en Aragón*, 421–22.
31. Conde et al., "Fonts per a l'estudi," 41; *Cortes*, 19: 453.
32. AHCB: Procesos de Corts, 1436, 5v, doc. 98 in Madurell Marimón, *Mensajeros Barceloneses*, 172; *Dietari de la Diputació del General*, 106.
33. AHCB: Procesos de Corts, 1436, 25v, 12 November 1435, doc. 107 in Madurell Marimón, *Mensajeros Barceloneses*, 179–80.
34. Coroleu and Pella y Forgas, *Las Cortes Catalanas*, 249–53.
35. On the Catalan and Valencian sessions, see *Doña María de Castilla*, 115, 123–28; *Alfonso the Magnanimous*, 213. For details on the Aragonese meetings, see Sánchez Aragonés, *Cortes, monarquía y ciudades en Aragón*, 421–22; *Los Trastámaras*, 393–98; *Història de Catalunya*, 2: 54–55.
36. *Alfonso the Magnanimous*, 200–209.
37. ARV: MR 9050, fol. 5r–7v, 20 January 1436; *Doña María de Castilla*, 98; *Alfonso the Magnanimous*, 220–21.
38. ARV: MR 9050, fol. 9v–12r; *Doña María de Castilla*, 90–93.
39. Conde, et al., "Fonts per a l'estudi," 42.
40. Sánchez Aragonés, *Cortes, monarquía y ciudades en Aragón*, 221–22, 422; and *Cortes del Reino de Aragón, 1357–1451. Extractos y fragmentos de procesos desaparecidos*, ed. Angel Sesma Muñoz and Esteban Sarasa Sánchez (Valencia: Anubar, 1976), 139. See also *Los Trastámaras*, 397–98.
41. Sánchez Aragonés, *Cortes, monarquía y ciudades en Aragón*, 222–23, 423; *Los Trastámaras*, 398–402.
42. Sánchez Aragonés, *Cortes, monarquía y ciudades en Aragón*, 146–51, 223–39, 423–24; *Los Trastámaras*, 407–9.
43. See, for example, ACA: C Cur 3200, 80v–81r, 12 July 1453, María to Alfonso: "E la dita Cort ha respost que ells hoien ab dolor e tristor aquesta demanda car tota hur consolacio esperen per la presencia de vostra Real persona."
44. Madurell Marimón, *Mensajeros Barceloneses*. See also *Alfonso the Magnanimous*, 364–65.
45. ARV: MR 9050, 14v–15r, 3 October 1440; *Doña María de Castilla*, 94. On the symbolism of the royal body, see Ernst Kantorowicz, *The King's Two*

Bodies: A Study in Mediaeval Political Theology (Princeton, N.J.: Princeton University Press, 1967), 207–32.

46. *Kingdom of Naples*, 170–77; Ryder, "Evolution of Imperial Government," 350–51.

47. ACA: C Sec 3227: 43v–44v, 22 April 1449; 75r–76r, 24 July 1449; 93r–v, 21 October 1449; 95r, 29 October 1449; 99v–100v, 6 December 1449; 104r–105r, 24 January 1450; 121r–123v, 6 February 1450; and 134v–136v, 3 September 1450.

48. Claude Carrère, *Barcelone: centre èconomique à l'époque des difficultés, 1380–1462*, 2 vols. (Paris: Mouton, 1967), 656–63, 691–718; Mario del Treppo, *Els mercaders catalans i l'expansió de la corona catalano-aragonesa al segle XV*, trans. Jaume Riera i Sans (Barcelona: Curial, 1976); originally published as *I mercanti catalani e l'expansione della Corona d'Aragona nel secolo XV* (Naples: L'Arte Tipografica Napoli, 1972), 160–240, 255–77, 535–53; idem,"The 'Crown of Aragon' and the Mediterranean," *Journal of European Economic History* 2 (1973): 161–85; and Luis de Valdeavellano, *Curso de história de las instituciones Españolas: de los origines al final de la Edad Media*, 2nd ed. (Madrid: Editorial Revista de Occidente, 1970), 594–95, 605–12.

49. *Alfonso the Magnanimous*, 370–74; Alan Ryder, "Cloth and Credit: Aragonese War Finance in the Mid-Fifteenth Century," *War and Society* 2, 1 (May 1984): 1–21.

50. *Kingdom of Naples*, 174.

51. *Medieval Crown of Aragon*, 141, 143, 145.

52. ACA: C Cur 2652, 89r–v, 11 June 1444, cited in *Alfonso the Magnanimous*, 267.

53. ACA: C CSS 2690, fol. 178v, 14 October 1445; and fol. 183v, 22 October 1445, cited in Ryder, "Evolution of Imperial Government," 336. See also *Alfonso the Magnanimous*, 269; *Doña María de Castilla*, 93–94.

54. For instance, Juan wrote the Barcelona town council concerning a dispute with Genoa (AHCB: LRO-A, no. 638, 15 May 1451); he requested that the town council permit a Florentine ship working on his behalf to dock and unload its contents (AHCB: LRO-A, no. 669, 15 July 1451); he wrote often concerning Castile (AHCB: LRO-A, no. 625, 4 December 1450; no. 640, 15 June 1451; no. 641, 7 September 1451). See also *Mensajeros Barceloneses*, doc. 283 (AHCB: LC VI-15, 135r–v, 28 September 1450), for Valencia; doc. 372 (AHCB: LCO X-21, 202r–203v, 19 and 23 October 1451) for Aragón.

55. ACA: C Sec 2695, 131r–v, 16 December 1438, transcribed and trans. Ryder in *Alfonso the Magnanimous*, 367.

56. ACA: C Cur 2660, 117r–v, 10 December 1453, transcribed and trans. Ryder in *Alfonso the Magnanimous*, 367.

57. Alfonso's illegitimate son Ferran governed as one of his lieutenants in Italy before he was endowed the duchy of Calabria. *Alfonso the Magnanimous*, 221, 230–31, 239–40, 268, 350–57, 304–11, 400–430.

58. ACA: C Cur 2651, 30v–31r, 14 March 1438, doc. 128 in Madurell Marimón, *Mensajeros Barceloneses*, 190.

59. *Doña María de Castilla*, 29-39; Andrés Giménez-Soler, "Retrato his-

torico de la reina doña María," *Boletín de la Real Academia de Buenas Letras de Barcelona* 1 (1901–2): 71–81; and Ferran Soldevila, "La reyna María, muller del Magnánim," *Memorias de Real Academia de Buenas Letras de Barcelona* 10 (1923): 213–345, esp. 285–89.

60. The clearest description of her health comes from September 1446, when her physician Gabriel García prepared a report of her health for the members of the Corts in Barcelona to explain why she was too ill to preside. He concluded that she suffered from an inflammatory disease (*mirarchia*), suffocation of the womb, syncope (fainting), unnatural contractions or spasmodic agitations of her limbs. ACA Leg, Caja 5, 1446; transcribed and trans. into Spanish by Lluís Comenge, *La medicina en el reinado de Alfonso V de Aragón* (Barcelona: Espasa, 1903), 29–30.

61. ACA: C PCC 3319, 2v–13v, 28 April 1453 to 20 October 1453. See also Lalinde Abadía, *La institución virreinal*, 85–86.

62. *Alfonso the Magnanimous*, 366.

63. Sánchez Aragones, *Cortes, monarquía y ciudades en Aragón*, 145.

64. *Kingdom of Naples*, 431.

65. *Los Trastámaras*, 373–75, 726–28; *Medieval Crown of Aragon*, 145.

66. "E que plagues a Déu que tals pràtiques de porrogacions e dissolucions de Corts, fossen dejus terra e no fossen axí introduhïdes e praticades segons són molt enamigues de la honor e glòria del dit senyor e de tota cosa públiqua de tots sos regnes e terres.... E més deuen induhir lo dit senyor a venir, perque vist personalment la molt alta senyora reyna, ab la qual segons Déu e lo gran deute de matrimoni requer, és tengut fer personal e acomplida residència." Instructions from the Consell de Cent to the Catalan ambassadors in Naples, Arxiu de la Catedral de Barcelona, 24 July 1438, doc. 131, Madurell Marimón, *Mensajeros Barceloneses*, 191–94.

67. ACA: C Var 3277, 19r–27r. *Cortes*, 20: 349–443; Conde et al., "Fonts per a l'estudi," 42; Coroleu and Pella y Forgas, *Las Cortes Catalanas*, 253–55; *Doña María de Castilla*, 121. For Alfonso's final campaigns to secure Naples, see *Alfonso the Magnanimous*, 239–51.

68. *Cortes*, 20: 349–443; ACA: C Div 3162, fols. 66v, 80; *Doña María de Castilla*, 121.

69. *Doña María de Castilla*, 94; *Alfonso the Magnanimous*, 240.

70. "Supliquen los dits couocats que lo dit jurament vostra senyoria faça continuar los dits conuocats que lo dit proçes de la dita Cort e liurar aquell a la dita Cort auctenticament ... placia vos, Senyora, prestar lo dit jurament e manar aquell continuar en lo dit proces ab les saluetats e protestacions apres de aquell offeridores e continuadores, e a part esser ne fetas vna e moltes cartes publiques liuradores a la dita Cort e a altres qui lan volran." *Cortes*, 20: 426.

71. ARV: MR 9050, 3v–4r, 24 May 1432.

72. "E aqui mateix la molt alta senyora Reyna, lochtinent dessus dita ... ab les suas man corporal tocats, tenir e inuiolablament obseruar e fer obseruar e tenir als prelats, religiosos, clergues, richs homens, barons, nobles, cauallers, homens de paratge e a ciutats, viles e altres lochs de Cathalunya ... tots los Vsatges de Barchinona, consitucions e capitols de les Corts de Cathalunya, libertats, priuilegis, vsos e consuetuts." *Cortes*, 20: 427.

73. "Lo qual jurament mana la dita Senyora en lo proces de la dita Cort esser continuat e esser ne feta carta publica vna e moltes liuradoras a la dita Cort e altres qui lan volran." *Cortes*, 20: 427, 429.

74. "Consenten per aquesta vegada tant solament conuocacio, congregacio e celebracio de la present Cort, protestant expressament, retenint e saluant a la dita Cort e als conuocats en aquella e al dit Principat, e als Braços, staments e singulars de aquell que per lo dit consentiment fet per aquesta vegada tant solament e per les dites causes e rahons no sia fet algun preiudici, nouacio o derogacio, tacitament o expressa, directament o indirecta, als dits Vsatges, constitucions, capitols, priuilegis, vsances, consuetuts, pratiques e altres libertats ne al dit Principat, Braços, staments e singulars de aquell en vnuiuersal e en particular." *Cortes*, 20: 430.

75. "No fo es de sa intencio fer preiudici algu al dit Principat de Cathalunya ne als singulars de aquell vuiuerslament o particular, e per mes seruar indemne lo dit Principe e singulars de aquell, plau a la dita senyora Reyna e consent que per la dita conuocacio e per qualseuol actes en la present Cort fets e fahedors ne per lo dit consentiment per los del dit Principat ne las Vsatges de Barchinona, constitucions de Cathalunya, priuilegis, pratiques, vsances e consuetuts o altres drets del dit Principat, generalment o particular." *Cortes* 20: 431.

76. 11 April 1440: "Los senyors deputats provehiren misser Francesch Torres, doctor, de esser advocat de General en la cort de la senyora reyna axi en defensar les constitucions de Cathalunya com en altra manera, sens empero preiuidici de qualsevol provisio sobe aço feta a misser Anthoni Amat," *Dietari de la Diputació del General*, 129; 1 February 1441: "Los senyors deputats provehiren a lur beneplacit misser Luis de Castell de esser advocat a defendre constitucions e usatges en la cort de la senyora reyna, stant la dita cort fora Barchinona, e sens preiudici de altres provisions sobre aço fetes e sens salari del General, ans les parts instants haien aquell acontentar." *Dietari de la Diputació del General*, 137.

77. The occurences are too numerous to list. See, for example, ACA: G N-660, 74v–76r, 26 November 1449, from the diputats del general to Galceran de Requesens. The diputats argue that the royal agents collecting the *remença* redemption payment are acting "contra les constitucions del Rey en Jacme primer en la cort de Leyda." See also Coroleu and Pella y Forgas, *Las Cortes Catalanas*, 253–55.

78. ACA: G N-655, 51r–v, doc. 153 in Madurell Marimón, *Mensajeros Barceloneses*, 211.

79. *Cortes*, 21: 1–3; *Dietari*, 152; Rycraft, "The Role of the Catalan 'Corts,'" 253.

80. AHCB: LRO-A, no. 438, 22 August 1442, doc. 160 in Madurell Marimón, *Mensajeros Barceloneses*, 215.

81. *Cortes*, 21: 1–189; Conde et al., "Fonts per a l'estudi," 43; Coroleu and Pella y Forgas, *Las Cortes Catalanas*, 255–59; *Doña María de Castilla*, 121.

82. Madurell Marimón, *Mensajeros Barceloneses*, 31–32.

83. *Cortes*, 20: 449; 21: 79, 94, 101, 156–57.

84. ACA: C Inst 2939, 54r–v, transcribed and trans. Ryder in *Alfonso the Magnanimous*, 369.

85. *Alfonso the Magnanimous*, 369–70.

86. Ibid., 358–67.

87. Mieres was also Alfonso's legal counsel to the office of the Reial Patrimonio and in that capacity wrote on feudal and seigneurial landholding and the status of the *remença* peasants. For his comments on the Corts, see Frandicso Elías de Tejada, *Las doctrinas políticas en la Cataluña medieval* (Barcelona: Aymé, 1950), 189–99; Lalinde Abadía, "Los Parlamentos," 162–63.

88. Elías de Tejada, *Las doctrinas políticas en la Cataluña medieval*, 189, 194–99; Lalinde Abadía, "Los Parlamentos y demas instituciónes representativas," 162.

89. Joan Ros, a representative of the Barcelona Consell de Cent at the Corts in Perpinyà in 1450, accused María of stalling and buying time while she waited for a letter from Alfonso. AHCB: LCO X-20, 71r–v, 13 March 1450.

90. Theresa Earenfight, "María of Castile, Ruler or Figurehead? A Preliminary Study in Aragonese Queenship," *Mediterranean Studies* 4 (1994): 45–61.

91. He does not, however, cite any provision specifically. AHCB; LCO X-19: 41r–v, 16 March 1449; 42r–v, 18 March 1449; AHCB: LC VI-14, 34v–35r, 20 March 1449.

92. Her last request for his return was dated 2 May 1450. ACA: C Sec 3227, 120r–v.

93. Ferran married Isabel of Clermont; María, the eldest daughter, married Leonello d'Este, marques of Ferrara; and her younger sister Leonor married Mariano Marzano, son of the duke of Sesa and prince of Rossano. *Doña María de Castilla*, 80.

94. AHCB: LCO X-12, 88r–v, 18 August 1442; X-13, 24r–v, 15 March 1443; X-13, 31r–v, 4 April 1443; X-14, 55r–56v, 9 April 1444; and X-13, 71r–74v, 11 May 1444. These letters were printed as docs. 159, 166, 169, 185, and 187 in Madurell Marimón, *Mensajeros Barceloneses*, 221–23, 226–27, 243–45, 249–56.

95. The correspondence concerning the *maridatges* is lengthy, but pertinent letters are ACA: C Cur 3201, 90v, 5 October 1448; Sec 2699, 164r–166v, 5 February 1449; Cur 2655, 54r–55v, 1 March 1449; Cur 2656, 172v, 20 April 1449; Sec 3227, 53r–55v, 9 June 1449; Sec 3227, 57r–58v, 30 June 1449; Sec 3227, 76v–83r, 10 August 1449; Sec 3227, 95v, 29 October 1449. See also *Alfonso the Magnanimous*, 274–75; and *The Kingdom of Naples*, 215–16.

96. AHCB: LCO X-20, 4 September 1450, doc. 274 in Madurell Marimón, *Mensajeros Barceloneses*, 322–25.

97. Speaking on behalf of the city of Tortosa, the members of the Consell de Cent of Barcelona protested the request in a letter to María on 13 September 1449. ACHB: LC, VI-14, 124v–125v. A week later, they relayed to her similar complaints from the townspeople of Lleída; AHCB: LC VI-14, 135v–136r, 27 September 1449.

98. ACA: C Sec 86r–87r, 3 September 1449.

99 Sánchez Aragones, *Cortes, monarquía y ciudades en Aragón*, 205.

100. Similar attempts date to the end of the fourteenth century. María Teresa Ferrer i Mallol, "El patrimoni reial i la recuperació dels senyorius jurisdiccionals en les estats catalano-aragoneses a la fi del segle XIV," *Anuario de Estudios Medievales* 7 (1970–71): 351–491.

101. "Possitis eciam procuratorem vel procuratores constituere et substituere cum illa potestate quam eis concedere volueritis sive dare tam super jurisdiccionis exercicio quam aliud quovismodo." *Cortes*, 13: 85.

102. *Kingdom of Naples*, 205–208.

103. Corts of Barcelona (1422), cap. 26; *Constitucions*, 109.

104. *Alfonso the Magnanimous*, 43, 49–51, 65.

105. Santiago Sobrequés i Vidal, "Política remensa de Alfonso el Magnánimo en los últimos años de su reinado (1447–1458)," *Anales del instituto de estudios gerundenses* (1960): 177–54, especially 123–25; *Alfonso the Magnanimous*, 389–90.

106. Besalú faced similar opposition in Mallorca in 1450. ACA: C Sec 3227, 107r–108r, 4 February 1450.

107. *Cortes* 21: 322, 394, 425.

108. *Cortes*, 13: 73, 77, 97–98, 112, 153, 156, 160, 164–65, 187, 411–12. See also *Constitucions*, 73, 77, 93–94, 97–98, 107, 109, 112, 144, 153, 156, 160, 187, 288, 292, 400, 411–12, 508–9.

109. These suits were especially numerous in the Ampurdà, in the locales of Verges, La Tallada, Bellcaire, Albons, Monells, Ullastret, La Pera, Palau Sator, Sant Pere Pescador, Les Olives, and Pelacals. The documents are numerous and contained in several registers. Among the most important are ACA: C Sec 2699, 155r–157v, 25 January 1449; Cur 2656, 165r–v, 26 February 1449; Cur 2655, 54v–55v, 1 March 1449. See also María's orders to her royal officials: ACA: C Cur 3203, 11v–12v, 14 October 1448; 18v, 26 October 1448; 30r, 23 December 1448; and 60r, 5 April 1449. Sobrequés i Vidal, "Política remensa de Alfonso el Magnánimo," 122; Santiago Sobrequés i Vidal and Jaume Sobrequés i Callicó, *La guerra civil catalana del segle XV*, 2 vols. (Barcelona: Edicions 62, 1973), 1: 15–16.

110. There were three Jaume Ferrer's in fifteenth-century Catalunya, all of whom worked in the service of the Crown and with the remença peasants. The eldest was a lawyer who worked for Martí; his son, also a lawyer, worked for Alfonso and María; and his son was a royal seribe who played an important part in the preparation of the Sentencia Arbitral in 1486. Sobrequés i Vidal and Sobrequés i Callicó, *La guerra civil catalana*, 1: 17.

111. Sobrequés i Vidal and Sobrequés i Callicó, *La guerra civil catalana*, 1: 16–19.

112. ACA: C Cur 2653, 187r–195v.

113. He later promised that this information would be made public, but it is not clear that it ever was. *Cortes*, 21: 497. Sobrequés i Vidal, "Política remensa de Alfonso el Magnánimo," 125–26; Sobrequés i Vidal and Sobrequés i Callicó, *La guerra civil catalana*, 1: 17.

114. ACA: C Cur 3203, 11v–12v, 14 October 1448. Sobrequés i Vidal, *Els barons de Catalunya* (Barcelona: Editorial Teide, 1957), 203–5.

115. AHCB: LC VI-13, 169v–170r, 17 October 1448.

116. "E com les dites coses fets por lo dit Procurador Reyal . . . sian contra usatges de Barchinona constitucions e capitols de Corts de Cathalunya . . . vulls la dita prouisio e tots los actes fets un virtut de aquella reuocar ab tot effecte e manar

al dit Procurador Reyal que ho torn al primer e degut stament." AHCB: LC VI-13, 110r–111r and 111v–112r, 24 May 1448.

117. ACA: C Cur 3203, 18v, 26 October 1448.

118. Sobrequés i Vidal, "Política remensa de Alfonso el Magnánimo," 123; *Alfonso the Magnanimous*, 389–90.

119. On the French ambassadors, see AHCB: LC VI-13, 174r–175r, 31 October 1448.

120. ACA: G N-657 fols. 185v–186r, 19 November 1448, from the Archbishop of Tarragona on behalf of the Diputació del General to Jofre d'Ortigues, *regent canceller* for Alfonso.

121. ACA: C Sec 3227, 10v–11v, 29 August 1448.

122. ACA: G N-657, 56v–57v, 27 April 1448; 67v–68r, 22 April 1448; 68v–69v, 24 May 1448.

123. ACA: C Cur 3203, 37r, 4 February 1448; 39r–v, 17 February; 41r–v, 18 February; 42v–43r, 20 February.

124. ACA: C Cur 3203, 30r, 23 December 1448; 175v, 11 July 1450; 176v–177r, 13 July 1450.

125. ACA: G N-657, 165v–167v, 7 October 1448.

126. AHCB: LC VI-6, 179r–179v, 8 November 1448; 190r–v, 7 December 1448; 195v–196r, 17 December 1448.

127. ACA: C Cur 3203, 60v, 7 April 1449.

128. ACA: C Cur 3203, 42r, 19 February 1449.

129. "Sitis eciam super omnes prelatos et religiosas personas in hiis in quibus Nos eis preficimur et super Duces, Comites, Vicecomites nobiles, barones et milites, infancones," but also "Possitis inquam homagia et fidelitas a feudarariis Nostris in dictis regnis, Principatu et insulis recipere seu recipi facere et investitura feudadariis polliceri juribus nostris regiis et laudimiis, tercis, et foriscapitis in omnibus semper salvis." *Cortes*, 13: 84–85.

130. The body of the letter reads: "Confiant de vostra clemencia . . . tant humilment com poden supplicar a vostra gran Senyoria sia de sa merce vulle desempatxar lo dit Comte en tal forma que sia a seruen del molt Alt lo Senyor Rey e de vos Senyora mol excellent," and closes with "Vostres humils seruidors e vessalles qui besants vostres mans humilment se recomanem en vostra gracia e merce los Consellers de Barchinona." AHCB: LC VI-13, 195v, 16 December 1448.

131. ACA: C Cur 3203, fols. 87r–v, María to all concerned in the dispute with Pallars.

132. For Girona, Vic, Osona, and Lleída, see ACA: C Cur 3204, 67v, 27 July 1448. For the bishop of Urgell, see ACA: C Sec 3227, 13r, 5 August 1448; 13r–v, 28 August 1448; 14v–15r, 29 August 1448 (addressed to both the bishop of Urgell and the count of Pallars); 16v–17r and 18r–v, 12 September 1448. For the count of Cardona, see ACA: C Cur 3204, 28 May 1448. For Pallars, see ACA: C Sec 3227, 24v–25r, 3 October 1448, for the Consell de Cent, ACA: C Sec 3227, 8r, 16 August 1448 (with a copy to the Diputació del General); 10v–12v, 29 August 1448; and for the Diputació del General, ACA: C Sec 3227, 7v, 16 August 1448.

133. ACA: C Sec 3227, 29v–31v, 14 October 1448.

134. ACA: C Sec 3227, 24r, 3 October 1448; ACA: C Sec 3227, 33r, 3 November 1448.

135. Most of the correspondence from Alfonso to María is contained the following registers: ACA: C Cur 2653 (1447–48), 2654 (1447), and 2655 (1447–52). For most of María's letters to Alfonso, see ACA: C Cur 3203 and Sec 3227.

136. Carrére, *Barcelone*, 656–63, 691–718.

137. Batlle i Gallart, *La crisis social y económica*, 1: 17–20; Alan Ryder, *The Wreck of Catalonia: Civil War in the Fifteenth Century* (Oxford: Oxford University Press, 2007), 40–50.

138. Batlle i Gallart, *La crisis social y económica*, 1: 135–44, 155–64, 190–94; idem, *Retorn a la 'Busca' i la 'Biga': els dos partits de la Barcelona medieval* (Barcelona: Institut d'Historia Medieval, Universitat de Barcelona, 1982); idem, "El sindicato del pueblo de Barcelona en 1454," *VI Congreso de Historia de la Corona de Aragón* (Madrid: 1959), 291–304.

139. He replaced María as lieutenant general of Catalunya in 1453; and was appointed governor of Mallorca in 1454. Santiago Sobrequés i Vidal, "Entorn del llinatge dels Requesens," in *Societat i estructura política de la Girona medieval* (Barcelona: Editorial Curial, 1975), 303–13.

140. Carme Batlle i Gallart, who has studied the Biga-Busca conflict in detail, believes that Requesens masterminded the confrontation and that Alfonso played no direct role. Ryder disagrees, noting that Alfonso's correspondence shows him to be actively involved every step of the way. Batlle i Gallart, *Crisis social y económica*, 1: 37; *Alfonso the Magnanimous*, 383.

141. Jaime Vicens Vives, "Alfonso el Magnánimo y Barcelona," in *Obra Dispersa de Jaume Vicens Vives*, 2 vols. (Barcelona: Editorial Vicens-Vives, 1967), 1: 251–60; *Alfonso the Magnanimous*, 382–88.

142. AHCB: LC VI-14, 173r–v, 10 December 1449; VI-15, 26v–27r, 23 March 1450; docs. 217 and 218 in Madurell Marimón, *Mensajeros Barceloneses*, 286–87.

143. "E a que lo dit senyor [Alfonso], me replicà, que no curàs de res, que vertaderament ell amave e volia amar aquexa ciutat, e la tractarie bé." AHCB: LCO X-21, 182r–185r, 19 September 1451, doc. 366 in Madurell Marimón, *Mensajeros Barceloneses*, 376–87; quote 386.

144. *Alfonso the Magnanimous*, 384.

145. Batlle i Gallart, *Crisis social y económica*, 1: 208–17.

146. "E oyt plenament aquell en tot ço e quant nos ha volgut dir de part de aquells," ACA: C Cur 2657, 70r–v, 7 August 1448, from Alfonso to María.

147. Officials would be instructed in advance to act only on those letters that contained some innocuous phrase. *Alfonso the Magnanimous*, 385.

148. *Alfonso the Magnanimous*, 384–85.

149. Batlle i Gallart, *Crisis social y económica*, 1: 182–89.

150. *Cortes*, 22: 1–2. AHCB: LRO A-574, 30 January 1449, from María to the Consell de Cent of Barcelona; ACA: C Cur 3201, 132v–133r, 30 January 1449, María to the towns.

151. *Cortes* 22: 1–23, 82–4. For Alfonso's letter supporting her authority to preside, see ACA: C Sec 2699, 154r–155r, 22 January 1449.

152. *Cortes* 22: 23–55.
153. *Cortes* 22: 55–57.
154. Alfonso to the Corts and prelates: ACA; C, Cur 2661, 31r–32r, 31 August 1453.
155. Augustí Durán i Sanpere, *Barcelona i la seva història*, 3 vols. (Barcelona: Editorial Curial, 1972–75), 3: 65–134; Mary Faith Mitchell Grizzard, *Bernardo Martorell, Fifteenth-Century Catalan Artist* (New York: Garland, 1985), 215–20; Juan Ainaud de Lasarte, *La pintura catalana: de l'esplendor del Gòtic al Barroc* (Geneva: Skira; Barcelona: Carrogio, 1990), 78–83. In addition to his manuscript illuminations, Martorell is well known for his altar panels (*retaules*), including *Sant Jordi i la Princessa*, commissioned in 1435 by the Diputació del General for their headquarters at the Palau de la Generalitat (now in the collection of the Chicago Art Institute); the *Retaule de la Transfiguració* (ca. 1445) in the cathedral of Barcelona; and the *Retaule* de Sant Pere (ca. 1437–44) in the cathedral of Girona. Judith Berg Sobré, *Behind the Altar Table: The Development of the Painted Retable in Spain, 1350–1500* (Columbia: University of Missouri Press, 1989), 288–97.
156. Donald Kagay, ed. and trans., *The Usatges of Barcelona: The Fundamental Law of Catalonia* (Philadelphia: University of Pennsylvania Press, 1994), 1–3, 52.
157. Nancy Rubin, *Isabella of Castile: The First Renaissance Queen* (New York: St. Martin's Press, 1991), 23.
158. Augustí Durán i Sanpere argued that this painting may be as accurate a representation of María of Castile as we are likely to have: "Reportage gráfic d'una ceremònia oficial . . . no sembla una representació arbitrari, sino real i històricament auténtica." *Barcelona i la seva història*, 3: 104, 107–9. Art historian Mary Mitchell Grizzard has described this image of María as "not idealized . . . her face bears an overall expression of gentleness and dignity. It is a possible portrait; if so, it is the only one of María in existence, in contrast to so many of her husband." *Bernardo Martorell*, 216. Durán i Sanpere sidesteps the question of physical verisimilitude by emphasizing the historicity of the event. Grizzard, however, is mistaken on two counts. First, it must be an idealized image. In 1448, María was forty-seven years old and this picture depicts a young-looking woman. Moreover, in real life María's face bore the scars of a childhood bout with smallpox, but Martorell paints a clear-skinned face. Second, there is one other image of the queen, a miniature from a book of privileges of a Catalan confraternity; the artist of this image probably borrowed heavily from Martorell. *Doña María de Castilla*, 35; Soldevila, "La reyna Maria," 235–61; and Giménez-Soler, "Retrato histórico," 71–81.
159. Grizzard, *Bernardo Martorell*, 215–20; Durán i Sanpere, *Barcelona i la seva història*, 3: 101–109.
160. Joan Landes, "The Public and the Private Sphere: A Feminist Reconsideration," introduction to *Feminism, the Public and the Private* (Oxford: Oxford University Press, 1998), 135–63.
161. Jürgen Habermas, *Structural Transformation of the Public Sphere*, 1962, trans. Thomas Burger (Cambridge: MIT Press, 1989), 16.
162. Habermas, *Structural Transformation of the Public Sphere*, 30. For a discussion of royal rhetoric in sermons and public pronouncements, see Suzanne

198   Notes to Pages 100–103

F. Cawsey, *Kingship and Propaganda: Royal Eloquence and the Crown of Aragon, c. 1200–1450* (Oxford: Oxford University Press, 2002).

163. For feminist responses to Habermas, see the essays in *Feminists Read Habermas: Gendering the Subject of Discourse*, ed. Johanna Meehan (New York: Routledge, 1995), especially Meehan's introduction, 1–20; and Landes, "The Public and the Private Sphere," 135–63.

164. Habermas, *Structural Transformation*, 30.

165. Foucault notes that "power is neither given, nor exchanged, nor recovered, but rather exercised . . . it exists only in action . . . [it] is above all a relation of force." Michel Foucault, *Power/Knowledge: Selected Interviews and Other Writings, 1972–1977*, ed. Colin Gordon and trans. Colin Gordon, Leo Marshall, John Mepham, and Kate Soper (New York: Pantheon, 1980), 89–90, 98.

Chapter 5. The Struggle to Liberate the Remença *Peasants, 1446–53*

1. Paul Freedman, *The Origins of Peasant Servitude in Medieval Catalonia* (Cambridge: Cambridge University Press, 1991), 89–118; Jaime Vicens Vives in *Historia de los remensas en el siglo XV* (Barcelona: 1945), 23–26; Eduardo Hinojosa y Naveros, *El régimen señorial y la cuestión agraria en Cataluña durante el Edad Media* (Madrid: Victoriano Suárez, 1905), 6–7; Alan Ryder, *The Wreck of Catalonia: Civil War in the Fifteenth Century* (Oxford: Oxford University Press, 2007), 30–39. Thomas Bisson, using royal documents, described the peasants' perspective, with an emphasis on their experience of power and coercion in *Tormented Voices: Power, Crisis, and Humanity in Rural Catalonia, 1140–1200* (Cambridge, Mass.: Harvard University Press, 1998). For a comparison to peasants and enserfment elsewhere in Europe, see Robert Brenner, "Agrarian Class Structure and Economic Development in Preindustrial Europe," *Past and Present* 70 (1976): 30–75; R. H. Hilton, *Bond Men Made Free: Medieval Peasant Movements and the English Rising of 1381* (New York: Viking, 1973), 121.

2. "Existe un vasto periodo desconocido que abarca unos 40 años, o sea la época de María de Luna hasta 1448, aunque parece evidente que se trató de un periodo de calma legislativa, de una época de sorda y subterránea agitación," in "Política remensa de Alfonso el Magnánimo en los últimos años de su reinado (1447–1458)," *Anales del instituo de estudios gerundenses* (1960): 117–54.

3. Freedman, *Origins of Peasant Servitude*; Pierre Bonnassie, *La Catalogne du milieu du Xe à la fin du XIe siècle: croissance et mutations d'une société*, 2 vols. (Toulouse: Association des Publications de l'Université de Toulouse-Le Mirail, 1975–76), 205–319; idem, *From Slavery to Feudalism in South-Western Europe*, trans. Jean Birrell (Cambridge: Cambridge University Press, 1991); Archibald Lewis, *The Development of Southern French and Catalan Society, 718–1050* (Austin: University of Texas Press, 1965), 264, 267, 273–76; and Josep Salrach, *El procés de formació nacional de Catalunya (segles VIII–IX)*, 2 vols. (Barcelona: Edicions 62, 1978), 136–9. Two older works by Vladimir Piskorski, *Origen e importancia de los seis malos usos en Cataluña*, trans. Julia Rodríguez Danilevsky (Kiev: 1899) and *La servidumbre en Cataluña en la Edad Media* (Kiev: 1901) are still valuable.

4. Freedman, *Origins of Peasant Servitude*. For Freedman's provocative comparison of the *remença* wars with the German peasant revolts in the early modern period, see "The German and Catalan Peasant Revolts," *American Historical Review* 98:1 (February 1993): 39–54. See also Antoni Jordà i Fernández, "Los remensas: evolución de un conflicto jurídico y social del campesinado catalán en la Edad Media," *Boletín de al Real Academia de Historia* 187:2 (1990): 217–97.

5. M. Mercè Homs i Brugerolas, *El sindicat remença de l'any 1448* (Girona: Ajuntament de Girona, 2005) contains many document transcriptions.

6. Vicens Vives, *Historia de los remensas*, 43–66, 347–65; idem, *El gran sindicato Remensa* (1488–1508) (Madrid: Impresor de Sucessores Juan Sánchez de Ocañayia, 1954). See also Concepción Fort Melia, "La Diputación de Catalunya y los payeses de remensa: la Sentencia Arbitral de Barcelona (1463)," in *Homenaje a Jaime Vicens Vives* (Barcelona: 1965), 1: 431–44; and M. Fila Golobardes, *Els remences dins el quadre de la pagesia catalan fins el segle XV* (Figueras: Arts Gràfiques Traiter, 1970).

7. In 1986, the entire volume 118 of the *Revista de Girona* was devoted to the *Sentencia*: Jordi Canal i Morell, "El conflicte remença vist pels historiadors dels segles XIX i XX," 57–63; Josep Canal i Roquet, "Els remences a les Valls d'Hostoles i d'Amer," 50–56; Paul Freedman, "Catalunya nova i Catalunya vella a l'edat mitjana: dues Catalunyas?" 29–35; Joaquim Nadal i Farreras, "Remences i no remences, una revolució agrària dels segles XIV–XV: una commemoració," 26–27; Josep M. Pons i Guri, "Relació jurídica de la remença i els mals usos a les terres gironines," 440–43; Eva Serra i Puig, "El 500è aniversari de la Sentència de Guadalupe: els usos polítics d'una commemoració," 28–31. See also Gaspar Feliu i Montfort, "El pes econòmic de la remença i dels mals usos," *Anuario de estudios medievales* 22 (1992): 145–60; Eva Serra i Puig, "Remences, una ocasió per tornat-hi a pensar," *L'Avenç* 93 (1986): 46–52; idem, "La crisi social agrària de la Baixa Edat Mitjana: els remences," *Cuadernos de Historia Económica de Cataluña* 19 (1978): 47–56; and Jaume Sobrequés i Callicó, "En torno al problema remensa," *Hispania* (Instituto Zurita, Madrid) 40 (1980): 428–35.

8. Santiago Sobrequés i Vidal, "Los origines de la revolución catalana del siglo XV: las cortes de Barcelona de 1454–58," *Estudios de Historia Moderna* 2 (1952): 1–96; and Santiago Sobrequés i Vidal and Jaume Sobrequés i Callicó, *La guerra civil catalana del segle XV*, 2 vols. (Barcelona: Edicions 62, 1973), 11–39.

9. *Pagesos i senyors a la Catalunya del segle XVII: baronia de Sentmenat 1590–1729* (Barcelona: Editorial Critica, 1988).

10. Francisco Monsalvatje y Fossas, *Colección diplomatica del condado de Besalú*, 26 vols. (Olot: Noticias Históricas, 11 [1901], 12 [1902], 13 [1906], and 20 [1910]). Julián de Chía, *Bandos y bandoleros en Gerona: Apuntes históricos desde el siglo XIV a mediados del XVII*, 3 vols. (Girona: 1888–90).

11. José Coroleu, *El feudalismo y la servidumbre de la gleba en Cataluña* (Girona: 1878).

12. *Historia del Ampurdán. Estudio de la civilización en las comarcas del noroeste de Cataluña* (Barcelona: Luis Tasso y Serra, 1883), 2nd ed., facsimile (Olot: Aubert, 1980).

13. Joaquim Camps i Arboix, *Verntallat, cabdill dels remences*, prologue Jaume

200 Notes to Pages 104–106

Vicens i Vives (Barcelona: Areos, 1955); idem, *La reivindicació social dels remences* (Barcelona: Dalmau, 1960); Josep M. Llorens Rams, "El mon agrari baix-medieval a la comarca de la Selva i el conflicte remença," *Aixa* 1 (1987): 23–30.

14. Ryder, *The Wreck of Catalonia*.

15. Teresa Vinyoles Vidal, *Història de les dones a la Catalunya medieval* (Lleída: Pagès, 2005), 108–21.

16. *Constitucions*, 346–47; Feliu i Montfort, "El pes economic de la remença," 145–60; Hinojosa y Naveros, *El régimen señorial*, 189; Pons i Guri, "Relació jurídica de la remença," 440–43; Freedman, *Origins of Peasant Servitude*, 17, 121–35; *The Usatges of Barcelona: The Fundamental Law of Catalonia*, ed. Donald Kagay (Philadelphia: University of Pennsylvania Press, 1994), 67, 75–76, 86, 88–9; Vicens Vives, *Historia de los Remensas,* 27–36.

17. *Cortes*, 1: 86; Hinojosa y Naveros, *El régimen señorial*, 213–16; Vicens Vives, *Historia de los Remensas*, 33–34; Freedman, *Origins of Peasant Servitude*, 172–78.

18. Sobrequés i Callicó, "La crisi social agrària de la Baixa Edat Mitjana: els remences," 47; Freedman, *Origins of Peasant Servitude*, 121–35; Hinojosa y Naveros, *El régimen señorial*, 216–25. On Jaume's reign, see *Medieval Crown of Aragon*, 58–85; *History of Medieval Spain*, 333–49.

19. *Cortes*, 1: 147; *Constitucions*, 347; Alfonso García Gallo, *Manual de historia del derecho español*, 2nd ed., 2 vols. (Madrid: 1964), 754.

20. A letter of commendation of 1285 illustrates this personal bond: "Vobis facio homagium manale. . . . Et ego predictus Arnaldus de Planis . . . promitto tibi Bartolomeo Nonel, quod quando tu volueris exire de meo dominio et servitute, solvam faciam et redam te, et omnem prolem a te natam et nascituram et omnes res tuas mobiles et inmobiles, franchum liberum quitium et absolutum . . . cum v solidos Barchinonensis de terno quo nobis vel nostris dare tenearis et nichil aliud in morte nec in vita." Hinojosa y Naveros, *El régimen señorial*, 87, n. 1; reprinted in García Gallo, *Manual de historia de Derecho español*, 754–55. Although these letters were from an early period, because the commendation was for the individual as well as his family ("et omnem prolem a te natam et nascituram"), this letter served as the basis for servitude for generations of peasants.

21. The price of redemption on the lands of the Abbot of Sant Martí in 1218, the redemption was fixed at fifteen *solidos*, but in Barcelona in 1285 it was five *solidos*. It is difficult to know for certain whether such variations reflect local conditions, change over time, or adjustment for currency fluctuations. The letter of 1218 is printed in Monsalvatje, *Colección diplomtica del condado de Besalú*, 9: appendix 33, 277–78 and reprinted in García Gallo, *Manual de historia de Derecho español*, 753–54; for an example of a letter of redemption (from Girona, ca. 1190), see 484–85. For a table of redemption prices before 1283, see Freedman, *Origins of Peasant Servitude*, 227–30.

22. Freedman, *Origins of Peasant Servitude*, 131–39, 149–53; Vicens Vives, *Historia de los remensas*, 33–34.

23. On the effects of the plague in Catalunya, see *Medieval Crown of Aragon*, 165; Claude Carrère, *Barcelone: centre économique a l'époque des difficultés, 1380–1462*, 2 vols. (Paris: Mouton, 1967), 656–717; Feliu i Montfort, "El pes econòmic

de la remença," 145–60; Freedman, *Origins of Peasant Servitude*, 154–78; *Spanish Kingdoms, 1250–1516*, 2: 29; Vicens Vives, *Historia de los remensas*, 34–36; Pierre Vilar, "Le declín catalan de Bas Moyen-Âge," *Estudios de Historia Moderna* 6 (1956–59): 3–68.

24. Santiago Sobrequés i Vidal, *Els barons de Catalunya* (Barcelona: Editorial Teide, 1957), 139–42; Sobrequés i Vidal and Sobrequés i Callicó, *La guerra civil catalana*, 1: 20–24, 30–39.

25. Sobrequés i Vidal and Sobrequés i Callicó, *La guerra civil catalana*, 1: 17–39. The authors claim that by 1462 the small rural towns had grown strong enough to comprise a veritable "fourth estate" that posed a serious threat to Barcelona and Girona, which were fractured and weakened by partisan disputes.

26. Feliu i Montfort, "El pes econòmic de la remença," 150–59; Freedman, *Origins of Peasant Servitude*, 166–68; Jaime Vicens Vives, *Els Trastámares, el segle XV* (Barcelona: Editorial Teide, 1956), 26–27.

27. María Teresa Ferrer i Mallol has made a strong case against any link between the recuperation of royal patrimony and the issue of peasant servitude before 1410. "El patrimoni reial i la recuperació dels senyorius jurisdiccionals en les estats catalano-aragoneses a la fi del segle XIV," *Anuario de Estudios Medievales* 7 (1970–71): 351–451, esp. 380, 430–48.

28. Angus MacKay, *Spain in the Middle Ages: From Frontier to Empire, 1000–1500* (London: Macmillan, 1977), 178; Freedman, *Origins of Peasant Servitude*, 184.

29. Carmen Batlle i Gallart, *La Crisis social y económica de Barcelona a mediados del siglo XV*, 2 vols. (Barcelona: Consejo Superior de Investigaciones Cientificas, 1973), 171, 217, 338–70; Vicens Vives, *Historia de los Remensas*, 64–66; Sobrequés i Vidal and Sobrequés i Callicó, *La guerra civil catalana*, 1: 26–37.

30. Pierre Vilar, *La Catalogne dans l'Espagne moderne*, 3 vols. (Paris: SEVPEN, 1962), 379–80, 467–71. This phrasing recalls Rodney Hilton's "continuous Jacquerie" in Naples in *Bond Men Made Free*, 111. For a multifaceted comparison of these revolts, see *The English Rising of 1381*, ed. R. H. Hilton and T. H. Aston (Cambridge: Cambridge University Press, 1984), especially 1–8, 74–83, 143–64; and Michel Mollat and Philippe Wolffe, *Popular Revolutions of the Late Middle Ages* (London: Allen and Unwin, 1973).

31. Barbara Hanawalt noted similarities with English peasants and the *remences*, especially in the attitude of the peasants toward the king as the person who would right the wrongs and act as protector. "Peasant Resistance to Royal and Seignorial Impositions," in *Social Unrest in the Late Middle Ages*, ed. Francis X. Newman (Binghamton: State University of New York Press, 1986), 23–47. See another work in the same volume by J. A. Raftis, "Social Change versus Revolution: New Interpretations of the Peasant's Revolt of 1381," 3–22.

32. A transcription of the letter is contained in Montsalvatje y Fossas, *Noticias históricas*, vol. 13, document no. 1729, 169–71; Vicens Vives, *Historia de los remensas*, 43–51; Freedman, *Origins of Peasant Servitude*, 179–83.

33. Chía, *Bandos y bandoleros en Gerona*, 1: 260; 2: 62; Freedman, *Origins of Peasant Servitude*, 182.

34. Benedict was Aragonese, born Pedro Martínez de Luna in 1328 or 1329.

He was elected pope in 1394, in the midst of the schism, on the promise that he would step down peacefully when the time came. He did not do so and was deposed in 1417; he died in 1422. José Angel Sesma Muñoz, *Benedicto XIII: la vida y el tiempo del Papa Luna* (Zaragoza: Caha de Ahorros de la Inmaculada, 1987). For an overview of his writings on the *remences*, see Freedman, *Origins of Peasant Servitude*, 182–83.

35. Fidel Fita, "Lo Papa Benet XIII y los Pagesos de Remensa," *Renaixensa* 11 (1875): 11–16, 81–85, 122–30; Aurea Lucinda Javierre Mur, *María de Luna, reina de Aragón* (Madrid: Consejo Superior de Investigaciones Científicas, 1942), 85–91; Freedman, *Origins of Peasant Servitude*, 183; Sobrequés i Vidal, "Política remensa de Alfonso el Magnánimo," 120–22.

36. Mark Meyerson, "Defending Their Jewish Subjects: Elionor of Sicily, Maria de Luna, and the Jews of Morvedre," in *Queenship and Political Power in Medieval and Early Modern Spain*, ed. Theresa Earenfight (Aldershot: Ashgate, 2005), 55–77; Nuria Silleras-Fernández, "Spirit and Force: Politics, Public and Private, in the Reign of Maria de Luna (1396–1406)," in Earenfight, *Queenship and Political Power in Medieval and Early Modern Spain*, 78–90.

37. ACA: C Cur 3203, 43v–44r, 21 February 1449.

38. AHCB: LC VI-15, 149r–v, 19 October 1450.

39. Claude Carrère ascribed relative peace in the countryside to this upturn, especially the devaluation of the currency in 1413 that lightened the peasants' burden by reducing the real value of their fixed payments. *Barcelone*, 2: 703–7.

40. *Cortes*, 11: 226–7; Freedman, *Origins of Peasant Servitude*, 184.

41. These fees were known as *luïcions*. Like the recuperation of royal patrimony, this issue often became entangled with that of the *remences*, many of whom were on lands subject to luïcion transactions. For the sake of clarity in this study, I will treat it as a separate issue. Chía, *Bandos y bandoleros en Gerona*, 2; 64; Sobrequés i Vidal, "Política remensa de Alfonso el Magnánimo," 122; Sobrequés i Vidal and Sobrequés i Callicó, *La guerra civil catalana*, 1: 15.

42. Chía, *Bandos y bandoleros en Gerona*, 2: 64; Sobrequés i Vidal and Sobrequés i Callicó, *La guerra civil catalana*, 1: 15.

43. *Cortes*, 17: 180–83; *Constitucions*, 348–49. Alfonso's confirmation of the statute is in *Cortes*, 18: 205. Canal i Roquet, "Els remences a les Valls d'Hostoles i d'Amer," 54; Freedman, *Origins of Peasant Servitude*, 196–97.

44. Hernández-León de Sánchez reported that María presided over a Corts in Valencia in 1443 but said nothing of what was accomplished. *Doña María de Castilla*, 121–22. María Rosa Muñoz Pomer and María José Carbonell Boria, "Las *Cortes* Valencianas medievales: aproximación a la historiografía y fuentes para su estudio," in *Les Corts a Catalunya*, ed. Direcció General del Patrimoni Cultural (Barcelona: Generalitat de Catalunya, 1991), 279.

45. Chía, *Bandos y bandoleros en Gerona*, 2: 64; Sobrequés i Vidal and Sobrequés i Callicó, *La guerra civil catalana*, 1: 15.

46. Alan Ryder, "Cloth and Credit: Aragonese War Finance in the Mid-Fifteenth Century," *War and Society* 2, 1 (May 1984): 1–21, especially 10–11. Hillgarth also believes that Alfonso's motivations were purely financial. *Spanish Kingdoms*, 2: 260.

47. He seemed forever preoccupied with money, but starting in 1437, after the defeat at Ponza, the problem became more acute. Ryder, "Cloth and Credit," 6–7.

48. On the financing of the Italian campaigns, see Ryder, "Cloth and Credit," 11–12.

49. Ryder, "Cloth and Credit," 3–11.

50. He encountered fewer difficulties in Aragón and Valencia, due in part to their more robust economies and their greater willingness to give in to his needs. *Medieval Crown of Aragon*, 143–45.

51. For a comparison to France, see Elizabeth A. R. Brown, "Royal Commissioners and Grants of Privilege in Philip the Fair's France: Pierre de Latilli, Raoul de Breuilli, and the Ordonnance for the Seneschalsy of Toulouse and Albi of 1299," *Francia* 13 (1985): 151–90.

52. *Cortes*, 21: 191–502. Rafael Conde, Ana Hernández, Sebastià Riera, and Manuel Rovira, "Fonts per a l'estudi de les Corts i els Parlaments de Catalunya," *Les Corts a Catalunya*, 43; José Coroleu and José Pella y Forgas, *Las Cortes Catalanes* (Barcelona: Revista Historica Latina, 1876), 259–64; *Dietari de la Diputació del General de Cathalunya*, ed. Arxui de la Corona d'Aragó, vol. 1: 1411–1458 (Barcelona: Diputación Provincial de Barcelona, 1974), 173.

53. ACA: C Litt 2940, 23r–v, 11 December 1446, transcribed and trans. Ryder in *Alfonso the Magnanimous*, 369.

54. In a letter to María written on 11 December 1446, he told of troubles with Pope Eugene, the duke of Milan, and the commune of Genoa that caused him to spend not only time and energy but also money. ACA: C Litt 2940, 22r–v, transcribed and trans. Ryder in *Alfonso the Magnanimous*, 270.

55. Letter from Alfonso, via his emissary Joan de Marimón, dated 23 October 1447: ". . . fora content scriura a la senyora reyna d'equí continuàs la Cort." AHCB: LCO X-17, 153r–v, document 206 in Madurell Marimón, *Mensajeros Barceloneses*, 279–80.

56. Letter from Alfonso to María, 17 January 1447: "nos no volem quens façen ne trameten armadad ne embaxada ne façen res que sia o redunas en despeses del general." ACA: C Cur 2654, 108v.

57. *Cortes*, 21: 394, 425. Sobrequés i Vidal and Sobrequés i Callicó, *La guerra civil catalana*, 1: 15, 17.

58. AHCB: LC VI-14, 164r–v, 19 November 1449.

59. Pella y Forgas, *Historia del Ampurdán*, 2: 666.

60. The diputats del general wrote to the bailiff of Bellver, a royal town, to request the return of remença peasants who had fled there from the lands of the viscount of Illa-Canet, who was then one of the three executive diputats. ACA: G N-657, 76v–77r, 1 June 1448.

61. These actions resonate deeply even today, with echoes of the Ku Klux Klan in the United States. Pella y Forgas, *Historia del Ampurdán*, 2: 51; Freedman, *Origins of Peasant Servitude*, 184; Sobrequés i Vidal, "Política remensa de Alfonso el Magnánimo," 118–19; Vicens Vives, *Historia de los Remensas*, 56–57.

62. They did not refer to *remences* per se, but "homens propris se aiustaren e fou prop seguirsen un gran scandol," which may indicate that the unrest was not

204 Notes to Pages 114–116

strictly confined to the *remences* and may not have involved them at all. *Cortes*, 21: 475.

63. *Cortes* 21: 473–76. Sobrequés i Vidal, "Política remensa de Alfonso el Magnánimo," 119.

64. "Com los mals juristes sien causa de la destrucció del món e és fama que en . . . Catalunya ne haie molts de tals." AHCB: LC VI-13, 9r–10r, 3 September 1447; *Cortes* 21: 473–76.

65. "lo dit Senyor ha gran voluntat poder lo dit Principat e altres terres e vassalls seus en aquelles parts visitar e ho haguera sens lur supplicacio ia executat si la pau de Ytalia se fos seguida, en la qual lo dit Senyor, ab gran voluntat ha treballat e treballa e ha confiança en nostre Senyor Deu que prestament aquella se seguira, la qual seguida per manera quel dit Senyor puxa lo seu regne de Sicilia [Naples] dexa far lexar en repos durant la absencia sua enten ab la ajuda de Deu anar visitar lo dit Principat e los regnes e terres seus de part della." *Cortes* 21: 495, 497, 3 January 1448; Sobrequés i Vidal, "Política remensa de Alfonso el Magnánimo," 125–26; Sobrequés i Vidal and Sobrequés i Callicó, *La guerra civil catalana*, 1: 17

66. Pere de Besalú went on to have a distinguished career in Alfonso's government. In 1450 he was named governor of Majorca and procurador reial of Sardinia and was granted substantial property in Sicily. Juan II named him Gran Senschal and Conservador of Sicily in 1462, but had to relinquish his property there when Juan granted it as a lordship to his Fernando. Besalú died shortly thereafter, perhaps as early as 1463. Sobrequés i Vidal, "Política remensa de Alfonso el Magnánimo," 125–26.

67. *Dietari de la Diputació*, 180–81; Conde et al., "Fonts per a l'estudi," 43.

68. ACA: C Cur, 2656, 120r–121r, 14 April 1448.

69. ACA: G N-657, 182v–186v, 19 November 1448; 193v–195r, 7 December 1448; 195r–v, 9 December 1448; N-658: 29r–v, 27 January 1449.

70. ACA: C Div 3154, 9r, 14 January 1451.

71. Chía, *Bandos y bandoleros en Gerona*, 2: 69; Monsalvatje, *Colección diplomática del condado de Besalú*, 2: 26; Sobrequés i Vidal, "Política remensa de Alfonso el Magnánimo," 128–29; Sobrequés i Vidal and Sobrequés i Callicó, *La guerra civil catalana*, 1: 18–19; Vicens Vives, *Historia de los Remensas*, 57. For a breakdown of the remença population in the northeast, see Pella y Forgas, *Historia del Ampurdán*, 577–629.

72. A 1460 redaction of this grant appears in Freedman, *Origins of Peasant Servitude*, appendix 1, 224–26.

73. ACA: C Cur 2657, 85v.

74. ACA: C Cur 2657, 75r, 7 September 1448; and Cur 3203, 11v–13v, 14 October 1448. The debt to him was nearly paid on 22 July 1449. ACA: C Sec 3227, 68r–v. Ryder, "Cloth and Credit," 11.

75. Chía, *Bandos y bandoleros en Gerona*, 2: 68; Monsalvatje, *Colección diplomática del condado de Besalú*, 2: 25; Sobrequés i Vidal, "Política remensa de Alfonso el Magnánimo," 129; Sobrequés i Vidal and Sobrequés i Callicó, *La guerra civil catalana*, 1: 20; Vicens Vives, *Historia de los Remensas*, 58.

76. Pella y Forgas, *Historia del Ampurdán*, 2: 666; Vicens Vives, *Historia de los Remensas*, 57.

77. Francesch Carreras y Candi, "Barcelona," vols. 3 and 4 of *Geografía general de Catalunya*, prologue by Jaume Sobrequés i Callicó (11 vols., reprint of original, undated, nineteenth-century ed., Barcelona: Edicions Catalanes, 1980), 504–5; AHCB: LC VI-13, 189r–v, 6 December 1448; ACA: G N-657, 193v–195v, 7 December 1448.

78. ACA: G N-657, 182v–186r, 19 November 1448.

79. She moved her court there after a severe earthquake destroyed parts of Barcelona. *Dietari de la Diputació*, 181.

80. ACA: G N-657, 186r–v, 19 November 1448.

81. "Ab totes nostres forces obuiar als dits preiudicis encare hauem plen de vostar excitacio e com dels dits afers hauer lo sentiment que a vosaltres de aquelles hauer es pertinent." AHCB: LCO X-18, fol. 164, 7 November 1448; ACA: G, N-657, 184r–185v, 19 November 1448.

82. ACA: G N-660, 106r–107v, 16 December 1449.

83. Castelló, a lawyer, was regent chancellor and assessor to the governor of Rosselló and Cerdanya. Both Foxa and Giganta were chancery officials. ACA: C Sec 3227, 35v–38r, 30 December 1448.

84. ACA: C Cur 2657, 70r–v, 7 December 1448.

85. ACA: G N-657, 195r–v, 9 December 1448; AHCB: LC VI-13: 195r, 16 December 1448 and 197r, 30 December 1448.

86. Sobrequés i Vidal, "Política remensa de Alfonso el Magnánimo," 130; Sobrequés i Vidal and Sobrequés i Callicó, *La guerra civil catalana*, 1: 21.

87. ACA: G N-658, 9r–11r, 9 January 1449.

88. "Si algunes coses apres en los dits afers se son innouades lo que no sentim deuien ne hauer auisats a nos qui jassie entenam en mudar en aquexa ciutat nos e nostre consistori la dita mutacio precipitarien tan e tanta porie esser la dita nouitat." ACA: G N-658, 4r.

89. Sobrequés i Vidal, "Política remensa de Alfonso el Magnánimo," 129.

90. ACA: C Div 3148, 189v–190r, a letter patent from María to the sindichs and all royal officials working with the *remences*. The proceeds were to be deposited with Johan and Bernat Banqueres, merchant bankers in Barcelona who also held bills of exchange from Alfonso. ACA: C Div 3149, 155v–156r. Sobrequés i Vidal and Sobrequés i Callicó, *La guerra civil catalana*, 1: 22–23; Vicens Vives, *Historia de los remensas*, 58.

91. ACA: C Sec 3227, 53r–55v, 9 June 1449. In her letter to Berenguer de Montpalau she stated that it was "quasi miracle" considering the objections of the diputats and the Consell de Cent.

92. This information was recorded on the verso of the letter, along with the date received. See, for example, AHCB: LC VI-15, 46v–47v, 28 April 1450.

93. ACA: G N-658, 31v–32r, 30 January 1449.

94. Sobrequés i Vidal and Sobrequés i Callicó, *La guerra civil catalana*, 1: 22.

95. Alfonso to Galceran de Requesens and Antoni Cerda, the bishop of Lleída, ACA: C Sec 2699, 154r–155r, 22 January 1449. María to the Consell de Cent of Barcelona, AHCB: LRO A-574, 30 January 1449; María to the towns. ACA: C Cur 3201, 132v–133r, 30 January 1449; *Cortes*, 22: 1–2.

206 Notes to Pages 118–121

96. AHCB: LCO X-19, 41r–v, 16 March 1449; *Cortes*, 22: 20–23; Conde, et al., "Fonts per a l'estudi," 43. The delays were met, of course, with formal protests from the Diputació. ACA: G N-658, 82r–84r, 22 April 1449.

97. AHCB: LCO X-19, 94, 8 May 1449.

98. María to Berenguer de Montpalau on 30 April 1449, ACA: C Sec 3227, 44v–48v. Vicens Vives, *Historia de los Remensas*, 61, n60.

99. AHCB: LC VI-15, 59v–60v, 15 May 1450. See also Sobrequés i Vidal and Sobrequés i Callicó, *La guerra civil catalana*, 1: 25.

100. AHCB: LCO X-20: 18r–v, 22 January 1450; 22r–v, 31 January 1450.

101. ACA: G N-658, 28v–29r, from the archbishop of Tarragona to the viscount of Illa-Canet, 27 January 1449. This end-run had already been proposed on 9 January: "Si la dita Senyora Reyna no fara o no volra fer prouisio alguna sobre los dits afers, lo dit Noble vezcomte dient que los dits deputats per la dita raho han trames al Senyor Rey, suplich a la dita Senyoria li placie manar e fer sobreseure en los dits acted e procehiments en lo interim tro lo qui es anat al dit Senyor sie retornat." ACA: G N-658, 9v–11r. *Dietari de la Diputació*, 185–86; Sobrequés i Vidal, "Política remensa de Alfonso el Magnánimo," 130; Sobrequés i Vidal and Sobrequés i Callicó, *La guerra civil catalana*, 1: 21.

102. For the report of his meeting with Coma and Montbui from the bishop to the Consell de Cent, see AHCB: LCO X-19, 21r–v, 4 February 1449. ACA: C Cur 3203, 32r–v, letter close from María to the vicar of Girona, 17 January 1449. For the bishop's response, see Pella y Forgas, *Historia del Ampurdán*, 2: 666; Vicens Vives, *Historia de los remensas*, 57.

103. ACA: C Cur 3203, 38v–39r, 14 February 1449. Montbui, according to diputats del general, was in the direct employ of the *remences*: "va per lo dit Principat salariat per los dits pagesos vertaderament se pot dir." ACA: G N-658, 58r–63v, 13 March 1449. See also AHCB: LC VI-14, 45r–v, 9 April 1449 and 184r, 2 January 1450.

104. AHCB: LC VI-14: 45r–v, 9 April; 46v–47v, 12 April 1449; 184r, 2 January 1450.

105. ACA: C Cur 2656, 172r, 20 April 1449; Cur 2658, 3v, 16 May 1449.

106. ACA: C Cur 2655, 59v–60r, 2 April 1449.

107. ACA: C Cur 3203, 98r, 7 June 1449.

108. ACA: C Cur 3203, 43v–44r, 21 February 1449.

109. ACA: C Cur 2656, 162v–163r, 27 February 1449.

110. "E deuen pensar que en preclamar los dits pagesos libertat ne en esser administrada justicia per ehibicio de la qual son constituits los regnes e senyories e que axi egualment si tractat lo pobre com lo rich e lo chich com lo gran." ACA: C Cur 2656, 164v–165r, 29 February 1449.

111. AHCB: LCO X-19, 59.

112. ACA: G N-658, 28v–29r, 27 January 1449. It is not known whether this embassy ever reached Naples; there is no mention of it beyond this one reference. Sobrequés i Vidal thinks that economic difficulties may have prevented it from sailing. "Política remensa de Alfonso el Magnánimo," 132; Sobrequés i Vidal and Sobrequés i Callicó, *La guerra civil catalana*, 1: 21.

113. ACA: G N-658, 75r–84r, 9 April 1449.

114. "Han posat la terra en gran bullici et pertorbació, en tal que mai los antics ho veeren, Déu los ho perdó." Carreras Candi, "Barcelona," 538–39.

115. ACA: C Cur 3203, 59r–v, 31 March 1449; Sec 3227, 60v–62v, 4 July 1449; Cur 3203, 105r, 6 July 1449.

116. ACA: G N-658, 71v–72r, 1 April 1449 and N-658, 75r–78v, 9 April 1449; AHCB: LCO X-19, 97, 15 May, 1449; ACA: G N-660, 117v–118v, 3 January 1450.

117. ACA: G N-660, 106r–107v, 16 December 1449. This is one of the rare letters that specifically cites the violations.

118. Alfonso to Perot Mercader (treasurer general) on 9 March 1449, ACA: C Cur 2657, 231r–v; María to the procurador of the Abbey of Sant Joan de les Abadesses, 20 March 1449, ACA: C Div 3151, 10r; María to the Consell de Cent of Barcelona, 18 June 1449 ACA: C Cur 3203, 101v–102r; María to the vicar of Vilafranca del Penedés, 14 July 1449, ACA: C Div 3150, 106v–107r; María to Galceran Oliver, her treasurer, concerning Vic, Vilafranca del Penedés, Martorell, Santboy, and Barcelona on 16 July 1449, ACA: C Sec 3227, 66v–67r; María to Galceran Oliver, 3 September 1449, ACA: C Sec 3227, 86r–87r; María to Galceran de Requesens, 29 October 1449, ACA: C Cur 3203, 130v–131r; María to the vicar of Cervera, 8 November 1449, ACA: C Div 3151, 139v–140r.

119. ACA: C Cur 2656, 172r, 20 April 1449; AHCB: LC VI-14, 90v–92r, 8 July 1449.

120. ACA: C Cur 3203, 63r–65r, 16 April 1449; Cur 3203, 79v–80r, 6 May 1449.

121. ACA: G N-658, 94v–95r, 13 May 1449.

122. María to Joan de Montbui, 14 March 1449, ACA: C Cur 3203, 51v–52r; María to Pere de Santcliment, 20 June 1449, ACA: C Cur 3203, 101r–v; María to Joan Sabastida, 26 June 1449, ACA: C Div 3150, 98r–v; María to Galceran de Requesens, 6 August 1449, ACA: C Sec 3227, 71r–v; María to Jaume Ferrer, ACA: C Cur 3203, 130r–v, 20 October 1449.

123. AHCB: LC VI-14, 68v–69r, 14 May 1449.

124. ACA: C Cur 3203, 118v, 11 September 1449. The lords of Terrassa, Sabadell, and Montcada used this as a defense of their actions. AHCB: LC VI-14, 169v, 4 December 1449. So too, the abbot of Santes Creues, ACA: G N-660, 125r–v, 12 January 1450.

125. ACA: C Cur 3203, 184v–185r, 19 August 1450.

126. ACA: C Sec 3227, 76v–83r, 10 August 1449.

127. ACA: C Sec 3227, 86r–87r, 3 September 1449.

128. ACA: C Div 3151, 139v–140r, 8 November 1449.

129. "dels dits dipputats e conseller de Barchinona e barons, cauellers, e gentils homens qui ab terrors e altres vies meten mal cor als Sindichs e homens de la dita remença veent que aço redundaua en gran dan e detriment de les coses que seran beneffici de la iusticia e gran seruey e util de vostar excellencia . . . vista per tenor de les dites supplicacions e protests llur gran passio e praticha insolita aquella humil supplich vulla prouehir sobre aço lo que ha sguard e la iusticia e descarrech dels entreuenints en lo negoci que reuiudato en gran merit honor e seruey e util de vostra excellencia." ACA: C Sec 3227, 109r.

Notes to Pages 122–123

130. ACA: C Sec 3227, 111v–112r, 3 March 1450; Sec 3227, 112r–113r, 13 March 1450.

131. For Alfonso's letters to María: ACA: C Sec 3227, 106r–108v, 4 February 1450, and 110r–v, 19 February 1450. And, for the Consell de Cent's response: AHCB: LC VI-15: 46v–47v, 28 April 1450; 65r–66r, 23 May 1450. The following letters have been published in Madurell Marimón, *Mensajeros Barceloneses*: AHCB: LCO X-20: 213r–v, 12 September 1450; 250r–v, 18 October 1450, 277r–v, 11 November 1450; AHCB: LC VI-15: 152v–153, 26 October 1450; documents 280, 298, 308, and 315; pages 331–33, 342–43, 348–49, 352–54.

132. ". . . que es causa de fer perdre la reputacio e cor als qui ensemblants fets ponderosos nos cancellan creem al demeys haurets fet les prouisions de la dita restitucio vinguem ab alguna justificaccio." ACA: C Sec 3227, 145r–146r, 7 December 1450. For other letters to Alfonso in support, see ACA: C Sec 3227: 118r–v, 8 April 1450; 119v–120r, 20 April 1450.

133. ACA: C Div 3151, 186v–187r, 6 February 1450.

134. ACA: C Div 3152, 52r–53r, 10 February 1450.

135. The diputats del general outline their demands and strategy to Pere Dusay, a member of the Consell de Cent, a diputat del general appointed to meet with María. ACA: G N-660, 189r–192r, 10 March 1450. For the opinions of the Consell de Cent, see AHCB: LC VI-15, 65r–66r, 23 May 1450.

136. *Cortes* 22: 29, 32, 34, 41. Freedman, *Origins of Peasant Servitude*, 173, 199. Pertinent passages in Mieres's work on the *remences* are reprinted in García Gallo, *Manual de Historia de Derecho Español*, 96–97, 940.

137. *Cortes* 22: 56–7. Joan Ros, a jurist working on behalf of the Consell de Cent reported to them the events of the opening session. AHCB: LCO X-20, 65, 6 March 1450.

138. Peter Rycraft, "The Role of the Catalan 'Corts' in the Late Middle Ages," *English Historical Review* 89 (1974): 241–69, esp. 266; Ryder, *The Wreck of Catalonia*, 51–54.

139. AHCB: LC VI-15, 31r–32r, 27 March 1450. ACA: C Sec 3227, 115r–v, 28 March 1450; Sec 3227, 116r–v, 8 April 1450; and Sec 3227, 117r–v, 9 April 1450. Jesús Lalinde Abadía, "Los Parlamentos y demas instituciones representativas," in *La Corona d'Aragona e il Mediterraneo: aspetti e problemi comuni, da Alfonso il Magnanimo a Ferdinando il Cattolico (1416–1516)* [IX Congreso de Historia de la Corona de Aragón] 4 vols. (Naples: Società Napoletana di Storia Patria, 1978), 2: 103–79.

140. *Cortes* 22: 62–63

141. Ibid., 71–75.

142. On 23 May 1450, the Consell de Cent reiterated their desire for a resolution in the Corts. AHCB: LC VI-15, 65r–66r.

143. From Vinyes, AHCB: LCO X-19: 41r–v, 16 March 1449; 42r–v, 18 March 1449; 57r–v, 29 March 1449. From Deztorrent, AHCB: LCO X-19: 95r–v, 12 May 1449. From Ros, AHCB: LCO X-20: 65r–v, 6 March 1450; 69r–v, 12 March 1450; 81r–v, 13 March 1450. From Felip de Ferrara, AHCB: LCO X-20, 68r–v, 11 March 1450. From the Consell de Cent, AHCB: LCO X-19: 58r–v, 29 March 1449; 94r–v, 8 May 1449; 97r–v, 14 May 1449; 99r–v, 18 May 1449.

144. AHCB: LC VI-15, 41v–42v.
145. *Cortes* 22: 23–55.
146. AHCB: LCO X-20, 71r–v, 13 March 1450; AHCB: LCO X-20, 68r–v, 11 March 1450.
147. ACA: C Sec 3227, 109v–110r, 19 February 1450; ACA: G N-661, 12r–v, 9 May 1450.
148. AHCB: LC VI-15, 27r–28v, 24 March 1450; ACA: C Sec 3227, 119r, 15 April 1450.
149. ". . . los dits honorables sindichs de aquesta ciutat . . . mostren gran odi a aquesta ciutat e entre los altres sindichs de leyda e de perpinya." AHCB: LC VI-15, 95r–96r, 15 July 1450; and 174v–175v, 12 December 1450.
150. ACA: C Div 3155, 57v–58r, 15 May 1450; Sec 3227, 132r–v, 12 August 1450.
151. ACA: C Sec 3227, 123v–125r, 7 June 1450.
152. ACA: C Div 3155, 97v–98r, 30 June 1450.
153. ACA: C Sec 3227, 125v–126v.
154. ACA: C Sec 3227, 134v–136v, 3 September 1450.
155. ACA: C Sec 3227, 128v–129r.
156. ACA: C Sec 3227, 156r–v, 30 July 1450.
157. ACA: C Sec 3227, 129r–130r, 2 August 1450.
158. ACA: C Sec 3227, 134v–136v, 3 September 1450.
159. "Significara lo dit senyor rey que hauria mester cccc m. florins que servissen axí per quitar e recobrar son patrimoni." *Llibre de les solemnitats de Barcelona*, vol. 1, *1424–1546*, ed. Agustí Duran i Sanpere and Josep Sanabre (Barcelona: Institució Patxot, 1930), 189–90.
160. Sobrequés i Vidal and Sobrequés i Callicó, *La guerra civil catalana*, 1: 28–29.
161. ACA: C Div 3155, 194v–195r. For the original decree, see ACA: C Cur, 3155, 57v–58r, 15 May 1450.
162. ACA: C Div 3155, 195r–v, 30 March 1452.
163. Sobrequés i Vidal and Sobrequés i Callicó, *La guerra civil catalana*, 1: 28–29.
164. ACA: C Sec 3227, 170r–172v, 21 October 1452.
165. "Apres del dit acte, o reuocacio, los dits sindichs de les remences sentint se grandissimament agreujats de aquella son vinguts a mi dients que yo vull cessar, o dilatar ultra del degut llur justicia, e que per aquesta raho ells son en punt que no gossen anar per la terra per dubte de llurs principals que com saben senyor son en nombre circa de xxxx Milia homes los quals pensen que per culpa llurs sindichs aquest negoci se dilate, e supliquam continuament." ACA: C Sec 3227, 174r–175r, 16 June 1453.
166. He notified María in February. ACA: C Sec 2700, 17v, 15 February 1453.
167. On the unrest, see ACA: C Var 2939, 155r–158r 26 January 1453.
168. He kept changing the date of his return, and in August 1453 he extended the deadline for his return to August 1454. Sobrequés i Vidal and Sobrequés i Callicó, *La guerra civil catalana*, 1: 29.

210 Notes to Pages 127–129

169. "Affermen hauer despeses grans quantitats de peccunia e que aço no passa sens gran carrech de les consciencies vostra e mia segons pus largament vostra alteza haura poscut veure en dites mies letres a les quals me reffer." ACA: C Sec 3227, 175v–176r.

170. ACA: C Cur 2661, 29r–30v, 30 August 1453; Cur 3215, 84v, 27 September 1453; AHCB: LRO A-654, 1 November 1453.

171. Miriam T. Shadis, "Berenguela of Castile's Political Motherhood: The Management of Sexuality, Marriage, and Succession," in *Medieval Mothering*, ed. John Carmi Parsons and Bonnie Wheeler (New York: Garland, 1996), 335–58.

172. ACA: C Cur 3200, 84v–85r, 2 October 1453. Her departure was noted in the *Dietari de la Diputació*, 208.

173. Alfonso issued the privilegio to Requesens on 31 August 1453. ACA: C Cur 2661, 29r–30v. That same day he notified the clergy, nobles, and members of the royal council of Catalunya. ACA: C Cur 2661, 31r–32r. On 1 November 1453, María sent a letter to the Consell de Cent formally notifying them that she had turned over the government to Requesens. AHCB: LRO A-654.

174. Santiago Sobrequés i Vidal, "Entorn del llinatge dels Requesens," in *Societat i estructura política de la Girona medieval* (Barcelona: Editorial Curial, 1975), 303–13; *Los Trasámaras*, 632–35.

175. ACA: C Cur 2661, 33r, 13 September 1453.

176. *Dietari de la Diputació*, 208–9.

177. ACA: C Sec 3227, 180v, 20 October 1453.

178. ACA: C Sec 3227, 181r–v, 26 October 1453. He reiterated his difficulties on 1 December 1453. ACA: C Sec 3227, 182r–v. See also Batlle i Gallart, *La Crisis social y económica de Barcelona*, 2: 442–44.

179. *Dietari de la Diputació*, 215; Vicens Vives, *Els Trastàmares*, 164–7; idem, *Juan II de Aragón: Monarquía y revolución en la España del siglo XV* (Barcelona: Editorial Teide, 1953).

180. *Dietari de la Diputació*, 216–17.

181. "Catalunya se veu totalment roïnada e perduda per l'absència del seu gloriós princep e senyor, lo senyor rey," in *Parlaments a les Corts Catalans*, ed. Ricard Albert and Joan Gassiot, Els Nostre Classics 19, 20 (Barcelona: Imprenta Varia, 1928), 214.

182. Sobrequés i Vidal and Sobrequés i Callicó, *La guerra civil catalana*, 1: 27–29.

183. The situation was an extremely complicated squabble that involved Juan of Castile; his son, Enrique, who did not get along well with his father; Juan's highly unpopular favorite, Alvaro de Luna; Juan of Navarre and his son Carlos of Viana, whose relationship was still troubled; and Enrique, infante of Aragón. Vicens Vives, *Juan II de Aragón*, 150–57; *Alfonso the Magnanimous*, 273; Ferran Soldevila, "La reyna María, muller del Magnànim," *Memorias de Real Academia de Buenas Letras de Barcelona* 10 (1923): 213–345, especially 225–34.

184. *Alfonso the Magnanimous*, 421.

185. *Doña María de Castilla*, 96–97; Soldevila, "La reyna María," 250.

186. The new woman in Alfonso's life, Lucrezia d'Alagno, came from a modestly wealthy but very ambitious Neapolitan family. Pope Calixtus (Alfonso Borja),

formerly bishop of Valencia, had close ties to both the Aragonese court in Rome and the Alagno family, but flatly refused to consider an annulment. *Alfonso the Magnanimous*, 393–400.

187. *Dietari de la Diputació*, 248–49.

188. "E la reyna se incliná en terra, e, estant axi, per lo majordom li fonch mes lo mantel de maregues, prim, damunt, e la senyora na Maça li mes lo vel negre al cap; e de det fonch messa la senyora en lo retret, e aqui ella se esmortí dues vegades, e de continent foren tanquades totes les finestres del real." Soldevila, "La reyna María," 258, from the *Dietari* of her chaplain; *Alfonso the Magnanimous*[430].

189. *Alfonso the Magnanimous*, 429.

190. Her will was drawn up at the Monasterio del Carmen in Zaragoza on 21 Feb 1457 (ARV 472, fol. 5), cited in *Doña María de Castilla*, 145–46.

191. José Toledo Girau, ed., *Inventarios del Palacio Real de Valencia a la muerte de doña Maria, esposa de Alfonso el Magnánimo* (Valencia: Anales del Centro de Cultura Valenciana, anejo n. 7, 1961).

192. *Doña María de Castilla*, 155–56.

193. *Alfonso the Magnanimous*, 428–29.

Chapter 6. Queenship, Kingship, and the Dynamics of Monarchy

1. Louise Fradenburg, "Rethinking Queenship," in *Women and Sovereignty*, ed. Louise Fradenburg (Edinburgh: University of Edinburgh Press, 1991), 1–13, esp. 7.

2. *Medieval Crown of Aragon*, 146–47; *Alfonso the Magnanimous*, 360–71; *Los Trastámaras*, 725–28.

3. "Indecents, impertinents e inhonestissimes mes encara son molt insoportables ala magestate e dignitat real." AHCB: LCO 20, fol. 48–54, not dated but likely before March 1450. See *Alfonso the Magnanimous*, 363.

4. Alan Ryder, *The Wreck of Catalonia: Civil War in the Fifteenth Century* (Oxford: Oxford University Press, 2007), 109–50.

5. *Spanish Kingdoms*, 2: 272–94.

6. *Anales*, 3: 304; Nuria Coll Juliá, *Doña Juana Enríquez, lugarteniente real en Cataluña, 1461–68*, 2 vols. (Madrid: 1953), 1: 77–82.

7. Jesús Lalinde Abadía, "Virreyes y lugartenientes medievales en la Corona de Aragón," *Cuadernos de Historia de España* (Buenos Aires) 31 (1960): 98–172, esp. 112, 162–64.

8. Coll Juliá, *Doña Juana Enríquez*, 2: 47–53, 225–30.

9. Ibid., 78–104.

10. Coll Juliá, *Doña Juana Enríquez*, 1: 83–120, 169–201, 325–26 and 2: 7–40, 105–20.

11. ACA: C 3412: fol. 33v (6 March 1465); document 68 in Coll Juliá, *Doña Juana Enríquez*, 2: 395–402. Fernando served as lieutenant in Catalunya (1461–62) and Sicily (1463–68).

12. Coll Juliá, *Doña Juana Enríquez*, 2: 121–221.

13. Peggy Liss, *Isabel the Queen*, 1992, 2nd ed. (Philadelphia: University of Pennsylvania Press, 2004).

14. Lalinde Abadía, "Virreyes y lugartenientes," 167–69.

15. Theresa Earenfight, "Two Bodies, One Spirit: Isabel and Fernando's Construction of Monarchical Partnership," in *Queen Isabel I of Castile: Power, Patronage*, ed. Barbara Weissberger (Woodbridge: Boydell and Brewer, 2008), 1–18.

16. Lalinde Abadía, "Virreyes y lugartenientes," 168–69; idem, *La institución virreinal en Cataluña (1471–1716)* (Barcelona: Instituto de Estudios Mediterráneos, 1964, 159–64; Alan Ryder, "The Evolution of Imperial Government in Naples Under Alfonso V of Aragon," in *Europe in the Late Middle Age*, ed. John Rigby Hale, John Roger Loxdale Highfield, and Beryl Smalley (Evanston, Ill.: Northwestern University Press, 1965), 332–57, esp. 357.

17. Jane de Iongh, *Margaret of Austria, Regent of the Netherlands*, trans. M. D. Herter Norton (New York: Norton, 1953).

18. Daniel R. Doyle, "The Body of a Woman But the Heart and Stomach of a King: Mary of Hungary and the Exercise of Political Power in Early Modern Europe" (Ph.D. dissertation, University of Minnesota, 1996).

19. Joan Reglà, *Felipe II y Cataluña* (Madrid: Sociedad Estadal para la Conmemoración de los Centenarios de Felipe II y Carlos V, 2000), 48–52; Jordi Buyreu Juan, *La Corona de Aragón de Carlos V a Felipe II* (Madrid: Sociedad Estadal para la Conmemoración de los Centenarios de Felipe II y Carlos V, 2000), 17–37.

20. Henry Kamen, *Philip of Spain* (New Haven, Conn.: Yale University Press, 1997).

21. Eleanor Goodman, "Conspicuous in Her Absence: Mariana of Austria, Juan José of Austria, and the Representation of Her Power," in *Queenship and Political Power in Medieval and Early Modern Spain*, ed. Theresa Earenfight (Aldershot: Ashgate, 2005, 163–84. See also Helen Nader, ed., *Power and Gender in Renaissance Spain: Eight Women of the Mendoza Family, 1450–1650* (Urbana: University of Illinois Press, 2004); Magdalena Sánchez, *The Empress, the Queen, and the Nun: Women and Power at the Court of Philip III of Spain* (Baltimore: Johns Hopkins University Press, 1998); Jorge Sebastián Lozano, "Choices and Consequences: The Construction of Isabel de Portugal's Image," in Earenfight, *Queenship and Political Power in Medieval and Early Modern Spain*, 145–63.

22. On absolutist monarchy in the sixteenth century, see Charles Jago, "Habsburg Absolutism and the Cortes of Castile," *American Historical Review* 86, 2 (1981): 307–26; I. A. A. Thompson, *Crown and Cortes: Government, Institutions, and Representation in Early Modern Castile* (Aldershot: Ashgate, 1993). On favorites and secretaries, see James M. Boyden, *The Courtier and the King: Ruy Gómez de Silva, Philip II, and the Court of Spain* (Berkeley: University of California Press, 1995); John Elliott, *The Count-Duke of Olivares* (New Haven, Conn.: Yale University Press, 1986); Antonio Feros, *Kingship and Favoritism in the Spain of Philip III, 1598–1621* (Cambridge: Cambridge University Press, 2000); Hayward Keniston, *Francisco de los Cobos, Secretary of the Emperor Charles V* (Pittsburgh: University of Pittsburgh Press, 1960).

23. Pierre Bourdieu, *Outline of a Theory of Practice*. Trans. Richard Nice (Cambridge: Cambridge University Press, 1977); Michel de Certeau, *The Practice of Everyday Life*, trans. Steven Rendall (Berkeley: University of California Press, 1984).

24. Michel Foucault, *The History of Sexualty*, vol. 1, *An Introduction* (1976; New York: Random House, 1978), 100.

25. It is a dialectic of system and practice possessing a real but "thin" coherence that is continually put at risk by the dynamic range of practices which makes it subject to transformation. William H. Sewell, Jr., "The Concept(s) of Culture," in *Beyond the Cultural Turn*, ed. Victoria E. Bonnell and Lynn Hunt (Berkeley: University of California Press, 1999), 43–52.

26. Marshall Sahlins, *Islands of History* (Chicago: University of Chicago Press, 1985), xi–xiii, 73–103, 138–55.

Bibliography

I. UNPUBLISHED ARCHIVAL SOURCES

Barcelona
Arxiu de la Corona d'Aragó
    Cartas reales de Alfonso IV (V) Cajas 1–18 (1416–58)
    Legislació Caja 5 (1446)
Arxiu de la Corona d'Aragó, Cancilleria *Registers*
    Comune 3055–3094 (1447–53)
    Comune Sigilli Secreti 3218–3219 (1422–44)
    Curia 2653–2661 (1447–53), 3200–3216 (1447–55 to 1453–54)
    Curiae Sigilli Secreti 2690 (1442–46)
    Diversorum 3146–3160 (1448–56)
    Domine Regine 3108 (1416), 3109 (1418–19), 3162 (1416–18)
    Gratiarum 1685 (1338)
    Itinerum 3260–3261 (1420–23)
    Litterarum et albaranorum 2940 (1446–53)
    Oficialum 3114 and 3115 (1442–56)
    Pecuniae 2412 (1412)
    Promiscuum Curie et Comune 3319 (1453)
    Secretorum 2697 (1452), 2699 (1447–49), 2700 (1453), 3227 (1448–54)
    Varia 2939 (1440–53)
Arxiu de la Corona d'Aragó, Generalitat registers
    "N" *Series* N-656 (1146–47) to N-663 (1452–53)
Arxiu Historíc de la Ciutat de Barcelona, Consell de Cent registers
    Deliberations: 1433–7
    Lletres Reials Originales
        Serie A: #351–700, 19 August 1439 to 11 November 1456
        Serie B: #701–757, 11 December 1456 to 4 September 1458
    Lletres Closes: VI-13 (1447–49), VI-14 (1449–50), VI-15 (1450–51), VI-16 (1451–52), VI-17 (1542–43)
    Lletres Comunes Originales: Cota X-17 (1447), Cota X-18 (1448), Cota X-19 (1449), Cota X-20 (1450), Cota X-21 (1451), Cota X-22 (1452), Cota X-23 (1453)
Valencia
    Arxiu Reial de Valencia, Maestre Racional registers, 9050 (legajo 401)

216   Bibliography

II. PUBLISHED PRIMARY SOURCES

Beccadelli, Antonio (Panormita). *De dictis et factis Alphonsi regis Aragonum et Neapolis.* Pisa: Gregorius de Gentius, 1485.

Carreres Zacarés, Salvador, ed. *Ensayo de una Bibliografia de Libros de Fiestas celebradas en Valencia y su antiguo reino.* 2 vols. Valencia: Hijo de F. Vives Mora, 1926.

Constitucions e altres drets de Catalunya. 3 vols. Barcelona: 1588, 1704. Facsimile edition, Barcelona: Romargraf, 1973.

Cortes de los antiguos reinos de Aragón y de Valencia y principado de Cataluña. 23 vols. Vols. 12–13, 1416–58. Madrid: Real Academia de la Historia, 1915.

Cortes del Reino de Aragón, 1357–1451. Extractos y fragmentos de procesos desaparecidos. Ed. Angel Sesma Muñoz and Esteban Sarasa Sánchez. Valencia: Anubar, 1976.

Crónica de Enrique III de Castilla. In *Biblioteca de Autores Españoles,* vol. 68. Ed. Cayatano Rosell. Madrid: Real Academia Española, 1953.

Crónica de Juan II de Castilla. Ed. Juan de Mata Carriazo y Arroquia. Madrid: Real Academia de la Historia, 1982.

Dietari del capella d'Alfons V el Magnanim. Ed. María Desamparados Cabanes Pecourt. Zaragoza: Anubar Ediciones, 1991.

Dietari de la Diputació del General de Cathalunya. Ed. Arxui de la Corona d'Aragó. Vol. 1, *1411–1458.* Barcelona: Diputación Provincial de Barcelona, 1974.

Eiximenis, Francesch. *Regiment de la cosa pública.* Ed. Daniel de Molins de Rei. Barcelona: Editorial Barcino, 1927.

García Gallo, Alfonso, ed. *Manual de historia del derecho español.* 2nd ed. 2 vols. Madrid: San Pedro, 1964.

Gíménez-Soler, Andrés. *Itinerario del rey don Alfonso de Aragón i de Napoles.* Zaragoza: Mariano Escar, 1909.

Kagay, Donald, ed. and trans. *The Usatges of Barcelona: The Fundamental Law of Catalonia.* Philadelphia: University of Pennsylvania Press, 1994.

Llibre de les solemnitats de Barcelona. Vol. 1, *1424–1546.* Ed. Agustí Duran i Sanpere and Josep Sanabre. Barcelona: Institució Patxot, 1930.

Madurell Marimón, José María. *Mensajeros Barceloneses en la Corte de Napoles de Alfonso V de Aragón, 1435–1458.* Barcelona: Consejo Superior de Investigaciones Científicas, 1963.

Manual de Novells Ardits, vulgarment apellant Dietari del Antich Consell Barceloní. Vol. 2, *1446–1477.* Ed. D. Frederich Schwartz y Luna and Francesch Carreras y Candi. Barcelona: Henrich, 1893.

Monsalvatje y Fossas, Franciso. *Colección diplomatica del condado de Besalú.* 26 vols. Olot: Noticias Históricas, vol. 11 (1901); 12 (1902); 13 (1906); 20 (1910).

Parlaments a les Corts Catalans. Ed. Ricard Albert and Joan Gassiot. Els Nostre Classics 19, 20. Barcelona: Imprenta Varia, 1928.

Pedro IV, King of Aragon (Pere III of Aragon). *Chronicle.* Trans. Mary Hillgarth, intro. and notes J. N. Hillgarth. 2 vols. Toronto: Pontifical Institute of Mediaeval Studies, 1980.

Rubio y Cambronero, Ignacio. *La Deputació del General de Catalunya en los siglos XV y XVI.* 2 vols. Barcelona: Diputació Provincial, 1950.

Rubriques de Bruniquer: Ceremonial dels Magnífichs Consellers y Regiment de la Ciutat de Barcelona. 5 vols. Barcelona: Henrich y Campanyía, 1912–16.

Tomich, Pere. *Histories e conquestes dels reys d'Aragó e comtes de Catalunya.* Valencia: Anubar, 1970; facsimile edition of the 1534 edition.

Turell, Gabriel. *Recort; obra feta per Gabriel Turell de la ciutat de Barcelona en l'any 1476.* Barcelona: Biblioteca de "L'Avenç," 1894.

Valla, Lorenzo. *Gesta Ferdinandi regis Aragonum.* 1445. Ed. Ottavio Besomi. Padua: In aedibus Antenoreis, 1973.

Zurita, Geronimo. *Anales de la Corona de Aragón.* 1562–82. Ed. Angel Canellas López. 8 vols. Zaragoza: 1967–77.

III. Secondary Sources

Ainaud de Lasarte, Juan. *La pintura catalana: de l'esplendor del Gòtic al Barroc.* Geneva: Skira; Barcelona: Carrogio, 1990.

Amelang, James. *Honored Citizens of Barcelona: Patrician Culture and Class Relations, 1490–1714.* Princeton, N. J.: Princeton University Press, 1986.

Aram, Bethany. *Juana the Mad: Sovereignty and Dynasty in Renaissance Europe.* Baltimore: Johns Hopkins University Press, 2005.

Aurell, Martin. *L'empire des Plantagenêt: 1154–1224.* Paris: Perrin, 2003.

Baldwin, John W. *The Government of Philip Augustus: Foundations of French Royal Power in the Middle Ages.* Berkeley: University of California Press, 1986.

Barber, Richard. *Edward, Prince of Wales and Aquitaine.* New York: Scribner's, 1978.

Batlle i Gallart, Carme. "El bisbe Arnau Roger de Pallars i la seu d'Urgell (1437–61)," *Estudios Históricos y Documentos de los Archivos de Protologos* 6 (1978): 216–35.

———. *La crisis social y económica de Barcelona a mediados del siglo XV.* 2 vols. Barcelona: Consejo Superior de Investigaciones Científicas, 1973.

———. *L'expansió baixmedieval (segles XIII–XV).* Vol. 3 of *Història de Catalunya.* Ed. Pierre Vilar. Barcelona: Edicions 62, 1988.

———. "Una famlilia barcelonesa: les Deztorrent." *Anuario de Estudios Medievales* 1 (1964): 471–88.

———. "La oligarquía de Barcelona a fines del siglo XV: el partido de Deztorrent," *Acta historica et archaeologia mediaevalia* 7–8 (1986–87): 321–35.

———. *Retorn a la 'Busca' i la 'Biga': els dos partits de la Barcelona medieval.* Barcelona: Institut d'Historia Medieval, Universitat de Barcelona, 1982.

———. "El sindicato del pueblo de Barcelona en 1454." *VI Congreso de Historia de la Corona de Aragón.* Madrid: 1959. 291–304.

Batllori, Miquel, Ernest Belenguer, Robert I. Burns, *et alii. Història del País Valencià.* Vol. 2, *De la conquesta a la federació hispànica.* Barcelona: Edicions 62, 1989.

Beaune, Colette. *The Birth of an Ideology: Myths and Symbols of Nation in Late-*

Bibliography

Medieval France. Trans. Susan Ross Huston. 1985. Berkeley: University of California Press, 1991.

Bedos Rezak, Brigitte. "Women, Seals, and Power in Medieval France." In *Women and Power in the Middle Ages*, ed. Mary Erler and Maryanne Kowaleski. Athens: University of Georgia Press, 1988. 61–82.

Bendix, Reinhard. *Kings or People: Power and the Mandate to Rule.* Berkeley: University of California Press, 1979.

Beneyto-Perez, Juan. "Jaime Callis y su 'Tratado de las Cortes.'" *Recueil de Travaux d'Histoire et de Philologie* 3rd ser. 45 (1952): 55–65.

Bertrán Roigé, Prim. "La pretendida coronación de Juan I y el estamento nobiliario de Aragón." *Hidalguía* 240 (1993): 691–703.

Bisson, Thomas N. *The Medieval Crown of Aragon.* Oxford: Clarendon Press, 1984.

———. *Tormented Voices: Power, Crisis, and Humanity in Rural Catalonia, 1140–1200.* Cambridge, Mass.: Harvard University Press, 1998.

Blythe, James M. "Women in the Military: Scholastic Arguments and Medieval Images of Female Warriors." *History of Political Thought* 22, 2 (Summer 2001): 242–69.

Bofarull y Mascaró, Próspero de. *Los condes de Barcelona vindicados.* 2 vols. Barcelona: Monmany, 1836.

Bonnassie, Pierre. *La Catalogne du milieu du Xe á la fin du XIe siècle: croissance et mutations d'une société.* 2 vols. Toulouse: Publications de l'Université de Toulouse-Le Mirail, 1975.

———. *From Slavery to Feudalism in South-Western Europe.* Trans. Jean Birrell. Cambridge: Cambridge University Press, 1991.

Borreson, Kari. *Subordination and Equivalence: The Nature and Role of Women in Augustine and Thomas Aquinas.* Trans. C. H. Talbot. Washington, D.C.: Catholic University of America Press, 1981.

Boswell, John. *The Royal Treasure: Muslim Communites in the Crown of Aragon in the Fourteenth Century.* New Haven, Conn.: Yale University Press, 1977.

Bourdieu, Pierre. *Outline of a Theory of Practice.* Trans. Richard Nice. Cambridge: Cambridge University Press, 1977.

Boyden, James M. *The Courtier and the King: Ruy Gómez de Silva, Philip II, and the Court of Spain.* Berkeley: University of California Press, 1995.

Bratsch-Prince, Dawn. "A Reappraisal of the Correspondence of Violant de Bar (1365–1431)." *Catalan Review* 8 (1994): 295–312.

———. "A Queen's Task: Violant de Bar and the Experience of Royal Motherhood in Fourteenth-Century Aragon." *La Corónica* 27, 1 (1998): 21–34.

———. *Violante de Bar (1365–1431).* Trans. María Morrás. Madrid: Ediclás, 2002.

Brenner, Robert. "Agrarian Class Structure and Economic Development in Preindustrial Europe." *Past and Present* 70 (1976): 30–75.

Brown, A. L. "Parliament, c. 1377–1422." In *The English Parliament in the Middle Ages*, ed. R. G. Davies and J. H. Denton. Philadelphia: University of Pennsylvania Press, 1982. 109–40.

Brown, Elizabeth A. R. "The Ceremonial of Royal Succession in Capetian France: The Double Funeral of Louis X." *Traditio* 34 (1978): 227–71.

Bibliography 219

————. "Royal Commissioners and Grants of Privilege in Philip the Fair's France: Pierre de Latilli, Raoul de Breuilli, and the Ordonnance for the Seneschalsy of Toulouse and Albi of 1299." *Francia* 13 (1985): 151–90.

Bullough, Vern L. *The Subordinate Sex*. Urbana: University of Illinois Press, 1973.

Burns, James Henderson. *Lordship, Kingship, and Empire: The Idea of Monarchy, 1400–1525*. Oxford: Clarendon, 1992.

Burns, Robert Ignatius. *The Crusader Kingdom of Valencia: Reconstruction on a Thirteenth-Century Frontier*. 2 vols. Cambridge, Mass.: Harvard University Press, 1967.

Cadden, Joan. *Meanings of Sex Difference in the Middle Ages: Medicine, Science, and Culture*. Cambridge: Cambridge University Press, 1993.

Camps i Arboix, Joaquim. *La reivindicació social dels remences*. Barcelona: Dalmau, 1960.

————. *Verntallat, cabdill dels remences*. Prologue Jaume Vicens i Vives. Barcelona: Areos, 1955.

Canal i Morell, Jordi. "El conflicte remença vist pels historiadors dels segles XIX i XX." *Revista de Girona* 118 (1986): 57–63.

Canal i Roquet, Josep. "Els remences a les Valls d'Hostoles i d'Amer." *Revista de Girona* 118 (1986): 50-56.

Canellas, Beatrice and Alberto Torra. *Los Registros de la Cancillería de Alfonso el Magnánimo*. Madrid: Ministerio de Educación, Cultura y Deporte, Centro de Publicaciones, 2000.

Canellas López, Angel. "Alfonso el Magnánimo e Aragón." In *Estudios sobre Alfonso el Magnánimo* (Barcelona: Universidad de Barcelona, 1960), 7–24.

Cantavella, Rosanna and Lluïsa Parra, eds. *Protagonistas femenines a la "Vita Christi."* Barcelona: La Sal, 1987.

Carmona Ruiz, María Antonio. *María de Molina*. Barcelona: Plaza Janés, 2005.

Carpenter, David. *The Minority of Henry III*. Berkeley: University of California Press, 1990.

Carpenter, Jennifer and Sally-Beth MacLean, eds. *Power of the Weak: Essays in the History of Medieval Women*. Urbana: University of Illinois Press, 1995.

Carreras y Candi, Francesch. *Barcelona*. Vols. 3 and 4 of *Geografía general de Catalunya*. Prologue Jaume Sobrequés i Callicó. 11 vols. Reprint of undated nineteenth-century edition. Barcelona: Edicions Catalanes, 1980.

————. "Hegemonía de Barcelona en Cataluña durante el siglo XV." *Discurso leído ante la Real Academia de Buenas Letras de Barcelona* (14 May 1898). Barcelona: Jesús Roviralta, 1898.

————. "Redreç de la reyal casa: ordemanements de Pere 'Lo Gran' e Anfós 'Lo Llibcral.' *Boletín de la Real Academia de Buenas Letras de Barcelona* 39, 3 (1909): 97–108.

Carrère, Claude. *Barcelone: centre économique a lépoque des difficultés, 1380–1462*. 2 vols. Paris: Mouton, 1967.

Caspi-Reisfeld, Karen. "Women Warriors During the Crusades, 1095–1254." In *Gendering the Crusades*, ed. Sarah B. Edgington and Sarah Lambert. New York: Columbia University Press, 2002. 94–107.

220   Bibliography

Cawsey, Suzanne F. *Kingship and Propaganda: Royal Eloquence and the Crown of Aragon, c. 1200–1450*. Oxford: Oxford University Press, 2002.

Certeau, Michel de. *The Practice of Everyday Life*. Trans. Steven Rendall. Berkeley: University of California Press, 1984.

Chaney, William. *The Cult of Kingship in Anglo-Saxon England*. Berkeley: University of California Press, 1970.

Chía, Julián de. *Bandos y bandoleros en Gerona: Apuntes históricos desde el siglo XIV a mediados del XVII*. 3 vols. Girona: Paciano Torres, 1888–90.

Chibnall, Marjorie. *The Empress Matilda: Queen Consort, Queen Mother, and Lady of the English*. Oxford: Blackwell, 1991.

———. "The Empress Matilda and Her Sons." In *Medieval Mothering*, ed. John Carmi Parsons and Bonnie Wheeler. New York: Garland, 1996. 279–94.

Chojnacki, Stanley. "Dowries and Kinsmen in Early Renaissance Venice." *Journal of Interdisciplinary History* 5 (1975): 572–600.

Collins, Roger. "Queens-Dowager and Queens-Regent in Tenth-Century León and Navarre." In *Medieval Queenship*, ed. John Carmi Parsons. New York: St. Martin's Press, 1993. 79–92.

Coll Juliá, Nuria. *Doña Juana Enríquez, lugarteniente real en Cataluña, 1461–68*. 2 vols. Madrid: Consejo Superior de Investigaciones Científicas, 1953.

Comenge i Ferrer, Lluís. *La medicina en el reinado de Alfonso V de Aragón*. Barcelona: Espasa, 1903.

Conde, Rafael, Ana Hernández, Sebastiá Riera, and Manuel Rovira. "Fonts per a l'estudi de les Parlaments de Catalunya. Catáleg dels processos de Corts i Parlaments." In *Les Corts a Catalunya*. Ed. the Direcció General del Patrimoni Cultural. Barcelona: Generalitat de Catalunya, 1991. 25–61.

Corell Ruiz, Luis. *Una copia del testamento de Catalina de Lancaster*. Valencia: Instituto Valenciano de Estudios Historicos, 1952.

Coroleu, José. *El feudalismo y la servidumbre de la gleba en Cataluña*. Girona: 1878.

Coroleu, José and José Pella y Forgas. *Las Cortes Catalanas*. Barcelona: Revista Historica Latina, 1876.

Les Corts a Catalunya. Ed. the Direcció General del Patrimoni Cultural. Barcelona: Generalitat de Catalunya, 1991.

Cosandey, Fanny. *La Reine de France: symbole et pouvoir, XVe–XVIIIe siècle*. Paris: Gallimard, 2000.

Costa Gomes, Rita. *The Making of Court Society: Kings and Nobles in Late Medieval Portugal*. Trans. Alison Aiken. Cambridge: Cambridge University Press, 2003.

Crawford, Katherine. *Perilous Performances: Gender and Regency in Early Modern France*. Cambridge, Mass.: Harvard University Press, 2004.

Cruz, Anne J. "The Female Figure as Political Propaganda in the 'Pedro el Cruel' Romancero." In *Spanish Women in the Golden Age: Images and Realities*, ed. Magdalena S. Sánchez and Alain Saint-Saens. Westport, Conn.: Greenwood, 1996. 69–89.

Cuadrada, Coral. "El greuges del Sagramental en les Corts catalanes (segles

Bibliography 221

XIV–XV)." In *Les Corts a Catalunya*. Ed. Direcció General del Patrimoni Cultural. Barcelona: Generalitat de Catalunya, 1991. 208–16.

Davies, R. G. and J. H. Denton, eds. *The English Parliament in the Middle Ages*. Philadelphia: University of Pennsylvania Press, 1982.

Dillard, Heath. *Daughters of the Reconquest: Women in Castilian Town Society, 1100–1300*. Cambridge Iberian and Latin American Studies. Cambridge: Cambridge University Press, 1984.

Douglas, Mary. *How Institutions Think*. Syracuse, N.Y.: Syracuse University Press, 1986.

Doyle, Daniel R. "The Body of a Woman but the Heart and Stomach of a King: Mary of Hungary and the Exercise of Political Power in Early Modern Europe." Ph.D. dissertation, University of Minnesota, 1996.

Dualde, Manuel and José Camarena. *El Compromiso de Caspe*. Zaragoza: Institución Fernando el Católico, Diputación Provincial de Zaragoza, 1971.

Duggan, Anne J., ed. *Queens and Queenship in Medieval Europe*. Woodbridge: Boydell, 1997.

Durán Gudiol, Antonio. "El rito de la coronación del rey en Aragón." *Argensola: Revista de Ciencias Sociales del Instituto de Estudios Altoaragoneses* 103 (1989): 17–39.

Durán i Sanpere, Augustí. *Barcelona i la seva història*. 3 vols. Barcelona: Editorial Curial, 1972–75.

Earenfight, Theresa. "Absent Kings: Queens as Political Partners in the Medieval Crown of Aragon." In *Queenship and Political Power in Medieval and Early Modern Spain*, ed. Theresa Earenfight. Aldershot: Ashgate, 2005. 33–51.

———. "María of Castile, Ruler or Figurehead? A Preliminary Study in Aragonese Queenship." *Mediterranean Studies* 4 (1994): 45–61.

———. "Political Culture and Political Discourse in the Letters of Queen María of Castile." *La corónica* 32, 1 (Fall 2003): 135–52.

———. "Two Bodies, One Spirit: Isabel and Fernando's Construction of Monarchical Partnership." In *Queen Isabel I of Castile: Power, Patronage*, ed. Barbara Weissberger. Woodbridge: Boydell and Brewer, 2008. 3–18.

———. "Without the Persona of the Prince: Kings, Queens and the Idea of Monarchy in Late Medieval Europe." *Gender & History* 19, 1 (April 2007): 1–21.

———, ed. *Queenship and Political Power in Medieval and Early Modern Spain*. Aldershot: Ashgate, 2005.

Echevarría Arsuaga, Ana. *Catalina de Lancaster: reina regente de Castilla, 1372–1418*. Hondarribia: Nerea, 2002.

———. "Catalina of Lancaster, the Castilian Monarchy, and Coexistence." In *Medieval Spain: Culture, Conflict, and Coexistence: Studies in Honour of Angus McKay*, ed. Roger Collins and Anthony Goodman. Basingstoke: Palgrave, 2002. 79–122.

———. "The Queen and the Master: Catalina of Lancaster and the Military Orders." In *Queenship and Political Power in Medieval and Early Modern Spain*, ed. Theresa Earenfight. Aldershot: Ashgate, 2005. 91–105.

Elías de Tejada, Francisco. *Las doctrinas políticas en la Cataluña medieval.* Barcelona: Ayma, 1950.

Elliott, John Huxtable. "A Europe of Composite Monarchies." *Past & Present* 137 (November 1992): 48–71.

———. *The Revolt of the Catalans: A Study in the Decline of Spain (1598–1640).* Cambridge: Cambridge University Press, 1963.

———. *The Count-Duke of Olivares.* New Haven, Conn.: Yale University Press, 1986

Erler, Mary, and Maryanne Kowaleski, eds. *Women and Power in the Middle Ages.* Athens: University of Georgia Press, 1988.

Estow, Clara. *Pedro the Cruel of Castile, 1350–1369.* Leiden: Brill, 1995.

———. "Widows in the Chronicles of Late Medieval Castile." In *Upon My Husband's Death: Widows in the Literature and Histories of Medieval Europe,* ed. Louise Mirrer. Ann Arbor: University of Michigan Press, 1992. 153–67

Facinger, Marion. "A Study of Medieval Queenship: Capetian France, 987–1237." *Studies in Medieval and Renaissance History* 5 (1968): 3–47.

Feliu i Montfort, Gaspar. "El pes econòmic de la remença i dels mals usos." *Anuario de Estudios Medievales* 22 (1992): 145–160.

Feros, Antonio. *Kingship and Favoritism in the Spain of Philip III, 1598–1621.* Cambridge: Cambridge University Press, 2000.

Ferrer i Mallol, María Teresa. "El patrimoni reial i la recuperació dels senyorius jurisdiccionals en les estats catalano-aragoneses a la fi del segle XIV." *Anuario de Estudios Medievales* 7 (1970–71): 351–491.

———. "Origen i evolució de la Diputació del General de Catalunya." In *Les Corts a Catalunya,* ed. Direcció General del Patrimoni Cultural. Barcelona: Generalitat de Catalunya, 1991. 152–59.

Fila Golobardes, M. *Els remences dins el quadre de la pagesia catalan fins el segle XV.* Figueras: Arts Gràfiques Traiter, 1970.

Fita, Fidel. "Lo Papa Benet XIII y los Pagesos de Remensa." *Renaixensa* 11 (1875): 1–130.

Font i Rius, José María. "Las instituciones de la corona de Aragón en la primera mitad del siglo XV." In *Ponencias del IV Congreso de la História de la Corona de Aragón.* Barcelona: Comisión Permanente de los Congresos de la Corona de Aragón, 1976. 209–23.

———. "Origines del regimen municipal de Cataluña." *Anuario de Historia del Derecho Español* 16 (1945): 388–529; 17 (1946): 229–585.

Fort Melia, Concepción. "La Diputación de Catalunya y los payeses de remensa: la Sentencia Arbitral de Barcelona (1463)." In *Homenaje a Jaime Vicens Vives.* Barcelona, 1965. 1: 431–44.

Foucault, Michel. *The History of Sexuality.* Vol. 1, *An Introduction.* New York: Random House, 1978; original French edition, 1976.

———. *Power/Knowledge: Selected Interviews and Other Writings, 1972–1977.* Ed. Colin Gordon, trans. Colin Gordon, Leo Marshall, John Mepham, and Kate Soper. New York: Pantheon, 1980.

Fradenburg, Louise Olga. "Rethinking Queenship." In *Women and Sovereignty,* ed. Fradenburg.

Bibliography

———, ed. *Women and Sovereignty*. Edinburgh: University of Edinburgh Press, 1991.

Freccero, Carla. "Marguerite de Navarre and the Politics of Maternal Sovereignty." In *Women and Sovereignty*, ed. Louise Olga Fradenburg. Edinburgh: University of Edinburgh Press, 1991. 133–49.

Freedman, Paul. "Catalunya nova i Catalunya vella a l'edat mitjana: dues Catalunyas?" *Revista de Girona* 118 (1986): 29–35.

———. *The Origins of Peasant Servitude in Medieval Catalonia*. Cambridge: Cambridge University Press, 1991.

———. "The German and Catalan Peasant Revolts." *American Historical Review* 98, 1 (February 1993): 39–54.

Fuster, Joan. "Jaume Roig i Sor Isabel de Villena." *Revista Valenciana de Filología* 5 (1955–58): 227–60.

Gaibrois de Ballasteros, Mercedes. *María de Molina, tres veces reina*. Madrid: Espasa-Calpe, 1936.

García Gallo, Alfonso. "El derecho de sucesión del trono en la corona de Aragón." *Anuario de Historia del Derecho Español* 36 (1966): 5–187.

———. "Los orígenes de la administración territorial de las Indias." *Anuario de Estudios del Derecho Español* 15 (1944): 16–100.

Garcia Llauradó, J. "Nueva interpretación de la enfermedad de la Reina Doña María de Castilla, esposa del Magnánimo." *Medicina clínica* 19 (1952): 192–98.

Garlick, Barbara, Suzanne Dixon, and Pauline Allen, eds. *Stereotypes of Women in Power: Historical Perspectives and Revisionist Views*. Westport, Conn.: Greenwood, 1992.

Gathagan, Laura. "Embodying Power: Gender and Authority in the Queenship of Mathilda of Flanders." Ph.D. dissertation, City University of New York, 2002.

Gay Escoda, Josep María. "La creació del dret a Corts i el control institicional de la seva observança." In *Les Corts a Catalunya*, ed. Direcció General del Patrimoni Cultural. Barcelona: Generalitat de Catalunya, 1991. 86–96.

Geertz, Clifford. "Centers, Kings, and Charisma: Reflections on the Symbolics of Power." In *Local Knowledge*. New York: Basic Books, 1983. 121–46.

Giesey, Ralph. *If Not, Not: The Oath of the Aragonese and the Legendary Laws of Sobrarbe*. Princeton, N.J.: Princeton University Press, 1968.

———. *The Juridic Basis of Dynastic Right to the French Throne*. Transactions of the American Philosophical Society n.s. 51, part 5. Philadelphia: American Philosophical Society, 1961.

Gillingham, John. *The Angevin Empire*. 2nd ed. New York: Oxford University Press, 2001.

Giménez-Soler, Andrés. "Retrato histórico de la reina doña María." *Boletín de la Real Academia de Buenas Letras de Barcelona* 1 (1901–2): 71–81.

Gómez Mampaso, María Valentina. "La mujer y la sucesión al Trono." In *Nuevas perspecitivas sobre la mujer*, ed. María Angeles Durán. 2 vols. Madrid: Universidad Autónoma de Madrid, 1982. 1: 127–35.

González Antón, Luis. *Las Cortes de Aragón*. Zaragoza: Librería General, 1978.

———. "Primeras resistancias contra el lugarteniente general-virrey en Aragón." *Aragón en la Edad Media* 8 (1984): 303–14.

Goodman, Eleanor. "Conspicuous in Her Absence: Mariana of Austria, Juan José of Austria, and the Representation of Her Power." In *Queenship and Political Power in Medieval and Early Modern Spain*, ed. Theresa Earenfight. Aldershot: Ashgate, 2005. 163–84.

Goody, Jack. "Inheritance, Property, and Women: Some Comparative Considerations." In *Family and Inheritance: Rural Society in Western Europe, 1200–1800*, ed. Jack Goody, Joan Thirsk, and E. P. Thompson. Cambridge: Cambridge University Press, 1976. 10–36.

———. *Succession to High Office*. Cambridge: Cambridge University Press, 1966.

Goody, Jack, Joan Thirsk, and E. P. Thompson, eds. *Family and Inheritance: Rural Society in Western Europe, 1200–1800*. Cambridge: Cambridge University Press, 1976.

Green, Monica H., ed and trans. *The "Trotula": A Medieval Compendium of Women's Medicine*. Philadelphia: University of Pennsylvania Press, 2001.

Grizzard, Mary Faith Mitchell. *Bernardo Martorell, Fifteenth-Century Catalan Artist*. New York: Garland, 1985.

Habermas, Jürgen. *Structural Transformation of the Public Sphere*. 1962. Trans. Thomas Burger. Cambridge, Mass.: MIT Press, 1989.

Haluska-Rausch, Elizabeth. "Unwilling Partners: Conflict and Ambition in the Marriage of Peter II of Aragon and Marie de Montpellier." In *Queenship and Political Power in Medieval and Early Modern Spain*, ed. Theresa Earenfight. Aldershot: Ashgate, 2005. 3–20.

Hanawalt, Barbara. "Peasant Resistance to Royal and Seigniorial Impositions." In *Social Unrest in the Late Middle Ages*, ed. Francis X. Newman. Binghamton, N.Y.: Center for Medieval and Renaissance Studies, 1986. 23–47.

Hanley, Sarah. "Identity Politics and Rulership in France: Female Political Place and the Fraudulent Salic Law in Christine de Pisan." In *Changing Identities in Early Modern France*, ed. Michael Wolfe. Durham, N.C.: Duke University Press, 1997. 78–94.

Hauf, Albert G. *D'Eiximenis a Sor Isabel de Villena: Aportació a l'estudi de la nonstra cultura medieval*. Valencia: Institut de Filologia Valenciana, 1990.

Hernández Calleja, Ana. "Tipología de los procesos de Cortes." In *Les Corts a Catalunya*, ed. Direcció General del Patrimoni Cultural. Barcelona: Generalitat de Catalunya, 1991. 62–70.

Hernández-León de Sánchez, Francisca. *Doña María de Castilla, Esposa de Alfonso el Magnánimo*. Valencia: Universidad de Valencia, 1959.

Hillgarth, Jocelyn N. "The Problem of a Catalan Mediterranean Empire 1229–1327." *English Historical Review* Supplement 8 (1975).

———. *The Spanish Kingdoms, 1250–1516*. 2 vols. Oxford: Clarendon Press, 1976–78.

Hilton, R. H. *Bond Men Made Free: Medieval Peasant Movements and the English Rising of 1381*. New York: Viking, 1973.

Hilton, R. H., and T. H. Aston, eds. *The English Rising of 1381*. Cambridge: Cambridge University Press, 1984.

Bibliography

Hinojosa y Naveros, Eduardo de. *El régimen señorial y la cuestión agraria en Cataluña durante el Edad Media.* Madrid: Victoriano Suárez, 1905.

Hollister, C. Warren, and John W. Baldwin. "The Rise of Administrative Kingship: Henry I and Philip Augustus." *American Historical Review* 83 (1978): 867–905.

Homs i Brugerolas, M. Mercè. *El sindicat remença de l'any 1448.* Girona: Ajunatament de Girona, 2005.

Howell, Margaret. *Eleanor of Provence: Queenship in Thirteenth-Century England.* Oxford: Blackwell, 1998.

Hughes, Diane Owen. "From Brideprice to Dowry in Mediterranean Europe." *Journal of Family History* 3 (1978): 262–96.

Humphrey, Patricia. "Ermessenda of Barcelona: The Status of Her Authority." In *Queens, Regents, and Potentates,* ed. Theresa M. Vann. Denton, Tex.: Academia Press, 1993. 15–35.

Huneycutt, Lois. "Intercession and the High Medieval Queen: The Esther Topos." In *Power of the Weak: Essays in the History of Medieval Women,* ed. Jennifer Carpenter and Sally-Beth MacLean. Urbana: University of Illinois Press, 1995. 126–46.

Iongh, Jane de. *Margaret of Austria, Regent of the Netherlands.* Trans. M. D. Herter. New York: Norton, 1953.

Jamison, Evelyn. "The Administration of the County of Molise in the Twelfth and Thirteenth Centuries." *English Historical Review* 176 (1929): 529–59; 177 (1930): 1–34.

Jago, Charles. "Habsburg Absolutism and the Cortes of Castile," *American Historical Review* 86, 2 (1981): 307–26.

Javierre Mur, Aurea Lucinda. *María de Luna, reina de Aragón.* Madrid: Consejo Superior de Investigaciones Científicas, 1942.

Jordà i Fernández, Antoni. "Los remensas: evolución de un conflicto jurídico y social del campesinado catalán en la Edad Media." *Boletín de al Real Academia de Historia* 187, 2 (1990): 217–97.

Jordan, Constance. "Woman's Rule in Sixteenth-Century British Political Thought." *Renaissance Quarterly* 40, 3 (1987): 421–51.

Kagay, Donald. "Countess Almodis of Barcelona: 'Illustrious and Distinguished Queen' or 'Woman of Sad, Unbridled Lewdness.'" In *Queens, Regents, and Potentates,* ed. Theresa M. Vann. Denton, Tex.: Academia Press, 1993, 37–47.

———. "The Development of the Corts in the Crown of Aragón, 1064–1327." Ph.D. dissertation, Fordham University, New York, 1981.

Kantorowicz, Ernst. *The King's Two Bodies: A Study in Mediaeval Political Theology.* Princeton, N.J.: Princeton University Press, 1957.

Keniston, Hayward. *Francisco de los Cobos, Secretary of the Emperor Charles V.* Pittsburgh: University of Pittsburgh Press, 1960.

Kern, Fritz. *Kingship and Law in the Middle Ages.* Oxford: Oxford University Press, 1956.

Kibler, William W., ed. *Eleanor of Aquitaine: Patron and Politician.* Austin: University of Texas Press, 1976.

226   Bibliography

Kleinschmidt, Harald. *Understanding the Middle Ages: The Transformation of Ideas and Attitudes in the Medieval World.* Woodbridge: Boydell, 2000.

Krieger, Leonard. "The Idea of Authority in the West." *American Historical Review* 82, 2 (1977): 249–70.

Kuehn, Thomas. *Law, Family, and Women: Toward a Legal Anthropology of Renaissance Italy.* Chicago: University of Chicago Press, 1991.

Lalinde Abadía, Jesús. *La gobernación general en la Corona de Aragón.* Madrid: Consejo Superior de Investigaciones Científicas, 1963.

———. *La institución virreinal en Cataluña (1471–1716).* Barcelona: Instituto de Estudios Mediterráneos, 1964.

———. "Las instituciones de la Corona de Aragón en el siglo XIV." *VIII Congreso de Historia de la Corona de Aragón.* 3 vols. Valencia, 1970. 2, part 2: 9–52.

———. *La jurisdicción real inferior en Cataluña ("Corts, veguers, batlles").* Barcelona: Ayuntamiento de Barcelona, 1966.

———. "Los Parlamentos y demas instituciones representativas." In *La Corona d'Aragona e il Mediterraneo: aspetti e problemi comuni, da Alfonso il Magnanimo a Ferdinando il Cattolico (1416–1516). IX Congreso de Historia de la Corona de Aragón.* 4 vols. Naples: Societá Napoletana di Storia Patria, 1978. 2: 103–79.

———. "Virreyes y lugartenientes medievales en la Corona de Aragón." *Cuadernos de Historia de España* (Buenos Aires) 31 (1960): 98–172.

Lalou, Elisabeth. "Le gouvernement de la reine Jeanne, 1285–1305." *Cahiers haut-marnais* 167 (1986): 16–21.

Lander, J. R. "Henry VI and the Duke of York's Second Protectorate, 1455–56." In *Crown and Nobility, 1450-1509*, ed. J. T. Lander. Montreal: McGill-Queen's University Press, 1976. 74–93.

———. *Government and Community: England, 1450–1509.* Cambridge, Mass.: Harvard University Press, 1980.

Landes, Joan. "The Public and the Private Sphere: A Feminist Reconsideration." Introduction to *Feminism, the Public and the Private*, ed. Joan Landes. Oxford: Oxford University Press, 1998. 135–63.

Lehfeldt, Elizabeth A. "Ruling Sexuality: The Political Legitimacy of Isabel of Castile." *Renaissance Quarterly* 53 (2000): 31–56.

Levin, Carole. "John Foxe and the Responsibilities of Queenship." In *Women in the Middle Ages and Renaissance*, ed. Mary Beth Rose. Syracuse, N.Y.: Syracuse University Press, 1986. 113–33.

Lewis, Andrew W. "Anticipatory Association of the Heir in Early Capetian France." *American Historical Review* 83 (1978): 906–29.

———. *Royal Succession in Capetian France: Studies in Familial Order and the State.* Cambridge, Mass.: Harvard University Press, 1981.

Lewis, Archibald. *The Development of Southern French and Catalan Society, 718–1050.* Austin: University of Texas Press, 1965.

Lewis, P. S. *Later Medieval France: The Polity.* London: Macmillan, 1968.

Leyser, Karl. *Rule and Conflict in an Early Medieval Society.* London: Blackwell, 1989.

Lightman, Harriet. "Political Power and the Queen of France: Pierre DuPuy's

Treatise on Regency Government." *Canadian Journal of History* 21 (1986): 299–312.

———. "Sons and Mothers: Queens and Minor Kings in French Constitutional Law." Ph.D. dissertation, Bryn Mawr College, 1981.

Linehan, Peter. "Frontier Kingship: Castile, 1250–1350." In *La Royauté sacrée dans le monde chrétien*, ed. Alain Boureau and Claudio Sergio Ingerflom. Paris: École des Hautes Études en Sciences Sociales, 1992. 71–79.

———. "The Politics of Piety: Aspects of the Castilian Monarchy from Alfonso X to Alfonso XI." *Revista Canadiense de Estudios Hispánicos* 9:3 (Spring 1985): 385–404.

Liss, Peggy. *Isabel the Queen*. 2nd ed. Philadelphia: University of Pennsylvania Press, 2004; first edition, 1992.

Llorens Rams, Josep M. "El mon agrari baix-medieval a la comarca de la Selva i el conflicte remença." *Aixa* 1 (1987): 23–30.

López Díaz, María Isabel. "Arras y dote en España. Resumen histórico." In *Nuevas perspectivas sobre la mujer*, ed. María Angeles Durán. 2 vols. Madrid: Universidad Autónoma de Madrid, 1982. 1: 83–106.

LoPrete, Kimberly A. *Adela of Blois, Countess and Lord (ca. 1067–1137)*. Dublin: Four Courts Press, 2007.

———. "Adela of Blois and Ivo of Chartres: Piety, Politics, and the Peace in the Diocese of Chartres." *Anglo-Norman Studies* 14 (1991): 131–52.

———. "Adela of Blois as Mother and Countess." In *Medieval Mothering*, ed. John Carmi Parsons and Bonnie Wheeler. New York: Garland, 1996. 313–33.

Macho y Ortega, Francisco. "Documentos relativos a la condición social y jurídica de los mudéjars aragonese." *Revista de Ciencias Jurídicas y Sociales* 5 (1922): 143–60, 444–64.

MacKay, Angus. "Signs Deciphered: The Language of Court Displays in Late Medieval Spain." In *Kings and Kingship in Medieval Europe*, ed. Anne Duggan. London: Centre for Late Antique and Medieval Studies, 1993. 287–304.

———. *Spain in the Middle Ages: From Frontier to Empire, 1000–1500*. London: Macmillan, 1977.

Major, J. Russell. *Representative Institutions in Renaissance France, 1421–1559*. Madison: University of Wisconsin Press, 1960.

Marongiu, Antonio. *Medieval Parliaments: A Comparative Study*. Trans. S. J. Woolf. London: Eyre and Spottiswoode, 1968.

Martindale, Jane. "Succession and Politics in the Romance-Speaking World." In *England and Her Neighbors 1066–1453*, ed. Michael Jones and Malcolm Vale. London: Hambledon Press, 1989. 19–41.

Masia de Ros, Angeles. "El maestre racional en la Corona de Aragón. Una pragmatica de Juan II sobre dicho cargo." *Hispania* 10 (1950): 25–60.

Maurer, Helen E. *Margaret of Anjou: Queenship and Power in Late Medieval England*. Woodbridge: Boydell, 2003.

Mayer, Hans Eberhard. "Studies in the History of Queen Melisende of Jerusalem." *Dumbarton Oaks Papers* 26 (1972): 93–182.

McCartney, Elizabeth. "Ceremonies and Privileges of Office: Queenship in Late Medieval France." In *Power of the Weak: Studies on Medieval Women*, ed. Jennifer Carpenter and Sally-Beth MacLean. Urbana: University of Illinois Press, 1995. 178–219.

McCracken, Peggy. *The Romance of Adultery: Queenship and Sexual Transgression in Old French Literature.* Philadelphia: University of Pennsylvania Press, 1998.

McLaren, A. N. *Political Culture in the Reign of Elizabeth I: Queen and Commonwealth, 1558–1585.* Cambridge: Cambridge University Press, 1999.

McNamara, Jo Ann and Suzanne Wemple. "The Power of Women Through the Family in Medieval Europe, 500–1100." In *Women and Power in the Middle Ages*, ed. Mary Erler and Maryanne Kowalski. 83–101 (originally published in *Feminist Studies* 1 (1973): 126–41).

Meehan, Johanna, ed. *Feminists Read Habermas: Gendering the Subject of Discourse.* New York: Routledge, 1995.

Menache, Sophia. "Isabelle of France, Queen of England: A Reconsideration." *Journal of Medieval History* 10 (1984): 107–24.

Meyerson, Mark. "Defending Their Jewish Subjects: Elionor of Sicily, Maria de Luna, and the Jews of Morvedre." In *Queenship and Political Power in Medieval and Early Modern Spain*, ed. Theresa Earenfight. Aldershot: Ashgate, 2005. 55–77.

Mollat, Michel and Philippe Wolffe. *Popular Revolutions of the Late Middle Ages.* London: Allen and Unwin, 1973.

Muñoz Pomer, María Rosa and María José Carbonell Boria. "Las Cortes Valencianas medievales: aproximación a la historiografía y fuentes para su estudio." In *Les Corts a Catalunya*, ed. Direcció General del Patrimoni Cultural. Barcelona: Generalitat de Catalunya, 1991. 270–81.

Myers, A. R. "Parliament, 1422–1509." In *The English Parliament in the Middle Ages*, ed. R. G. Davies and J. H. Denton. Philadelphia: University of Pennsylvania Press, 1982. 141–84.

Myers, Henry. *Medieval Kingship.* Chicago: Nelson-Hall, 1982.

Nadal i Farreras, Joaquim. "Remences i no remences, una revolució agrària dels segles XIV–XV: una commemoració." *Revista de Girona* 118 (1986): 26–27.

Nader, Helen, ed. *Power and Gender in Renaissance Spain: Eight Women of the Mendoza Family, 1450–1650.* Urbana: University of Illinois Press, 2004.

Nederman, Cary J. and N. Elaine Lawson. "The Frivolities of Courtiers Follow the Footprints of Women: Public Women and the Crisis of Virility in John of Salisbury." In *Ambiguous Realities: Women in the Middle Ages and Renaissance*, ed. Carole Levin and Jeanie Watson. Detroit: Wayne State University Press, 1987. 82–98.

Nelson, Janet L. "Early Medieval Rites of Queen-Making and the Shaping of Medieval Queenship." In *Queens and Queenship in Medieval Europe*," ed. Anne J. Duggan. Woodbridge: Boydell, 1997. 301–15.

———. "Gendering Courts in the Early Medieval West." In *Gender in the Early Medieval World*, ed. Leslie Brubaker and Julia M. H. Smith. Cambridge: Cambridge University Press, 2004. 185–97.

Nieto Soria, José Manuel. *Ceremonias de la realeza: Propaganda y legitimación en la Castilla Trastámara.* Madrid: Nerea, 1993.

———. *Fundamentos ideológicos del poder real en Castilla (siglos XIII al XVI)*. Madrid: Ediciones de la Universidad Complutense, 1988.

———. "Del rey oculto al rey exhibido: Un síntoma de las transformaciones políticas en la Castilla bajomedieval." *Medievalismo* 2, 2 (1992): 5–27.

Oakley, Francis. *Kingship: The Politics of Enchantment*. Malden, Mass.: Blackwell, 2006.

O'Callaghan, Joseph F. *The Cortes of Castile-León, 1188–1350*. Philadelphia: University of Pennsylvania Press, 1989.

———. *A History of Medieval Spain*. Ithaca, N.Y.: Cornell University Press, 1975.

———. *The Learned King: The Reign of Alfonso X of Castile*. Philadelphia: University of Pennsylvania Press, 1993.

———. "The Many Roles of the Medieval Queen." In *Queenship and Political Power in Medieval and Early Modern Spain*, ed. Theresa Earenfight. Aldershot: Ashgate, 2005. 21–32.

Okin, Susan Moller. *Women in Western Political Thought*. Princeton, N. J.: Princeton University Press, 1976.

Oleart i Piquet, Oriol. "Organització i atribucions de la Cort General." In *Les Corts a Catalunya*, ed. Direcció General del Patrimoni Cultural. Barcelona: Generalitat de Catalunya, 1991. 15–24.

Oliveri, Mario. *The Representatives: The Real Nature and Function of Papal Legates*. Gerrards Cross: Van Duren, 1980.

Palacios Martín, Bonifacio. *La coronación de los reyes de Aragón, 1204–1410*. Valencia: Anubar, 1975.

Paro, Gino. *The Right of Papal Legation*. Washington: Catholic University of America Press, 1948.

Parsons, John Carmi. *Eleanor of Castile: Queen and Society in Thirteenth-Century England*. New York: St. Martin's Press, 1995.

———. "Family, Sex, and Power: The Rhythms of Medieval Queenship." In *Medieval Queenship*, ed. John Carmi Parsons. New York: St. Martin's Press, 1993. 1–11.

———. "Piety, Power, and the Reputations of Two Thirteenth-Century English Queens." In *Queens, Regents, and Potentates*, ed. Theresa M. Vann. Denton, Tex.: Academia Press, 1993. 107–23.

———. "The Pregnant Queen as Counsellor and the Medieval Construction of Motherhood." In *Medieval Mothering*, ed. John Carmi Parsons and Bonnie Wheeler. New York: Garland, 1996. 39–61.

———. "The Queen's Intercession in Thirteenth-Century England." In *Power of the Weak: Essays in the History of Medieval Women*, ed. Jennifer Carpenter and Sally-Beth MacLean. Urbana: University of Illinois Press, 1995. 147–77.

———. "Violence, the Queen's Body, and the Medieval Body Politic." In *"A Great Effusion of Blood"? Interpreting Medieval Violence*, ed. Mark Meyerson, Daniel Thiery, and Oren Falk. Toronto: University of Toronto Press, 2004. 241–67.

———, ed. *Medieval Queenship*. New York: St. Martin's Press, 1993.

——— and Bonnie Wheeler, eds. *Medieval Mothering*. New York: Garland, 1996.

Bibliography

Pella i Forgas, José. *Historia del Ampurdán: Estudio de la civilización en las comarcas del noroeste de Cataluña*. Barcelona: Luis Tasso y Serra, 1883. 2nd ed., facsimile. Olot: Aubert, 1980.

Phillips, William D. *Enrique IV and the Crisis of Fifteenth-Century Castile (1425–1480)*. Cambridge, Mass.: Medieval Academy of America, 1978.

Piskorski, Vladimir. *Origen e importancia de los seis malos usos en Cataluña*. Trans. Julia Rodríguez Danilevsky. Kiev, 1899.

———. *La servidumbre en Cataluña en la Edad Media*. Kiev: 1901.

Pons i Guri, Josep M. "Relació jurídica de la remença i els mals usos a les terres gironines." *Revista de Girona* 118 (1986): 440–43.

Poulet, André. "Capetian Women and the Regency: The Genesis of a Vocation." In *Medieval Queenship*, ed. John Carmi Parsons. New York: St. Martin's Press, 1993. 93–116.

Procter, Evelyn. *Curia and Cortes in León and Castile, 1072–1295*. Cambridge: Cambridge University Press, 1980.

Pugh, T. B. "Richard Plantagenet (1411–60), Duke of York, as the King's Lieutenant in France and Ireland." In *Aspects of Late Medieval Government and Society*, ed. J. G. Rowe. Toronto: University of Toronto Press, 1986. 107–41.

Quilligan, Maureen. *The Allegory of Female Authority: Christine de Pizan's "Cité des dames."* Ithaca, N.Y.: Cornell University Press, 1991.

Raftis, J. A. "Social Change versus Revolution: New Interpretations of the Peasant's Revolt of 1381." In *Social Unrest in the Late Middle Ages, ed.* Francis X. Newman. Binghamton, N.Y.: Center for Medieval and Renaissance Studies, 1986. 3–22.

Reilly, Bernard. *The Kingdom of León-Castilla Under Queen Urraca, 1109–1126*. Princeton, N.J.: Princeton University Press, 1982.

Richardson, Henry G. and G. O. Sayles. *The Administration of Ireland, 1172–1377*. Dublin: Dublin Stationary Office for the Irish Manuscripts Commission, 1963.

———. *The Governance of Mediaeval England from the Conquest to Magna Carta*. Edinburgh: Edinburgh University Press, 1963.

Riquer, Martí de. *Aproximació al Tirant lo Blanc*. Barcelona: Quaderns Crema, 1990.

Rodríguez López, Ana. "Dotes y arras en la politica territorial de la monarchía feudal castellan, siglos XII–XIII." *Arenal: Revista de Historia de las Mujeres* 2, 2 (1995): 271–93.

Rosaldo, Michelle Zimbalist and Louise Lamphere, eds. *Women, Culture, and Society*. Stanford, Calif.: Stanford University Press, 1974.

Rubin, Nancy. *Isabella of Castile: The First Renaissance Queen*. New York: St. Martin's Press, 1991.

Rubio y Cambronero, Ignacio. *La Deputació del General de Catalunya en los siglos XV y XVI*. 2 vols. Barcelona: Diputació Provincial, 1950.

Rucquoi, Adeline. "De los reyes que no son taumaturgos: los fundamentos de la realeza en España." *Relaciones* 51 (1992): 54–100.

Ruiz, Teofilo. "Unsacred Monarchy: The Kings of Castile in the Late Middle Ages." In *Rites of Power: Symbolism, Ritual, and Politics since the Middle*

Ages, ed. Sean Wilentz. Philadelphia: University of Pennsylvania Press, 1985. 109–44.

Russell, Peter E. *The English Intervention in Spain and Portugal in the Time of Edward III and Richard II*. Oxford: Oxford University Press, 1955.

Rycraft, Peter. "The Role of the Catalan 'Corts' in the Late Middle Ages." *English Historical Review* 89 (1974): 241–69.

Ryder, Alan. *Alfonso the Magnanimous: King of Aragon, Naples, and Sicily, 1396–1458*. Oxford: Clarendon Press, 1990.

———. "Cloth and Credit: Aragonese War Finance in the Mid-Fifteenth Century." *War and Society* 2, 1 (May 1984): 1–21.

———. "The Evolution of Imperial Government in Naples under Alfonso V of Aragon." In *Europe in the Late Middle Ages*, ed. John Rigby Hale, John Roger Loxdale Highfield, and Beryl Smalley. Evanston, Ill.: Northwestern University Press, 1965. 332–57.

———. *The Kingdom of Naples Under Alfonso the Magnanimous*. Oxford: Clarendon Press, 1976.

———. *The Wreck of Catalonia: Civil War in the Fifteenth Century*. Oxford: Oxford University Press, 2007.

Sablonier, Roger. "The Aragonese Royal Family Around 1300." In *Interest and Emotion: Essays on the Study of Family and Kinship*, ed. Hans Medick and D. W. Sabean. Cambridge: Cambridge University Press, 1984. 210–39.

Sahlins, Marshall. *Islands of History*. Chicago: University of Chicago Press, 1985.

Salicrú i Lluch, Roser. "La coronación de Ferran d'Antequera: l'organització i els preparatius de la festa." *Anuario de estudios medievales* 25, 2 (1995): 699–759.

———. "Las demandas de la coronación de Fernando I en el reino de Aragón." In *Aragón en la Edad Media: Homenaje a la profesora Carmen Orcástegui Gros*. Zaragoza: Universidad de Zaragoza, 1999. 1409–27.

Salrach, Josep. *El procés de formació nacional de Catalunya (segles VIII–IX)*. 2 vols. Barcelona: Edicions 62, 1978.

Sánchez, Magdalena. *The Empress, the Queen, and the Nun: Women and Power at the Court of Philip III of Spain*. Baltimore: Johns Hopkins University Press, 1998.

Sánchez Aragones, Luisa María. *Cortes, monarquía y ciudades en Aragón durante el reinado de Alfonso el Magnánimo (1416–1458)*. Zaragoza: Institución Fernando el Católico, 1994.

Sans i Travé, Josep María and Consepció Ballart i Marsol. "El catàleg de Diputats i Oidors de Comptes de la Generalitat de Catalunya (1359–1710) de Pere Serra i Postius." *Estudis Històrcs i Documents dels Arxius de Protocols* 8 (1980): 63–118.

Sarasa Sánchez, Esteban. "Las Cortes de Aragón en la edad media (estado de la cuestión y planteamiento general)." In *Les Corts a Catalunya*, ed. Direcció General del Patrimoni Cultural. Barcelona: Generalitat de Catalunya, 1991. 296–303.

Saxonhouse, Arlene. *Women in the History of Political Thought: Ancient Greece to Machiavelli*. New York: Praeger, 1985.

Scott, Joan W. *Gender and the Politics of History*. New York: Columbia University Press, 1988.

Searle, Eleanor. "Women and the Legitimisation of Succession at the Norman Conquest." *Anglo-Norman Studies* 3 (1980): 159–70.

Sebastián Lozano, Jorge. "Choices and Consequences: The Construction of Isabel de Portugal's Image." In *Queenship and Political Power in Medieval and Early Modern Spain*, ed. Theresa Earenfight. Aldershot: Ashgate, 2005. 145–63.

Serra i Puig, Eva. "La crisi social agrària de la Baixa Edat Mitjana: els remences." *Cuadernos de Historia Económica de Cataluña* 19 (1978): 47–56.

———. "El 500é aniversari de la Senténcia de Guadalupe: els usos polítics d'una commemoració." *Revista de Girona* 118 (1986): 28–31.

———. *Pagesos i senyors a la Catalunya del segle XVII: baronia de Sentmenat 1590–1729*. Barcelona: Editorial Critica, 1988.

———. "Remences, una ocasió per tornat-hi a pensar." *L'Avenç* 93 (1986): 46–52.

Sesma Muñoz, José Angel. *Benedicto XIII: la vida y el tiempo del Papa Luna*. Zaragoza: Caha de Ahorros de la Inmaculada, 1987.

———. "El sentimiento nacionalista en la Corona de Aragón y el nacimiento del la España moderna." In *Realidad e imagines del poder: España a fines de le Edad Media*, ed. Adeline Rucquoi. Valladolid: Ambito, 1987. 215–31.

Sevillano Colom, F. "Apuntes para el estudio de la cancillería de Pedro IV el Ceremonioso." *Anuario de la Historia del Derecho Español* 20 (1950): 137–241.

———. "De la canicllería de la Corona de Aragón." In *Martínez Ferrando, archivero: miscelénea de estudios dedicados a su memoria*. Barcelona: Atenas, 1968. 451–80.

———. "Las cancillerías de Fernando I de Antequera y de Alfonso V el Magnánimo." *Anuario de la História del Derecho Español* 35 (1965): 169–216.

Sewell, William H. Jr. "The Concept(s) of Culture," in *Beyond the Cultural Turn*, ed. Victoria E. Bonnell and Lynn Hunt. Berkeley: University of California Press, 1999. 43–52.

Shadis, Miriam T. "Berenguela of Castile's Political Motherhood: The Management of Sexuality, Marriage, and Succession." In *Medieval Mothering*, ed. John Carmi Parsons and Bonnie Wheeler. New York: Garland, 1996. 335–58.

———. "Motherhood, Lineage, and Royal Power in Medieval Castile and France: Berenguela de León and Blanche de Castile." Ph.D. dissertation, Duke University, 1994.

Shideler, John. *A Medieval Catalan Family: The Montcadas, 1000–1230*. Berkeley: University of California Press, 1983.

Silleras-Fernández, Núria. *Power, Piety, and Patronage in Late Medieval Queenship: Maria de Luna*. New York: Palgrave Macmillan, 2008.

———. "Queenship en la Corona de Aragón en la Baja Edad Media: estudio y propuesta terminológica." *La corónica* 32, 1 (Fall 2003): 119–33.

———. "Spirit and Force: Politics, Public and Private, in the Reign of Maria de Luna (1396–1406)." In *Queenship and Political Power in Medieval and Early Modern Spain*, ed. Theresa Earenfight. Aldershot: Ashgate, 2005. 78–90.

———. "Widowhood and Deception: Ambiguities of Queenship in Late Medieval Crown of Aragon." In *Shell Games: Scams, Frauds, and Deceits (1300–1650)*, ed. M. Crane, M. Reeves, and Richard Raiswell. Toronto: Centre for Renaissance and Reformation Studies, 2004. 187–205.

Sinués Ruiz, Atanasio and Antonio Ubieto Arteta, eds. *El Patrimonio Real en Aragón durante la edad media*. Zaragoza: Anubar, 1986.

Sobré, Judith Berg. *Behind the Altar Table: The Development of the Painted Retable in Spain, 1350–1500*. Columbia: University of Missouri Press, 1989.

Sobrequés i Callicó, Jaume. "La crisi social agrária de la Baixa Edat Mitjana: els remences." *Cuadernos de Historia Económica de Cataluña* 19 (1978): 47–56.

———. *El pactisme a Catalunya: una praxi política en la història del pais*. Barcelona: Edicions 62, 1982.

———. "El pactisme en l'origen de la crisi política catalana: les Corts de Barcelona de 1413." In *Les Corts a Catalunya*, ed. Direcció General del Patrimoni Cultural. Barcelona: Generalitat de Catalunya, 1991. 79–85.

———. "En torno al problema remensa." *Hispania* (Instituto Zurita, Madrid) 40 (1980): 428–35.

Sobrequés i Vidal, Santiago. *La alta nobleza del norte en la Guerra Civil Catalana de 1462–1472*. Zaragoza: Institución Fernando el Católico, 1966.

———. *Els barons de Catalunya*. Barcelona: Editorial Teide, 1957.

———. *Els barons de Catalunya i el Compromís de Casp*. Barcelona: Rafael Damau, 1966.

———. *El compromís de Casp e la noblesa catalana*. Barcelona: Curial, 1973.

———. "Entorn del llinatge dels Requesens." In *Societat i estructura política de la Girona medieval*, ed. Santiago Sobrequés i Vidal. Barcelona: Curial, 1975. 303–13.

———. "Una illustre família banyolina: els Samasó." In *Societat i estructura política de la Girona medieval*, ed. Santiago Sobrequés i Vidal. Barcelona: Curial, 1975. 285–300.

———. "Los origines de la revolución catalana del siglo XV: las cortes de Barcelona de 1454–58." *Estudios de Historia Moderna* 2 (1952): 1–96.

———. "La petita noblesa catalana i l'interregne de 1410–1412." *Estudis d'Historia Medieval* 3 (extract). Barcelona: Institut d'Estudis Catalans, 1970.

———. "Política remensa de Alfonso el Magnánimo en los últimos años de su reinado (1447–1458)." *Anales del instituto de estudios gerundenses* (1960): 117–54.

Sobrequés i Vidal, Santiago and Jaume Sobrequés i Callicó. *La guerra civil catalana del segle XV*. 2 vols. Barcelona: Edicions 62, 1973.

Soldevila, Ferran. *Història de Catalunya*. 3 vols. Barcelona: Editorial Alpha, 1934.

———. "La reyna Maria, muller del Magnánim." *Memorias de Real Academia de Buenas Letras de Barcelona* 10 (1923): 213–345.

Stafford, Pauline. *Queen Emma and Queen Edith: Queenship and Women's Power in Eleventh-Century England*. Oxford: Blackwell, 1997.

———. *Queens, Concubines, and Dowagers: The King's Wife in the Early Middle Ages*. Athens: University of Georgia Press, 1983.

234 Bibliography

————. "Sons and Mothers: Family Politics in the Early Middle Ages." In *Medieval Women: Essays Presented to R. M. T. Hill*, ed. Derek Baker. Oxford: Clarendon Press, 1978. 79–100.

Stalls, William Clay. "Queenship and the Royal Patrimony in Twelfth-Century Iberia: The Example of Petronila of Aragón." In *Queens, Regents, and Potentates*, ed. Theresa M. Vann. Denton, Tex.: Academia Press, 1993. 49–61.

Strayer, Joseph Reese. "Normandy and Languedoc." In *Medieval Statecraft and the Perspectives of History*. Princeton, N.J.: Princeton University Press, 1971. 44–59.

Strohm, Paul. "Queens as Intercessors." In *Hochon's Arrow: The Social Imagination of Fourteenth-Century Texts*, ed. Paul Strohm. Princeton, N.J.: Princeton University Press, 1992. 95–120.

Suárez Fernández, Luis, Angel Canellas López, and Jaime Vicens Vives. *Los Trastámaras de Castilla y de Aragón en el siglo XV: Juan II y Enrique IV de Castilla (1407–1474), El compromiso de Caspe, Fernando I, Alfonso V, y Juan II de Aragón (1410–1479)*. Vol. 15 of *Historia de España*, ed. Ramón Menéndez Pidal. Madrid: Espasa-Calpe, 1964.

Suárez Fernández, Luis Campisto, and Juan Regla Campisto. *España cristiana, crisis de la reconquista, luchas civiles: Pedro I, Enrique II, Juan I y Enrique III de Castilla (1350–1406); Pedro IV el ceremoioso, Juan I y Martín de Humano de Aragon (1336–1410); Carlos II el malo (1332–1387); y Carlos el noble de Navarra (1361–1425)*. Vol. 14 of *Historia de España*, ed. Ramón Menéndez Pidal. Madrid: Espasa-Calpe, 1966.

Tanner, Heather J. "Queenship: Office, Custom, or Ad Hoc? The Case of Queen Matilda III." In *Eleanor of Aquitaine, Lord and Lady*, ed. Bonnie Wheeler and John Carmi Parsons. New York: Palgrave Macmillan, 2003. 133–58.

Taylor, Craig. "The Salic Law and the Valois Succession to the French Crown." *French History* 15:4 (2001): 358–77.

Thirsk, Joan. "The European Debate on Customs of Inheritance, 1500–1700." In *Family and Inheritance: Rural Society in Western Europe, 1200–1800*, ed. Jack Goody, Joan Thirsk, and E. P. Thompson. Cambridge: Cambridge University Press, 1976. 177–91.

Thompson, E. P. "The Grid of Inheritance: A Comment." In *Family and Inheritance: Rural Society in Western Europe, 1200–1800*, ed. Jack Goody, Joan Thirsk, and E. P. Thompson. Cambridge: Cambridge University Press, 1976. 328–60.

Thompson, I. A. A. *Crown and Cortes: Government, Institutions, and Representation in Early Modern Castile*. Aldershot: Ashgate, 1993.

Toledo Girau, José, ed. *Inventarios del Palacio Real de Valencia a la muerte de doña Maria, esposa de Alfonso el Magnánimo*. Valencia: Aneles del Centro de Cultura Valenciana, anejo n. 7, 1961.

Torre y del Cerro, Antonio de la. "Orígenes de la Deputació del General de Catalunya." *Discurso leído en la Real Academia de Buenas Letras de Barcelona*, November 18, 1923. Barcelona: Atlas Geográfico, 1923.

Trenchs Odena, José, and Antonio María Aragó. *Cancillerías de la Corona de*

Aragón desde Jaime I a la muerte de Juan II. Vol. 1 of *Folia Parisiensia.* Zaragoza: Institución Fernando el Católico, 1982.

Trenchs Odena, José, and Vicente Pons Alós. "La nobleza valenciana a través de las convocatorias a Cortes (siglos XV–XVI)." In *Les Corts a Catalunya*, ed. Direcció General del Patrimoni Cultural. Barcelona: Generalitat de Catalunya, 1991. 368–83.

Treppo, Mario del. "The 'Crown of Aragon' and the Mediterranean." *Journal of European Economic History* 2 (1973): 161–85.

———. *Els mercaders catalans i l'expansió de la corona catalano-aragonesa al segle XV.* Trans. Jaume Riera i Sans. Barcelona: Curial, 1976. (Originally published as *I mercanti catalani e l'expansione della Corona d'Aragona nel secolo XV.* Naples: L'Arte Tipografica Napoli, 1972).

Udina Martorell, Federico. "Importáncia i influéncia de la Cort General i la Diputació del General a Catalunya." In *Les Corts a Catalunya*, ed. Direcció General del Patrimoni Cultural. Barcelona: Generalitat de Catalunya, 1991. 129–41.

———. "La organización político-administrativa de la Corona de Aragón (1416–1516)." In *La Corona d'Aragona e il Mediterraneo: aspetti e problemi comuni, da Alfonso il Magnanimo a Ferdinando il Cattolico (1416–1516). IX Congreso de Historia de la Corona de Aragón.* 4 vols. Naples: Societá Napoletana di Storia Patria, 1978. 2: 49–83.

Ullmann, Walter. *A History of Poltical Thought: The Middle Ages.* Harmondsworth: Penguin, 1975.

Valdeavellano, Luis G. de. *Curso de história de las instituciones españolas: de los orígines al final de la Edad Media.* 2nd ed. Madrid: Editorial Revista de Occidente, 1970.

VanLandingham, Marta. "The Hohenstaufen Heritage of Costanza of Sicily and the Mediterranean Expansion of the Crown of Aragon in the Later Thirteenth Century." In *Across the Mediterranean Frontiers*, ed. Dionisius Agius and Ian Richard Netton. Turnhout: Brepols, 1997. 87–104.

———. "Royal Portraits: Representations of Queenship in the Thirteenth-Century Catalan Chronicles." In *Queenship and Political Power in Medieval and Early Modern Spain*, ed. Theresa Earenfight. Aldershot: Ashgate, 2005. 109–19.

———. *Transforming the State: King, Court and Political Culture in the Realms of Aragon, 1213–1387.* Leiden: Brill, 2002.

Vann, Theresa M. "The Theory and Practice of Medieval Castilian Queenship." In *Queens, Regents, and Potentates*, ed. Theresa M. Vann. Denton, Tex: Academia Press, 1993. 125–47.

———, ed. *Queens, Regents, and Potentates.* Denton, Tex.: Academia Press, 1993.

Vicens Vives, Jaime. "Alfonso el Magnánimo y Barcelona." In *VI Congres d'historia de la Corona d'Arago* (Cagliari: Artes Graficas Arges, 1957). Reprint in *Obra dispersa de Jaume Vicens Vives*, ed. M. Battloni and E. Giralt. 2 vols. Barcelona: Editorial Vicens-Vives, 1967. 1: 251–60.

———. *An Economic History of Spain.* Trans. F. M. López-Morillas. Princeton, N. J.: Princeton University Press, 1969.

Bibliography

————. *El gran sindicato Remensa (1488–1508)*. Madrid: Impresor de Sucessores Juan Sánchez de Ocañayia, 1954.

————. *Historia de los remensas en el siglo XV*. Barcelona: 1945.

————. *Juan II de Aragón (1398–1479): Monarquía y revolución en la España del siglo XV*. Barcelona: Editorial Teide, 1953.

————. "Precedentes mediterráneos del virreinato Colombino." *Anuario de Estudios Americanos* 5 (1940): 571–614.

————. "La transformació de la generalitat medieval." In *Obra dispersa de Jaume Vicens Vives*, ed. M. Battloni and E. Giralt. 2 vols. Barcelona: Editorial Vicens-Vives, 1967. 1: 30–43.

————. *Els Trastámares, el segle XV*. Barcelona: Editiorial Teide, 1956.

Vicens Vives, Jaime. Luís Suárez Fernández, and Claude Carrére. "La economía de los paises de la Corona de Aragón en la baja Edad Media." In *Obra dispersa de Jaume Vicens Vives*, ed. M. Battloni and E. Giralt. 2 vols. Barcelona: Editorial Vicens-Vives, 1967. 2: 220–37. (Originally published in *VI Congres d'historia de la Corona d'Arago*. Cagliari: Artes Graficas Arges, 1957).

Viera, David J. and Jordi Piqué-Angordans. *La dona en Francesc Eiximenis*. Barcelona: Curial, 1987.

Vilar, Pierre. *La Catalogne dans l'Espagne moderne*. 3 vols. Paris: SEVPEN, 1962.

————. "Le déclin catalan de Bas Moyen-Âge." *Estudios de Historia Moderna* 6 (1956–1959): 3–68.

Vinyoles Vidal, Teresa. *Història de les dones a la Catalunya medieval*. Lleída: Pagès, 2005.

Wallace-Hadrill, J. M. *The Long-Haired Kings*. London: Metheun, 1962.

Warren, W. L. *Henry II*. Berkeley: University of California Press, 1973.

Webster, Jill. *Francesc Eiximenis: La societat Catalana al segle XIV*. 1967. 2nd ed. Barcelona: Edicions 62, 1980.

Weissberger, Barbara. *Isabel Rules: Constructing Queenship, Wielding Power*. Minneapolis: University of Minnesota Press, 2004.

Wemple, Suzanne Fonay. *Women in Frankish Society: Marriage and the Cloister, 500–900*. Philadelphia: University of Pennsylvania Press, 1981.

Wheeler, Bonnie and John Carmi Parsons, eds. *Eleanor of Aquitaine, Lord and Lady*. New York: Palgrave Macmillan, 2003.

Wood, Charles T. "The First Two Queens Elizabeth, 1464–1503." In *Women and Sovereignty*, ed. Louise Fradenburg. Edinburgh: University of Edinburgh Press, 1991. 121–31.

————. *The French Apanages and the Capetian Monarchy, 1124–1328*. Cambridge, Mass.: Harvard University Press, 1966.

Index

advocat fiscal, 54
Alfons I, king of the Crown of Aragon (r. 1104–34), 22
Alfons II, king of the Crown of Aragon (r. 1162–96), 25, 175n42
Alfons III, king of the Crown of Aragon (r. 1285–1391), 41, 162n37, 175n42
Alfons IV, king of the Crown of Aragon (r. 1299–1336), 28, 48
Alfonso IX, king of León (r. 1188–1230), 23, 25, 160n15
Alfonso X, king of Castile (r. 1252–84), 22, 26
Alfonso XI, king of Castile (r. 1312–50), 23, 172n10
Amay, Pere, 115
Añon, García Aznar de, 93
apanage(s), 28, 45, 50
Aragón, kingdom, 2–3, 6, 25, 27, 29, 33, 35, 38–40, 43, 47–49, 56–58, 66, 68–70, 72, 74–77, 80–82, 133-34, 139, 151n6
Audiència, 10, 52–56, 80, 84, 91, 121, 177n73, 178n74

Catalina of Lancaster, queen of Enrique III, king of Castile (1372–1418), 5, 13–14, 19–24, 27, 36
Chancery (Cancillería), 2, 10, 15, 32–33, 40, 42, 52–53, 55, 58, 90, 117, 171n126
Clement VII, pope, 108
Coma, Jacme, 115, 117, 119
Compromise of Caspe, 24, 31, 59, 110, 169n109
Consell de Cent, 11, 16, 36, 42, 54, 60–61, 70, 72–75, 81–82, 85, 89, 92–96, 98, 102, 114, 116–18, 120–26, 128, 135–36, 143, 188n13
Consell e Audiència, 1, 10, 15, 33–34, 52–56, 80, 84, 91, 114, 121, 131, 177n73, 178n74

Constança, daughter of Pere IV, king of the Crown of Aragon, 26
Constança of Sicily, queen of Pere III, king of the Crown of Aragon, 30
Constanza of Castile, duchess of Lancaster, 5, 19, 22
contractual monarchy, 7, 13–14, 18, 30, 51, 59, 64–66, 82, 101, 134–44. *See also* monarchy; pastism; queenship
Corbera, Bernat Joan, count of Módica, 74, 119
Cortes of Aragón, 3, 48–49, 72, 81–82; at Tamarit (1367), 49; at Zaragoza (1388), 50; at Maella (1423), 58, 66–67; at Teruel (1427), 67; at Monzón and Zaragoza (1435–36), 58, 70, 73–77, 116; at Alcañiz (1436), 74–75; at Alcañiz and Zaragoza (1441), 58, 77; at Zaragoza (1446–50), 89, 139
Cortes of Castile, 51
Corts of Catalunya, 2–3, 11, 15–16, 30–31, 36–38, 40–42, 48–49, 52, 54, 57–70, 72, 102, 109–10, 128–29, 132–37, 140–43; at Barcelona (1419–20), 57; at Tortosa (1420), 110; at Tortosa and Barcelona (1421–23), 58, 65–66; at Tortosa (1430), 58; at Barcelona (1431); at Tortosa (1432), 111–12; at Barcelona (1436), 70–73, 75–76, 80; at Tortosa (1439), 58, 83–84; at Lleída (1439–40), 58, 82–83; at Tortosa (1442–43), 58, 84–88; at Barcelona (1446–48), 58, 91, 113–17; at Perpinyà-Barcelona-Vilafranca del Penedès (1449–53), 58, 88–89, 92, 97–98, 118–27
Corts of Valencia, 3, 48, 58, 68, 73, 80–81; (1435–36), 75–76
Crexells, Bertran, 112, 115
council, royal. *See* Consell e Audiència

Deztorrent, Pere, 116, 123
Diputació del General, 11, 62–63, 65,

Diputació del General (*continued*)
72–76, 84, 87, 91, 93–94, 112, 116–23,
129, 134, 137, 142, 155n51, 197n155
diputats del general, 62–63, 84, 113–20,
135
Dusay, Pere, 93

Edward, Prince of Wales, 19, 21–22, 46–47
Eiximenis, Francesch, 64–65
Eleanor of Aquitaine, queen of Henry II,
king of England, 13, 21, 127
Elionor of Sicily, queen of Pere IV, king of
the Crown of Aragon, 30, 49, 51, 58, 86
Enrique III, king of Castile (r. 1379–1406),
5, 19–23, 25, 28
Enrique of Trastámara, *infante de Aragón*,
master of Santiago, 28, 36, 39, 67, 70,
80, 83
d'Entença, Teresa, queen of Alfons III,
king of the Crown of Aragon, 41, 48

Fernando I, of Antequera, king of the
Crown of Aragon (r. 1412–16), 5, 20,
24, 28, 31, 37, 52, 110
Fernando II, king of the Crown of Aragon
(r. 1479–1516), 17–18, 22, 44, 104,
138–40, 211n11
Fernando III, king of Castile (r. 1217–52),
23, 25, 127
Fernando IV, king of Castile (r. 1295–
1312), 23
Ferran, son of Alfonso V of the Crown of
Aragon, duke of Calabria (r. 1443–58),
and king of Naples (1458–94), 36–37,
52, 88–89, 190n57
Ferrer, Jaume, 91–94, 109, 113–14, 124–
25, 194n110
Ferrera, Felip de, 54, 99, 123
Foix, count of, 67, 92, 137
Folc, Joan Ramón (II), count of Cardona,
60, 93–94
Fonolleda, Arnau, 96, 115
Foxa, Johan de, 117
Funes, Juan de, 67

Gallach, Joan de, 91
García I Sánchez, king of Navarre (r.
926–70), 23
Giganta, Francesch, 117
Gilabert, Ramon, 125

Giovanna II, queen of Naples (r. 1414–35),
38

Henry II, king of England (r. 1152–89),
43–44, 46, 127
Hijar, Margarita de, 37
Hostalrich, Berenguer de, 35

infantes de Aragón, 28, 36, 39. *See also*
Enrique of Trastámara; Juan of Navarre;
Pedro
Isabel I, "la Católica," queen of Castile (r.
1474–1504), 3, 9, 17–18, 20, 22, 44,
140–41
Isabel of Portugal, empress of Carlos V,
140
Isabel de Villena, 9

Jaume I, king of the Crown of Aragon (r.
1213–76), 23, 25–27, 47
Jaume II, king of the Crown of Aragon (r.
1291–1327), 30, 41, 48, 116
Jimena González, queen of Garcia Sánchez
II, king of (Pamplona) Navarre, 23
Joan I, king of the Crown of Aragon (r.
1387–96), 24, 31, 41, 49–51, 53, 55,
108
John, king of England (r. 1199–1216),
44, 46
John of Gaunt, duke of Lancaster, 5, 19,
21–22, 46
Juan I, king of Castile (d. 1390), 23
Juan II, king of Castile (r. 1406–54), 5,
16–17, 23–25, 27–29, 67, 76, 129
Juan, *infante de Aragón*, king of Navarre
(r. 1425–79) and Crown of Aragon (as
Juan II, r. 1458–79), 8, 17, 28, 39, 41,
56, 58, 62, 67–70, 74–77, 80–83, 87,
104, 113, 128–29, 133, 137–40, 143.
See also *infantes de Aragón*
Juana, "la Loca," queen of Castile (r.
1516–55), 3
Juana Enríquez, queen of Juan II, king of
the Crown of Aragon (1425–68), 17,
30, 41, 138–40
justiciar, 43, 46

kingship, contractual, 1, 15, 30, 52,
64–65, 101–2, 134–36, 140–42.
See also pactism

Leonor, illegitmate daughter of Alfonso V, king of the Crown of Aragon, 37, 88–89
Leonor of Albuquerque, queen of Fernando I, king of the Crown of Aragon (1374–1435), 14, 20, 28, 31–32, 36–37, 39, 169n92
Leonor of Castile, queen of Jaume I, king of the Crown of Aragon, 26
Leonor of Castile, queen of Alfons IV, king of the Crown of Aragon, 28
lieutenant: general, Crown of Aragon (*lloctinent general*), 1–5, 8–10, 13–19, 31–33, 35, 38–55, 57–59, 61–103, 107, 125, 127–43, 159n8, 173n26, 175n42, 176nn49, 57, 177n63, 190n57, 211n11; governmental, 14–15, 18, 42–48. *See also* protector; queen-lieutenant; regent; seneschal
Llull, Berenguer, 99

mals usos, 105, 107–8, 17, 122, 129, 137
Margaret of Austria, regent of the Netherlands, 140–41
Margarida of Prades, queen of Martí, king of the Crown of Aragon, 41, 50
Margarit, Joan Moles de, bishop of Perpinyà, 92, 128
maridatge, 88–89
María, illegitimate daughter of Alfonso V, king of the Crown of Aragon, 37, 88–89
Maria de Luna, queen of Martí, king of the Crown of Aragon, 31, 41, 50–51, 58, 62, 103, 108–9, 113
María de Molina, queen of Sancho IV, king of Castile, 23, 51
María of Aragón, queen of Juan II, king of Castile, 28
Marimon, Joan, 109, 114
Marquilles, Jaume, 98–99
Martí, king of the Crown of Aragon (r. 1396–1410), 24, 31, 41, 50–51, 62, 9, 102, 108–9
Martorell, Bernat, 98–99, 125, 144
Martorell, Joanot, 9
Mary of Hungary, 140
Mendoza, Pedro González de, 27
Mestre Racional, 10, 52–54, 56–57, 71, 78
Mieres, Tomás (*Apparatus super Constitutionibus Curiarum Generalium Cathalonie*), 86–87, 122, 193n87

monarchy. 2–4, 7, 12–21, 24, 26–27, 42, 51, 64–66, 100–101, 131–44. *See also* contractual monarchy; pactism; queenship
Montcada, count of, 60, 116, 118
Montbui, Joan de, 91, 93–94, 119, 121, 124
Montpalau, Berenguer de, 35, 79
Morera, Pere, notary for remences, 115

Naples: Alfonso's court in 2, 8, 10, 15, 17, 34–35, 53–58, 71–72, 76–81, 88–89, 91, 96–97, 112–14, 117–21, 124–26, 131–38, 171–72n9; conquest of, 15, 38, 68, 70–71, 76–77, 84–85; kingdom of, 1, 5–6, 18, 38, 40, 43, 52
notary for the *remences*, 115, 117, 119. *See also* Pere Morera; Jacme Coma

Oliver, Galceran, 89, 121–22

pactism, 30, 64; *See also* contractual monarchy; monarchy; queenship
Pallars: count, 60, 91–96, 113–14, 121, 139; county, 90–91, 93–94, 118. *See also* Arnau Roger IV
Parlement of Barcelona, 50
patrimony, royal, 28–29, 32, 45, 54, 57, 72, 139; recuperation of, 89–95, 106, 112–13, 125
Pau, Bernat de, bishop of Girona, 111, 119
Pedro, *infante de Aragón*, 28, 36, 39, 67. See also *infantes de Aragón*
Pedro I, "the Cruel," king of Castile (r. 1350–69), 5, 19, 27
Pere III, king of the Crown of Aragon, (r. 1276–85), 30, 47–48, 116
Pere IV, king of the Crown of Aragon (r. 1336–87), 24–26, 30, 33, 49, 51, 86, 116
Perpinyà, 33, 54, 58, 88, 92, 115–16, 118, 123–24, 128. *See also* Corts at Perpinyà
Petronila, queen of Ramon Berenguer IV, king of the Crown of Aragon, 25, 51, 151n2
Philip Augustus, king of France (r. 1180–1223), 44–46
Philippa of Lancaster, queen of João I, king of Portugal, 21, 153n19
Pinós i Fenollet, Galceran de, viscount of Illa-Canet, 60, 117–20, 124

Ponza, battle of, 15, 70–71, 85
protector, 45, 92. *See also* lieutenant;
 queen-lieutenant; regent
Puigpardines, Hug de, 35
Pujades, Mateu, 7

queen-lieutenant, 1–5, 8–10, 13–19,
 31–33, 35, 39–44, 48–52, 61–103, 125,
 127–43. *See also* lieutenant; protector;
 regent
queen-regent, 1, 3, 20–27, 45, 48, 50–51,
 127, 141, 162n34, 172n10
queenship, 3–5, 8, 12–18, 19–23, 27,
 31–32, 42, 47, 51, 98–101, 131–44. *See
 also* contractual monarchy; pactism

Ram, Pere, 67, 114
Ramiro, king of the Crown of Aragon (r.
 1134–37), 25
Ramón Berenguer IV, king of the Crown of
 Aragon, 25
remença, remences, 3, 12, 14, 16, 36, 50,
 72, 95, 101–30, 133–35, 137, 139, 143.
 See also notary for the *remences*; sindich
 of the *remences*
Requesens, Galceran de, 85, 93, 96–97,
 119–20, 128
Reverdit, Gueraldona Carlina, 36, 169n103
Rocabertí, viscount, 60
Roger, Arnau (IV), count of Pallars, 60,
 91–96, 113–14, 121, 139
Roger, Arnau, bishop of Urgell, 91–94,
 116
Roig, Jaume, 9
Romeu, Pere, 99
Ros, Joan, 123–24
Ruiz de Corella, Joan, governor of Valen-
 cia, 125

Salic Law, 26, 163n39
Salvador, Simon, bishop of Barcelona, 83
Sancho III Garcés, el Mayor, king of Na-
 varre (r. 1000–1035), 23, 172n10
Sancho IV, king of Castile (r. 1284–95),
 23, 51, 172n10
Santcliment, Pere de, 114
Sant Trinitat (Valencia), 9, 154n45
Sapila, Bernat, 99
Scayó, Barthomeu, 114
seneschal, 43, 46. *See also* lieutenant

Senesterra, Bernat, 55
Sentencia Arbitral de Guadalupe (1486),
 104
Seriat, Ramon (*remença* peasant), 115
Serra, Pere, 99
Sibila de Fortià, queen of Pere IV king of
 the Crown of Aragon (?–1406), 30
sindich of the *remences*, 115. *See also* Amay;
 Seriat

tall, 113, 115, 117–26
Toda Asnúrez, queen of García I Sánchez,
 king of Pamplona (Navarre), 23
Tomich, Pere (*Histories e conquestes dels reys
 d'Aragó e comtes de Catalunya*), 6
Turrell, Gabriel (*Recort*), 6

Urraca, queen of León-Castile (r. 1109–
 26), 3, 22
Urraca Fernández, queen of Sancho II,
 king of Pamplona (Navarre), 23
Urrea, Pere de, archbishop of Tarragona,
 109
Urgell, Jaume of, 24, 70
Usatges of Barcelona, 63–64, 80, 83, 86,
 88, 98, 136

Valencia: city, 3, 6, 8–10, 27–38, 57–58,
 75, 83, 90–91, 112, 129–30; kingdom,
 2, 6, 10, 33, 35, 3–40, 43, 47–48,
 56–58, 68–70, 75–76, 80–81, 85, 90,
 125, 134, 155n50. *See also* Corts of
 Valencia
Valla, Lorenzo, 6, 153n26
vicar (*veguer*), 53, 57, 60, 90, 94, 115–16
viceroy, 18, 44, 46, 50, 52, 66, 82, 92,
 140–41
Vila, Jaume, 122, 124–25
Vilademany i de Blanes, Arnau de, 119,
 124
Vilalba, Marc de, abbot of Montserrat, 61
Vinyes, Antoni, 71, 85, 88, 96, 123
Violant of Bar, queen of Joan I, king of the
 Crown of Aragon, 30, 41, 50
Violant of Hungary, queen of Alfonso X,
 king of Castile, 26
Visconti, Filippo Maria, 74, 76

Zurita, Geronimo (*Anales de la Corona de
 Aragón*), 6

Acknowledgments

A project such as this is never simply a solitary endeavor, but one that thrives in the creative brainstorming of conferences, seminars, e-mails, and lunches and dinners at home and abroad. My colleagues are models of generosity and collegiality, and I cannot thank them enough except to name them and return the favor in the future. I owe much to a great many people and institutions, but most of all Joseph F. O'Callaghan, now Emeritus Professor of History at Fordham University, whose work inspired mine and without whom this book would not have been possible. He is deeply learned, open-minded, and critical without being judgmental, and this work owes much to his insights on medieval Spain, monarchy, and institutions. I remain inspired by his ethics and humanity that are evident in all his work. Also at Fordham, Maryanne Kowaleski, Fr. Louis Pascoe, Dan Smail, and the late Fr. Albert Loomie were unfailingly generous critics who pushed me in unexpected directions and whose perceptive suggestions gave this book a depth and richness it might not otherwise have had. Robert Berkhofer III, María Bullon-Fernández, Brian Catlos, David Cope, Steve Donatelli, Ana Echevarria Arsuaga, the late Elka Klein, Adam Kosto, Elizabeth Lehfeldt, Jacquelyn Miller, Helen Nader, Isabel O'Connor, William D. Phillips, Lucy Pick, Allyson Poska, Shelley Roff, Nancy Rubin, Teofilo Ruíz, Miriam Shadis, Núria Silleras-Fernández, David Cloyce Smith, Marta VanLandingham, Barbara Weissberger, and Rebecca Winer gave me invaluable advice on theorizing the monarchy in the Crown of Aragon in terms of gender, power, and political discourse.

This book would have been unthinkable without the librarians at Fordham University, Seattle University, the New York Public Library, the Consejo Superior de Investigaciones Científicas in Barcelona, the Biblioteca de Catalunya, and archivists at the Arxiu de la Història de la Ciutat de Barcelona, the Arxui Reial de Valencia, and the Arxiu de la Corona d'Aragó, especially Beatrice Canellas and Alberto Torra, whose meticulous work on the registers of Alfonso V and María of Castile made my own research so much easier. I have received generous grants of time and money from Fordham University, the Fulbright Fellowship Program, the National

Endowment for the Humanities, the Program for Cultural Cooperation between United States' Universities and Spain's Ministry of Education, Culture and Sports, and Seattle University.

It is conventional to thank friends and family, and it is so much more than just a list of names. Friends are my lifeline and my comic relief and they remain close to me even when I'm on another continent. I would never have known Barcelona had it not been for Benet and Carme, who first suggested that I come to Barcelona, and to Susan and Pedro, and Joan Webb, who took me into their homes and made me fall in love with the city and its vibrant culture. They are, to quote a slogan from the 1992 Barcelona Summer Olympics when I first met María of Castile in the old Arxiu de la Corona d'Aragó, *amics per sempre. Moltes gràcies per tot.* Love and thanks to Catherine, David, Gail, Joe, June, Kevin, Martha, Nancy, Scott, Sonja, and Victoria.

Last, never least, I was blessed to be born into a big boisterous family who quite literally were always there when I needed them. Many of my fondest memories of my family take place in a kitchen, with my mother and father, brothers and sisters and their spouses and partners and children cooking, laughing, talking fast and over one another about love and work while trying not to burn down the house. I cannot express my love and gratitude enough except to say that this book is as much theirs as it is mine, and especially it belongs to my father and mother who gave me more than they could ever have imagined and to whom this book is dedicated.